The Great American Transit Disaster

 HISTORICAL STUDIES OF URBAN AMERICA

Edited by Lilia Fernández, Timothy J. Gilfoyle, and Amanda I. Seligman
James R. Grossman, Editor Emeritus

Recent titles in the series

Claire Dunning, *Nonprofit Neighborhoods: An Urban History of Inequality and the American State*

Tracy E. K'Meyer, *To Live Peaceably Together: The American Friends Service Committee's Campaign for Open Housing*

Mike Amezcua, *Making Mexican Chicago: From Postwar Settlement to the Age of Gentrification*

Arnold R. Hirsch, *Making the Second Ghetto: Race and Housing in Chicago, 1940–1960, With a New Afterword by N. D. B. Connolly*

William Sites, *Sun Ra's Chicago: Afrofuturism and the City*

David Schley, *Steam City: Railroads, Urban Space, and Corporate Capitalism in Nineteenth-Century Baltimore*

Rebecca K. Marchiel, *After Redlining: The Urban Reinvestment Movement in the Era of Financial Deregulation*

Steven T. Moga, *Urban Lowlands: A History of Neighborhoods, Poverty, and Planning*

Andrew S. Baer, *Beyond the Usual Beating: The Jon Burge Police Torture Scandal and Social Movements for Police Accountability in Chicago*

Matthew Vaz, *Running the Numbers: Race, Police, and the History of Urban Gambling*

Ann Durkin Keating, *The World of Juliette Kinzie: Chicago before the Fire*

Jeffrey S. Adler, *Murder in New Orleans: The Creation of Jim Crow Policing*

David A. Gamson, *The Importance of Being Urban: Designing the Progressive School District, 1890–1940*

Kara Murphy Schlichting, *New York Recentered: Building the Metropolis from the Shore*

A complete list of series titles is available on the University of Chicago Press website.

The Great American Transit Disaster

A CENTURY OF AUSTERITY,
AUTO-CENTRIC PLANNING,
AND WHITE FLIGHT

Nicholas Dagen Bloom

The University of Chicago Press   CHICAGO AND LONDON

The University of Chicago Press, Chicago 60637
The University of Chicago Press, Ltd., London
© 2023 by The University of Chicago
All rights reserved. No part of this book may be used or reproduced in any manner whatsoever without written permission, except in the case of brief quotations in critical articles and reviews. For more information, contact the University of Chicago Press, 1427 E. 60th St., Chicago, IL 60637.
Published 2023
Paperback edition 2024

33 32 31 30 29 28 27 26 25 24   1 2 3 4 5

ISBN-13: 978-0-226-82440-6 (cloth)
ISBN-13: 978-0-226-83662-1 (paper)
ISBN-13: 978-0-226-82441-3 (e-book)
DOI: https://doi.org/10.7208/chicago/9780226824413.001.0001

Library of Congress Cataloging-in-Publication Data

Names: Bloom, Nicholas Dagen, 1969– author.
Title: The great American transit disaster : a century of austerity, auto-centric planning, and white flight / Nicholas Dagen Bloom.
Other titles: Historical studies of urban America.
Description: Chicago : The University of Chicago Press, 2023. | Series: Historical studies of urban America | Includes bibliographical references and index.
Identifiers: LCCN 2022029933 | ISBN 9780226824406 (cloth) | ISBN 9780226824413 (ebook)
Subjects: LCSH: Urban transportation—United States—History.
Classification: LCC HE308 .B56 2023 | DDC 388.40973—dc23/eng/20220812
LC record available at https://lccn.loc.gov/2022029933

Contents

Introduction * 1

Pre–World War II

PART I
Urban Transit Rise and Decline * 21

CHAPTER 1
Baltimore: City Leaders versus Private Transit * 25

CHAPTER 2
Chicago: A Limited Public Commitment to Transit * 38

CHAPTER 3
Boston: Reverse Engineering Public Transit * 52

The Postwar Transit Disaster, 1945 to 1980

PART II
Unsubsidized Private Transit * 69

CHAPTER 4
Baltimore: Urban Crisis, Race, and Private Transit Collapse * 73

CHAPTER 5
Atlanta: Race, Transit, and the Sunbelt Boom * 114

PART III
"Pay as You Go" Public Transit * 147

CHAPTER 6
Chicago: The Failure of "Pay as You Go" Public Transit * 149

CHAPTER 7
Detroit: Racism and America's Worst Big-City Transit * 189

PART IV
Public Transit That Worked Better * 223

CHAPTER 8
Boston Pioneers Public Regional Transit * 227

CHAPTER 9
San Francisco: Deeply Subsidized Public Transit * 258

Conclusion: Beyond Transit Fatalism * 288

Acknowledgments * 293
Notes * 295
Index * 351

INTRODUCTION

Transit riding is a needlessly draining and frustrating experience in most American cities. Even at peak times, buses and trains rarely run when and where everyday riders need to go, including between the suburbs where most Americans now live, work, and shop. When car drivers can otherwise speed to their destinations outside rush hours, transit customers often find themselves stranded with minimal or no service. To make matters worse, travel by transit usually involves time spent in an uncomfortable environment, such as bus stops without shade or rain protection. Transit agencies go through the motions of printing schedules and deploying buses or trains, but their service has become irrelevant to most Americans. Substandard bus and train services help sell cars in the United States, with record car ownership partly driven by the lack of a decent alternative.

The twentieth-century collapse of American mass transit not only makes life miserable for remaining riders but adds to the nation's severe environmental and social problems. Low or no ridership on transit contributes to automobile-related smog, greenhouse gas emission, and water pollution. The low-density, automobile-based society has spread highways and suburban development across some of the country's best farmland and fragile natural habitats. Socially, urban highways and roadways reduce the quality of life in many urban, often nonwhite, neighborhoods. The noise, pollution, and speeding traffic contribute to public health problems like asthma and pedestrian death or injury. Transit-dependent residents of both cities and suburbs, disproportionally nonwhite, face mobility hurdles accessing better jobs thanks to limited service. Automobiles offer advantages in terms of speed and convenience, but they come at a high environmental and social price.[1]

Many American academics, planners, and politicians have resigned themselves to the notion that wholesale loss of transit quality in the United States was an inevitable outcome of the rise of cars, highways, and suburbs. Considerable evidence, however, points to policies that could have balanced investments between transit and automobiles. American cities like San Francisco, New York, Boston, Seattle, and Portland (Oregon) have developed and maintained decent bus and rail service within the context of primarily auto-centric regional transportation systems. The view from abroad offers even more compelling counterexamples of equalized transit and automobile development. Just to the north, cities like Toronto and Montreal built successful postwar rapid and bus transit systems despite regional suburbanization. European leaders made even more ambitious transit investments that kept the sector a well-funded, reliable public service even as the number of car owners has increased. London, for instance, had removed all the streetcars from city streets by 1952, but its Underground, commuter rail, and bus systems remained essential for millions of citizens. Modern urban societies, in sum, can have both automobiles *and* subways, plentiful buses, and electric trams.[2]

Most Americans are all too eager to blame the auto industry for the lopsided mobility options available today. The influential American "streetcar conspiracy" is still widely accepted in planning circles, and the popular press blames an all-powerful automotive industry for transit's undoing. Like any good conspiracy theory, there is enough truth to make the more extreme claims believable. Companies such as Standard Oil, General Motors (GM), Mack Truck, and Firestone Tire and Rubber bankrolled the transit operator National City Lines (NCL). In the first two postwar decades, the NCL and its subsidiaries (such as American City Lines) oversaw the accelerated replacement of streetcars with buses in about forty-five urban transit systems, including Baltimore, Philadelphia, and Los Angeles. The automobile companies also ceaselessly advertised their wares and lobbied successfully for highways. However, in his widely cited 1974 Senate report, legislative analyst Bradford Snell turned these facts into a more dramatic story, blaming the automotive sector, NCL, and buses for destroying transit quality nationally. Los Angeles became his prime example of the environmental damage wrought by the conspiracy, claiming that NCL had despoiled a paradise: "the noisy, foul-smelling buses . . . turned earlier patrons of the high-speed rail system away from public transit and, in effect, sold millions of private automobiles."[3]

Scholars ever since have tried to separate fact from fiction. The cultural and political power of the automotive sector was tremendous but blaming it for all that ails American mobility is nonsense. Urban historian

Scott Bottles, in his study of interwar Los Angeles, acknowledged that the private auto "provided the owner with unequaled mobility" compared to streetcar networks. Driving or supporting highways was a rational choice for American urbanites and did not require a corporate conspiracy. Snell also overlooked the inconvenient fact that NCL's forty-five systems, including major cities like Baltimore and Saint Louis, were a fraction of the 1,200 transit systems nationwide. Yet, almost all non-NCL private and public managers also substituted streetcars with buses, usually with local solid political support.[4] Finally, while streetcars had certain advantages (such as energy efficiency and capacity), Snell and other streetcar fans exaggerated the unsuitability of buses as mass transit options. By 1930, for instance, bus lines had already demonstrated their utility, carrying 2.5 billion passengers, a substantial increase from just 404 million in 1922. Postwar buses, both electric and diesel, were large, comfortable, and dependable.[5] Cities such as San Francisco, Toronto, and London developed and sustained well-planned, comprehensive bus systems in the postwar period. In sum, most dimensions of the streetcar conspiracy fall apart upon close inspection.[6]

If American society is to move beyond a conspiracy-driven transit fatalism and thus reinvest in alternative mobility, a good starting point is getting the national history right. How did a nation that had built its cities around transit technology end up destroying its transit companies and abandoning so many of its transit-oriented neighborhoods? And why did the nation's metropolitan areas so conspicuously fail, given their overall wealth, to achieve a better balance between private and collective transportation? Reviewing the case studies, readers of this book will see that bus and rail service was not necessarily doomed to occupy the lowest possible level of public service. Instead, city and state leaders, riders, planners, and voters made crucial decisions about the future quality of mass transit.[7]

Elected leaders, including mayors, governors, city councilors, and state representatives across the nation, ignored the need for subsidies and public ownership as transit slid downhill. Politicians frequently championed anti-transit policies such as heedless streetcar removal, regressive transit taxes, and unprecedented highway programs. City planners endorsed auto-based suburbanization, low-density zoning, and destructive center-city redevelopment. Technocratic traffic administrators, who viewed cars and trucks as their primary responsibility, pushed for streetcar track removal, one-way streets, and repaving to speed up city traffic. Multiple generations of private and public transit system executives destroyed their agencies in the name of short-term goals such as profits, economizing, and right-sized service levels. Downtown business elites frequently fomented against public ownership and, at best, promoted prestige high-speed rail lines of marginal utility for everyday riders. Millions of ordinary city and suburban residents said yes to highways and no to transit commutes, transit-rich central neighborhoods, transit subsidies, fair housing, higher-density housing, and robust regional transit agencies.

The following case-study narratives focus on three themes that explain the wide range of anti-transit policy in the United States. The first was the dominance of *austerity* funding that required private and public transit to be operated for too long on a "pay as you go" basis instead of as a subsidized municipal service. The second, *auto-centric planning*, was the widespread opinion among the elite, politicians, and the public that the modern city should be redesigned from the ground up to prioritize auto-centric, low-density environments. The third was the *white flight* from cities, encouraged by multiple public policies, leading to center-city residential and commercial decline that robbed transit companies of riders, fares, and regional political support. These three long-term factors, still dominating American public policy and social conditions, were the driving force behind America's dramatic, unparalleled, and sustained loss of mass transit mobility.

The Great American Transit Disaster returns to the locus of transit operations—transit agencies, local and state government, planning agencies, and neighborhoods—to reconstruct a composite national perspective on American mass transportation policy. The book draws on a vast store of professional transit industry books and articles, transit agency and city planning reports, census records, extensive newspaper coverage, and published work in urban history. The debates in daily newspapers over the quality and future of transit prominently featured in the following chapters provide overwhelming evidence that transit disinvestment was a widely publicized and debated dimension of city life. Americans worked hard collectively and openly to destroy their transit systems.[8]

Austerity or "You Get What You Pay For"

This book explores the relationship between public policy and agency finances across multiple cities and decades. Good or better systems were usually subsidized; so-called bad ones were underfunded and forced to subsist on fares in the crucial postwar decades (ca. 1945 to 1970). The three categories identified by this study are *unsubsidized private systems* like Baltimore or Atlanta; *unsubsidized public systems* like Chicago and

Detroit; and *subsidized public systems* like those in Boston, New York, and San Francisco. The columns and rows of figures in annual reports summarized regularly in detail in local newspapers spoke directly to the prospects of transit companies and agencies. The public and politicians refused to face facts.

Americans of the late nineteen and early twentieth centuries took for granted the existence of profitable traction companies that offered cheap, citywide, round-the-clock service without tax support. City governments bestowed generous transit franchises that empowered private companies with the right to design, build, and operate transit lines on selected streets and private rights-of-way. City leaders expected that private capital, attracted by the prospect of a captive market on crucial routes, would finance the building of lines in exchange for these rights. Indeed, fares covered the entire cost of operations, modernization, stockholder dividends, and taxes for decades.⁹

The transit companies, starting in the 1830s, first equipped the rails with networks of passenger cars pulled by horses along fixed tracks. Later in the nineteenth century, companies in big cities like Chicago and San Francisco with heavy ridership switched to passenger cars pulled by moving underground cables. After 1890, nearly every transit company in the nation changed its service to faster, more reliable electric streetcars powered by overhead lines. Transit operators carried urbanites far beyond the walking limits that had hemmed in urban growth for centuries.

Access to the countryside for urban masses created opportunities for profit beyond what could be expected in collecting modest fares. Businesspeople in the land development business, often in league with transit companies, bought up land in anticipation of the families arriving on the rails. Transit companies frequently built competing, duplicative tram lines in city centers to whisk their customers to the urban periphery. Some center-city neighborhoods close-in had too many lines, while others further out had very few. With the private sector financing development, low fares, and profit as the driving motivation, few city governments intervened to demand long-term transit planning during the boom years.

Transit owners for decades evaded the trend to municipal ownership. Large-scale public control and investment in water supplies, for instance, grew directly from the manifest failure of private water companies to deliver sufficient clean water to growing cities. Transit companies, in contrast, met the growing customer demand for decades and encouraged urban expansion with impressive technologies like electric streetcars. These wealthy and powerful companies also resisted public purchase with every political and legal tool at their disposal.[10] Transit as a profitable private enterprise distinguished the United States from much of Europe. According to historian Jon Teaford, European riders enjoyed slightly lower fares under municipal ownership, but at the cost of innovation and supply. Europeans mostly walked or rode slow horse-drawn cars. At the same time, their American counterparts—in cities from small to large—increasingly substituted walking for fast rides on privately operated electric streetcar systems operating "on a scale that dwarfed networks in comparable European municipalities."[11] Total streetcar ridership increased in the United States from 2 to 15.5 billion passengers between 1890 and 1920.[12]

Private transit built American cities and suburbs, but growing rider dissatisfaction led to Progressive-era regulation. Traction monopolists had built a market and a new way of living, but they inflamed customers by failing to replace older equipment, rationalize networks, or invest in faster elevated or subway lines. Newly empowered public service commissions began regulating fares, corporate consolidation, and service levels; city governments frequently taxed transit companies to pay for parks and road repairs. However, regulation remained weak because the wealthy companies had influential supporters in government and commissions. Companies were also entitled to profits through their franchise agreements. A few Progressives and socialists still clamored for outright municipal ownership, but most politicians and voters disagreed.

As complaints about transit service quality mounted before World War II, just a few cities like New York, Boston, and San Francisco finally entered the public transit business. Citizens and leaders in most other cities ignored massive ridership losses from automobile competition and auto-centric policies in the crucial period from 1945 to 1970. Voters, mayors, and city councils stubbornly rejected public ownership or tax support for private transit despite obvious signs of systemic collapse. Transit in most American cities thus remained in private hands until the 1960s and 1970s. Private companies, left to their own devices, responded postwar in predictable ways to their declining market share and lack of support: less service and higher fares, substitution of streetcars with buses, and deferred maintenance on remaining legacy rail lines and bus service. Service reduction predictably accelerated ridership loss. Failing private companies refused to extend anything but limited bus service to expanding suburbs, leaving most transit a center-city service.

Public buyouts of private companies took place only after decades of devastating losses to service and ridership in cities such as Baltimore (1970), Salt Lake City (1970), Atlanta (1971), Houston (1974), Indianapolis (1975), and many more. The terms of emerging public ownership, moreover, undid many potential benefits to riders. City and state officials mostly refused to create robust new taxes or divert sufficient general revenue to the new public transit agencies. Poorly subsidized public ownership in hundreds of additional cities thus proved insufficient to stabilize service or reach new markets. Government officials also signed off on pay and benefits for public transit workers, thus avoiding damaging strikes, without backing up these deals with public money. Cities and states limited their support despite the poor record of long-term unsubsidized public ownership in cities like Detroit (1922) and Chicago (1947). Transit had gone from one crisis, bankrupt private ownership, to another, underfunded public ownership.

The failure of city and state officials to stabilize transit ridership and transit's reputation narrowed the dividends of new federal transit funding beginning with the Urban Mass Transportation Act of 1964 (and expanding substantially in 1970 and after). Federal funds helped buy a new generation of buses in most cities, a welcome improvement for long-suffering riders. Cities with legacy transit, like Chicago and New York, devoted their federal funds to rehabilitation of aging rail networks. In many more cities, like Baltimore and Atlanta, civic leaders deployed valuable federal capital funding to building limited and expensive new rail lines that ultimately attracted few riders. Because federal operating funds proved modest and transient (roughly 1974–80), most transit agencies still pursued austerity management policies thanks to lackluster farebox collection and insufficient local and state subsidies. Mass transit's poor service, minimum rail network, and limited ridership made deep federal investment risky compared to other national priorities.

Cities like San Francisco, Boston, and New York profited long term because their respective city or state governments became intimately and reputationally involved when most city residents depended upon transit. The development of expensive subways or tunnels, necessitated by overcrowded downtowns or significant geographical barriers in these cities, required greater capital than private operators would provide unaided. By incorporating transit in government operations so early, city leaders put transit on a more level playing field with other city services in legislation, annual budgets, and the minds of voters and elected officials. City leaders diverted tax revenues early to support transit development in Boston, San Francisco, and New York. Public funds allowed for service consistency during decades of ridership losses. New federal capital funding, building on decades of local pro-transit funding choices, could be deployed

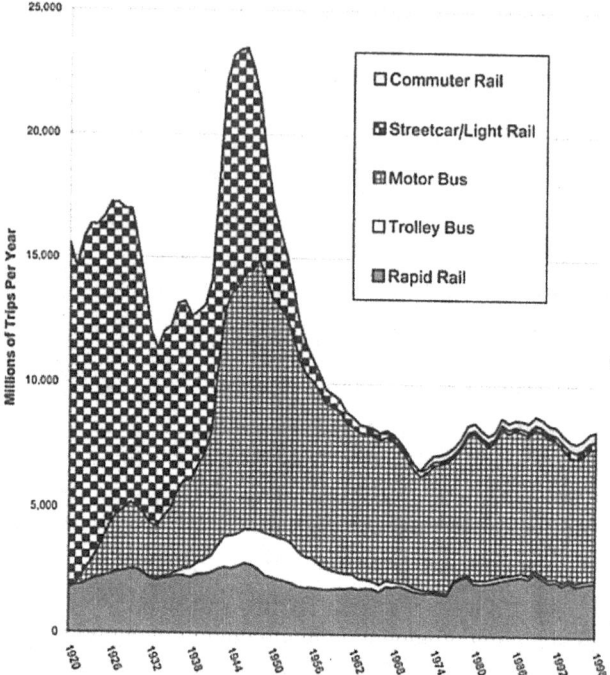

FIGURE 1. The twentieth-century collapse of American transit is reflected on this chart derived from selected American Public Transit Association data. Only rapid rail was relatively consistent due to the modernization of legacy systems in cities like New York, Boston, and Chicago. Reprinted with permission from *Making Transit Work: Insight from Western Europe, Canada, and the United States.* Special Report 257. Committee for an International Comparison of National Policies and Expectations Affecting Public Transit (Transportation Research Board, National Research Council National Academy Press, Washington, DC, 2001).

to sustaining and expanding transit offerings rather than trying to attract hypothetical suburban riders from their cars (as in Baltimore, Atlanta, and many other cities).[13]

San Francisco residents, for instance, have benefited without much interruption from electric streetcars, reliable buses, and electric trolleybuses (buses powered by overhead electric wires) since the 1920s. The region, thanks to subsidies, even built a new rapid rail system (Bay Area Rapid Transit [BART]) in the postwar decades. New York sustained a massive subway system and rescued private commuter rail, despite the 1960s and 1970s urban financial and demographic crisis. Despite regional sprawl and highway development, Boston's Massachusetts Bay Transportation Authority (MBTA) has sustained comprehensive service—on streetcars, buses, trolleybuses, commuter rail, and subways.

Quality transit like this can exist alongside an automotive society, but taxpayers must support it. Waiting for an elevated level of federal funding that will single-handedly pay for creating and maintaining high-quality transit in hundreds of cities was a losing strategy for American cities like Baltimore and Detroit.[14]

Auto-Centric City Planning

As early as the 1920s, leaders and an emerging generation of planners and traffic engineers throughout the nation believed that only retrofitting traditional downtowns and neighborhoods for cars would sustain urban health. Officials demanded the removal of streetcar tracks in neighborhoods and downtowns to speed up car and truck traffic, ignored remaining transit rider demands, and mostly succeeded in junking the streetcar lines by the 1960s. Mayors and city councils rejected available opportunities for streetcar modernization and acceleration (i.e., tunnels or separated lines) in all but a few cities. Planning to make buses run rapidly, such as exclusive busways, were often considered but rarely constructed. In many cases, city governments commissioned detailed proposals for rapid transit, but these were usually shelved when the cost estimates came in.[15] City officials, however, found the money for citywide networks of paved streets, boulevards, and parkways and planned for regional-scale highways long before the federal interstate system of the 1950s.[16]

While waging war on downtown streetcars, planners, real-estate interests, and city leaders endorsed zoning rules that dispensed with the existing laissez-faire transit-oriented growth regime. As documented in the enduring classic *Streetcar Suburbs*, the Gilded Age was America's last transit golden age thanks to the freedom given to property owners to determine the type and density of development near rail. But the rise of carefully planned lower-density suburbs created an alluring model of living in the first half of the twentieth century. Real-estate and city leaders made low-density residential development the central pillar of citywide zoning regulation widely adopted at the time: "By 1926 the 426 zoned municipalities had a total of more than 27 million inhabitants, over half the total urban population of the United States."[17] Zoning prevented the development of sufficient density on the urban fringe and in the suburbs to support transit service on a "pay as you go" model. The economic logic of city and suburban transport, including commuter rail, interurbans, and streetcar lines, collapsed.[18]

Transit companies from the 1920s onward were now looking at a maximum number of riders throughout their service areas, mostly at rush hours, no matter how rapid or frequent the service. Only a few big cities, with a tradition of dense urban development, took an alternative approach. New York, Chicago, Boston, and San Francisco made more generous provisions for citywide multifamily housing, commerce, or industry, with long-term benefits for transit. But even where center-city zoning was friendlier to transit, as in Chicago, the more rapidly growing suburbs tightly locked down future development. The strict regulations sent a solid message to transit operators that future investment was futile. Redlining compounded transit disinvestment by encouraging long-term population and commercial abandonment of many neighborhoods best served by transit.

Postwar local policies of car-friendly urban renewal further damaged the viability of mass transit. Local officials worked closely with state and federal officials to clear neighborhoods to make way for wide arterials and urban interstate networks.[19] The Housing Acts of 1949 and 1954, encouraging slum clearance and redevelopment, built on long-standing civic priorities to rebuild downtowns and clear poor and Black families from desirable central locations. Large-scale redevelopment that moved ahead intentionally reduced the density of more impoverished, transit-riding populations living near convenient transit nodes and central business districts (CBDs). Replacement by low-density housing projects (public and private), shopping centers, or new college or hospital campuses usually included ample parking space and easy access to highways. After World War II, the clearance projects sometimes forced transit route changes or elimination to make way for wider streets, forbidding superblocks, and elevated or depressed roadway sections.[20]

The massive citizen pressure from freeway revolts and anti–urban renewal opinion finally forced politicians to reconsider their auto-centric policies and reliance on federal highway programs. The federal government in 1974 helped the emergent pro-transit movement when it permitted diversion of highway funds to transit. A few cities grudgingly scaled back urban renewal policies or highways. City leaders in New York, Boston, and San Francisco—under enormous public pressure—aided transit by canceling more center-city expressways than was typical nationally. If done early enough and on a large scale, actions like these were effective in preserving density and urban vitality. These cities are also notable for housing stabilization and affordable housing programs that stabilized neighborhoods near transit.[21] Researchers Erick Guerra and Robert Cervero highlighted in a national study that "higher densities tend to improve transit's cost-effectiveness, in spite of higher capital costs." Densely populated central city neighborhoods that evaded the postwar wrecking ball remain the core of transit ridership today.²²

However, a transit renaissance was usually too late for a genuine revival in most cities as the mainstream transit habit was lost, and minimal bus service remained. When the federal government in the 1960s and 1970s began covering a higher percentage of capital costs per project, federal capital grants paid for new buses in most cities and helped stabilize legacy transit in cities such as Boston, Chicago, San Francisco, and New York. Elsewhere, however, civic leaders often prioritized federal grants for new rapid or light-rail systems that consultants believed would attract higher-income suburban riders back to transit and city centers. Yet the capital grants that flowed to cities like Baltimore and Atlanta built

FIGURE 2. Baltimore's African American defense workers during World War II rode electric trolleybuses, gasoline buses, and old streetcars (all visible in the background).

only one or two rail lines rather than comprehensive, citywide systems of value to city residents.²³ Rail made a modest comeback nationally thanks to federal investment, but insufficient attention to planning, density, and zoning usually led to mediocre ridership on the new rail systems.²⁴

White Flight from Transit

Race and the white preference for highly segregated public spaces were crucial factors in the American transit disaster. Racial conflict became an underlying, if rarely acknowledged, factor in transit disinvestment as cities changed over the century. For decades, annual reports of transit companies and most transit coverage avoided discussing the racialized dimension of transit. In the official story, ridership losses resulted from automobile ownership, rising fares, less service, population decline, and mismanagement rather than racism. Aligning transit decline with neighborhood census patterns and other sources tells another story.

American mass transit's so-called golden age was a comparatively socially homogeneous one characterized primarily by tightly packed cars of native whites and new immigrants primarily from Europe. When American cities were majority white in the early twentieth century, transit riders filled the booming streetcars and rapid lines. The growing African American populations in southern and northern cities in the industrial era also took advantage of these systems at their height. Still, their presence disrupted the social homogeneity preferred by many white riders. The responses to integrated ridership were different in the North and South, but the outcome was much the same. Transit became a second-tier public service in the United States disproportionately utilized by poor, nonwhite riders.

In the early twentieth century, southern cities, comparatively small but growing fast, developed with streetcar infrastructure. The Jim Crow laws that mandated extreme segregation on public transit harshly maintained dividing lines as the Black population increased. Pioneering activists began targeting transit because of these seating rules, making transit an essential battleground for civil rights battles of the postwar period. Boycotts and legal challenges in cities like Montgomery and Atlanta eventually led to judicial decisions mandating the end of Jim Crow policies. The right to travel on mass transit in dignity in the South understandably took precedence over concerns about dramatic losses to the quality of service, encouraged by white local officials, taking place simultaneously as civil rights battles. Sadly, by the time Jim Crow was gone, so was much of the better-quality transit system that whites had once enjoyed.²⁵

Southern whites chose to address mandated integration by doubling down on transit disinvestment, urban renewal, automobiles, and suburbia. The southern transit strategy, much like that in the North, relied on mass migration to restricted suburbia and limiting remnant transit. Glitzy projects like Atlanta's Metropolitan Atlanta Rapid Transit Authority (MARTA) focused on attracting whites back to separate, higher-speed rail lines even though many white suburbs in Atlanta refused to participate in developing the new system. The legacy of southern disinvestment in transit is evident in the minor role of mass transit across almost all southern states today. The Atlanta story, told here, illustrates the racial divisions over transit in the South and the failure of transit development to keep pace with blistering economic growth in the Sunbelt. Very few urban travelers, of any race, use transit anywhere in the Sunbelt.[26]

The conditions in northern and mid-Atlantic cities were no less fraught, and the outcome of failing to deal with racial hatred was quite similar to the South. At the turn of the century, the small minority ridership in northern cities benefited from extensive, low-cost transit systems. Racial tension, however, increased on transit in the North with the Great Migration. Whites attacked Black riders who had to cross color lines to travel from overcrowded ghetto districts to work and play. The infamous postwar race riots in Chicago, for instance, prompted the editorial board of the *Chicago Tribune* in 1919 to flirt with calls for northern legal "segregation." The editorial board believed that "if a colored person cannot enter a streetcar without this being the signal for shooting and furor, how long will it be before public policy and the protection of life and property makes necessary another system of transportation."[27]

The North demurred from implementing Jim Crow, but the prediction of the need for "another system of transportation" was prescient. White leaders in the North left transit a low priority as neighborhoods, and transit patronage changed, and most whites found the social distance they wanted in their cars. Indeed, as white families in the North moved rapidly to new car-based subdivisions, both within city limits and in independent suburbs in the early twentieth century, they took with them both their fares and their political pressure for transit improvements and subsidies. White families also added new pressure for costly city expenditures on new parkways, highways, and roads. They ably resisted the rising calls for regional transit and taxation when asked at the ballot box.

At first, private and public transit companies operating on typical "pay as you go" models cut service faster in whiter semi-suburban areas rather than closer-in areas with growing Black populations. Black riders paid the bills. But companies could not sustain such a targeted strategy after cutting the least-patronized service. As whites stopped riding—and as white majorities rejected bonds, general fund subsidies, or taxes for transit—managers made deeper cuts. The white mayors elected everywhere until the late 1960s always placed transit at a low priority. Almost all transit systems eventually cut to the bone comprehensive, expensive-to-operate streetcar and trolleybus options. Bus systems often debuted at a high-quality level, with new buses and lots of them, but managers eventually cut back bus service to match declining profits and ridership.

Redlining discouraged investment and renovation in older city neighborhoods with legacy transit and growing Black populations. Property owners took advantage of widespread housing discrimination by charging Black families higher rents than was justified for substandard accommodation. When the buildings finally wore out, many owners just abandoned their properties. City officials, meanwhile, stood by while owners discriminated based on race and egregiously violated building codes. City leaders focused on clearing and rebuilding Black neighborhoods, usually near the CBD. In the wake of clearance were empty lots and lower-density housing, industrial, or commercial projects. Small and large stores along transit lines that had successfully served straphangers lost clientele. As stores closed, opportunities in entry-level retail employment also evaporated, erasing what was once a fixture of working-class social stability. Long-term unemployment reduced the number of daily riders who once traveled by tram to factories, warehouses, and downtowns.

The combination of these factors was dreadful for transit in the 1960s and 1970s. The declining population density was evident in neighborhoods in Rustbelt cities like Baltimore, Cleveland, and Philadelphia and Sunbelt cities like Los Angeles and Atlanta. These broader trends in Black areas directly impacted transit service because these were often the neighborhoods with the most remaining lines and riders. Only in cities where a small white elite still rode legacy rail systems (New York, Boston, Chicago, Philadelphia, and San Francisco) was saving and subsidizing transit a pressing issue.

The urban disorder that accompanied disinvestment was another strike against transit. The riots of the 1960s in American cities dealt a death blow to many struggling neighborhoods reliant upon transit and scared off many residual white riders. Rising crime on transit vehicles further hurt transit's reputation and competitiveness. Transit managers responded by creating transit police forces and exact change requirements that protected drivers from stickups. But the damage to transit's reputation was done. Transit experts dreamed up a horrible name for the remaining transit consumers in most cities: "captive" riders. By this, they meant those who could not drive a car because of being too old, too young, too poor, or having a disability.[28]

Racial fractures along regional lines impacted all transit service. The dying private transit companies and most newly created public agencies extended few lines anywhere postwar. The potential links to prospering suburban offices, factories, malls, and light industrial parks were usually absent, cut, or limited given the limited density and potential ridership. Suburbanites actively resisted regional cooperation to improve transit, even if white people might also have benefited from a transit option. Declining connectivity robbed African American newcomers of affordable, dependable, and extensive mass transit systems that had once well served poor and working-class white families as steppingstones to the American dream. Reverend Martin Luther King Jr. in 1968 believed that "if transportation in American cities could be laid out so as to provide an opportunity for poor people to get to meaningful employment, then they could begin to move into the mainstream of American life."[29] Transit collapse was a significant source of the "spatial mismatch hypothesis" (1968) that identified the distance between poor urban neighborhoods and booming suburban employers as essential in growing urban poverty.[30]

When African Americans finally achieved electoral success in the 1960s and 1970s, mayors overseeing urban decline had limited resources to deal with the issue. Moreover, only a few transit agencies benefited significantly from regional and state taxation. White suburban and rural voters refused to endow almost all regional transit agencies with the subsidies, taxing power, or land-use controls that could have enabled successful operation. Many middle-class Black families had also turned to cars and stopped riding as service declined by the 1970s and 1980s; more prosperous Black neighborhoods, often suburban in style, almost always had high car usage. Integrating transit agency workforces and leadership was sometimes as important politically as bus service quality. For mayors, it was often best to keep a transit authority at arm's length, push for hiring of Black citizens, or make requests for additional state or federal aid.

The racial dimension became even more pronounced with the arrival of federal capital funds in the 1960s and 1970s. White elites, who had mostly ignored the decline of streetcar and bus systems, often invested the new capital funds in expensive rapid transit systems designed to link cities and suburbs. Reverend King highlighted the racial issue in Atlanta, observing that "the rapid-transit system has been laid out for the convenience of the white upper-middle-class suburbanites who commute to their jobs downtown. The system has virtually no consideration for connecting the poor people with their jobs. There is only one possible explanation for this situation, and that is the racist blindness of city planners."[31] Yet African American mayors like Maynard Jackson in Atlanta, Coleman Young in Detroit, and Tom Bradley in Los Angeles ultimately promoted the same downtown-suburban linked rail systems favored by the white business community.

Local Stories and National Patterns

Transit history looks different when viewed with practices and trends like zoning, regional planning, and white flight. Newspapers for decades hammered transit managers for failing their riders or financial mismanagement, but angry editorial writers and reporters rarely considered the troubled context in which transit operated. Too little attention was devoted to the transit operations' social, political, and economic challenges. The following chapters use a case-study historical approach that interweaves the story of mass transit management and development with local politics, planning, and demography.

Part 1 briefly explores how choices made before World War II influenced the conditions for postwar transit operations and development. Baltimore, Chicago, and Boston case studies show the early patterns as cities pursued different subsidy and public management strategies. Despite fundamental differences, and Boston's pioneering role in launching regional transit subsidy, these cities shared the national interwar trend to automobiles, car-centric planning, and racial separation.

Part 2 on unsubsidized private transit utilizes Baltimore and Atlanta to illustrate the depressing fate of hundreds of private transit systems in the period of postwar decline. NCL ran Baltimore's lines during the postwar decades while two local private companies ran the Atlanta system. Despite the conventional wisdom that NCL in Baltimore would stand out for anti-streetcar animus, the disinvestment in these cities looks similar. Both Baltimore's and Atlanta's private managers sequentially slashed streetcars, trolleybuses, and high-quality buses during the postwar decades. Service in both cities failed to keep pace with sprawl. Public managers in these cities who followed the private companies lacked the necessary funding to compete for customers. They made poor choices in spending federal subsidies on expensive fixed-rail systems in the 1970s and 1980s. Underperforming public transit agencies like those in Baltimore and Atlanta were too common.

Part 3 on "pay as you go" public transit features Chicago and Detroit as case studies of publicly owned transit systems forced to subsist on fares during the crucial postwar era of decline. These cities are part of a smaller but essential subset of big cities, including Cleveland and Seattle, which made a painfully slow transition to transit as a subsidized municipal responsibility. Modest victories in these cities, such as extensions of a few postwar rapid lines, were undermined by more significant cuts to streetcars, electric trolley coaches, and buses. The public transit companies lacked the long-term funding or planning power to avoid decline. The arrival of federal and state funding, absent local or regional subsidies, proved insufficient to build or maintain high-quality service. Cities like these have a great deal to teach contemporary city officials, transit advocates, and planners struggling with so-called dysfunction in transit operations. Most of America's poorly performing public transit agencies are simply underfunded, just as Chicago and Detroit have been for decades. However, Seattle of late has demonstrated that it is never too late to reinvest in transit.

Part 4 on subsidized public transit reconstructs Boston's and San Francisco's stories to show that a moderately subsidized alternative existed quite early within the broader austerity, pro-automobile planning consensus. By preserving more of their transit network than was typical, these two cities share a great deal with transit in America's biggest city, New York. The three cities alone account for a disproportionate share of all US transit riders because of a century of investments made to modernize their systems. Because New York's transit system history has received so much previous attention, I focus on Boston and San Francisco as exemplars of an achievable American approach to balanced investment on transit and roads.[32]

Transit managers and city officials in Boston, New York, and San Francisco initially made similar decisions to their peers in Baltimore or Chicago. For instance, they heedlessly ripped out their streetcars and prioritized auto-centric planning such as highways and urban renewal for decades. Thankfully, however, these cities had underlying advantages that compensated for these errors. Among these were sustained population density near transit, well-heeled transit activists, significant geographical barriers to car commuting (bodies of water and crowded downtowns), and vibrant service economies. But these lucky advantages only turned into more dependable, affordable, and comprehensive service thanks to transit-friendly public policies, including local or regional transit taxation, supportive state government, more capacious zoning, and highway cancellation. Cities that have learned from best practices in these cities—such as Seattle, Portland, and Los Angeles—are finally reaping the rewards from more stable funding and transit-first planning initiatives.

The case studies collectively include cities of varied sizes, regions, demographics, and economic vitality to provide a broadly representative sample of urban transit in the twentieth century. The cities are primarily large, such as Chicago, but Atlanta was comparatively small for the history described here. Regional diversity is reflected in northern, southern, midwestern, and western case studies. Some cities are majority Black, like Baltimore, Detroit, and Atlanta, while others are more ethnically mixed, such as Boston and San Francisco. In terms of economics, the book includes declining Rust Belt cities like Chicago, Detroit, and Baltimore; comparatively stable cities like San Francisco and Boston; and a rapidly growing Sunbelt city like Atlanta.

Contextual and geographic differences impacted transit performance, but these case-study cities and hundreds of others all struggled during the shift from rail to rubber. The case studies foreground the wide range of policy options available to citizens and leaders, now mostly forgotten, that might have led to a better balance between transit and automobility. Americans ignored transit problems and created cities favorable to cars thanks to public policy choices rather than inevitability or secret conspiracies. The same mobility, planning, and social decisions are before Americans today as they face the challenge of meeting equity goals and a global climate crisis.

Pre–World War II

PART I

Urban Transit Rise and Decline

Across the nation, interwar city transit riders enjoyed a remarkable variety of transportation options at low fares: streetcars of a staggering variety and age, modern gas buses, electric trolleybuses, and in a few big cities, rapid elevated lines and subways. Even most suburbs still benefited from service provided by streetcars and interurbans (trolley service linking towns and cities). But such a large and impressive mobility infrastructure rested on shallow foundations. The three significant factors of transit collapse—austerity, auto-centric planning, and racial conflict—emerged during these interwar years.

Austerity was an emerging obstacle as traction companies encountered new revenue losses, bankruptcy, and receivership. The short era of robust profits, the late nineteenth century to the 1920s, created such a negative image of traction executives and shareholders that they blinded politicians to a workable private-public partnership during a sustained period of corporate decline. The director for research of Baltimore's faltering private-sector United Railways in 1934 explained the problem succinctly: "The average man's mind is filled with the suspicion and prejudice that are the outgrowth of evils associated with the promotional stage of street railways of 25 or 30 years ago, when they were in a boom period."[1]

Local leaders consistently rejected transit subsidies from the city, suburban, or state budgets. They viewed traction companies as unfeeling, mismanaged monopolies that only victimized the riding public rather than providing an essential public utility on a for-profit basis. They mostly ignored the plans for rapid transit they had commissioned and took active steps to reduce downtown transit lines to speed up autos. Local and state politicians set in motion decades of *extreme* service decline and disinvestment. A downward spiral ensued without subsidies, fare increases, tax relief, or access to public credit. During the interwar years, the refusal to stabilize bankrupt companies emboldened vulture corporations like NCL during the 1940s. Again, alternative financial choices existed, but most local officials ignored them.

The rise of popular, local, auto-centric city planning contributed directly to the growing transit crisis during the interwar years. Between 1920 and 1929, car ownership dramatically increased, rising from one auto for every thirteen Americans to one for every five.[2] The *Electric Traction and Bus Journal* in 1934 admitted that "the public certainly does not ride streetcars due to preference over the automobile."[3] American urban society became a car culture not only because of Detroit's aggressive marketing and the public appetite for driving but because local officials decided to make driving competitive, and in many cases superior in comfort and speed, to transit. The interwar era's critical efforts were smooth paving, street widening, sidewalk narrowing, electric traffic signals, streetcar track removal, and limited-access parkway development. Interwar auto-centric planning was a choice, not a mandate, often requiring generous local government outlays—just not on transit.

Zoning, a powerful planning tool widely adopted in the 1920s, prevented the development of dense peripheral areas within expanding city limits or densification of older neighborhoods required for good transit service. The emerging city planning profession in the United States, which one might have hoped could see beyond the auto-mania of the day, endorsed auto-centric planning. John Nolen, a founder of the field, showed a flair for suburban town planning, favored decentralization, and in 1931 claimed that subways were "evidence of an unsuccessfully planned city." Even avant-garde planning of the time, as embodied in Clarence Stein's Radburn, New Jersey, project, envisioned an urban future of decentralized, auto-centric garden cities and peripheral social housing. Leading planner Harland Bartholomew eventually soured on decentralization. In 1932, for instance, he encouraged rapid transit to slow the "disintegration of the larger central areas of cities." Yet, he was a voice in the wilderness.[4]

During this period, patterns of racialized public policy began undermining the notion of transit as a citywide urban utility. White leaders during the interwar years encouraged racist policies that starkly divided areas: restrictive covenants, single-family zoning, school segregation, and redlining. These efforts left transit, which still traversed the city, in a precarious position. Streetcars became some of the few shared interior spaces that Americans encountered daily. The high-profile riots in Chicago and Jim Crow on transit in the South overshadowed the widespread shift of whites to auto-centric single-family areas poorly served by the older transit networks. Black newcomers to cities, by contrast, crowded into restricted neighborhoods well served by transit and poorly suited to car ownership. Thus, the pattern of white suburban drivers and Black center-city riders began its inexorable rise. This division would undermine political support for transit in the postwar decades within cities and across metropolitan areas.

CHAPTER 1

Baltimore: City Leaders versus Private Transit

The political war on streetcars, first United Railways and then its successor the Baltimore Transit Company (BTC), was part of a broader, multi-decade attempt to modernize what many Baltimore city leaders considered to be an old-fashioned, second-tier, racially divided metropolis. The sense of comparative urban inferiority that drove the city's anti-transit movement was typical of Baltimore. Yet the regulatory failure, auto-centric planning, anti-streetcar stance, resistance to public ownership, and racial tensions reflected conditions in many American cities.

Baltimore's impressive residential, industrial, and commercial growth in the late nineteenth century had been enabled, in part, by expanding streetcar networks. Baltimore residents of the turn of the century benefited from the city's web of streetcar lines for work, play, and commerce. The streetcars daily funneled hundreds of thousands of riders from their homes to center-city docks, warehouses, stores, offices, and factories. On evenings and weekends, city residents out for a fun time rode streetcars to shopping and urban amusements. Builders surrounded the expanding trolley routes with block after block of compact row houses. Stores and businesses also followed the streetcar lines outward.[1] The older, centrally located row houses, usually subdivided into apartments, packed the streetcar lines with customers. Yet even newer town-house developments further out, for a higher-class buyer seeking light and air, were dense enough to support transit before widespread auto ownership. Most trolley lines ran in the middle of streets or boulevards, but many peripheral lines sped along exclusive rights-of-way. By the early twentieth century, growing numbers of upper-class Baltimoreans rode the streetcars to and from leafy suburbs of single-family homes, like Roland Park or Mount Washington, just beyond the city's borders.

City leaders, over the decades and in step with a national practice, failed to exercise their regulatory power constructively and proactively over granting franchises for new lines. An industry representative like Dean Locke, of the United Railways would justifiably pin the blame for the disjointed system on regulatory failure. Streetcars, according to Locke, may have "added value to outlying property... and central values rose" yet "little or no thought was given either to the control of construction or to the planning of new lines as parts of a citywide system of local travel. For the most part, present street railway systems consist merely of a grouping of former separate lines built with little regard to a community plan or to the future."[2] After unification and electrification in the 1890s under the United Railways, the Baltimore system still sprawled over 324 line miles with 1,278 streetcars. Residents in tightly packed neighborhoods close-in often had their pick from lines just a few blocks apart. However, as the lines reached out from the central city, enormous gaps opened, making everyday transit less convenient for fast-growing suburban areas. City leaders, as much as the transit companies, had neglected to direct the growth of an integrated, customer-friendly network.

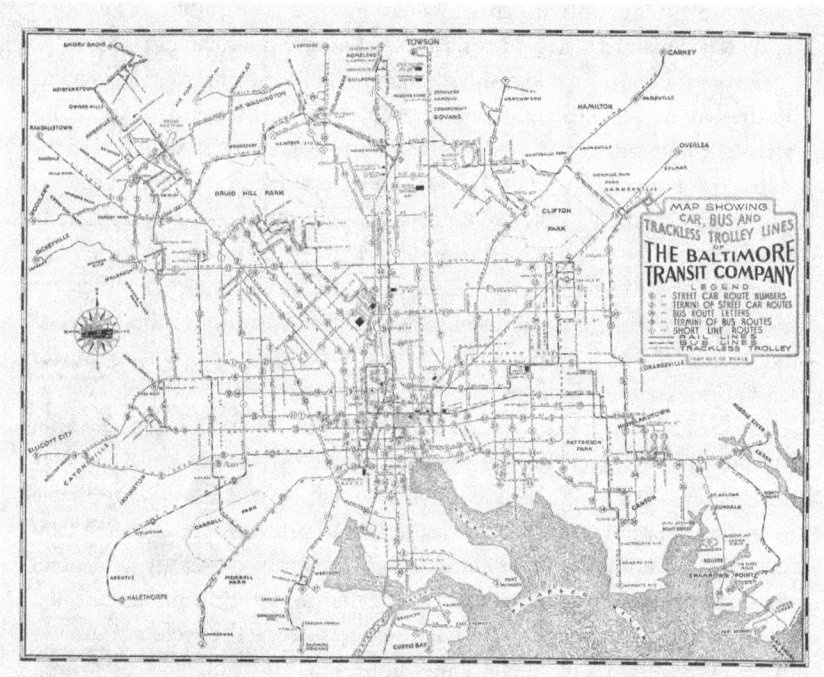

FIGURE 3. The Baltimore Transit Company's system in 1941, still mostly streetcars, remained extensive in the central neighborhoods where most riders still lived.

Like most American cities, Baltimore failed to move transit under municipal sponsorship during the high point of progressive reform. Transit had the dubious distinction of being a public utility or service with significant and regular profits for private investors. Progressive innovation focused on public control of expensive services that directly impacted public health or welfare and seemed unlikely to yield enormous profits. Municipal responsibility for money-losing citywide services in roads, water, sewers, parks, public schools, and public health was widely accepted by the early twentieth century in cities like Baltimore and many others. The city, for instance, had taken over water service from a private company in 1854 and, by the early twentieth century, spent millions on building a network of vast reservoirs, pipes, and treatment plants. Profitable transit companies, by contrast, buoyed by fares from their captive markets, operated with few restraints and resisted regulation. Transit even made money for cities by paying Baltimore city park taxes and facilitating land development.

United Railways used its new monopoly position to sustain a profitable enterprise and left in place the uncoordinated trackage and routes it absorbed in the early twentieth century. Management then squeezed every penny of service it could from its aging equipment.[3] The State of Maryland finally created the Public Service Commission (PSC) in 1910 to police the United Railways. Like most public utility commissions of the time, the PSC focused on issues like route frequency and capacity rather than long-term planning. In 1920, for instance, an editorial in the *Baltimore Sun* observed that "residents of Northeast Baltimore are compelled to ride to the center of the city in order to reach Southeast Baltimore." Even worse, "millions of dollars' worth of property in the old city of Baltimore lies unimproved because it is not accessible, and in the ten years of its existence the Public Service Commission has never made the slightest effort to compel extensions of the car line within the old city for the benefit of the public." The PSC, hamstrung by the power of the United and franchise agreements mandating an agreed-upon rate of profit, rarely pushed back.[4] The United Railways management in 1931 eventually looked back with regret on this cozy arrangement: "The street railways were prosperous during the long years of non-competition, growing revenue and ease of financing, and the public heaped upon them a burden of taxes and expenses of various kinds."[5]

That transit taxes supported parks and other city infrastructure development meant little to transit customers struggling to move around on slow and aging streetcars. Politicians also became dangerously reliant on transit taxes, just as they did in other cities. In the years to come, even as the company faltered, leaders fiercely resisted any tax reductions that might, in their view, boost profits without service improvement. The city might have, for instance, designated these taxes for a rapid transit system, downtown tunnel system, crosstown routes, or other modernization strategies. Between 1900 and 1935, for example, United Railways had paid park or gross receipts taxes of $30 million (about $560 million in current dollars), not including additional paving charges for which the company was responsible.[6] Chicago, by contrast, created a traction fund that diverted a portion of the taxes on the private companies to system upgrades, funds that helped pay for a center-city subway during the 1930s.

Auto-Centric Planning and Racial Conflict

The growing enthusiasm for city planning was another strike against transit. The rise of modern zoning in the 1910s and 1920s, promoted by city leaders, threatened the ecology of transit by halting the densification of many neighborhoods near existing transit while, at the same time, banning much of any multifamily housing in newly annexed peripheral areas. Baltimore's assistant civil engineer Jefferson C. Grinnalds was a leading advocate for zoning. He shaped Baltimore's local code as secretary of the city's Zoning Board from 1923 to 1954. His pinched urban vision was typical of his contemporaries in the emerging city planning profession. He had nothing but disdain for the crowded downtowns and cramped row houses of the streetcar city. Those of his class had looked on with fear as "speculators converted some three-story houses into walk-ups" and older areas lost respectability with the arrival of poor whites from Appalachia, immigrants, and Black migrants. In his perfectly zoned city, by contrast, not only would business districts decentralize, but "high class residential districts can be preserved for their rightful use. Areas can be assigned to unbroken rows of brick houses. Apartment houses can be segregated."[7]

White flight from Baltimore's most transit-oriented neighborhoods was a crucial underlying attraction of zoning to city officials, real-estate interests, and citizen groups. Flight reshaped the city's west side in the early twentieth century, with many whites bolting from once fashionable areas such as Mount Royal and Bolton Hill to larger homes with lawns in streetcar suburbs like Windsor Hills and Forest Park. Their departure created opportunities for a rising class of Black families to leave behind alleys for better town houses on main streets.[8] Baltimore in 1920 counted 108,322 African American residents among its population of 733,826, or 14.76 percent.[9] Pennsylvania Avenue on the near west side of downtown, traversed by streetcars and surrounded by most of the city's Black population, had by the 1920s become the heart of Baltimore's segregated "Harlem" according to the *Sun*: "Along it are the clothing stores, the groceries, the markets, the confectionaries, the theaters, the hotels and restaurants which cater to the tastes of the inhabitants," many of them run by white ethnic immigrants.[10] The Black population achieved some geographic expansion on both the east and west sides, but the aging row-house housing stock within the expanded boundaries was dangerously overcrowded.[11] By 1940, on the west side (then 70.2 percent Black), the population density was 51,654 persons per square mile, a remarkably high figure for a low-rise city. Citywide, Black residents had jumped to 19.3 percent in 1940, or one in five city residents.[12]

Real-estate interests and residents of areas facing racial change were desperate for new ways to limit the spread of Black people from the restricted ghettos. Most whites viewed vibrant Black neighborhoods as evidence of weakening white control over urban space. Some white neighborhoods adopted restrictive covenants after development. Yet it was often hard to get all owners to sign on, given the potential future profits in renting or selling to Black families. The Supreme Court's 1917 ruling, *Buchanan v. Warley*, overturned a noxious 1910 Baltimore City law that aimed to create a legal basis for long-term residential segregation. The decision potentially unleashed a wave of new Black renters, buyers, and transit riders in white neighborhoods.[13]

Many whites in neighborhoods attacked Black families with the audacity to seek better housing across the color line and would do so for decades, but the rapid growth of the Black population overawed informal regulation in many close-in neighborhoods.[14] Racist property owners, therefore, hoped that zoning might now protect "purely white neighborhoods from a negro invasion." The Supreme Court in 1917 may have ruled that racial categories in zoning laws were illegal, but the higher income level of whites meant that a zoned single-family residence area in new districts was effectively out of reach for most Black families. In sum, for many white Baltimoreans, zoning was a long-sought tool of segregation.[15]

City leaders like Grinnalds were particularly concerned about the future development in the New Annex, a massive expansion of Baltimore's city boundaries in 1918, including primarily undeveloped land and a few elite, segregated suburban areas like Roland Park (1891). Roland Park's curvilinear streets, landscaped streetcar boulevard, single-family homes with setback and design controls, and strict limits on other uses proved influential. E. H. Bouton, president of the Roland Park Company and an overt racist, added racially restrictive covenants to the even more exclusive Guilford (1911).[16] The design innovation and social engineering reflected in these elite suburbs reflected national trends as the emerging field of planning, according to historian Mark Foster, devoted more energy to decentralization and "shaping suburban environments" than to "reconstructing urban cores." Most planners also endorsed social exclusivity along racial and class lines.[17]

Typical developers of the era rarely duplicated the exclusive social and design standards of a Guilford or Roland Park in Baltimore's more modest and numerous residential suburban "cottage" or row-house developments. The availability of inexpensive automobiles during the interwar years "encouraged home building away from the streetcar lines."[18] Municipal zoning, substituting cost and ground coverage factors for explicit segregationist policy, careful design, or covenants, was a possible way to take some of Roland Park's standards citywide for both new vacant areas and older middle-class communities facing pressure for land subdivision and additional density.[19] Bouton was a central figure in the pressure for citywide zoning, serving on the first commissions charged with developing the zoning maps.[20] Real-estate interests and city leaders promoted zoning "restrictions as to certain classes of dwelling within certain areas, which would forbid, for instance, the erection of houses in rows in neighborhoods where the cottage plan prevails."[21] The older row house, packed with ethnic or Black families, had become the dominant image of urban decay, much as the tenement was in other cities. The limited row-house growth permitted in future neighborhoods was unwelcome news for transit.

Baltimore's first zoning regulations approved in 1923 divided the city into distinct areas for residences, business, and manufacturing and set overlapping regulations within those districts on building height and ground coverage. Densification of existing areas was now difficult, spelling trouble for transit's future. The city, which never had many large apartment houses to begin with, permitted high-density apartment towers in just a few choice locations near Druid Hill Park and Johns Hopkins University. Low-density residence designations dominated the New Annex, including ample ground coverage requirements "so as to exclude row houses from the suburbs." A few enterprising developers found space or lobbied for variances for additional high-quality row houses, and large apartment buildings did prove popular with developers and the public where narrowly allowed, but the detached home on its own lot emerged dominant in Baltimore's undeveloped areas. City officials ignored transit's need for future density to create a more segregated environment by both race and class.[22]

In 1940, after the 1920s boom and a decade of Depression, zoning had worked as an effective tool for shaping low-density peripheral development. Forty-five square miles of the city's outer districts, mostly former New Annex areas, housed 180,000 people (98.1 percent white) at an average population density of just 3,947 persons per square mile—much lower than the intensive streetcar systems of the central districts. These density levels increased slightly postwar as the remaining undeveloped lands sprouted more car-friendly developments, but not by much.[23]

Many whites simply left the city during the interwar years, mostly thanks to cars, for a semirural suburban existence in Baltimore County. The county's population during the interwar years grew larger and whiter. The county in 1920 was 12.16 percent Black but by 1940 had dropped to 6.74 percent Black, despite a doubling of the total population from 1920 to 1940 from 74,817 to 155,000. While some streetcar lines reached out to the county in Towson and Catonsville, most commuter rail lines had already failed. Remaining private bus lines offered limited coverage, and driving in most areas was required. The county adopted its own zoning code in 1945, with a heavy bias to maintaining its rural and suburban character. The county's auto-centric suburban landscape would eventually draw out hundreds of thousands of white city residents seeking their private yards and freestanding homes.[24]

Some whites also hoped to use government power to enforce segregation on transit. Transit was one of the few racially integrated public services in Maryland when department stores, railway cars, and schools were segregated. While southern-identified and surrounded by even more extreme segregation in the rest of Maryland, the city did not enforce Jim Crow laws on mass transit.[25] This liberality bothered State Delegate Michael Noon of Baltimore who proposed a bill in 1924 "to extend segregation law to city transportation"[26] The idea of separate cars for white and Black passengers failed, but the bill got a full hearing.[27] The Twenty-Fourth Ward Democratic Club, in a working-class white area on the south side of the harbor, endorsed the bill, probably reflecting broader support.[28] The inability of white racists to secure separate cars or seating may have accelerated flight from transit; at minimum, the effort indicates a high level of discomfort in certain neighborhoods.

The Emerging Auto-Centric Mindset

Local politicians in the interwar years abetted white flight from transit and from the city center to the New Annex and the county by building better streets and traffic controls. During these years, the ceaseless increase in cars and white flight disrupted a precarious streetcar city equilibrium.

Between 1915 and 1925, Baltimore's ratio of car ownership zoomed up from one to thirty persons per car to one to ten.[29] The United Railway's peak ridership of 254 million riders arrived and passed in 1920.[30] Between 1920 and 1925, the United lost thirty million annual revenue passengers, mostly to private automobiles.[31] Losses in non–peak hour riders, crucial to profitable operations, damaged operations in Baltimore and other cities. As the company admitted, "The courtin' couple that used to go trolley ridin' of an evening, now uses the flivver."[32] Individual streetcar fares were cheap, but automobiles were competitive in price for family travel. And in many cases, the trip in a car was also faster thanks to alternative routes.[33]

The city was behind on high-speed parkways and highways compared to Chicago or New York,[34] but street widening, traffic control, and paving were already civic priorities. The transit companies got the message. Dean Locke of United Railways in 1934 protested that "public officials and civic leaders have endeavored to provide street improvements and other public works to facilitate automobile travel." The obsessions of elected officials with roads and the prosperous masses, in the eyes of transit executives, meant that they ignored "the needs of those who travel in public vehicles." The evidence of this auto mania was the politicians' refusal to make "provisions for the safety and convenience of public transit patrons, such as special right of way treatment, safety zones, etc., which could be included at almost negligible cost at the time the improvements are made."[35] City leaders doubled down on road improvements. They widened Franklin Street, for instance, in the 1930s to help drivers "skirt the congested center of the city and get through town at a fast clip."[36] Widened and paved roads could have been designed to accommodate future streetcar lines as had been done in the past or in interwar European urban extensions during this time.

The battle for Baltimore's scarce downtown road space, like other cities, pitted rail versus autos. Sixteen different streetcar lines, served by hundreds of trams, screeched daily up and down a hilly and congested CBD of just under half a square mile. Decongesting downtown became a multidecade political crusade in Baltimore and every American city. Politicians and traffic experts disproportionately focused on removing streetcars rather than the problems caused by the rapidly growing number of private automobiles. In a sign of transit problems to come, transit consultants hired by the city in 1926 recommended consolidating streetcar routes despite carrying 70 percent of riders into the CBD on a tiny fraction of the total vehicles. The report also highlighted the potential for additional bus service to free roads from streetcars, tracks, and riders.[37]

City leaders also openly disregarded expensive rapid transit alternatives for disentangling downtown snares. The general manager of the United Railways in 1920, for instance, called subways or elevated rapid transit lines "the only real remedy" to relieve downtown congestion. Rapid transit of this kind would, however, be expensive and meant "the municipality ... would be called upon to finance such an undertaking." Multiple proposals for publicly funded rapid transit in Baltimore fell on deaf ears, often the case in other cities. City leaders and voters were unwilling to move transit into the municipal expenditure column. Given the decentralization underway during the interwar years, their caution is understandable. However, by not investing in a high-quality rapid system, they left Baltimoreans without any demonstration of what rapid transit might deliver to their city.[38]

United Railways still dominated urban mobility in the 1920s, but as in other cities, the popularity of cars undermined ridership. The boom in car ownership, better roads, and emphasis on low-density development directly threatened the viability and importance of rail mass transit. As losses continued, the executives reduced service in step: "A streetcar system, like any other business, must 'cut its cloth to suit the garment,' and many economies have been instituted. When fewer people ride fewer cars must be operated because it is the operation of cars that entails most of a street railway's expense."[39] Management in the 1920s began experimenting with substituting streetcar lines in fashionable areas with upscale, more expensive to ride bus service, a typical approach in cities at the time. The company also introduced electric trolleybuses that promised to reduce expensive track maintenance costs, utilize existing power generation capability, and capitalize on city investments in paved roads. However, the United deferred investment in new equipment and cut service.[40] Between 1920 and 1933, the company cut service 19 percent, mostly before the Great Depression. The average age of streetcars in the inventory was twenty-two years by 1935. No wonder riders were angry.[41]

Downward Spiral

The Depression was another hit for a transit company beset by ridership decline, auto competition, and park taxes. Many Baltimoreans could no longer afford their cars, so they grudgingly returned to streetcars. Yet mass unemployment so severely reduced the total transit ridership (including leisure) that the company was worse off than before. Raising fares was one option to restore profits as ridership tanked. The Supreme Court in 1930 ruled that the PSC of Maryland's refusal to raise fares was "confiscatory" because it provided less than the 7.44 percent returns promised in the franchise agreements. The company promptly raised fares to ten cents. Court rulings in favor of transit companies for fare increases were common in this time, as political leaders tried to wiggle out of binding franchise contracts made some years before.[42] United Railways was not, however, able to benefit for very long from these additional revenues because of declining Depression ridership; the company even reduced fares 25 percent in 1934 in a desperate bid to draw back riders.[43]

Local tax reduction offered a potential path to restore the company's profitability during the worst economic days the country had ever seen. The United Railway's request for tax reduction in 1931 made a strong case that the transit taxes paid by mostly working-class fares flowed primarily to the benefit of automobile users: "The public must recognize the fact that the street railway is a public servant, conferring very definite and important benefits to the community, and that the whole community should bear the paving costs, snow removal and park taxes, etc., and other burdens imposed on the street railway and now borne almost wholly by the car rider."[44] United Railways was still paying about $1 million per year in city park taxes imposed decades before when the streetcar system was a big moneymaker.[45] City leaders ignored the pleas in 1931 for tax relief during a national economic crisis and provided no subsidies, setting the stage for dramatic and unsettling corporate reconstruction.

Ridership had plummeted from the 1920 high of 254 million to just 104 million riders in 1933, a roughly 60 percent decline. The entire enterprise was in danger.[46] United Railways put on a good front for a few years of the Depression and even tried to maintain service quality but entered receivership in 1933. The publicly supervised reorganization that ended that receivership in 1935 created the successor BTC, slightly reduced park taxes, reorganized the company's debt and accelerated bus substitution and other economies. The top-to-bottom reorganization aimed to restore profitability and thus keep the trains running. A key element was significant reductions in future returns to company investors. In Baltimore and many other American cities, the destruction of shareholder and bondholder value in transit companies during this period was satisfying to many political leaders who had condemned the monopoly companies and their profits. Investor haircuts, however, slashed the number of potential future investors, the value of companies like BTC, and their ability to finance improvements privately.[47]

Without hope of public support and much lower ridership now a permanent situation, the BTC reorganization set in motion the destruction of the comparatively high-cost streetcar system. Only packed cars had justified the massive infrastructure required to keep a streetcar system in action. Moreover, streetcar substitution with buses directly aligned with the city's goals of reducing trackage in the downtown to speed up automobile traffic. The reorganization plan authored in 1935 by court-appointed special master Charles W. Chase of the Indianapolis Street Railway System, and endorsed by the local judge supervising the receivership, called for a five-year plan of reducing the streetcar network to just 189 miles, primarily the popular "trunk" routes, 150 miles of trackless electric service, and eighty-nine miles of gasoline bus routes. The reorganization program envisioned BTC spending millions on new equipment to shift from streetcar majority to minority. The plan echoed substitution choices made across the country during this time.[48]

If city leaders had carried out the plan with strong public regulation and financial support, the modernization plan might have created a high-

FIGURE 4. Electric trolleybuses (also known as trackless trolleys or trolley coaches) replaced streetcars on many routes in Baltimore and other cities.

quality system. The introduction of new electric trolleybuses on some lines, in Baltimore as in many other cities, improved service quality when they replaced ancient streetcars. Some gas bus additions were genuine upgrades, like a sorely needed crosstown east–west travel route in prosperous northern Baltimore. However, the newly minted BTC removed tracks for short-term cost cutting, often under city pressure, rather than as part of a long-term plan.

BTC promised "to retain and improve its busiest streetcar routes using PCC cars." PCC (President's Conference Committee) cars were quieter, wider, and more comfortable one-person-operated trams. Their leather seats, additional windows, wider doors, better heating, and smoother ride aimed to compete with automobiles for customers. Developed cooperatively by the desperate streetcar industry, and reflecting the best of

FIGURE 5. Older streetcars en route to the defense plants in World War II Baltimore.

American industrial design know-how, they represented a breakthrough in transport technology that influenced transport design for decades to come. The PCCs were of tremendous quality, but most private streetcar operators were too broke (or committed to rubber-tired vehicles) to buy that many of them in the 1930s.[49] The BTC, for instance, purchased only a limited number PCCs. In 1945, PCC cars were just 275 out of a 1,040 streetcar fleet, reflecting the small number of PCC cars purchased during the preceding decade. The rest of the 1940s streetcar fleet was mostly composed of aging equipment that paled compared to the appeal of comfortable, streamlined automobiles. The city leadership stood by while the company failed to carry out the modernization program as recommended and offered no financial support for modernization. Nor did the BTC build the massive electric trolley system to replace streetcars recommended in the reorganization.[50]

The failure to trash half or more of the streetcar lines as recommended turned out to be a mixed blessing during the war years. BTC achieved record ridership during World War II, as did most transit companies, due to booming wartime industries and federal restrictions on gas and motor vehicle production. Like all transit companies of the time, the BTC packed the factory-bound riders into whatever old streetcar and bus equipment it could find. Crowding served the war effort, and there was no alternative for BTC given the limited production of new vehicles during the war. Still, obsolescent equipment helped render transit riding even less appealing. The crowded and racially mixed street cars repelled many racist whites who had to ride because of wartime rationing.

BTC remained an easy takeover target as the war wound down. By failing to invest in transit, city leaders set the stage for NCL in 1944. Even more broadly, municipal investment in roads and zoning put transit at a disadvantage. The extreme segregation city leaders had promoted created contrasting urban spaces: one, primarily white, suburban-style, and increasingly auto-centric; the other, increasingly minority, densely packed in older row housing, and dependent on transit or walking. Politicians, who could see the growing popularity of cars, chose auto-friendly policies because they were the ones that they and their white constituents favored.

CHAPTER 2

Chicago: A Limited Public Commitment to Transit

A century ago, Chicago thrived thanks to streetcars and elevated lines that helped build the city's dense neighborhoods, industrial concerns, and downtown skyscraper Loop. In 1926, for instance, the Chicago Surface Lines (CSL) streetcar companies could still boast of running the "largest streetcar system in the world," offering the attractive possibility "to ride 37 miles on Surface Lines on the payment of one fare." Best of all, "no place in the city is more than a short walk from streetcar service."[1] The CSL network of streetcars crisscrossed the city at regular half-mile intervals and along the few diagonal streets.[2]

Many Chicagoans had been complaining about CSL's old and slow streetcars for decades, but they could not complain about the quantity or comprehensiveness of service. Even more remarkable, the city government had provided almost no local funding to support the development or maintenance of the streetcars, elevated, interurban, or commuter rail service. The lack of subsidy was typical nationally, but it contrasted with the situation in rival cities of New York or Boston, which started subsidizing and financing the rapid transit network development at the turn of the century.

Chicago threw away its leading national and global position in urban mass transit starting in the 1920s. As different as Chicago was in size, industrial strength, and density from Baltimore or cities like it, the forces behind the wrecking of a citywide system are familiar: a city government and planning consensus obsessed with road improvements; a city government and populace that delayed public ownership and remained solidly opposed to subsidy; regional zoning that undermined ridership by limiting future suburban density; and emerging racial tensions and restrictions that undermined neighborhoods and eventually diminished white support for mass transit. The interwar years of disinvestment and the failure to modernize proved crucial to setting the extreme era of postwar decline in motion.

The decline of Chicago's transit took place in the context of urban leadership that had otherwise progressively expanded the role of government to make a more livable city. Among these outstanding accomplishments was a twenty-six-mile system consisting of eight parks, nineteen boulevards, and six squares that today make up the Chicago Park Boulevard System Historic District. City politicians and voters approved bond issues (1905, 1915, 1923, and 1927) for park expansion and other improvements, including a regional forest preserve beyond the city's borders.[3] The city government's leadership was crucial to developing the massive Chicago Sanitary and Ship Canal that reversed the Chicago River's flow to preserve the quality of drinking water taken from Lake Michigan. The Municipal Sanitary District built the canal between 1889 and 1907 for over $31 million. A city that had dawdled on public education compared to some was by the 1920s finally educating its working class in a massive, if uneven, free school system that enrolled about four hundred thousand students. In 1887 the city had successfully developed publicly owned electric power, demonstrating "the practical value of municipal ownership of public utilities."[4] Over the decades, city and state leaders created new agencies to develop and manage these projects, aggressively pushing at the state's limits on the city's bonding capacity. The voters mostly approved.[5]

Notably absent from the list of public investments was mass transit. In the late nineteenth century, the city government and private rail interests worked together to build three tunnels for mass transit and other vehicles under the Chicago River to relieve pressure on overcrowded bridges. Still, in most other respects, the city left the companies in the driver's seat.[6] After all, the transit business was a profitable private industry intricately linked to real-estate speculation. Traction entrepreneurs, to whom the city had granted franchises (the first of which was inked in 1858), took advantage of the terrain and regular grid of streets as they extended innovative technologies, including horsecars, cable cars, electric streetcars, and elevated lines in the nineteenth and early twentieth centuries. According to transit historian Alan Lind, the flat five- to fifteen-mile-wide Chicago Plain on which the city rose "helped in the rapid settlement of outlying areas. The street railways aided this dispersion of the population by making it possible for workers to live many miles away from their work yet reach it in a reasonable time."[7]

New residential, commercial, and industrial districts in Chicago rose along the lines, creating a complex web of uses across the city's fast-growing neighborhoods. In the minds of Chicago riders, who otherwise benefited from the extensive networks built without taxation, the owners were greedy, unfeeling capitalists. The streetcars and cable cars were agreed to be crowded, unheated, poorly maintained, and slowed by surrounding traffic. As in New York, the elevated lines were a cheap solution to faster transit favored by private interests looking to speed up riders with moderate capital outlays (compared to subways). Thanks to their relative speed, the elevated lines were instantly popular, but they were usually overcrowded, polluting eyesores to some, and they created a racket in the areas they served.

As in Baltimore and most other cities in the second half of the nineteenth century, Chicago's public officials encouraged the multiple surface lines and elevated companies to compete against each other by granting franchises that allowed them to develop nearby without coordinated fares or routes. City leaders frustrated over traction business practices in early twentieth-century Chicago, as elsewhere, focused on regulatory efforts like transit taxes, franchise terms, fares, and transfer privileges. Consolidation of surface transit under monopolist Charles Yerkes in the late nineteenth century and elevated lines under Samuel Insull in the early twentieth potentially allowed city leaders to reshape the network in a more rational, public-focused system. Yet the advocates of long-term planning had limited success facing off against powerful new monopolies. For instance, transit operators and city leaders failed to follow through on multiple plans to create a downtown streetcar subway system connected to the tunnels under the Chicago River. Such a system would have further expedited surface journeys and boosted capacity, but would have required city subsidy (as in Boston). The failure to expand the elevated rapid system beyond a narrow band of the city's territory also limited future transit leaders' ability to create a modern, fast, citywide system to match the challenge of the auto age.

Some brave politicians had tried taking on the traction interests directly by promoting municipal ownership but failed thanks to a mix of corruption, voter fiscal conservatism, and bad political luck. It is revealing to learn that even Chicago's first franchise for street railways in 1858 included an option for municipal ownership. Decades of succeeding battles primarily focused on the scope and length of franchises to the various private companies that had built out the transit network on a for-profit basis. For instance, city leaders had enough work countering the attempts by traction companies to buy themselves absurd ninety-nine-year franchises. Having grown tired of the "utterly inadequate" service, the public voted (in 1902 and 1904) for municipal ownership. The Democratic platform in 1904–5 boldly called for public ownership citing the "beneficial results of municipal ownership in England, Germany and other European countries." Voters elected the Democrats on the platform, but they were to be disappointed once again.[8]

The city's voters were not necessarily reliable when genuine opportunities for municipal ownership advanced. In 1906 the city council was finally ready to spend $75 million to buy traction companies, but supporters could not win the 60 percent of voter support required by law. Instead, in 1907 the city council granted twenty-year franchise extensions and locked down the nickel fare and new provisions for future purchase and transit taxes. Voters approved this modest "settlement" of 1907. Voters also rejected public ownership in 1916 and 1925, despite strong support from elected officials.[9] During these battles, politicians had succeeded in just one central policy area: consolidation of surface transit in 1914, bringing a universal five-cent fare and new equipment. The multiple elevated lines followed suit in 1924, but these policies mostly blessed monopolies.[10]

During these years of political conflict, the private transit companies covered payrolls, built extensions, and paid taxes, dividends, bond interest, and principal reduction by collecting nickels and pennies from millions of daily users. In 1920, the four companies that made up CSL managed 1,059 miles of single-track surface lines. Chicago possessed 2.3 percent of all American surface track and accounted for 6.5 percent of all revenue passengers nationally! Its sixteen thousand employees in 1920 made it one of Chicago's more significant industrial concerns.[11] Between 1914 and 1926, CSL added 113 miles of extensions to emerging areas further out, mainly before 1920, and rebuilt 433 miles over the same period.[12] The Chicago Rapid Transit Company (CRT) maintained a system of elevated lines with about fifteen hundred cars threading their way through back alleys and over streets, on about two hundred miles of track, to converge and circle the famous center-city elevated tracks of the Loop. A few elevated and streetcar lines even crossed city lines and offered service to suburbs like Evanston and Cicero.

The streetcars and elevated lines prospered thanks to density and diversity of uses. Traction thrived in the most crowded neighborhoods near the elevated lines thanks to densities of between forty and fifty thousand persons per square mile that generated heavy, round-the-clock ridership. Chicago may have styled itself the "City of Homes," but in 1923, its 135,000 one-family dwellings (750,000 inhabitants) was dwarfed by 96,000 two-flat and 37,000 apartment buildings housing about two million of the city's growing population. Even the single-family homes were tightly

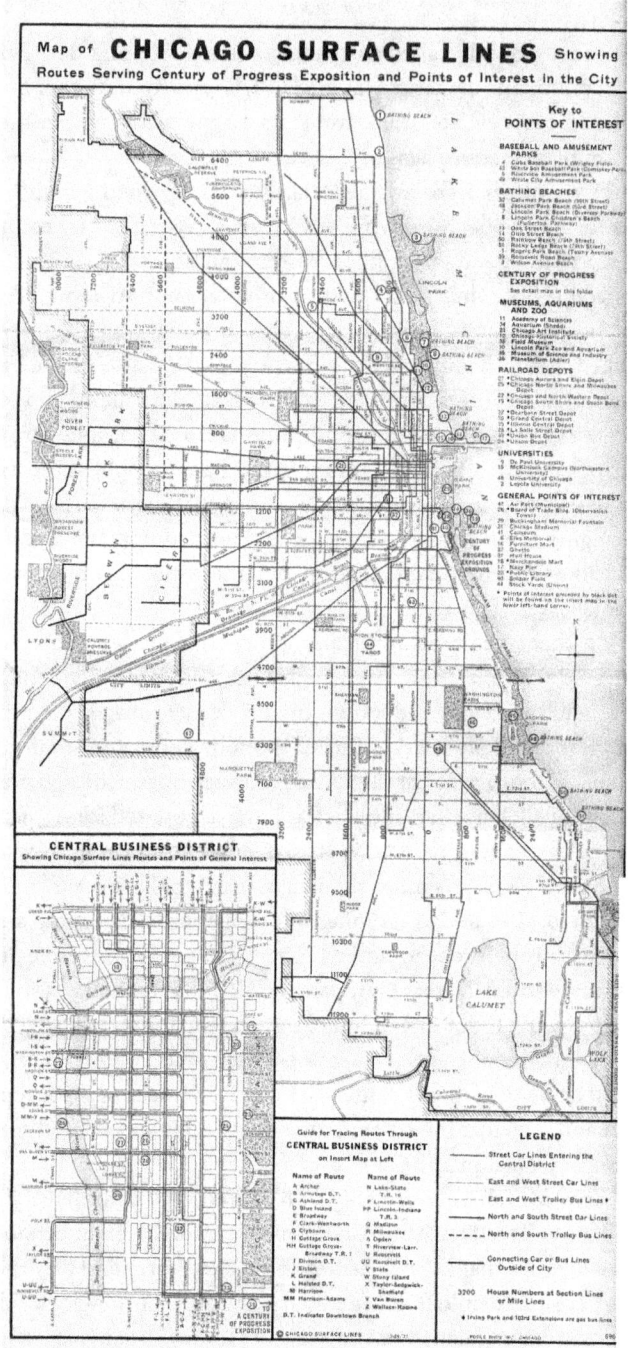

FIGURE 6. The extensive system of streetcars in Chicago, as illustrated on this 1933 map, provided citywide service. Source: Library of Congress.

packed into their lots. Only a few suburban-style areas, like Hyde Park, had larger lots and homes.[13] The city's rapidly developing Bungalow Belt reached levels of ten to twenty thousand persons per square mile thanks to closely packed bungalows and two-flats, providing sufficient density for streetcars.[14] In 1935, according to CSL management, 98 percent of the Chicago population and 84 percent of the city area were still "within three blocks of its gridiron of tracks and bus routes."[15]

Traction in a city like Chicago benefited from the multiple destinations and markets of these densely packed residents traversing the city around the clock. In striking contrast to the postwar situation of commuter-focused service, the dominant CSL boasted that it was mostly an interneighborhood system: "most of the passengers it carries are local riders going from one neighborhood to another. Only 18 percent of them enter the central business district."[16] Workers in massive numbers traveled both to large manufacturing districts on the South and West Sides and small factories and warehouses spread throughout neighborhoods citywide. Chicago's long neighborhood commercial strips paralleled streetcar and elevated lines and stops, with notable clusters at diagonal cross streets. In Chicago, for instance, "at least 75 neighborhood communities and shopping centers . . . developed around transfer points or terminals of local transit routes."[17] A remarkable sixty out of ninety-seven CSL routes in 1928 were transporting riders twenty-four hours a day with some important lines offering service at eight- or ten-minute intervals throughout the night! Imagine what a different kind of city this was.[18]

One of the factors contributing to transit's enduring popularity among whites in Chicago during the interwar years was the highly segregated landscape of the city. White ethnic immigrants had dominated since the city's founding before the Civil War, and the city's Black population remained under 2 percent before World War I. The wartime migration to Chicago of fifty thousand African Americans seeking industrial work set significant social and spatial changes in motion.[19] Transit emerged as a theater of conflict in 1919 riots in and around the South Side. According to the *Chicago Daily Tribune*, "Riots are increasing in violence and frequency, not alone because of neighborhood friction, but because of conflicts in interests which are extensions of neighborhoods life, such as bathing beaches and on streetcars."[20] An interneighborhood transit system threatened the white population's attempts to impose a color line.

But whites riding transit seeking social distance benefited during the interwar years from the fact that, while Jim Crow was absent in their northern city, city officials and average residents enforced segregation of Chicago's Black population at an extreme level. The Black population grew from 4.1 to 8.2 percent of the city's population between 1920 and 1940, but the space for living remained cramped.[21] Whites in Chicago succeeded in restricting the growth of Black neighborhoods through covenants, redlining, and intimidation during the interwar years. Many Black residents were on the South Side "Black Belt," and a growing Black population was on the Near West Side.[22] The outer Bungalow Belt to which many immigrants were moving, and almost all of the North, South, and West Sides—covered with an extensive web of streetcar lines—were at this time entirely white. Given the city's overall demographics, the robust interwar ridership pouring from these areas was primarily white. Wealthier whites also had options such as driving and riding higher-cost express elevated lines, bus lines, or commuter rail lines that linked all-white areas to offices downtown.[23]

The extreme segregation of the interwar years would have devastating long-term effects on transit. Areas like Bronzeville in the 1920s, well served by elevated and streetcar transit, sustained the shopping, social, and entertainment needs of a large and growing Black middle and working class. Yet, as in Baltimore, the ghettoization of the Black population, and emphasis on auto-centric planning for everyone else, laid the groundwork for postwar transit disinvestment. The neighborhoods on the South and Near West Sides were dangerously overcrowded, forcing residents to pay more than whites on a square foot basis. The declining quality of the housing stock helped justify white leaders' introduction of government-sanctioned redlining in the 1930s and postwar "slum clearance" for highways, subsidized housing, and urban renewal. Thanks to these policies, Black neighborhoods in the postwar years would lose population density and commercial vitality, leaving a massive rapid and surface transit system underutilized in key areas.

Transit and Auto-Centric City Planning in Chicago

Daniel Burnham's 1909 Plan of Chicago, which served as a blueprint for long-term infrastructure investment, took an uneven approach to a transit-oriented future. On the one hand, Burnham's plan encouraged separate "rights-of-way" for streetcars, provisions for streetcars in new boulevards, expansion of the elevated Loop westward, downtown tunnels for both streetcars (subway) and steam railroads to speed their passage, and grand new rail terminals to tie together both railroads and streetcars "with all parts of the city." At the same time, the thrust of the report was anti-transit. Underground tunnels downtown would be necessary to reduce the "excruciating" noise of elevated and streetcars that created "misery to a large majority of people" to make a city that would be "quiet, clean, and generally beautiful." The report's striking visuals and texts emphasized smooth central city diagonal boulevards, wider streets, and lakefront and regional parkways. Streetcars are notably absent from Jules Guerin's alluring renderings of the future city: pedestrians and groups of elegant horse-drawn carriages dominate the vistas. Transit has no individual chapter or even section in the plan, a strange oversight considering the crucial role still played by the systems at the time. No one who picked up the report would have any impression of the central role streetcars played in the city's life in 1909.[24]

The failure to highlight a bright transit future in the 1909 plan, and the preference for cars among city leaders, is reflected in the plan's long-term influence. Planning Commissioner Charles Wacker, with broad support, enthusiastically adopted the 1909 plan's auto-centric features in the succeeding years. City leaders focused on redeveloping Michigan Avenue as a boulevard, the lakefront and regional parkways, and the paving and widening of major streets such as Western Avenue. Transit, still in private hands, was ignored. The updated *Wacker's Manual of the Plan of Chicago* (1920) by planning publicist Walter Moody devoted extensive attention to roadways to resolve "congestion" and "crowding" to move "millions of people" in the future. But Wacker barely mentions streetcars or elevated lines despite their ability to manage crowds efficiently. Politicians devoted general revenues and voter-approved bonds to make these street improvements, including $8 million just on the Michigan Avenue improvement. Moody argued that "the community has ample financial ability to do this." In 1919, the state government approved Chicago's $27.5 million bond for road improvement even though the city had already exceeded its local borrowing power. The state government in 1913 also approved funding for "good roads for the entire state," including many of the outer drives.[25]

Chicago's leaders gave occasional nods to transit-friendly planning, including innovative traffic lights (1926) to prioritize major streetcar streets in the Loop, but in practice mostly ignored improvements that would have upgraded transit to a level competitive with automobiles. A 1916 Chicago Traction and Subway Commission, for instance, created a comprehensive rapid transit plan under the guidance of New York's William Barclay Parsons.[26] The plan, largely ignoring autos, focused on transit: "The main concern of the commission was to find a way to develop a unified system—to consolidate ownership; to protect the public interest; to expand service."[27] But the high price tag for an extended elevated loop, north–south subways, and downtown streetcar loop ($375 million) frightened city leaders. A series of follow-up plans in the 1920s (1923, 1927, and 1930) included recommendations for an expensive north–south subway. Only when the Public Works Administration showed up during the Great Depression did the city finally build the first phases of the downtown subway, and only then at a modest scale. In any case, the various transit plans failed to generate much excitement, as indicated by the lack of city funding or prioritization.[28]

A watershed in public commitment to high-speed driving was the 1939 Comprehensive Plan for Superhighways. According to the *Chicago Area Transportation Study* (1960), interwar planners developed the "first formal proposal for a system of special, new roadways. This report recognized that a new kind of facility that could cope with the flooding tide of automobiles and trucks was needed. The sportsman's car of 1909 was now mass-produced for millions. Street space was rapidly being used up. Special purpose roadways which would permit the smooth flow of vehicles appeared essential for the accommodation of the enlarged demands."[29] City officials were picking winners by planning and building great roads but making almost no provisions for mass transit.

These civic investments in better roads directly benefited cars and buses by the 1920s, to the detriment of the streetcars. The city's park boulevard system drew rubber-tired vehicles thanks to city investments in the 1920s in widened drives, better paving, stop signs, stoplights, and signal towers. By 1921, motor vehicles counted for 99 percent of boulevard traffic.[30] City and state leaders doubled down on internal combustion engines when it allowed private bus company companies to poach riders from CSL. The Illinois Commerce Commission, a state entity that regulated transit, in 1923 approved boulevard and park bus lines, which became Chicago Motor Coach (CMC). Comparatively luxurious and fast, CMC buses competed with streetcars and the elevated in many parts of town and expanded aggressively. The luxury coaches developed a strong following among women riders heading downtown for shopping.[31]

CSL and the city fought off major expansion in CMC service later in the 1920s through both legal challenges and political maneuvering. CSL launched its first bus route in 1927,[32] and boasted of a "lower rate of fare than the existing motor coach lines."[33] By 1930 CSL had also created "the largest trolley bus installation in the world."[34] CSL had risen to challenges and competition, but it was clearly struggling to keep up with changing technology and growing political support for rubber-tired vehicles of all kinds.[35]

Chicago's leaders made one prewar planning choice with long-term benefits for the transit system. Zoning was more pro-transit in Chicago than Baltimore, Detroit, Atlanta, and most other American cities. Chicago's major annexation (1889) led to the intensive development of vast territories before zoning more narrowly defined urban development. Chicago's 1923 zoning, as a result, was necessarily "sensitive to existing land uses, proximity to transportation networks, and distance to waterways." Even the massive Bungalow Belt on the city's periphery was built out at relatively high-density levels thanks to small homes on tiny lots.[36] Homer Hoyt explained that "the zoning law does not impose a very serious limit on the use of land, for if all the land in Chicago were built to the limit allowed by the zoning law, the entire population of the United States could be housed in the city."[37] Chicago's planners blessed existing uses and density through hierarchical zoning (residences allowed in the apartment, commercial, and industrial zones) and grandfathering existing nonconforming uses. Initial diversity of uses remained a hallmark of transit-friendlier cities like New York, San Francisco, Boston, and Chicago.[38]

The zoning code helped stratify the city by income, but many potential benefits of zoning for neighborhood stability were lost thanks to racist attitudes. The Chicago Real Estate Board had strongly supported city-sponsored racial zoning, but the 1917 *Buchanan v. Warley* decision (at least in the North) discouraged planners and city leaders from explicitly including racial categories in Chicago's zoning code.[39] Chicago's many racists had to find other means to zone out what some advocates called "undesirable neighbors." The real-estate industry in Chicago thus developed aggressive means of policing racial lines through redlining and racial deed restrictions and covenants. The expectation of racial segregation in Chicago created during the interwar years would encourage white flight, reduce housing quality for Black families, and undermine the vitality of central city areas with major transit lines.[40]

Restrictive zoning in the suburbs around Chicago, beginning in earnest during the interwar years, also made a significant difference to the future of city transit. The region's unparalleled industrial growth had spawned peripheral industrial towns, and in many cases, dense town centers developed naturally around commuter and rail lines. But the introduction of zoning put the brakes on rail-based densification that might have created a more transit-friendly region. The North Shore of Chicago, for instance, linked with commuter rail lines to the city center, developed as rural retreats for the wealthy. These communities, and similar ones like Forest Park and Riverside on the west, set the standard for the vast suburban belt encircling the city by creating zoning rules that disallowed anything but low-density development.[41]

Winnetka in Lake County, for instance, in 1921 passed a zoning resolution to preserve the area's spacious estates and homes. The zoning rules, developed by pioneering planner Edward H. Bennett, reflected the community's values: "Winnetka should remain country-like rather than suburban. For this reason, every effort should be made to control the density of its occupation." Industry would be strictly limited, and "single detached dwellings" prioritized on large lots. Apartments were to be "avoided," and if allowed, to rise no more than three stories. Attention was paid to diverting traffic around the village with new, good roads.[42]

Cumulative suburban zoning of this type—even in areas then served by interurbans, commuter rail, and a few elevated extensions—created a landscape perfectly positioned for the automobile age and poorly suited to future transit use and revenue. Suburban Lake County's density in 1940 was 257 persons per square mile, and just 121,000 people lived countywide. DuPage County's 101,000 residents resided at just 307 persons per square mile. Almost no Black residents lived in these areas at the time. Had zoning not developed in the early twentieth century, it is likely that Chicago-style density might have spread much more rapidly in the suburbs, or at least, developed around transit stations. Restrictive suburban zoning would become a hurdle in later attempts to improve regional transportation.[43]

Downward Spiral

Later attempts to build regional transit might have succeeded if the city's leaders had also better preserved high-quality transit during these years when most Chicagoans still rode. CSL experienced a steady increase in ridership on surface lines throughout the 1920s, rising from 743 million in 1920 to 897 million revenue passengers in 1929, its highest year of riding ever recorded.[44] Chicago was still well built for surface transit and doing better than most other American cities like Baltimore, where transit decline had otherwise set in by the mid-1920s. Chicago's transit companies nevertheless entered receivership during the interwar years despite heavy ridership. Why?

City leaders regulated the transit companies out of business. Chicago's mayors, the city council, and the Public Utilities Commission continued to intervene in counterproductive ways. The CSL, facing major postwar increases in labor and material costs, fought the commission and city government in the early 1920s in the courts to raise the universal nickel fare in place since 1914. The seven-cent fare CSL finally won in the 1920s through legal action failed in the long term to offset the typical annual increase of operating and capital costs, undermining the financial gains made by CSL's robust 1920s ridership.[45] Transit wages by 1926 had increased 175 percent since 1907, but the average fare per ride was just 28 percent higher.[46] The city also continued taxing the companies in ways that did not benefit most riders. Between 1915 and 1927, CSL alone had paid $113 million in total public benefits, including millions for snow removal, street paving, general taxes, and track removal for sewer work.[47]

The city leadership's worst failure was bankrupting companies despite having no approved backup public plan. The CSL leadership complained that the failure of the city in the 1920s to renew CSL's twenty-year franchise, initiated in 1907, made it "difficult to obtain money for development of the property to meet the city's growth."[48] Despite solid ridership, the outlook was dim due to low fares, taxes, and high costs. Receivership for CSL thus "began on December 15, 1926, when the Chicago Railways Company, one of its constituent companies, passed into the hands of the Court just prior to maturity of its bonded indebtedness."[49] CRT entered receivership in 1932. The surface and rapid companies did not emerge from receivership until 1947 with the launching of the Chicago Transit Authority (CTA) (discussed in chapter 6).[50]

The Depression further weakened the bankrupt companies and impacted the quality of service. CSL lost 29 percent of revenue passengers between 1929 and 1933 and reduced car miles operated by 12 percent.[51] In the early 1930s, the CSL admonished their twelve thousand employees to reach out to their neighbors to remind them that the Chicago system, offering up to a thirty-five-mile ride on a single fare, was "the greatest bargain in transportation of any local transportation system in the world." Such economy compared favorably with the "uneconomic . . . private automobile," with underestimated costs for ownership, parking, and repair. Managers thought autos "should be reserved for weekend pleasure jaunts and for other special uses."[52] Depression-era Chicagoans still appreciated the value proposition. By 1936 CSL was back to 80 percent of peak 1929 ridership. With its focus on Loop traffic and pricier ride, CRT had clawed back just 66 percent of peak elevated ridership of 1926.[53]

The receivership stabilized the companies, but the companies made few extensions, modernization of existing equipment slowed dramatically, and economizing became the watchword. CSL cut expenses by 16 percent between 1929 and 1940, sad news for riders seeking better equipment. Yet even this economizing failed to offset a stagnant fare of seven cents, a tax increase of 28 percent, and labor cost increase of 18 percent during that same period.[54] CSL paid its bills in receivership but slashed dividends and delayed interest on bonds. Multiple attempts to attract private capital back to transit failed as it had become clear that the sector was losing popularity and suffered from overregulation. Chicago's future as a densely populated city was also in doubt. Chicago's suburbs had continued to boom during the 1930s (11.5 percent). At the same time, the city itself grew by only twenty thousand individuals, a massive drop compared to the Roaring Twenties city population increase of 675,000.[55]

Standing in the way of a public takeover during the 1930s were familiar problems. City leaders were adamant that leaving receivership without unification of the street and rapid companies, including extensive bus substitution, was unsatisfactory. They also kept their eye on freeing up streets for auto and truck traffic, usually at the expense of rail. According to CSL executives, the city's meddling "greatly complicated the problem" of restoring the companies, forestalling a new day for mass transit. Mayor Kelly, in 1937, eventually commissioned a Comprehensive Local Transportation Plan that included system unification, modernization, and bus substitution.[56]

The $172 million modernization plan, developed by Philip Harrington, the city's subway and traction commissioner (and future CTA chairman), envisioned Chicago catching up with "the trend in local transit service throughout the country ... toward the abandonment of car lines and the substitution of buses." The plan would mean switching out 360 of 1,040 miles of streetcar track with buses for Chicago. New PCC cars would only replace about one thousand aging streetcars on the busiest routes. New express bus routes, some running on converted elevated lines, would "bring rapid transit to a large area of the city." The approximate 170 miles of remaining elevated lines would get new signals, one thousand new cars, and additional subway tunnels.[57] However, timid city leaders and the still bankrupt transit companies only made incremental changes during these years. Just two short stretches of downtown subways got started during the Depression thanks to the Works Progress Administration (WPA) and a traction tax.

New streetcars were potentially more transformative. CSL reported in 1937, after delivery of the first of the modern PCC cars, that "experience with the new streamlined cars on Madison Street has confirmed its belief that modern rail equipment compares favorably with modern automotive equipment in rider appeal, economy of street space, and economy of operation."[58] Competition with automobiles was on their minds. CSL management, still optimistic about rail in the future, believed that "from the standpoint of economy, both of street space and operating costs, rail operation where large numbers of passengers must be carried is far superior to bus operation." They offered a clear example of this financial and managerial advantage: "The Clark-Wentworth line, for instance, carries 30,000,000 more riders annually than are carried by the entire competitive bus systems." The slower and smaller buses of the time "would require approximately 10,000 buses to carry the riders now using the Surface Lines Daily."[59] Yet CSL ordered only a few hundred PCCs in a fleet of thousands of aging cars despite keeping "intact virtually the entire streetcar system." CSL did expand electric trolley coaches modestly, adding lines to serve some new areas.[60] Chicago, in sum, missed an excellent opportunity for creating and sustaining modern systems that could compete with cars.

As in Baltimore, retention of the streetcar system through World War II, and the temporary boom in ridership, reflected severe wartime restrictions rather than consumer preference. The streetcars and elevated lines gave their all for the war, but they were decades old, many made of wood and iron, and the patched-up streetcar track infrastructure was ready for renovation. CSL was finally allowed to increase the basic fare from seven to eight cents and agreed to add equipment.[61] As in Baltimore and so many other cities, crowded and uncomfortable wartime transit riding increased the postwar public appetite for driving. CSL executives warned that "with the removal of restrictions on travel in private vehicles and the end of war production . . . [u]nless an effective effort is made to retain a part of the new riding that has come during the war period, the renewed competition of the private auto will force the industry back to its unenviable status of the 1930s."[62] There were mixed signals as the war wound down. The impressive system of surface transit was on the line. CSL placed the nation's largest order for new equipment in 1945, with more PCC streetcars than buses, but the company also sought to convert twenty-two streetcar lines to bus service.[63]

Chicago in the interwar years was a middle ground between the extreme collapse in Baltimore and the start of deeper subsidies in Boston. City leaders desired streetcar removal but left the extensive transit system in a holding pattern, which effectively meant falling behind in the automobile era. The bankrupt companies, overall, failed to expand in terms of quality and speed, except for the short subway sections and modest bus and trolleybus extensions, leaving most customers riding aging and poorly maintained streetcars. City and state leaders made sure competing roads were smoother, faster, and broader. Despite their manifest advantages, they failed to provide exclusive lanes for buses or trams. By endorsing racial and class restrictions, city and suburban leaders laid the groundwork for housing exploitation, disinvestment, and white flight from areas rich in transit. Chicago had laid the groundwork for a steep decline.

CHAPTER 3

Boston: Reverse Engineering Public Transit

A few American cities pioneered public-subsidized and -operated transit in the late nineteenth and early twentieth centuries, including Boston, San Francisco, and New York. The process of bringing transit under the umbrella of municipal sponsorship was not an easy path or a foregone conclusion, even in these cities known today for their transit systems. Early public investments in subways in New York and Boston, for instance, required private operators to pay high rents or payments for system development rather than a public donation to the effort of building a modern transit system. And even when cities started building and running their lines in the early twentieth century, as did San Francisco (1912) and New York (1921), the new municipal lines covered only part of the city. The city-sponsored lines had as their primary target exacting revenge on the private traction companies given franchises decades before. Therefore, the rise of publicly supported transit was characterized by partial solutions and continuing political conflicts. American city leaders struggled to find the ideological justifications and financial resources to support their novel actions.

Boston's decision to begin subsidizing transit during the interwar years reflects the complicated process of bringing private transit under the public tent. The city's bankrupt transit system survived and expanded thanks to timely public subventions, setting a positive stage for postwar transit that few other cities matched. Unfortunately, the modest interwar subsidies did not pay for aggressive rapid expansion or prevent shortsighted economizing such as accelerated streetcar substitution. The moderately subsidized transit system also had to compete, as in other cities, with robust auto-centric planning, including a growing number of parkways and low-density zoning codes. And while the growing but comparatively small Black population was already concentrated in areas served by transit, just as in other cities, the benefits of living in these areas would be undermined postwar by redlining, white flight, and later, disruptive urban renewal.

Boston is more like a typical American city than many realize. Waterways required some heroic infrastructure on the eastern side of the city and along the Charles River. Yet, the region was not as geographically constrained as Manhattan or San Francisco. In fact, much of the region's populace had dispersed by the early twentieth century thanks to an extensive, complicated, and diverse private transit network spread over hundreds of square miles of land. Limited land regulation, political fragmentation, and comparatively few insuperable natural boundaries on the west, north, or south sides encouraged dispersal. By 1903 there were 2,621 miles of electrified streetcar lines, up from just 157 miles of lines in 1890.[1] Transit in Boston became a force for urban growth, with multiple centers and districts serviced by distinct kinds of transport, rather than central city concentration more characteristic of New York. In 1910, the city of Boston had only 670,000 residents in a metropolitan area of approximately 2.5 million inhabitants.[2]

Boston's downtown was much smaller than Manhattan because of the many commercial subcenters, industrial plants, universities, ports, and warehouses spread across the metropolitan area. Powerful and exclusive suburbs like Brookline and Newton, and independent working-class cities like Cambridge and Sommerville, absorbed much of the streetcar-era urban growth in the region. The urbanized areas of Boston, Somerville, Brookline, and Cambridge filled in with duplexes, triplexes, small and medium apartment houses, and single-family homes. Overcrowded tenements in center-city districts like Boston's West and North Ends, with densities in some tracts reaching as high as one hundred thousand per persons per square mile, were atypical. Suffolk County's population of 835,522 (comprising Boston, Chelsea, Revere, and Winthrop) was moderately settled at 13,830 persons per square mile in 1920. With large areas yet undeveloped, Middlesex County registered just 918 people per square mile (778,352 total) in 1920 even including densely populated cities like Cambridge. The centrally located wealthy suburb of Brookline housed residents at just 535 persons per square mile and fiercely resisted further urbanization. There was, therefore, adequate space for automobiles and future low-density development in Boston's vast sprawl.[3]

As in most American cities, the private sector had led the way in transit and real-estate development. The ancestors of today's Green Line streetcar and subway routes developed initially by Henry Whitney's West End company, were part of his land development scheme in Brookline and Boston, originating in 1886. Decades later, in 1966, MBTA planners still admired the West End lines because of their extensive system of separated routes (made even speedier once connected to the subway in 1897): "It is an outstanding system in that most of the route miles of the system are operated in subway, on private rights-of-way or in reserved medians of surface streets, and that it provides excellent downtown distribution." It is a shame that so few other Boston streetcar lines had their exclusive rights-of-way or subway connections, as the city might still benefit from such an arrangement today.[4]

Whitney built lines and successfully consolidated the other streetcar lines in the region. According to urban historian Sam Bass Warner, the "consolidation did, in fact, accelerate the rate of improvements in transportation" including electrification and ambitious line extensions. Whitney, "a champion of the suburban city," like many of his contemporaries, believed streetcars would deconcentrate overcrowded slums without the need for government interference. The working class would build new homes they would own, and public health and morals would inevitably improve. Warner makes a compelling case that Whitney's emphasis on the volume of passengers led him to carelessness concerning "the relationship of distance, cost, and fare per ride." The flat five-cent fare Whitney promoted as a benefit of his monopoly position would provide inadequate long-term profits for the system (as we shall see). The enormous number of streetcars converging on the downtown also snarled streetcar efficiency.[5]

The government became involved early in public transit development because the West End and predecessor companies were unwilling to invest in untested, expensive underground rapid lines despite the apparent need for faster CBD transit and underwater tunnels. The state legislature, voters, and Boston City Council agreed to create a Subway Commission in 1894 to build a subway and finance the improvements. In 1897, capitalists behind the Boston Elevated Railway Company outmaneuvered Whitney, leased the West End, and signed a contract with the commonwealth (the Massachusetts state government) to pay high subway rents to use the tunnels. Warner believed that "with this new operating company, the great subway and elevated projects were undertaken in a belated effort to solve downtown traffic problems."[6]

According to historian Lawrence Kennedy, a public-private partnership was crucial for the complex effort: "The public sector financed construction and maintained ownership of the rapid transit lines but leased the administration and management of the systems to private interests."[7]

The first section in the center-city subway opened in 1897 (America's first subway) and proved immediately popular. The public financed the subway construction, but as Kennedy notes, they stuck the elevated with the bill "to amortize the city debt incurred for the transit system."[8] The elevated agreed to serve passengers for a five-cent flat fee for twenty-five years. This shortsighted thinking kept public spending low but had two major impacts: greater financial instability for the private operator and a more limited system of rapid transit development than might have been hoped. The combination of high subway rents and low fares worked for only a few years when inflation was low and ridership astronomical.

The Boston Elevated private-public partnership would eventually develop the core of today's Red Line subway line, including sections between Harvard Square and Dorchester, the North/South Main Line elevated from Everett to Forest Hills, and the subway tunnel to East Boston. However, public financing plus fares were inadequate to build, finance, and operate a vast, modern regional rapid transit system that might have reached major population and industrial centers like Lynn in the north or Quincy in the south. The Boston Elevated leadership, for its part, had realized by 1910 that the five-cent fare barely justified expansion.[9]

The Boston Elevated, because of choices made by both politicians and private companies, thus remained primarily a slower-moving hub-and-spoke electric streetcar system after World War I. By 1918, the elevated had 3,372 streetcars in service versus just 391 rapid transit cars.[10] In most of the city, streetcar suburbanites still had to travel to or through the crowded center on comparatively slow streetcars no matter where they were headed. Moreover, few regional streetcar riders enjoyed the speedier service of dedicated rights-of-way and connecting downtown subway routes of the former West End lines. Chicago, for instance, had a more rational surface streetcar network allowing for citywide travel in many directions without traveling through the CBD. Streetcar riders in Boston were easy marks for auto dealerships and the emerging network of parkways and state highways.

There was even worse news for transit in just a few years. It was clear that by 1916 the company's managers had started to cut service and defer maintenance to try and maintain profitability. High fixed annual carrying charges, including millions in local taxes, street repairs, and subway rents, turned potential profits into losses. The National War Labor Board's decision to raise wages during World War I hastened collapse. The elevated's $5 million annual operating deficit in 1918 was unsustainable.[11] Executives looking back from a decade later painted a portrait of a wartime system in "disrepair" that "was approaching ruin.... The public of Greater Boston faced the menace of a broken service. Bound to a five-cent fare, earnings could not meet the demands for improved equipment and better service."[12] The elevated in 1918 may have carried 348 million revenue passengers total on rapid and surface streetcars but certainly did not do so in style. Because politicians could not easily ignore this transit-dependent majority, the early collapse of the transit company would prove to be a positive factor in public policy.[13]

Step One: Regional Taxation for Transit and Dividends

The commonwealth stepped in during 1918 for the "rehabilitation" of the Boston Elevated Railway Company.[14] The Public Control Act of 1918, "necessary to prevent bankruptcy" that the government had generated through its own policies, created a supervisory board for the Boston Elevated with trustees appointed by the governor.[15] The reconstituted elevated was not only entrusted to run the system and expand it but given the power to tax fourteen towns directly served by trains to make up any annual deficits. This was a revolutionary form of regional transit taxation.

The willingness of the commonwealth to step in on urban issues was typical in Boston, where white, Protestant, Republican reformers at the state level looked eagerly for ways to control the power of the Democratic Irish political class in Boston and other cities. Most of Eastern Massachusetts was urbanized, effectively making urban issues a state concern. In most American states, where rural voters held disproportionate power, state legislatures and governors ignored urban issues until the postwar urban crisis. Because most Boston-area transit riders were white (based on the city's demographics at the time), gaining city and regional and state support was also more straightforward than it would be decades later in regions more deeply divided by race.

The rehabilitated elevated company under state control paralleled other influential and well-regarded regional agencies that the state legislature and reformers designed to weaken local ethnic power, finance expensive improvements, and overcome the feuding between towns of the eastern region. Among these successful enterprises were the Metropolitan Sewerage Commission (1889), the Metropolitan Water Board (1895), and the Metropolitan Parks Commission (1892). These government entities, staffed with professionals in emerging fields like civil engineering and landscape architecture, had demonstrated the power of government to shape a higher quality of life by reducing pollution, guaranteeing clean water, and building parks and parkways. In this crucial moment of the transit crisis, Boston benefited from a strong tradition of state-controlled, reform-minded, urban governance. The unique political culture of the region made a difference.[16]

Advocates invented and popularized both social and economic justifications for this novel expansion of government in transit. The growing divide between elite drivers and everyone else, according to the *Boston Globe*, had already become apparent by 1918: "The essential thing is to see that satisfactory transportation facilities are provided for the people who, not being rich enough to own automobiles, must depend on the Boston Elevated." And in 1918, before the 1920s auto boom, that was still most of the region.[17] The newly appointed chair of the public-controlled elevated trustees, James F. Jackson, reinforced the social equity position: "Ninety-nine percent of the people who use street cars do so because they are obliged to, not because they simply want to. Many people now walk because they cannot afford the fare. People who settled in the suburbs on their faith in a low fare ought to be allowed to stay there."[18] That the region's vast population of low-income suburbanites in areas like Somerville and Cambridge already merited protection from fare increases is noteworthy given the subsequent history of regional support for transit. The emphasis on a low fare as a social right was typical nationally, including in New York, where for decades the nickel subway fare was a pillar of central city slum decongestion.

Transit's contribution to general urban prosperity was equally important. A prominent editorial in the *Globe* explained that under a "new theory . . . the public generally and . . . those people who benefit from operations of the road in other ways than by riding on its cars, should contribute to its income and thus relieve the passengers from a part of the burden." Advocates targeted "those real estate owners whose property has grown more valuable because of the Elevated lines being extended to it" and "those merchants whose shops are advantageously placed in relation to the subway and elevated stations and hence have attracted customers from the suburbs."[19] This style of general benefit argumentation resurfaced continuously over the decades in Boston and was seldom utilized or very effective in many other cities. The key was to have enough merchants who agreed with these statements. It certainly helped to make these arguments when Boston still had such a lively commercial center. Not that supporters convinced everyone. The Massachusetts Civic Alliance came out against the Public Control Act as an "arbitrary exercise of the power to charge the public, who must patronize the monopoly enough to provide the millions that these splendid dreams will require."[20]

Advocates made novel arguments publicly, but practically speaking, they treated the company's investors with kid gloves during and after the transition to public management. The state took control under "lease conditions,"[21] and thus agreed in 1918 to pay 6 percent annual dividends to mollify the shareholders. The trustees from the beginning were not happy about the payment requirements because of the strain it put on their budgets. They argued in 1918 that "subways are nothing more than highways under the surface" and "the public owes the same duty to furnish a highway for the streetcar rider that it owes the pedestrian or other traveler." They even demanded the "public treasury" reimburse the elevated for the approximate $2 million in annual rentals, but the commonwealth was not agreeable.[22] According to the elevated trustees, forced in 1940 to defend the generous payouts to investors, the agreement "was one of the terms in the public control act under which the owners turned over the entire management and operations of the company and its property to public trustees appointed by the Governor."[23] The Boston Elevated under public trusteeship paid $51 million in dividends from 1919 to 1947, money that might have gone to system modernization, reduced town assessments, or reduced fares. The trustees also made good on the annual subway rentals, which were another source of profit for investors.[24]

Under immense financial pressure from investors, the towns, and the commonwealth, the public trustees almost immediately raised the fares in 1918 from five to eight cents, despite popular pressure to hold the line on fares.[25] By 1919 the elevated had raised the fare again, as the drop-off in ridership and increasing costs continued to drag down finances. The typical rider (combining streetcar and rapid connections) was suddenly paying ten cents for a ride (although the single, local five-cent streetcar fare remained until the 1940s).[26] According to the trustees, looking back from 1928, the ten-cent fare was crucial to better financial performance throughout the 1920s. New York, by contrast, was stuck with the nickel fare until the 1940s, a key factor in bankrupting private transit companies. However, every transit economist will explain that there is a cost to transit fare increases where other options exist: lost ridership. Meanwhile, many of these fares in Boston ended up in investor pockets rather than improvements or services.[27]

The Public Control Act held the fourteen towns served directly by the elevated responsible for loans to cover annual operating deficits to calm investors.[28] Chairman James F. Jackson at first reassured the fourteen towns that the assessments were "temporary forced loans, and all must be paid back to the cities and towns before the fares can be lowered."[29] The outlook was much grimmer for the towns than Jackson admitted.

When fares were still low in the first year, the elevated racked up staggering losses; revenues failed to cover the cost of service and subway rental, taxes, and so on. Taxpayers in the fourteen towns thus helped clear the $4 million deficit in 1919 by "loaning" the elevated money: the city of Boston had to pony up $2.9 million, Cambridge $386,000, and Somerville $167,000 (as did the other eleven towns to a much lesser degree).[30] In 1921, according to company executives, "the tax-paying public urged the prompt reimbursement of their loan of 1919. This was their right under the statute."[31] But enforcing that right was another matter. By 1928, despite some robust early repayments to the towns, the elevated had only reduced the amount owed to the towns to $1.349 million. None of the towns were bankrupted by these payments, although many complained.[32]

The elevated took some steps in the interwar years to make their product more attractive thanks to the higher fares and government support. Boston began diverging from nearly every American city (except, for instance, San Francisco and New York). Despite the Boston region's typical investments in roads, zoning, and racial segregation, these transit investments also took place. The trustees, sensing the changing times, emphasized modernization, rapid transit development, and bus substitution of streetcar lines in a dawning age of automobility.[33]

The trustees, for instance, spent about $40 million on improvements to streetcars and equipment by 1928, including a fleet of modern steel cars that reflected faith in the viability of rapid rail systems.[34] Extension of rapid transit service on the Cambridge-Dorchester line to Ashmont also took place during the 1920s that would become the spine of the city's future subway system. An additional connection from Ashmont to the Mattapan neighborhood (1929), utilizing "high-speed" streetcars on a leafy private right-of-way for two and a half miles, provided an essential template for future development: "The Trustees emphasize this as highly significant and as an eloquent suggestion for the future development and improvement of the railway. The popular demand for rapid transit is accurately reflected in the liberal use of it as soon as it is provided." The trustees, therefore, sought "reasonable extension of rapid transit" to deal with congestion and suburban needs. With New York and San Francisco, Boston stands out among American transit operators in the period for achieving significant expansion in service during the 1920s. Public financial support was the key to growth in cities like these.[35]

As part of a national trend to save on labor and capital costs, decongest streets, and speed movement of transit, trustees aggressively pursued streetcar substitution with buses. Emerging public systems, including New York, Detroit, and San Francisco, also engaged in bus substitution.

FIGURE 7. The glamorous buses of the Boston Elevated in the 1940s.

The two-person rule for streetcar operation, no longer a requirement on modern cars but an item of faith of unionized workers, was a burden for every transit operator, public or private. Accordingly, the elevated management discovered that bus lines worked better financially than trams either "where traffic is not sufficient to warrant the heavy investment in track and electric system" or where overly congested streets slowed streetcars.[36] By 1924, buses annually traveled 890,901 revenue miles,[37] and by 1932, buses counted for 17 percent of the elevated company's mileage system-wide. Some of these substitutions were upgrades for riders, like introducing electric trolleybuses. Boston developed one of the country's most extensive systems of trackless trolleys during the 1930s. Managers kept these quiet and fast vehicles in service far longer than most other American operators.[38] Boston is another nail in the coffin of the streetcar conspiracy. A public trusteeship during the interwar years was already switching out streetcar lines for buses and trolleybuses. In sum, Boston's substitution was not all bad if paired, as in New York and San Francisco, with a broad public investment program.

The elevated notched some modest transit victories and pursued economies, but the small number of subsidies built into the public trusteeship had already shown signs of strain in the late 1920s. Ridership had picked up temporarily in the early 1920s thanks to an improving economy. Still, long-term ridership losses that set in were beyond the company's control. In 1919 and 1920, for instance, the trustees reported that "there were 600,000 fewer passengers carried upon Saturdays, Sundays and holidays" because "the automobile is in more general use as a substitute for the streetcar."[39] These were massive losses for off-peak ridership when considered on an annual basis. The elevated began a modest downward ridership trend thanks to the rise of the 1920s car culture. Profits declined steeply in the last half of the 1920s as riders departed, the fare remained at ten cents, and costs remained high.[40] The company was still paying about $9–$10 million *annually* in fixed charges, including subway rentals, real estate, and sales taxes, interest charges, dividends, and so on.[41] Labor costs were also rising fast in the 1920s as a public arbitration board mandated substantial raises for workers.[42]

Auto-Centric Planning

Thanks to state intervention, the elevated avoided bankruptcy and made some key investments. All the same, auto-centric infrastructure pulled out ahead of transit in this period in Boston, just as in other cities. State and local leaders had not made drivers subject to a "pay as you go" approach, with tolls or gas taxes. Voters statewide rejected a gasoline excise tax for roads in 1924 by a wide margin, and they only passed the first gas tax in 1929, one of the last states to do so.[43] To their credit, and rare in the American context, Boston's leaders invested in roads and zoning at the very same time they started to support and subsidize mass transit. But even beyond the question of subsidy was a more profound failure. In a transit-friendly region like Boston, the failure to coordinate road and transit development with each other or with the emerging practice of zoning set in motion big problems for transit operators.

For decades, city and state leaders had funded road improvements from general bond offerings or general revenues. The parkways, for instance, had developed in the late nineteenth century from proactive efforts by landscape architect Charles Eliot and supportive state officials to overcome the lack of sufficient open space in the densely settled and rapidly developing towns in the region. Eliot, in 1893, created an exciting plan for a regional belt of parks, including wild forests, lakes, riverbanks, and oceanfront beaches. A network of paved parkways, themselves linear parks, ideally provide scenic opportunities for city dwellers on limited-access drives between parks and along rivers and oceans. The state, which covered most of these parkways and parks, authorized the Metropolitan Park Commission, with leaders appointed by the governor, to develop this system for thirty-five communities (later thirty-nine) within ten miles of the statehouse. By 1900 the Metropolitan Park Commission (MPC) had succeeded brilliantly: 9,177 acres of parks, thirteen miles of waterfront, fifty-six miles of riverbank, and seven parkways for the tidy sum of $6.8 million dollars.[44]

However, as in Chicago and so many other cities, parkways originally designed for pleasure quickly became automobile highways. The parkway system, which eventually linked dense towns like Cambridge and Boston with distant working-class hubs like Revere, Quincy, and Lynn, offered incomparable travel speed for drivers and put the old streetcars to shame—and there were suddenly plenty of drivers. Massachusetts's auto registration increased from 3,772 cars in 1904 to 1,019,460 in 1929. No longer the plaything of the rich, the automobiles had become a mass product for the working and middle classes as well. Parkway advocates themselves admitted "that automobiles were overwhelming the metropolitan parkways." MPC had to repave its parkways with asphalt after 1905, and as early as the 1910s, the parkways "evolved from being leafy pleasure drives to commuter corridors." MPC widened and resurfaced them.[45]

The state government supplemented these efforts with newly designated and subsidized state highways commencing in the early twentieth century. These state highways, four lanes wide and paved, further opened new suburban areas for growth. The state's Department of Public Works, for instance, designated the now famous Route 128 in the 1920s; and it was so popular that work on a "high-speed version" began in 1936. According to James C. O'Connell's *The Hub's Metropolis*, the total impact of the auto-centric planning was that "parkways formed a network of landscaped greenways, which conveyed residents to parklands and paved the way for automobile commuting. The metropolitan park-and-parkway system produced a distinctive built landscape, with single-family and two-family homes and ample green space." It is worth noting that these substantial investments in roads took place at the very same time the state kept transit on a much shorter financial leash.[46]

New zoning rules also made transit less competitive in areas with significant development potential. The Tenement House Act of 1912, for instance, raised standards for multifamily housing, including fireproofing, open spaces, and setbacks. Suburban areas frightened of density and immigrants eagerly signed on. O'Connell explains that "adopting the Tenement House Act curtailed the construction of three-family homes and boosted single- and two-family houses." The state's granting of local control of subdivision review between 1891 and 1916 also undermined densification in towns that sought to retain a pastoral quality. Zoning was the watershed, however, just as it was in Baltimore and the Chicago region (and everywhere else in America). Widespread adoption of zoning by suburbs helped to "maintain a desired character and avoid the rapid changes that swept urban communities in the pre-zoning era." By 1928, twenty-eight Greater Boston towns had zoning. Even Brookline and Newton, excellently served by transit, adopted strict zoning "to restrict apartment buildings" then multiplying within their boundaries.[47]

In the 1920s, the elevated trustees acknowledged that zoning and new investments were working at cross-purposes. Boston's first zoning law, initiated in 1924, potentially undermined the rapid transit investment. The trustees had invested in a new rapid transit tunnel in Boston. They now worried that "an expensive rapid transit line such as the Dorchester Tunnel requires density of population to increase its traffic, and whereas in Cambridge there have grown up many apartment buildings, the zoning laws in Boston prevent such growth in Dorchester and unless changed will naturally retard the growth of riding" on the subway.[48]

The history of mass transit in the United States would have been quite different if city planning in these crucial years of zoning implementation had not worked at cross-purposes to prevent the development of densely populated neighborhoods. Even an urban region like Boston with subsidized transit has had challenges maintaining ridership because so many neighborhoods, even many with rapid transit, are still low or moderate density. New York's zoning, by way of contrast, allowed for the development of dense neighborhoods around the subway and elevated extensions in growing areas like the Bronx and Queens, without which the subway would have failed to capture sufficient ridership.

Parkways and zoning had a significant impact on interwar transit developments. Racial conflict was, by comparison, still a minor factor. In 1920, Boston had a much smaller Black percentage than Chicago, Baltimore, and many other American cities. Its suburbs were almost entirely white, and many zoned for higher-income residents. One might speculate that the primarily white riders from Brookline or Cambridge remained supportive of transit in the context of a continuing white-majority ridership on trains they rode. By 1940, the city's nonwhite population had grown in districts such as the South End and Roxbury, but housing segregation kept most of the city's neighborhoods and transit lines white.

Step Two: Regional Taxation + Public Financing + Economizing

Under the initial public trusteeship, the elevated had very few of the benefits of public ownership, such as tax exemption or access to general revenues, or of private companies, such as lower wages and benefits. The result was a publicly managed private company with growing financial problems.[49] The massive ridership losses in the early years of the Great Depression finally required the commonwealth to take a more aggressive role. Boston lost fewer riders than most cities during the Depression: between 1929 and 1933, the elevated lost 24 percent of its riders as compared to 44 percent in Baltimore, 29.7 in Chicago, and 51 percent in Detroit. Yet losing a quarter of Boston's paying transit customers was still bad news.[50] The elevated's lowest ridership point (before public ownership) was in the depths of the Depression, 1933, when just 267 million riders paid for a trip.[51]

The Depression created pressure to redesign the public trusteeship to put it on firmer financial footing. A 1931 state law extended public supervision for a total of twenty-eight years, retired $21 million in preferred stock with bonds issued by the Metropolitan District Commission (the merged agency handling sewers, waters, parks, and parkways created in 1919), and reduced shareholder dividend payouts from 6 to 5 percent. The trustees also used the proceeds from bond sales to cover the overdue $1.4 million still owed to the fourteen cities and towns. However, the fourteen towns remained responsible for covering future deficits and would be taxed even more in years to come. The commonwealth created a legal framework for public purchase of the elevated, but the state would not exercise the option until 1947.[52]

The commonwealth leaders were getting creative, but the elevated's fixed costs were still dragging down the system; without them, the system would have been running in the black. In 1932, fixed costs absorbed 35.3 percent of total revenues, including interest due on an accumulated $74 million in debt.[53] Transit managers and state legislators thus began even more aggressively using public credit to reduce the "excessive interest charges on bonds of the railway."[54] In a positive sign of subsidies to come, the commonwealth authorized the Metropolitan District to buy more elevated bonds to help pay down higher-interest debt. The management preferred this approach to "outright public ownership" because the state was essentially "acquiring ownership" over time. Once the elevated paid off the newly issued bonds, the Metropolitan District would hold the bonds, and thus, the public "acquires a large ownership of railway bonds representing property."[55] Between 1933 and 1945, refinancing saved $2.283 million in interest and over the lifetime of the bonds saved $9 million.[56] In 1931 the commonwealth also reduced the rental burden for new rapid transit routes. The elevated would also only pay subway rents if it had first covered all other operating costs. The region was reverse engineering a much more deeply subsidized system.[57]

Management, for its part, also cut costs to try and reduce the deficit. The elevated revenue slipped from $35 million in 1926 to $24 million in 1935 or 29.75 percent; accordingly, the trustees reduced operating costs in that time from $26 to $17 million, or 32 percent. But there were limits to cuts because, and this is a crucial elevated statement of policy from the era, "there is available for the residents of the district served a transportation system capable of carrying a vastly greater number of passengers than are using the system."[58] In other words, beyond ripping out lines and ending service to many communities, there was only so much economizing that could be done. The trustees refused to make the dramatic cuts, thus saving the system for future users. The trustees admitted that "the ultimate goal of a railway system operating without a deficit is not in view for the immediate future."[59]

The trustees saved the system, but they also accented Yankee frugality during these difficult years. Elevated riders still paid the lion's share of costs; most capital spending went to basic modernization; and total expansion during the era of public trusteeship was modest. Moreover, the biggest project of the Depression era, the development of the subway tunnel along Huntington Avenue, was a WPA-funded effort. Economies could only achieve so much, so the trustees necessarily turned to the fourteen towns to cover deficits; in so doing, they were able to keep the entire system intact. The amounts assessed were steep for the Depression: in 1932, the trustees levied $1.7 million; 1933, $2.75 million;[60] $1.39 million in 1935;[61] $2 million in 1936;[62] $1.70 million in 1937,[63] and so forth. The assessments could be charitably viewed as partial rebates by the towns to the elevated for the high real-estate taxes the company (still lacking tax exemption) had already paid the towns each year. Still, local officials did not necessarily see it that way.[64]

The politics of transit funding remained divisive during the rosier 1940s. When the war, according to executives, "restored an equilibrium between fixed and operating costs,"[65] the elevated wisely assessed no deficit on the towns between 1941 and 1945.[66] The towns, however, refused to pay $3.6 million worth of assessments run up before 1941. The trustees thus sued the towns for payment. They tried to shame them into supporting a "metropolitan" system "performing a greater and greater part of the job of transporting the public" during wartime.[67] In 1943, the trustees even paid $1.3 million in reimbursement to cities and towns, with the lawsuit ongoing, as a good-faith measure. Nonpayment of the deficit by the towns represented a threat to the company's survival because it raised questions among investors about the creditworthiness of the elevated.[68]

Ridership finally rebounded during the war thanks to restrictions and hit a new high of 433 million in 1946,[69] but the company's fundamentals remained so imbalanced that even record ridership could not right the ship. Operating costs, including local property taxes, were going up faster than revenues. The ten-cent fare had not been raised since 1919, even though the cost of nearly everything else, including labor, had increased. The trustees had depleted their reserve fund and in 1946 initiated the first new taxation on the towns since 1941. While a modest total charge of $787,000, it reignited anger from politicians and dramatized the need for action. The company finally ended the five-cent local fare in 1946 but was still losing money. The elevated desperately needed cash to pay bills and postponed payment of real-estate taxes. Nor could it borrow money because of town nonpayment of deficits still tied up in the courts. The trustees even threatened to force the towns to pay the interest on railway bonds.[70]

A rough landing to the interwar years obscured the accomplishment compared to most other cities. As in New York and San Francisco, public investment made a difference in the quality of transit. The elevated, just like transit operators in other cities, had to contend with ridership losses thanks to new parkways, highways, suburban development, and the Great Depression. By choosing public financing and subsidies so early, instead of prolonged bankruptcy in Baltimore and Chicago, the region's leaders tapped majoritarian demands for a better transit system. Fares remained low and ridership comparatively robust. Leaders continued building a regional rapid transit system when almost every other city buried the option. Even the process of bus substitution in Boston, an aspect of economizing, led to an excellent system of trolleybuses that provided decades of quality service. Public investments made in the interwar years thus laid the practical and ideological groundwork for developing an even more deeply subsidized transit system postwar.

The Postwar Transit Disaster, 1945 to 1980

PART II

Unsubsidized Private Transit

The losses piled up for private transit companies during the interwar years, but even in 1945, national transit quality could have gone either way. Most cities had not ripped out all their streetcars, some executives had partly modernized systems with buses and trolleybuses, and traction companies were coming off a wartime boom that had set ridership records. There was cautious optimism because American cities were still densely populated and commercially vibrant. If transit managers could somehow find a way to modernize their product, many thought they might retain riders. Had private transit operators faced the problem of declining ridership alone, they might have performed better. However, they met an overwhelming tide of anti-transit choices and patterns.

Austerity. Most American cities after World War II continued to rely on private-sector transit throughout the 1940s–1960s even after it was clear that only public operating and capital support could maintain quality urban transit systems. America's private-sector transit systems, responsible for almost every American system before the 1960s (and numbering about 1,200 at their height), were the first and most numerous victims of toxic local political culture. Local politicians drove the private-sector transit managers in nearly all regions out of business through auto-friendly policies, welcoming vulture capitalists like NCL, and openly ignoring transit problems. State and federal officials kept transit problems at a distance during these crucial years of decline. The widespread local resistance to public purchase of systems and subsidies allowed for zombie private transit service: just enough for so-called captive riders.

In full view of the public and usually with solid political support, virtually all postwar transit executives devised their short-term stratagems for staying in business. Private companies, both NCL and non-NCL, fast-tracked bus substitution of dense streetcar systems losing riders year over year, deferred investment in new and better equipment such as modern streetcars and electric trolleybuses, instituted high and constant fare increases, and uniformly made deep service cuts despite charging more per ride. Almost no private company invested in significant service extensions after World War II. Every step in the destruction of streetcars and other service reductions were fully encouraged in city halls and described in detail on the pages of daily newspapers.

Auto-centric planning. Before a complete federal interstate program, postwar city and state leaders prioritized larger and faster roadways in city centers and the suburbs. A powerful combination of local general revenues, bonds, state gas tax revenues, and growing federal support flowed to automotive infrastructure. City officials turned many local streets into high-speed routes by converting them to one-way traffic and using lights timed to reduce stopping. Complementing the fast roads was urbanism remade for cars: downtown redevelopment, urban renewal, or public and private housing with lots of parking. City and suburban leaders reinforced the restrictive interwar zoning that left most land zoned for single-family homes within city limits. Suburban leaders encouraged manufacturing, retail, and office parks distant from residences and existing transit lines in stand-alone greenfield sites. Planning choices like these accentuated the advantages of the automotive lifestyle and limited future ridership.

Racism. In the first postwar decade, the growing Black population remained concentrated in center-city neighborhoods with existing transit infrastructure. The initial areas of Black expansion frequently enjoyed access to good transit, and Black people continued to ride transit at higher levels than whites in center cities. The lower-income profile of many Black families usually put car ownership, although not necessarily carpooling, out of reach. As Black families still riding transit demanded integration in the South, whites first resisted the end of Jim Crow and then did everything they could to ruin the systems after they had exhausted legal challenges. As in Montgomery, some private bus systems ceased operations in response to integration requirements.

As the white families departed center cities across the nation, they took their tax dollars and transit fares. Once-thriving commercial districts, well served by transit, began to lose their customers, while bulldozers cleared others to make way for urban renewal or public housing.

Redlining, blockbusting, slum landlordism, and deindustrialization took a toll on center-city density by the 1960s and 1970s. Housing abandonment and social decline on a vast scale reduced transit demand overall. As Black families moved further out or suburbanized, they also rode transit at much lower rates. Due to these factors, private transit was overmatched in the postwar decades.

CHAPTER 4

Baltimore: Urban Crisis, Race, and Private Transit Collapse

Baltimore's extensive if outmoded transit system remained in place as the war wound down. In 1945, the BTC's system utilized 1,040 streetcars trundling along twenty-eight routes, 128 trackless trolleys quietly and rapidly serving three major routes, and a growing fleet of 242 motor buses plying nineteen routes citywide.[1] The amount of equipment and number of lines, albeit much worn down thanks to deferred maintenance and wartime crowds, spoke to the enduring quality of the service on offer for such a modestly sized city. However, city officials commanded streetcar removal during the first two postwar decades. They then turned a blind eye to poor-quality bus substitution and service by BTC, which had become an NCL subsidiary. The public buyout of BTC in 1970 took control of a much-diminished property that had, by every measure, failed to capture postwar ridership on a city or regional basis.

The grim and infuriating tale of unrelenting city political animus to transit that unfolds below reflects broader trends in postwar American cities, both under the sway of NCL subsidiaries and the more numerous locally held private transit companies. The Baltimore story of private transit destruction repeated hundreds of times across the nation. The individual details varied—timing, technology, company structure—but the pattern of public hostility to private transit dominated. It made a minor difference if the companies were well run or basket cases, if cities were large or small, or north, west, or south. City and state leaders across the country refused to step in and save failing private companies in a time of massive ridership losses; collective public policy choices ended up denying citizens quality transit.

Baltimore in the 1940s looked to have a bright future. Wartime industries in the shipyards and steel plants had rebuilt the regional economy and filled streetcars and buses. Neighborhoods were full and often over-

FIGURE 8. Defense workers rode interracial trams in Baltimore in 1943. Source: Library of Congress.

crowded. The troubled BTC, however, remained a sitting duck for vulture capitalists despite the brighter economy. BTC executives, for instance, were under no illusion about the war boom: "Our wartime business was abnormal. We can expect our normal business to be much less than during the war and immediate post-war periods."[2] As businesspeople, they knew that investing in an industry going through an artificial and temporary boom was reckless.[3]

In 1944, American City Lines, the investment arm of NCL, took a controlling interest in the BTC, and NCL executives took over BTC management in 1945. NCL was all-in on buses everywhere, but what transpired on the ground had very little connection to the streetcar conspiracy narrative. NCL executives made no secret in Baltimore or anywhere else, including Los Angeles, that bus substitution was the only path they saw to sustain profitability in an era of decline. The company, however, served as a handy tool for Baltimore's auto-centric political and social elite to scrape the city's streetcar system from the streets. Having refused to bail out the BTC either before or after the war, the city's leaders endorsed the harsh capitalist logic that NCL represented.[4]

With the purchase and management shift complete in 1945, the elected leadership's banging of the substitution drum accelerated the ripping out of so many streetcar lines so rapidly. Fred A. Nolan, the new NCL-installed president of BTC who had played a role in motorizing Detroit's streetcars, made clear that in Baltimore, the company was carrying out the will of local politicians and bureaucrats: "City authorities were first to launch these plans. Under date of May 21, 1945, the chief engineer of Baltimore city sent the Mayor a comprehensive program for one-way streets and substitution of free-wheel for fixed-wheel public transit lines on a number of important arteries."[5] In 1945, per the request of the chief engineer of the city, the BTC studied "removal of tracks from Charles Street, Saint Paul Street, Calvert Street . . . Reed Street" threading their way through densely built-up neighborhoods. The company, no surprise, was "happy to report that it can accomplish both the requests of the Council and Mr. Smith [chief engineer]."[6] Pulling streetcars off major streets would be "in accordance with the City's program" of one-way street development to accelerate traffic.[7]

The BTC's plan projected a reduction of streetcar lines citywide from twenty-seven to eleven, necessitating the rapid removal of 170 single-track miles to free up sixty miles of streets from tracks and trams.[8] BTC openly stated that their goal was "abandonment of more than half the rail operation in Baltimore City." They were not fans of electric trolleybuses either, given both the company's backing from the automotive sector and the trolleybuses' continuing reliance on expensive overhead electrical infrastructure.[9] The protracted negotiations in 1945–46 between the city government and BTC over final approval of such a dramatic change in service reflect unflagging city support for bus substitution. The city delayed approval until 1946 not because of the loss of half or more of its traditional transit service and all the difficulties dedicated riders might face, but over a dispute on streetcar taxation.[10] The city leaders were most concerned about the repaving costs of ripping out rail lines and the loss of streetcar taxes; service quality was not a sticking point in negotiations. The resulting compromise in 1946, accepted grudgingly by BTC, predictably did nothing for riders. Instead, the resolution taxed buses at a higher rate and tripled the streetcar tax, thus preserving transit as a net contributor to city revenues. Hiking up the streetcar tax made BTC even more eager to shutter remaining car lines, not that they needed any additional justification.[11]

The company openly celebrated "widespread public approval" of the final BTC substitution plan. BTC received support from the city council, the city planning commission, the Baltimore Association of Commerce, and the PSC: "Public hearings were held at which city officials, civic groups and individuals testified in favor of the program."[12] City and company leaders "kept in close touch with" city officials during the implementation.[13] The city government even joined with the BTC to fight a legal challenge by two of its shareholders who sought to stop the bus substitution program.[14] The story in Baltimore of public pressure for streetcar destruction was one repeated across the country. City officials planned for so-called modernization for decades in the interwar period and then worked closely with NCL and other local private-sector transit operators postwar to rid their cities of streetcars. Had NCL not existed in Baltimore or anywhere else, city leaders and transit managers would have removed just as many streetcar lines. Streetcar removal, for instance, proceeded just as rapidly without NCL subsidiaries in cities like Atlanta, Chicago, Detroit, and New York. American city leaders, almost without exception, ignored opportunities for streetcar modernization or acceleration in the race to clear streets of tracks and trolleys.

As in other cities, choosing the bus modernization program in Baltimore was much less costly than repairing the streetcar lines and buying new cars. BTC planned to spend approximately $7.5 million, as in 1945 the company had on hand only 242 motor buses and 128 trackless trolleys.[15] BTC in 1946 promised to buy "600 modern motor buses" to retain service quality.[16] The company placed its biggest order for new diesel buses with GM, one of its main investors, but the company would eventually throw in orders for Brill manufactured gas and trackless trolley models to defer criticism of its cozy relationship with GM.[17] The buses arrived slowly as the bus industry was unprepared for such rapid postwar conversion of streetcars. GM had wanted the streetcars gone, but the company leaders never dreamed they would be so successful so fast. The key to such quick removal in Baltimore and other cities was widespread city support for substitution.

Because the buses were still comparatively small, with at most forty-five seats (vs. fifty-four on the PCC cars) and little standing room, BTC had no choice but to preserve the trunk streetcar rail lines until the bus industry could supply the needed equipment.[18] BTC management, in the meantime, promised riders that consolidation of lines and bus substitution would not undermine service as impacted areas would remain "less than one-fourth of a mile from a public transit line." They claimed that "free-wheeling vehicles" delivered "better transportation at a lower cost per passenger," were better "able to travel in heavy traffic more expeditiously," dropped off riders more safely, and allowed for more rapid schedule adjustments. These were typical bus industry talking points at the time.[19] However, the company went too far when it spun a rosy future of "increased attractiveness of service" that would have people leaving their cars at home. More bus transit they claimed would benefit the city because it could "remedy traffic congestion . . . halt the trend toward decentralization . . . save and preserve downtown property values" and "halt the decay and deterioration of downtown business and shopping centers."[20]

Portions of this utopian description might have come to pass if, as in San Francisco or Boston, Baltimore's city government had stepped in to maintain bus and trolleybus service quality through the worst years of ridership losses. But Baltimore, like most American cities, failed to support high-quality, regional bus service. Some riders in Baltimore were also not buying the bus superiority argument. At a public meeting in North Baltimore in 1948, for instance, the public in attendance expressed their preference for modern PCC streetcars, the most modern and advanced car available. But public displeasure in a few meetings and local editorials was insufficient to stop the powerful combination of political substitution supporters and BTC.[21] Baltimore was not alone in emphasizing substitution, and most streetcar replacements were by non-NCL companies. Between 1946 and 1972, streetcar ridership nationally declined from about nine billion rides to just over two hundred million per year. After a while, there were almost no streetcars to ride anywhere in America.[22]

BTC reached 1946 streetcar replacement goals by 1948, faster than predicted. By 1948, just half of the city's streetcar system remained: nineteen streetcar lines versus twenty-eight gas and diesel bus lines and five trackless trolley routes. Even the busy Baltimore Street line, a crucial east–west connector through the downtown, was converted to buses in 1948. The BTC of 1948 operated more rubber-tired vehicles than streetcars in the fleet, a stunning reversal after decades of streetcar domination.[23] As substitution proceeded in 1947, with the arrival of new buses, BTC initially seemed to keep its promise that service would not suffer. Between 1946 and 1949 BTC increased vehicle miles of service—now a mix of bus and streetcar lines. However, company officials faced a bleak reality because patronage sank by 17 percent during that period.[24]

With the tracks gone from city streets and public consciousness, politicians and planners could more easily ignore advances in streetcar technology that might have updated lines and thus focus solely on roads and highways as the public mobility responsibility. Removing visually dominant, permanent, and dense streetcar lines sent a strong, negative signal to the public and property owners about the future of mass transit and neighborhoods built around tracks. Dense neighborhood shopping districts built for the streetcar era struggled when the lines disappeared so rapidly because they had been constructed without extensive parking and relied primarily on local patronage going to and from streetcars. New shopping centers, both within the city and in the suburbs, had super-abundant parking.

BTC, NCL, and other private companies oversold the transformative role of new buses. In Baltimore or any other city, buses did not drive ridership growth as predicted. Instead, ridership losses system-wide to automobiles aided the bus transition because, according to BTC officials, the "falling patronage released buses for other assignments." With continuing losses and no financial support from the city, "BTC management's concern was that too many transit lines continued to serve principal trunk routes to and from the central business district." The company cut service on downtown originating and converging lines in the late 1940s and early 1950s.[25] The BTC company, for instance, regularly cut service as the riders thinned out across the region: "Each fall and summer, schedules are lighter than for the previous corresponding period." BTC reduced vehicle miles operated from thirty-nine million in 1946 to twenty-eight million in 1954, a clear sign of reduced service quality for remaining riders.[26]

Not even buses, and those on a reduced scale, were sufficiently economical for a transit service in decline that lacked public subsidies and paid high taxes. In 1952, BTC reported that it had not paid a dividend to investors in five years despite cutting service, staff, and routes while raising fares. When the PSC in that year evaluated the company's request for another fare increase, it had to walk a fine line between preserving the for-profit principle of the franchise and mollifying unhappy riders. The PSC reprimanded company investors that "the mere fact that one is an owner of stock in a street railway does not per se entitle him to a dividend." In the end, however, the PSC signed off on a major fare increase so BTC can "operate profitably."[27] A 1953 PSC study nevertheless blamed the profit motive as the source of a downward spiral including "1) charging higher fares, 2) reducing service, and 3) ultimately serving only 'necessity passengers.'" The PSC that year absurdly recommended that the "natural remedy—and certainly the one most often suggested—is that the Company should increase its service." By this time, any increase or even stabilization of service in an era of significant ridership losses thanks to suburbanization and automobiles would have required a public subsidy. The PSC, however, left out politically controversial recommendations for subsidies or public ownership.[28]

Mayor Thomas D'Alesandro Jr. (1947–59) appointed Henry Barnes as traffic commissioner in 1953. Barnes was a rising star in traffic management who strongly supported streetcar substitution to speed up motor vehicles. In 1953, for instance, Barnes supported the BTC's goal of replacing a major crosstown streetcar route on North Avenue even though it was crucial to the network. BTC desired substitution of the North Avenue line to save money on the rail renovation and maintenance of electrical wire (about $211,000). The city council supported the removal of streetcars even though the PSC did not, pointing out that "there is still a place for both types of vehicles" (streetcars and buses) in the system. Speaking for the city government, Barnes exaggerated the public danger of the streetcar infrastructure. He claimed in a public hearing that "bus service on North Ave. would be safer than streetcars." He offered overly dramatic descriptions of private cars hitting streetcar pylons, killing drivers, and creating mayhem. The PSC agreed to the substitution only under pressure.[29]

Barnes was a friend to the BTC in the years that followed. By 1956 there were just three major streetcar lines thanks to the combination of BTC pro-bus policies and city government support. The BTC went ahead and cut one of the three streetcar lines in 1956, that running on Hartford Road, severing one of the last visible suburban-city transit links.[30] Mayor D'Alesandro credited Barnes in 1957 for helping "the transit company 'in case after case' to obtain PSC consent for bus conversion."[31]

Mayor D'Alesandro, while endorsing the streetcar replacement program, sensed during these years that the transit issue was a growing political liability. In 1955, he appointed Abel Wolman, a Hopkins professor famous for his pioneering research on sanitation, to chair a Committee on Mass Transit. The committee determined that the root of the problem was the "almost universal agreement that the problem of mass transit is essentially the province of the Transit Company and is to a minor extent the concern of public agencies." The committee's calls for public ownership to be vested in a Metropolitan Transportation Authority (MTA) was based on their analysis of the structural and political challenges to maintaining and developing rapid transit in an auto-dominated society: "We have reached the inescapable conclusion that this action is essential and inevitable, if imaginative, attractive service is to be continuously provided or recaptured." Public ownership, and the end of the onerous park taxes and charges, would give a new public transit company a "tax cushion" to restore financial and managerial soundness. The positive experience of publicly owned systems in Cleveland and Toronto demonstrated to the committee the benefits of "good, honest, and efficient management."[32] Wolman, influenced by his extensive experience in public infrastructure, "noted an analogy between a water supply system of the city, which is publicly owned and supported by the tax rate, and the mass transit system. Both of these service are, in his opinion, absolute necessities to a modern urban system."[33]

According to the most influential voices in the city, the Wolman Committee's promotion of public ownership had gone too far. Mayor D'Alesandro and Barnes both rejected the committee's calls for public ownership.[34] The BTC, for its part, preferred tax relief and a new MTA with a limited role in developing highway bus transit lanes and peripheral parking.[35] The powerful Greater Baltimore Committee (GBC)—a privately run advocacy group of the city's leading business interests and the dominant force behind the city's plans for urban renewal and highway development—also rejected the committee's push for municipal ownership: "It is apparent that public ownership of the transit system and the coordination of transit and traffic matters will not solve this problem." The GBC dismissed the value of an "all-powerful MTA." Like civic leaders before them, they endorsed the "elimination of streetcars" and supported new express bus service and off-peak transit promotion.[36]

Mayor D'Alesandro had encouraged the bus trend under Barnes's leadership. Yet his frustration grew in the late 1950s as he realized that BTC was not a dependable partner in service improvements—and thus a political liability. In a televised speech in 1957, he addressed those "who must stand out in the cold or rain, waiting and waiting for an overcrowded bus or streetcar. . . . Every day of your lives you are subjected to discomfort, inconvenience and the loss of valuable time because of one of the worst transit systems in America." D'Alesandro admitted that the BTC seemed to use the advantages in operations granted to it by the PSC and city—such as streetcar substitution, reduced stops, left-turn priority, and limited parking on certain routes—to reduce service and, as the mayor put it, "put more money into the transit company's pockets."[37]

The mayor delivered this 1957 heartfelt message to riders on local television in the shadow of his failure to gain state approval for a city vote on public ownership of transit in Baltimore. He had reversed course by this time on the issue, now arguing that "if we can't have responsible private ownership, then we must seek public ownership." Municipal ownership had already been successfully extended to water, education, and "other essential facilities worth hundreds of millions of dollars." His campaign for public ownership had foundered on politically motivated questions about the city's corruption and the opposition of the *Sun* editorial page. The state legislature would not even allow for a public vote on the proposed $25 million purchase. This was a last-ditch effort at public ownership for a mayor who had resisted public ownership for many years and overseen the loss of most of the streetcar system.[38] That the mayor in 1957 put Henry Barnes "in charge of all efforts to improve the transit picture" on the recommendation of the GBC was not comforting.[39]

Barnes's 1958 rapid transit plan, encouraged by the mayor, attempted to make the best of the bus-dependent system he and other city officials had brought forth. Buses had lost much of their initial shine in a city crowded with automobiles and trucks. Barnes believed that the remaining riders, about half of all those going to and from the CBD every day, would be well served by express bus lines and a new CBD bus terminal rather than rail, monorail, and other more expensive options then being discussed both in Baltimore and nationally. Exclusive busways in medians on expressways, linked to exclusive bus lanes through the downtown, would have the advantage of directly serving "suburban residential areas" rather than requiring rail, bus, and auto transfers: "The all-bus system provides its own feeder and rapid transit service in one package." Busways had a financing advantage in a society still resistant to funding transit because they were a "legitimate highway facility" and thus developable using "highway user funds" from the state and federal governments.[40] In total, he proposed forty-two miles of exclusive busways.[41]

The BTC was supportive of the busway plan should the city pay the bills, but the city took no action. A busway plan would have required public funds that elected officials still held back from the BTC.[42] Barnes nevertheless went ahead and created temporary bus lanes during rush hours in 1958–59 along sixteen downtown streets by limiting curbside parking. He claimed that along Charles Street, for instance, rush-hour bus lanes saved an average of about five minutes over eighteen blocks.[43] A few rush-hour bus lanes, and the reduction of the total number of stops to speed service, were not a true substitute for Barnes's elaborate busway program or a high-speed rail system. Even Barnes was pessimistic that transit would ever overcome the "great travel time differentials" that "exist in favor of the private automobile."[44]

With public ownership off the table, a stillborn bus rapid transit plan, and no additional financial relief in sight, BTC continued its service reduction strategy. Barnes's study of transit in 1958 inspired the company in 1959 "to effect . . . more than 50 per cent of the local route conversion and consolidations recommended" by the Department of Transit and Traffic, the main focus of which was to maintain "existing rates of fare" and "keep the Company in existence."[45] The company, for instance, discontinued the remaining sections of the once high-quality trackless trolley system in the late 1950s, with the last lines cut in 1959. BTC after 1959 might not have been shedding riders as it had for decades, down to one hundred million riders or so per year, but it had become a second-choice system in a region now dominated by automobiles. By 1959, BTC counted twenty-six bus routes and two streetcar lines on the books, but according to *Motor Coach Age*, only "about half of the bus lines were truly major ones, each needing 30 or more buses in peak hours, while a few were of moderate importance and the rest were quite minor, some requiring only a single bus."[46]

The promise that buses by design would be faster than streetcars, central to the substitution program in Baltimore and nationally, had run out of gas. In 1960, for instance, the average speed of buses was just ten miles per hour. The BTC admitted that grindingly slow bus speed "is where the competitive disadvantage of transit riding with the automobile may be most clearly seen." So much for the claims of buses as inherently superior to streetcars on city streets.[47] Independent analyst Jack L. O'Donnell, who had studied engineering and transportation at the University of Utah, offered a stimulating critique of the BTC and Barnes's "bus propaganda." In his letter to the head of the GBC in 1959, he observed that "Barnes and the local politicians seem bent on spending millions on freeways and encouraging more automobiles with subsidized busways to handle the poor stragglers who can't drive." The BTC in 1945 had "maintained that elimination of rail lines would result in an excellent low cost transit system," but, in fact, "there has been a steady decrease in average scheduled speed" and fewer riders. The BTC and city officials, according to O'Donnell, had oversold the benefits of bus substitution: "If buses were really the answer, wouldn't our *nearly* all bus system be *nearly* perfect now?"[48]

Reshaping Baltimore for Cars

BTC was going to lose many riders no matter what with the rise of the suburbs, but the extreme losses were an artifact of public policy. In 1949, for instance, Baltimore County officials initiated planning and funding for the Baltimore Beltway to link up suburban towns and, in the long term, allow residents to bypass the center city.[49] The thirty-two interchanges planned for the beltway would open hundreds of square miles for new subdivisions, many of which were likely to draw out white middle-class residents. County officials were in such a hurry that they allocated local funding for the first sections. After 1953, the state contributed significantly to the construction; and the beltway was eventually folded into the interstate highway network, providing the federal funding needed to complete an ambitious circumferential growth engine. The beltway, once combined with center-city highways, would allow for speed and range point to point impossible to duplicate by mass transit of the time.[50]

Highways and parkways also became a significant factor in transit decline within Baltimore City but limited-access roads had a rockier start. The many hills and valleys, complex politics, dense central neighborhoods, and limited funds meant that the city was comparatively slow to develop a high-speed road network. More people were driving in the town, but major north–south and east–west local streets were crowded with cars and trucks, many of which were simply crossing the city on their way elsewhere. Postwar city leaders, including the Planning Commission, favored the development of highways to link the downtown and port to the regional roadways.

The Planning Commission's ability to damage mass transit was apparent in their 1950 $214 million master plan for highway and parkway improvements. Rather than relying on the existing radial network of roads, the city would finally have a circulating web of parkways and widened streets that would intersect with new expressways. Such a system, much of which Baltimore leaders would build in one form or the other over the succeeding decades, was a transit killer. What became the Jones Falls Expressway (JFX) facilitated mobility in the wealthier, white northern sections of the city. The planned Inner Harbor Crossing (today's I-95 and Harbor Tunnel) would speed workers to and from the shipyards and steel mills and drivers around and away from the downtown. Road widenings within the city like Northern Parkway and today's Martin Luther King Jr. Boulevard (ringing part of downtown) created new boundaries and higher-speed routes. City leaders endorsed this massive road program, partly supported by general revenues, while the Planning Commission kept public transit planning at arm's length.[51]

The first of the major projects from this plan reflect how transit got the shaft from city leaders. The postwar priority was for the JFX, a high-speed (then forty-five miles per hour), four-to-six lane route following the then picturesque Jones Falls river valley. A century before, the valley had been the power source of the city's industrial revolution. Decaying mills, underutilized train lines, and a second-growth forest lined the valley's banks by the 1940s. City leaders believed the valley should become the site of the high-speed expressway path from the CBD to elite northern city neighborhoods, the Baltimore County suburbs, and York, Pennsylvania. Such a road would free up crowded city streets by drawing trucks from "congested North–South traffic arteries."[52]

City planners envisioned the JFX as a "highway of the future, complete with depressed roadbed, bridge underpasses and elaborate interchanges at six main streets."[53] In contrast to "pay as you go" models for transit, however, drivers on the JFX would not have to pay their way on the first expensive six miles of roadway. Mayor Thomas D'Alesandro dismissed the use of tolls to pay for the $30 million JFX because "the people are paying too much taxes now and should not be asked to pay a toll for using the streets."[54] The JFX's first six miles just to Roland Park required a $10 million city bond to be repaid out of general revenues, as well as millions in additional federal and state funds.[55] The mayor had much less concern for "double-taxed" transit riders, a portion of whose fares were still going to the city in the form of various taxes.

City officials initially made noises about the compatibility of the new JFX with bus mass transit, perhaps to assure tram and bus riders that they would not be left out: "City planners are now hoping to incorporate high-speed bus service and easy connections . . . in their No. 1 project—the proposed Jones Falls Expressway." Such plans would include "special stations off the road for buses" for dropping off passengers to be linked to neighborhoods by ramps or walkways.[56] The mayor, however, quickly threw cold water on the bus plan: "Space is not readily available for the off-street loading and unloading platforms," access to platforms would be "difficult and inconvenient," and "bus service is seldom feasible on highways."[57] Voters, by wide margins, approved the $10 million JFX bond without any provisions for transit. The first section of the JFX was not ready to open until about 1960 because of the complexity of threading a highway through the central city. Nevertheless, the city government by 1951 had established its priorities. Voters in 1951 also approved bonds for $5 million for private parking development. The millions, to be paid back by the garage operators, would add four thousand more off-street spaces downtown. Had there been less parking and at a higher price transit would have better retained its competitiveness.[58]

The JFX was just one of many postwar highway programs that left transit in the rearview mirror. The highway project most directly in competition with mass transit was the city leadership's tireless support for an east–west expressway. This highway would have displaced a massive, mostly Black population in east and west Baltimore, disrupted commerce, and undermined the attractiveness of mass transit. The plan had many incarnations over the decades, but all were bad for transit and the neighborhoods served best by it.

Mayor Theodore McKeldin (1943–47 and 1963–67) in 1944 had brought Robert Moses to town to promote highways.[59] Moses, mastermind of a multiple-decade parkway program in the New York City region, prepared auto-centric consultant reports for many cities during this time. Picking up on existing highway visions developed before he arrived in Baltimore, Moses called for $40 million for a massive east–west dual highway four hundred feet wide, much of it below grade. In classic Moses fashion, the plan ignored neighborhood life and would have required city leaders to demolish $7.3 million in property, much of it in poor, Black neighborhoods.[60] A city report in 1945 celebrated the benefits of associated slum clearance: "A trip afoot, making detours into the alleys, will be sufficient to convince most people of the need for cleaning out these slum areas." The plans failed to gain traction but never entirely died.[61]

City leaders continued promoting numerous east–west highway proposals into the 1970s, most of which required massive demolition of neighborhoods best served by transit and most riders. In 1964, pro-transit city councilman Thomas Ward, head of the City Council Public Transportation Committee, called for "mass transit . . . in the east–west expressway." Indeed, an exclusive transit lane was incorporated into official east–west transit plans but was never built.[62] The final approval of a broader city urban interstate program came in 1969. While some egregious harbor interstate connections were cut or modified to preserve historic, whiter areas, the "3-A" plans approved that year led to today's urban sections of I-95, I-395, the MLK widening, and the first phase of the east–west highway, or I-70.[63]

Neighborhood bulldozing on the east side for I-70 started in 1969, taking 971 houses, sixty-two businesses, and one school. Black residents on the west side had had enough and joined forces with anti-highway activists in other areas targeted for interstates.[64] The Movement against Destruction (MAD) in 1971, a coalition of anti-highway organizations, was not only opposed to "any expressway through the city of Baltimore" but demanded "an effective public transportation system."[65] As early as 1969, MAD had demanded "more buses, buses that run on schedule, better equipment . . . bus rights-of-way" and "shuttle buses from housing projects . . . where public transportation is most needed."[66] Thanks to opposition, city and state leaders only built a short section of I-70 in west Baltimore, known today locally as the "highway to nowhere." The entire west side expressway link was not finally canceled until the early 1980s.

The combined impact of highways in Baltimore, only slightly tamed by the freeway revolt, was disruption to many densely populated city areas and, more crucially, creating a faster and more reliable transportation system than downwardly mobile transit.[67]

Incremental changes to city streets were also disruptive to mass transit, often more directly impacting transit lines than the highway programs. Barnes was fanatic about the benefits of one-way streets throughout his tenure in Baltimore and other cities, including New York, viewing this strategy as key to speeding up city traffic. He had many allies in Baltimore as one-way streets had long been a civic priority. The PSC, for instance, approved his plan in 1954 that required extensive rerouting and abandonment of streetcar lines. Barnes called for the removal of streetcar lines and tracks or their relocation on one-way street conversions whenever possible. BTC was naturally unwilling to rebuild trackage on new routes since it was generally anti-streetcar. The speeding auto traffic on one-way streets, often facilitated with timed streetlights, also made neighborhoods less pedestrian-friendly.[68]

Wolman's Committee on Mass Transit (1955) had highlighted the auto-centric bias of the city's leadership. Wolman argued that the Planning Commission mistakenly viewed "transit planning as outside its province. Thus, its transportation plan is designed primarily for the movement of automobiles."[69] Even the pro-highway editorialists at the *Sun* in 1961 admitted that the highway regime was gobbling up resources that might have been spent on transit: "At some point the Baltimore area has to decide which it wants more, mass transportation or expressways. Trying to stimulate both private travel and mass transportation leads to foreseeable frustration. If, say, the proposed east–west expressway is to cost $200 million and for the same sum an extensive network of mass transit can be created, a choice is indicated, one that might save the city and suburbs from working simultaneously toward opposing goals."[70] The editorial board at the *Sun* was pretending a choice had not already been made for highways. By 1965, just 12.9 percent of person trips daily were by transit in the Baltimore metro area, while 81 percent were in cars.[71]

Racial Conflict

The dreadful state of race relations in Baltimore undercut the ability of privately run transit to sustain itself. When combined with pro-growth, low-density zoning, the city and county leadership's unwillingness to confront the corrosive impacts of racially based discrimination accelerated white flight from the most transit-rich areas. White families knew they could move to highly segregated areas further out that could be more easily defended from racial change. Opportunists in the city also took advantage of redline-fueled disinvestment to encourage contract buying, blockbusting, and racial steering that created a new generation of hyper-segregated, downwardly mobile neighborhoods with growing signs of abandonment. Slum landlords rented substandard, often overcrowded housing to Black families with few better choices. This disinvestment and exploitation occurred in neighborhoods with the most transit service and ridership.[72]

The city's racial makeup changed postwar. Baltimore City's total population between 1950 and 1970 dropped modestly from just 949,708 to 905,759 persons, but the racial balance shifted dramatically. Black residents in 1950 had risen to 23.8 percent or one in four city residents; by 1960, that figure was 34.7 percent or one in three city residents; and by 1970, Black residents comprised 46.4 percent or almost one in two city residents. Baltimore was on an accelerated timetable of racial division, both within the city and between city and suburban ring. In the long run, many American center cities looked a lot like Baltimore.[73]

Whites in more affluent areas like Guilford or Roland Park often maintained all-white neighborhoods through racial steering, existing covenants, or intimidation. The Supreme Court's 1948 *Shelley v. Kramer* decision, barring court enforcement of racist covenants, in practice allowed discrimination to continue because of the lack of city, state, or federal fair housing laws. Transit ridership in more affluent white areas by 1960 ranged from 5 to 20 percent of daily workers, with most in the teens. Postwar builders added mostly single-family homes and garden apartments, but just a few row houses and semidetached houses to the Annex areas. Density thus remained low thanks to established development patterns, restrictions, and city zoning. Except for the Black domestic help traveling to semi-suburban places like Roland Park by bus or streetcar during the daytime hours, these neighborhoods remained marginal transit markets.[74]

Central city working-class white areas were another declining market for transit. For instance, in working-class Hampden, tightly packed blocks of small, brick row houses had filled over many decades with white migrants to Baltimore from Appalachia. In Hampden, whites defended their turf postwar through discrimination, intimidation, and violence. These protected white areas, which once had been essential sources of ridership, had lower transit ridership levels than might be expected by their income levels and location, about 20 percent or fewer daily riders in 1960. The growing transportation divide between white and Black families in the city contributed to difficulties in generating political support in a city where white political machines dominated city government until the 1980s.[75]

The abandonment of transit was terrible news for the poor neighborhoods close-in. Neighborhoods within two miles of downtown, thick with transit lines, were dense by contemporary Baltimore standards. Transit remained central to the bulk of the city's large and rapidly growing Black population living in these areas, most of whom were priced out of car ownership. In 1960, 30–50 percent of daily workers in nonwhite central areas used transit daily.[76] An extensive study in 1959 of 815 acres in the northwest center-city neighborhoods of Mount Royal and Fremont gives a unique glimpse into the relationship between transit and neighborhood change. Mount Royal–Fremont was integrated, but not for long. In 1959, despite decades of attempts by the government and various neighborhoods to stabilize white residential occupancy through discriminatory tactics and zoning, the area "contained a population of about 64,000 persons of whom 13,000 . . . were white and 51,000 (80%) were nonwhite."[77]

The whites who remained in Mount Royal–Fremont had negative attitudes about their Black neighbors. An extensive survey of 2,300 householders reflected this reality: "About 29% of all white owner-households and 18% of all white renter-households stated that their neighbors were definitely undesirable. This is in sharp contrast to 9% of nonwhite owner-households and 6% of nonwhite renter-households stating the undesirability of their neighbors."[78] In Mount Royal–Fremont, these unhappy white residents had the income to buy and store cars and avoid transit, even though this was a densely populated area: "In the total area, 46% of the white households and 23% of the nonwhite households had cars."[79] These ownership figures stand out because, according to 1960 census figures, about one in two working adults still rode transit in the area. The remaining whites, down to just 20 percent of the population, could not have made up more than a small portion of the transit riders—even if every single white commuter rode transit.

Planners targeted transit-centric neighborhoods such as Mount Royal–Fremont for disruptive slum clearance and redevelopment, sharply dividing areas through public housing, private-sector urban renewal, and highway clearance. Just how ineffective these postwar policies had been in Mount Royal–Fremont, and many similar neighborhoods targeted for redevelopment became apparent in the late 1960s when the dust of postwar urban renewal had started to settle. Redevelopment failed to arrest most neighborhood decline and often worsened the housing situation of Black residents. According to Baltimore's League of Women Voters in 1966, "Clearance, relocation, and abandonment have reduced available low-income housing, pressuring conversion (one-family dwellings into multiple dwellings) which can bring about deterioration of these neighborhoods." That year, the city tolerated deplorable conditions, including 18 percent of the city's three hundred thousand housing units rating substandard and an estimated fifteen thousand unlivable and vacant. The city government allowed slum property owners to amass profits at the expense of Black resident health and finances. In sum, the city did little to stop neighborhoods with the most density and transit riders from steep decline.[80]

Whites could not contain the growing Black population postwar in the west and east side ghettos in the postwar years forever given the absolute increase in the Black population, rising Black income, loss of older units to clearance and disinvestment, and white flight to the periphery. White owners outside the racial dividing lines started selling or renting their properties postwar to Black families.[81] A rising Black working class, for instance, found their way to comfortable, relatively new row houses built to high standards for the white ethnics who had preceded them. Neighborhoods in Edmondson Village on the far west side transitioned between 1960 and 1970 from exclusively white to entirely Black. Transit ridership in areas like these after racial transition was moderate, between 20 and 40 percent, because the new homeowners and renters could afford cars. By 1970, the streetcars were gone, and buses ran less often. There also existed adequate space for cars thanks to moderate density. Regional employment had also decentralized, so transit lines still serving the downtown may have been less useful to rising Black families.[82]

Successful Black families also made inroads into elite single-family sections of the northwest and northeast, such as Ashburton, constructed originally in the interwar years for white middle-class residents. By 1960, the primarily white population (80 percent) of that neighborhood had only 19 percent daily transit ridership rates because of the higher income profile of residents and the lower-density suburban-style living. The white families departed in the 1960s with astonishing speed as Black families moved in. The Black population in Ashburton rose from 20 percent in 1960 to 99 percent in 1970. Even with a complete racial transition in the 1960s, transit ridership was at 20.61 percent in 1970, indicating that the Black middle class was also abandoning transit. More affluent Black Baltimoreans driving than riding transit augured poorly for the future when Black political power finally expanded.[83]

The impact of zoning and white flight on transit ridership increased

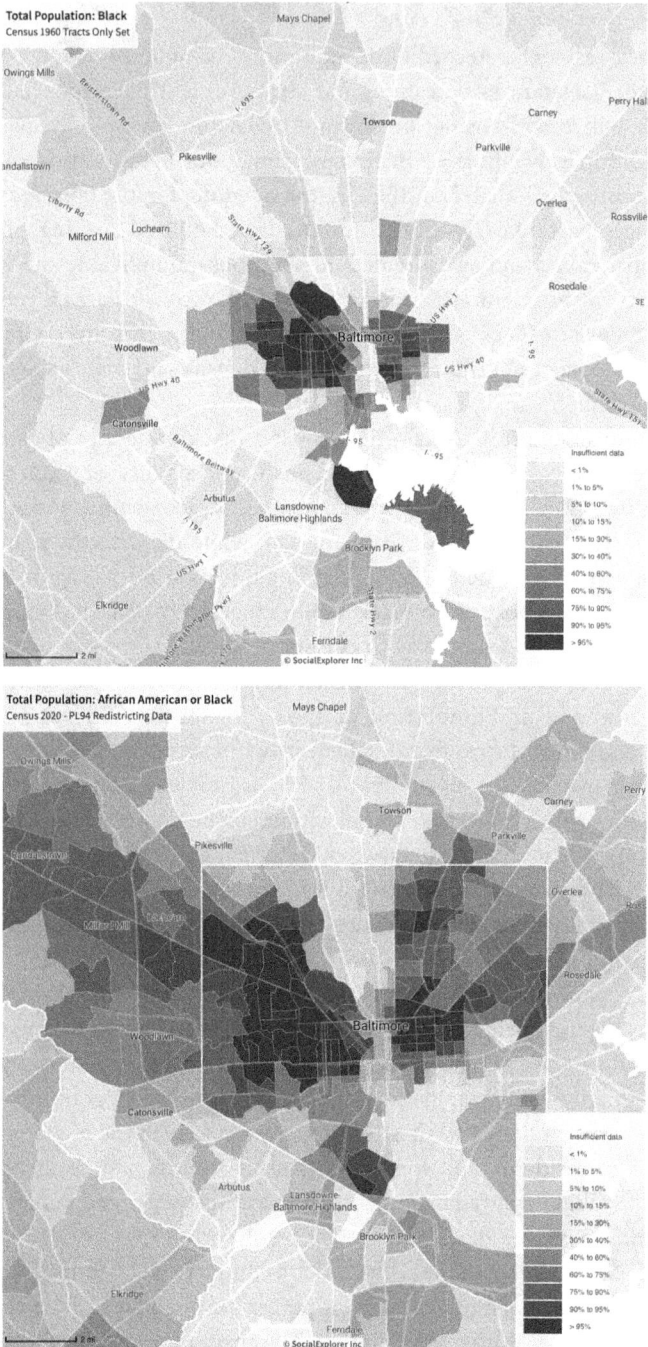

FIGURES 9A AND 9B. African American neighborhoods expanded postwar, eventually encompassing much of Baltimore's west and east sides. Source: Black, 1960/2020, Social Explorer, accessed June 27, 2021.

in the suburbs. Baltimore's suburban counties exploded postwar, adding three hundred thousand residents between 1940 and 1955, at the city's expense. In the Mount Royal–Fremont survey, for instance, "eleven percent stated a preference for the suburbs outside of Baltimore; this preference for suburban Baltimore included 20% of all white households and 7% of all nonwhite households."[84] In 1960, Black residents made up just 3.46 percent of Baltimore County's population or 17,054 out of 492,428 persons.[85] The League of Women Voters in 1966 reported that "housing is a limited commodity for Negroes due to the lack of open occupancy in the region."[86] The booming industrial and commercial centers "around the interchanges" of the new highways, according to Henry Barnes, meant that few white suburbanites would have to go downtown anymore.[87]

Sections of compact suburban neighborhoods from the streetcar era remained in areas like Catonsville, Dundalk, and Towson. Still, the county mostly sprawled outward thanks to its rural traditions and a low-density zoning code passed in 1945. Almost no one rode transit in the county thanks to the limited service, bias against transit, ease of driving, and, as discussed below, the severing of the last streetcar links between the city and county by BTC. As was typical nationally, a few private suburban bus companies offered limited service by the 1960s.[88] Baltimore County would join in as a member of the Metropolitan Transit Authority, but the appetite for what that authority should do was limited given the minimal role of suburban transit. Few supported buying out the failing BTC on an accelerated schedule, given the cost to do so and the substantial number of county residents who had recently fled the city and transit. Building better suburban-city connections was not a priority for most suburbanites.

Austerity and the Streetcar Coup de Grâce

The city government in the 1950s and early 1960s, despite clear signs of decline, refused to provide support, buy out the company, or reduce the annual taxes on transit. BTC was still paying high taxes to the city and state in the late 1950s. Despite losing half its ridership between 1950 and 1959, the taxes had gone up by two-thirds. The company's diversion of 12.46 percent of revenue to taxes stood out compared to other private-sector operators nationally. In Chicago, for instance, the publicly owned CTA was by this time paying just 1.28 percent of its revenue in taxes. In a typical year like 1959, by contrast, twenty-seven different transit taxes in Baltimore diverted a total of $2.661 million from service or profits.[89] The BTC failed to get subsidies and diverted money from fares to support other city services. BTC park taxes, the *Sun* acknowledged, were "a throwback to the vanished days when people generally ... used streetcars to get to the parks."⁹⁰

The company's leaders, desperate to convince city leaders of the company's value, began using social justice rationales for resisting the heavy weight of municipal taxation. The BTC cited reputable figures from the GBC in 1958 showing "that transit riders are generally in the low-income groups." Because the average bus rider had 60 percent less income than motorists, "the tax on transportation which Baltimore exacts is collected from those least able to afford it." Moreover, the tax-burdened riders "are not creating nor are they contributing to the traffic strangulation which besets Baltimore." The company in 1960 proposed $5.5 million in improvements for $1 million in annual tax relief. The upgrades were new express service routes, metropolitan route consolidation and extension, and final streetcar substitution.⁹¹ Sadly, the ensuing negotiation over tax breaks centered, at the city's insistence, on bus substitution and suburban-oriented express routes rather than genuine service improvements for typical city passengers. Had the company not been forced into offering the last streetcars in exchange for tax breaks, it would have left them in place long enough for federally funded renovation in the 1960s and 1970s.

The last streetcars still plying city streets remained a thorn in the side of Henry Barnes's center-city traffic acceleration plans, including ever more one-way streets. In 1959, the BTC rebuffed Barnes's requests to reduce or eliminate the Number 8 streetcar line whose tracks stood in the way of one-way street creation. They cited "grave financial problems" that would follow in the "conversion of the No. 8" line, including the loss of millions worth of "overhead structure, track structures, streetcars, substations, etc." as well as requiring millions in new buses. However, the company hinted that they remained open to the use of tax relief to fund the final substitution of streetcars.⁹²

The remaining streetcars and their tracks also stood in the way of the much-touted Charles Center urban renewal project developed by the powerful GBC. The CBD lacked the polish, modern office space, and views postwar corporations and GBC's influential real-estate and business leaders sought. Inspired by postwar redevelopment projects like Pittsburgh's Golden Triangle, the GBC had convinced city leaders to demolish a large section of the existing downtown to make way for a planned district. Charles Center would feature modernist towers and open plazas interconnected by grade-separated bridges and walkways. Office workers, speeding to and from the center on Barnes's new one-way streets, and the region's emerging expressway network, would find ample parking in structures integrated into the planned district.[93]

Streetcars not only stood in the way of additional one-way street development, but the height of streetcars and their accompanying wires impeded a plan for the dramatic two-story pedestrian bridge crossing over Fayette Street. These design issues could have been resolved with a higher bridge over the streetcar lines, or elimination of the bridge entirely, had the city desired a compromise. The real problem, however, was the art deco PCC cars trundling through downtown. Their increasingly poor and nonwhite riders undercut the image of auto-friendly, affluent office development desired in Charles Center. City leaders thus demanded that the BTC immediately cut the last two major trunk streetcar lines, the 8 and 15. The city's leaders in their haste overlooked crucial facts: these last two lines boasted strong city-suburban links and passed through a mix of neighborhoods in terms of density, social class, and race. They had exciting potential as modernized streetcar lines because they ran near where so much of the city's population lived. Boston, San Francisco, Toronto, and many cities across the globe took a breath and decided to renovate and upgrade at least a few well-used streetcar lines.

The BTC made a believable case that removing these lines was not their preferred step at that time; instead, they were moving forward only because of overwhelming pressure from city leaders to remove the lines and their need for tax relief to stay in business. The Number 8 streetcar line, according to the BTC, ran from rapidly growing suburban Towson, down busy York and Greenmount Avenues, "through the heavily populated central axis of Baltimore." The journey along this axis gathered riders of different races from a mix of poor, middle-class, and wealthy neighborhoods. Once downtown, the 8 crossed west on Fayette Street through downtown, heading west through densely populated, increasingly African American neighborhoods, all the way out to suburban, white Catonsville in Baltimore County. The 15 ran from downtown through the busy Belair commercial district, serving both low-income and suburban-style neighborhoods in its journey through central and northeast Baltimore.[94]

The BTC was never sentimental about streetcars. The company had reserved these lines only because they paid their way and boasted modern equipment, and because the substitutions would have been expensive. It was their hope, as well, that the city would bear any additional substitutional costs through tax relief or other measures. The BTC highlighted that the two remaining streetcar lines carried thirteen million riders per year, who paid $3.5 million annually in fares and alone counted for 17 percent of total system ridership. The lines were, explained BTC management, "trunk routes . . . with feeder bus lines at their outer ends and crosstown lines within the city." With only PCC cars on the lines, BTC could also justifiably claim that the "remaining streetcars used on these two lines are modern and attractive." Buses would be hard-pressed to handle the passenger volume. While the big fifty-four-passenger PCC streetcars were uneconomic on most other routes, those economies did "not exist" on those two lines. The BTC would need 111 fifty-one-seat buses to replace the 101 fifty-four-seat streetcars. So why was BTC going to change the workable formula on these two? The city leadership and planners wanted them gone according to the BTC statement:

> The reason for the proposed conversion of these lines now is not the condition of the streetcar system or prospect of operating income, *but the insistence of the City upon elimination of them to accommodate automobile traffic in downtown Baltimore.* Traffic Transit Commissioner Henry A. Barnes states that the success of the Charles Center and the Civic Center programs is dependent on the conversion of the two remaining lines to bus operation. This changeover would permit making Baltimore and Fayette Streets one-way arteries. David A. Wallace, Director of the Greater Baltimore Committee's Planning Council, also has emphasized that the entire Charles Center plan "depends quite heavily on increasing the number of one-way streets in the downtown area."[95]

The city kept the pressure on the BTC as negotiations continued over the amount of tax relief BTC would deserve for its cooperation.

Pro-streetcar modernization activist Jack O'Donnell became a one-man band for streetcar retention. He created his alternative analysis in 1962 and got a hearing at the Baltimore City Council to promote his ideas. Today, his thinking would be considered best practice and reflect his knowledge of modernization in cities like Toronto that retained streetcar lines while upgrading bus and rapid transit service.[96] O'Donnell made a compelling case that these two "heavily traveled" streetcar trunk lines, the 8 and 15, could become the backbone of a modernized surface rail system. The lines could also have been integrated into downtown plans to create a short downtown subway route (as was done in San Francisco and Boston). He proposed, in the meantime, that downtown Fayette Street could become an exclusive transit mall to improve the timeliness of service. Peripheral sections on the line could be configured to offer additional private rights-of-way. He called for "multi-car skip-stop trains" on the service front to give "all patrons semi-express rush hour service." New equipment such as "lightweight, fast accelerating, quiet, odorless one-man electric cars" would attract riders. BTC could also adapt PCC cars to include air conditioning and double doors.[97]

City leaders ignored O'Donnell's dissent, and even the company's compelling analysis of the enduring value of these lines, in a rush for urban renewal and traffic acceleration. Politicians dangled tax relief as the reward for substitution; sadly, the tax breaks were minor and in the name of service quality reduction. It is a shame that city leaders could not envision a constructive role for its remaining lines. Barnes, for instance, demanded to know "how far the city could go in forcing conversion of the streetcar lines." City Solicitor Francis Burch, digging into the franchise agreements, discovered that the city would need to give the BTC just two years notice to require the substitution.[98] Solicitor Burch in 1962, in fact, "drafted a ruling which could in effect force the BTC to convert its two remaining streetcar lines to bus operations." The pending expiration of the franchise gave the city leverage: "The city's immediate interest is to get the tracks off Fayette Street so that work can proceed on Charles Center plans to widen and lower the bed of that street."[99]

Mayor Grady in spring of 1962 announced that "the city will seek conversion of the BTC's last two streetcar lines to buses."[100] The newly created MTA (1961), described in more detail below, gave "qualified approval" to the BTC plan to remove the streetcar lines and replace the streetcars with 101 air-conditioned buses. The agreement also included less substantial and fleeting bus improvements such as express buses on the new JFX.[101] The city council gave final approval to the deal in December of 1962. The city gave only partial relief from taxes and charges, leaving BTC with its declining financial situation. The city would cover $2 million in rail removal costs,[102] and give an annual tax rebate of $285,000 for seven years. That the BTC accepted the deal reflects just how dreadful things had become for the company.[103]

The MTA celebrated the removal of the streetcar lines as a "major accomplishment" completed "in cooperation with the City of Baltimore." The MTA praised "The City Administration" for the tax credits and covering paving for a total cost of about $3.5 million.[104] The *Baltimore Sun* praised the deal for removing streetcar lines and encouraged "other proposals for further strengthening of the service" so that they might "avoid the course on which St. Louis is embarked—public ownership of a mass transportation system."[105] The *Sun* in 1962 published a flattering feature on Barnes as he departed for New York and a new job as traffic commissioner. Baltimore had secured his reputation as one of the era's most influential traffic planners. The article claimed that transit "service would be even worse today if Mr. Barnes had not taken a hand in rerouting and consolidating lines to get the most out of the buses on hand." It is hard to agree, in retrospect, with the city's newspaper of record.[106]

Downward Spiral

The reputation of private transit companies like the BTC hit new lows in the 1960s. Newspapers across the country were filled with articles about substandard and reduced service, management shortcomings, labor unrest, and perennial deficits. In Baltimore, the influential Citizens Planning and Housing Association described the hard truth: "so many potential mass transit riders have their minds poisoned against this mode of travel that it would be psychologically impossible to woo them back again." Those "who enjoy the freedom of their cars . . . never want to think again of waits on wet, cold or windy corners."[107] BTC, for instance, had limited success even with a new luxury service designed to entice drivers back to transit. A Metro Flyer highway express service from suburban Towson to downtown at rush hours in air-conditioned buses only attracted about five hundred riders daily, many of whom were nonwhite "domestic workers" reverse commuting from the center city. The peak hour service barely covered its cost. The troubles of the express service in Baltimore seem to have been typical for much-hyped highway bus lines.[108]

As in so many other cities, the problem in Baltimore was not only the speed, social segregation, and comfort of subsidized car travel on new highways but the rise of a multicentered metropolis. Baltimore's CBD, where most transit routes started and ended, had slipped in importance. By 1962 of the 1.9 million vehicle trips in metro Baltimore, just 7 percent traveled to or from the CBD. It was getting hard to imagine any transit service working well in such auto-centric geography.[109]

Experts confirmed the low quality of transit service. A 1964 study by transit consultant Parsons Brinckerhoff found that BTC's fleets were older than its peer companies. The number of buses (805 in 1964) and age (60 percent of the fleet was over fifteen years old) undermined service. BTC was no longer the central force in urban mobility in the city or region: transit counted for just 21 percent of all trips in Baltimore and just 38 percent of trips to the CBD. Even though ridership was no longer hemorrhaging, "the trend is levelling off, primarily due to the fact that transit captives (people who do not have a driver's license, such as children and elderly people) are becoming an increasingly greater proportion of transit riders."[110] The company was serving a narrow slice of city residents by the mid-1960s: "It was found that 85 percent of transit riders were necessity riders—persons who either did not have a driver's license or did not own an automobile."[111]

Parsons Brinckerhoff's consultants were realistic about what could be expected from a private company operating an unsubsidized public utility: "in terms of coverage, frequency of service, and loading practices . . . the service provided by the BTC is in keeping with reasonable standards for a free-enterprise operation that must live within its income." They identified high taxes as a drag on operations. The BTC paid operating taxes and license fees of $2.25 million in 1963 despite minor tax reductions related to the streetcar substitution project. High taxes and lack of subsidies penalized riders who were now paying fares higher than those in five comparable cities: "In most cities throughout the country, some type of tax relief has been given to transit operating companies." Parsons Brinckerhoff admonished city leaders as had Wolman a few years before: "A private transit company cannot be expected to operate at a deficit . . . in order to furnish services which the community deems essential, unless the community is willing to subsidize the service to the extent necessary."[112] BTC was not opposed to running socially important transit services; they just expected to be subsidized to do so. For instance, with federal support, the BTC developed services to "facilitate transportation from inner-city areas to suburban job opportunities," such as the new Social Security complex on the city's western edge.[113]

As in so many other cities, in Baltimore city leaders failed to act fast enough to save transit before it hit bottom. Because transit riders were such a small percentage of state residents by the 1960s, making a case for transit as a public responsibility among city and suburban drivers was a challenge. Baltimore's city council, for instance, passed multiple bills calling for public ownership of BTC in the 1960s but failed to follow through and refused to either drop taxes or make serious headway in this crucial initiative.[114] In 1965, a mayor's committee examining public ownership claimed there would be an extra $3 million or so available if the public owned the transit system because of relief from federal, state, city, and county taxes.[115] Yet city leaders did nothing.

The Limits of the MTA

The creation of the MTA in 1961 resulted from multiple pressures in the 1950s including the Wolman Committee report, Henry Barnes's push for an express bus system on a metropolitan scale,[116] downtown interests concerned about CBD vitality, and politicians aiming for regional traffic and transit solutions. From the beginning, however, there were vast differences in opinion among proponents about MTA operation scope. For instance, Republican mayoral candidate McKeldin in 1959 believed that an MTA should exclude "any form of subsidy or tax relief that would benefit stockholders of the Baltimore Transit Company" despite that company still running the region's mass transit.[117]

The MTA that emerged from state-level negotiations between 1959 and 1961 reflected a fractured metropolitan area and weak support for transit. A state-sanctioned commission first developed the draft legislation between 1959 and 1960 under the watchful eyes of notables such as Henry Barnes, the GBC leadership, and the Committee for Downtown. The proponents cited the success of metropolitan port authorities in Maryland and the regional transportation compact binding suburban counties and the District of Columbia.[118] The GBC, major business leaders, and Baltimore mayor Harold Grady successfully lobbied for the passage of the MTA legislation in 1961 in the hope that the new agency would "improve the mass transportation service available to the residents of the region."[119] The GBC believed mass transit was key to the "dramatic program for urban renewal, its success in attracting new people to live downtown" and "the success of Charles Center."[120]

Baltimore County business leaders (i.e., Bethlehem Steel) and community councils came out strongly for the MTA, not only because of expected commuting benefits, but because the MTA would help the region "compete favorably with other cities."[121] Private bus companies in the county were barely operating, limiting options for their employees. But suburban Anne Arundel County political leadership and citizen groups resisted joining even though the county was "a heavily suburbanized and industrialized part of a metropolis that has erased political boundary lines." The legislation that finally passed in 1961 excluded neighboring and rapidly growing Anne Arundel and Howard Counties.[122]

The MTA was a typically ineffectual regional transit agency, undertaking just enough regional transportation planning to qualify for growing federal grants. MTA, by legislative authorization, had many potential powers including long-term planning, eminent domain, regulation over all transit, and the right to buy and operate mass transit on a public basis. But the MTA legislation included familiar poison pills that set back any effort for public ownership. Struck from the final bill, for instance, was this key phrase: "The General Assembly recognizes its own obligation to provide for adequate mass transportation when private operation cannot or does not do so." Striking the phrase left state-level financial support in doubt. Legislators also took out the MTA's tax exemption. Lack of general fund support or tax exemption were significant barriers to creating a successful transit agency.[123]

That the MTA only served Baltimore City and County rather than the metropolitan area was a central problem given the economic interrelationship of many other counties. The city did not select the majority of board members, with two members for the city, two for the county, and one by the governor—despite most transit riders living in the city. The MTA took over regulation from the PSC, but it could not buy a transit system until 1963, and then only the BTC rather than suburban bus companies (and only with sign-off from at least one county member of the MTA). In this period, state legislatures frequently gave suburbs more power over transit than was warranted to buy off skeptical officials. This arrangement was the case in Baltimore, as even MTA supporters cited the many "safeguards ... incorporated in the bill to protect both the citizens and mercantile interests in Baltimore County." This suburban favoritism was as notable in transit-rich regions like New York and Chicago as in more car-dependent areas like Baltimore.[124]

The newly created MTA, dominated by members of the wealthy, white business classes in both the city and county, pushed back on public ownership throughout most of the 1960s even though it was the only organization, after 1963, empowered to take such action. The first head, lawyer Philip Heller Sachs, was a stalwart of pro-highway Citizens Planning and Housing Association (CPHA) and a leading member of the northwest Jewish community; none of the original five board members were mass transit professionals. The MTA in 1963 argued "that public ownership might prove expensive to taxpayers in the area and that loss of all taxes now paid by private enterprises to the city, County, and State and Federal governments would automatically occur." Worse, public ownership might require "heavy subsidies from local governments."[125]

The MTA resistance to public ownership aligned with business opinion. The GBC and downtown interests during the early phases of subway planning in 1967 (see below) remained steadfast in their "belief that a premature acquisition of the BTC and other private bus companies ... would serve no useful purpose in advance of the opportunity for an integrated" rail and rapid system. They believed that no "dramatic improvement" in service would be forthcoming in a stand-alone public bus system. This delay in public ownership was shortsighted, as the declining BTC was bound to alienate even more Baltimoreans before rapid rail development offered new service.[126]

By refusing to act on legislation that empowered it to take ownership, the MTA left the BTC to its own devices. BTC made more cuts, raised fares, and deferred maintenance. The company ordered some new GM buses, but by 1968 BTC had raised fares to thirty cents, one of the higher rates in the country and a rate out of line for the mostly poor Baltimoreans still riding. By 1969, BTC's eight hundred GM diesel buses served just twenty-seven routes, and just 16 percent of the city's working population used transit for commuting. BTC was now running a second-tier public service, and offering gimmicks like express bus service was editing at the margins.[127] An inspection of BTC's 773 buses by the PSC in 1969 discovered twenty-six needing major repairs and 77.3 percent of the whole fleet had broken or cracked windows.[128]

NCL by the late 1960s had mostly divested itself of the fading BTC, holding just 25 percent of the company.[129] In 1968, on revenue of just $21 million, the BTC was paying $2.5 million in combined city, state, and federal taxes, or 11.75 cents for every dollar of revenue. These taxes were far beyond the company's dividend to investors of just $781,000 for the year. The BTC had to cover the interest on $103 million in debt, much of which had been run up to pay for capital investments the city or state should have covered as part of a public commitment to transit.

Ridership had slipped to eighty-eight million passengers, down from about ninety-one million in 1967 and a fraction of its former glory. Attacks on staff by criminals in the late 1960s led to exact fare requirements (so drivers did not have to carry cash), and a damaging twenty-four-day strike that must have frustrated long-suffering riders. Baltimore's extensive riots in April of 1968, in part a response to the assassination of Martin Luther King Jr., damaged many neighborhoods best served by transit, including areas along Pennsylvania Avenue. BTC reported that the riots "caused serious disruptions to our service, made it necessary to temporarily reroute transit lines serving the affected areas, and resulted in considerable loss of revenue."[130] In 1969, the MTA signed off on a 1 percent system-wide service cut, which was modest compared to the 12.4 percent year-over-year rider loss between 1968 and 1969 (January–March).[131]

The MTA in 1970, with an eye to federal subsidies and relief from local taxes (ca. $3 million in 1969), finally paid $35 million for the BTC's remaining assets through condemnation proceedings.[132] The MTA gave millions for the keys to this threadbare kingdom and pledged to order hundreds of new buses. The MTA became the Mass Transit Administration in 1971 (now MDOT MTA) with authority over all transit in Maryland cities and began merging once independent suburban lines with BTC bus services.[133] The state government also began dedicating a small portion of transportation-related taxes (i.e., fuel) to the operation and capital needs of transit through the Transportation Trust Fund. Since the 1970s, however, the state has demonstrably failed to provide sufficient state capital or operating support to sustain or expand high-quality bus or rail service in the Baltimore region.[134]

Rapid Transit without a Transit Network

In Baltimore, Atlanta, and other cities that had mostly ignored transit, leaders did an about-face in the 1960s and 1970s. Enticed by federal capital grants, and hopeful that transit would spur downtown redevelopment, they spun out plans for new rail systems. Political elites optimistically believed that rail could overcome bus transit hesitancy among the mostly white middle and upper classes. Many hoped in the 1960s, as today, that transit might also address many of the urban social and environmental problems caused by freeways and suburbanization. Plans like these might have worked within a well-considered regional vision of urban development and growth. However, new rail lines usually operated in a public policy and planning vacuum in Baltimore, Atlanta, and most other cities.

Baltimore's MTA leadership shared the standard industry position in the postwar era that only rapid transit, not buses, could compete with cars and draw in suburbanites. For instance, glossy new rail stations would create a new image for downtown urban renewal projects like Charles Center.[135] Philip Heller Sachs, the first chairman of the MTA, aimed to create a transit system "designed not just to compete with the private auto but to better auto performance." He envisioned rapid transit with bus feeders and suburban parking lots playing a significant role in the daily commute to downtown.[136] The GBC, Baltimore's downtown redevelopment boosters who had resisted municipal transit ownership for years and encouraged highways, endorsed rapid transit because "we cannot depend on the automobile for mass transportation."[137] Mayor Thomas D'Alesandro III (1967–71) was another strong advocate of both Baltimore rapid transit and national federal funding that would help pay for such a system.[138]

The unrelenting MTA and elite pursuit of a Baltimore subway in the 1960s and 1970s ignored decades of analysis that had determined that rapid transit was of limited utility and would be expensive for the city. Moreover, these earlier studies took place when streetcar and bus transit was comparatively popular and extensive, creating opportunities for integration and feeders with new high-speed lines. Proposals for Baltimore subways from 1905, 1926, 1929, 1942, and 1951, among others, had failed to gain support. A report in 1955, for instance, noted that "Baltimore is far from an ideal city for the building of subways.... The streets are narrow; there are a number of hills . . . much rock would be encountered . . . and the spokes of a wheel passenger movement pattern make it difficult to contemplate that subways costing $250,000,000 or more are economically, politically, or physically justified."[139] Henry Barnes in 1958 had also warned against reliance on "existing rail lines" for rapid transit routes as "one becomes aware that in most instances these rights-of-way are located along parks, streams, and other sparsely populated areas." As it turned out, he predicted correctly that lines in such "inaccessible" locations would attract very few riders without feeder bus lines.[140] He was also skeptical "because the population density downtown is so much smaller than in New York." But his departure removed a prominent critic of rapid transit.[141]

The MTA brought in leading transportation planning firm Parsons Brinckerhoff to study options. The firm's analysis culminated in an exciting but deeply flawed 1965 study. The plan envisioned a magnificent regional system with six rapid rail corridors, about sixty-five miles long in total. Trains would zoom from the periphery, including stops in the suburbs, to connect with a primarily underground 7.5-mile "inner-city" subway loop with ten stations, two of them in the heart of the CBD. Many of the neighborhoods on this loop were dense, transit-rich historical neighborhoods. To run at the planned speed of seventy-five to eighty miles per hour, new rapid lines outside the subway loop would mostly skirt old streetcar routes for abandoned railroad rights-of-way above grade service. As might be expected, these higher-speed routes were not as conveniently located for the riders as the old streetcar lines. Riders would either have to walk longer or catch feeder buses, requiring the MTA or BTC to develop a robust bus network.[142] Parsons Brinckerhoff fondly imagined that by 1985 the completed system, extending in all points of the compass, would somehow be moving 387,000 passengers a day. These were ambitious figures given the highways, lack of density outside the core, declining race relations, and restrictive zoning in the region—factors all outside the control of the MTA. The fares from these passengers would theoretically cover the operating costs, leaving only the construction costs, a mere $697 million for the whole system, to be covered by government subsidies.[143]

The MTA and planners failed to understand the scale of the cliff on which Baltimore sat, rendering these early ridership projections and the financial model inaccurate. For example, Parsons ignored clear signs of the city's mounting problems in the 1960s. The consultants believed that the city would grow from 938,000 to 949,000 by 1980. In fact, the city's population slipped to 786,000 during that period.[144] The GBC claimed in 1966 that population projections "indicate a moderate increase in Baltimore City, reversing the declining trend recorded in the 1950–1960 period," but it was unclear why such optimism was warranted given the city's manifest problems. Baltimore County alone was projected to reach 880,000 inhabitants by 1980, many of whom were relocated city residents. The CBD's employment base was also projected to expand by only fifteen thousand workers, comprising just 88,850 workers in 1980, undermining the justification for an expensive, CBD-focused system.[145] In truth, the planners and many city leaders had an exalted faith in rapid transit's ability to arrest decentralization of population and employment. Baltimore's rapid rail, they predicted, would generate transit-oriented growth, reduce outward sprawl, increase transit corridor property values, and decongest downtown parking lots and streets. In other words, it would be a cure-all for what ailed Baltimore.[146]

The lavishly illustrated rendering of a new Charles Center subway station in one of the planning reports hints at the true agenda. As with the destruction of the last streetcar lines in the name of urban renewal, downtown interests were calling the tune for a planning concept that would put Baltimore on the national map. Advantages of rapid rail included "maintenance and possible improvement of the Area's competitive position in attracting its share of the nation's future economic growth." The planners claimed that "many cities which have constructed new or expanded rail rapid transit facilities have reported marked increase in real estate value in downtown areas and along the transit routes."[147] The Baltimore subway would "increase development opportunities" in the CBD, inner loop, and on the radial lines.[148] Business leaders sat on a committee to build support, including Albert Hutzler Jr. whose family still ran the anchor Hutzler's department store on Howard Street despite opening multiple suburban branches that drained downtown commercial vitality.[149] The references in the report to neighboring and competitor cities of Philadelphia and Washington, DC, then actively planning or developing rapid transit upgrades, helped light a fire under civic leaders. The planning documents reflect an elite, top-down approach that won politically but at the cost of planning for people.[150]

In a nod to realism, the consultants recommended that the development of the system should be staged, beginning with lines in northeast and northwest Baltimore. The MTA was even more cautious, and in 1967 recommended starting with the northwest line first. A northwest route did not have an immediate highway competitor and could leverage remaining bus riders still fairly numerous in the area. Thanks to political pressure, the MTA also promised an early rapid line connection to Anne

Arundel County.[151] The GBC and downtown interests were understandably displeased with the cutting of the inner-city subway loop: "it is our judgement that lack of completion of the inner city loop reduces the value of the system from the transit standpoint to the City of Baltimore." They had a point. Without an "inner-city" loop, many of the most densely populated neighborhoods, with many "necessity riders," lost potential service. How many white-collar workers could really be collected in the northwest to make the Charles Center stop worthwhile? Not that many, as it turned out.[152] Plans for "special bus facilities" on expressway expansions also remained aspirational, were never built, and were likely included to try and mollify critics who otherwise opposed the destructive east–west expressway.[153]

The planners and MTA deserve some credit for planning transit in the primarily Black, racially changing, northwest corridor despite their hopes for suburban patronage. An early Baltimore Metro document highlighted the ability of rapid lines to "improve the lives of those dependent on public transportation—the low-income family, the handicapped, the elderly, the young."[154] The MTA chose a promising route, but a single line's actual benefits to Black families were doubtful. According to the GBC in 1966, there needed to be more attention paid to "provision of public transportation service to accommodate the home-to-work travel of those of our citizens who live in the dense inner-city residential areas, and whose jobs or job potentials are in" the suburbs. This "growing segment" of the population had trouble finding work thanks to "the absence of adequate public transportation."[155] The growing opportunity presented by federal capital grants encouraged city officials in Baltimore and other cities to plan for expensive construction projects like a subway despite growing concerns about the ability of rail to serve decentralized regions including suburban employers. The "freeway revolt" was in full swing, and city officials across the nation were looking for less controversial projects that would still deliver federal grants, construction jobs, and downtown revitalization without displacing residents.[156]

Riders along the northwest line would either ride a bus to or leave their cars behind at stations. From there, they would speed quickly downtown with stops at the new state office complex near Bolton Hill, the Howard Street and Lexington Market shopping district, and finally, the CBD at Charles Center. By this time, the northwest section of town was divided between declining but dense African American areas like Old West Baltimore and low-density middle-class Black and Jewish neighborhoods further out. The Baltimore City Department of Planning, in fact, was concerned in 1970 about the small number of residents within walking distance of planned stations.[157] The planners believed that the city should "increase the densities in the areas in proximity to the transit stations." The Planning Department's 1970 station-area study was filled with intriguing ideas for building apartment and office buildings near stations as part of a program of "High Intensity Districts." Districts would be upzoned, assembled (through eminent domain and excess condemnation), incentivized (tax breaks, deferrals, etc.), and carefully designed. The city government, however, failed to heed their advice.[158]

The Baltimore rapid system development process, despite good intentions, reflected typical 1970s and 1980s political and cost-control problems. In early planning estimates, the mostly above-ground first train line would cost just $150 million and open by 1975, with the federal government picking up the tab for $60 to $80 million of the cost.[159] However, the single-line price inflated rapidly, gobbling up future capital funds that might have gone to buses rather than rail. By 1971, the MTA reiterated its support for the "practical" option of a twenty-eight-mile system, linking the northwest through downtown to the airport in Anne Arundel County. The MTA, however, cut the fourteen-mile line section to Anne Arundel County and Baltimore Washington International (BWI) Airport when "politicians there balked at plans for the rail line for political and, some feel, racial reasons." While at first demanding a line extension, Anne Arundel politicians and voters by the 1970s rejected closer contact with a city many had recently fled.[160]

The federal transit agency, the Urban Mass Transit Administration (UMTA), provided funding only for the abbreviated northwest route in 1975, and the state legislature approved its share of the line in 1976.[161] Dysfunctional local politics, rising labor costs, engineering challenges, and manufacturing delays slowed the development. The first eight miles of the Baltimore Metro system finally opened in 1983 and stretched from just Charles Center to a less than thriving district near Reisterstown Road, well within the city limits. At a total cost of $797 million, or about $100 million a mile, it was both one of the shortest new rapid systems in the county and one of the most expensive.[162]

Solid ridership might have justified high costs and delays, but the benefits of rapid rail were hard to see on the ground. George Tyson, a knowledgeable Baltimore resident who wrote a sharp critique of the planning in 1982, called the system "inappropriate to the area through which it is built. It is primarily a commuter railroad traversing an urban area which needs better local transit service."[163] Indeed, the focus was "special lots for suburban residents" even though lots around stations reduced potential inhabitants within walking distance.[164] Most stops in the system were also too far apart to offer convenient neighborhood service without a bus connection.¹⁶⁵ Metro promoters in 1983 claimed that Metro had inspired renovation of some central city real estate, a subsidized business park in the northwest, and a few new housing units, but in truth they had little to show given the scale of investment.¹⁶⁶

City leaders tried to put a good face on the impact, but it was undeniable to *Mass Transit* in 1983 that the rapid system mostly "runs through depressed, predominantly Black neighborhoods."¹⁶⁷ During the initial, limited daytime service period, MTA officials predicted they could reach twenty-five thousand riders in six months and forty-five to sixty-five thousand riders once full service with feeder buses were created. According to *Mass Transit*, however, these rider numbers were not anything close to the eighty thousand daily "figure tossed around in the early days when officials were trying to justify construction."¹⁶⁸ The planners and promoters had failed to consider the declining population and density in the corridor, the loss of the CBD's centrality in the region, and the unattractiveness of the system to auto-centric suburbanites. The famous Inner Harbor also lacked a stop; the nearest was at Charles Center, which meant that the line derived few benefits from the tourists flocking to James Rouse's Harborplace (1980) project. The lack of adequate local, state, and federal planning that might have stabilized center-city neighborhoods in crisis by investing in housing and cracking down on slum landlords also took its toll. By 1987, the first eight-mile section of Metro was moving just forty-five thousand riders a day, many fewer than initially projected and a small percentage of the total three hundred thousand riders using Metro bus services per day.¹⁶⁹

The disappointing results did not deter modest and expensive extensions of the Metro rapid line. City and state leaders diverted money from canceling the east–west I-70 in the city to the Metro. A total of $150 million in federal funds (of a $190 million project) would pay for a six-mile addition to Baltimore County that opened in 1987. However, the extension did not connect to an emerging edge city like Towson. Nor did the new stops along the line, primarily white areas such as Pikesville, rezone for additional density. The terminus in the county was along a highway and a "meadow" in suburban, lightly populated Owings Mills. The surrounding moderate-density housing subdivisions and strip malls did not relate to the transit stop. The Rouse Company, known for Harborplace, regional malls, and the new town of Columbia, Maryland, in Howard County, envisioned a "town center" shopping hub at Owings Mills. The wealthy Meyerhoff family promised a planned community surrounding the station. Rouse, however, only built a lackluster mall, and the planned residential community flopped. Various subdivisions, with lots of parking, slowly filled in the area.[170]

The growth of the rapid transit system stalled out, given the lackluster results. Federal funds for big-ticket rapid transit also dried up during the 1980s. The only addition since Owings Mills was short and expensive. A planned 1.6-mile subway extension from Charles Center to the vast Johns Hopkins University Hospital on the east side initially made sense as the university had become the city's largest employer. An extension like this could help low-income service workers from the west side access hospital jobs through rapid transit. Unfortunately, the short extension ended up as a complex and expensive ($325 million) engineering project and only opened in 1995. The extension was a deeply subsidized transit gift to Johns Hopkins University.[171]

The Baltimore Metro in October of 2019 was down to just 701,00 passengers total, or about twenty-two thousand riders a day on average, a typical ridership level preceding the pandemic.[172] The remaining Metro riders (about seven in ten of whom are Black) ride despite the limited connecting lines, minimum service, and the tragic housing disinvestment and failed neighborhood stabilization along the northwest corridor.[173] City officials have also targeted the Lexington Market and Howard Street shopping corridor for gentrification and redevelopment despite its longstanding role as core shopping area for African American Baltimoreans. Charles Center has meanwhile declined as a hub of the city's white-collar workforce. On the other end of the line, and forty years too late, Owings Mills is finally developing a small transit-oriented development. However, the new complex still relies on thousands of new parking spaces for guests and residents. The minimal ridership number for Metro looks even worse when one considers the regional population of 2.7 million inhabitants.

The contrast with the high-density, planned transit-oriented developments in the Washington, DC, suburbs, such as Rosslyn and Bethesda, reflects the missed opportunity in Baltimore's suburbs. But the Capitol region, while just a short drive away, benefited from the combination of a more extensive and deeply subsidized transit system, sufficient leadership in surrounding counties that provided annual subsidies and favored dense transit-oriented developments, and the recession-proof government service industry. Baltimore's mediocre heavy-rail experience and lackluster transit-related planning were more typical. Expensive rail investments in American cities postwar (Cleveland, Atlanta, Buffalo, Detroit, Miami, and Los Angeles) struggled in the United States thanks to some combination of bad timing, limited connecting service, high construction and operating costs, central city decline, suburban not-in-my-backyard-ism, and auto-centric development.[174]

Baltimore during the 1980s had the dubious distinction of also developing an underperforming light-rail system. Light-rail has many variations but is usually distinguished by large, multiunit electrified trams running in separate rights-of-way on the periphery (typically abandoned rail corridors) and in or along streets closer to the CBD. By 1984, UMTA counted fifty-three new-start rail projects nationally costing $19 billion, mostly light-rail.[175] The light-rail sector has grown even larger since the 1970s. The American Public Transit Association in 2019 documented the enduring popularity of both light-rail and downtown streetcars: "Of the 93 rail systems now operated by public transit agencies, only nine have been operating since the 19th century."[176] Light-rail plans help secure federal grants and are thought to attract more affluent suburban riders back to transit by connecting suburbs with attractions such as the CBD, stadiums, airports, and universities.

A quick look at Baltimore's long-term experience helps explain why light-rail so rarely performs as expected. Baltimore's famous "comeback" mayor, and later governor of Maryland, William Donald Schaefer, remained committed in the 1980s to rail as a way of bolstering downtown, the Inner Harbor, and a new Camden Yards stadium. He was also eager to procure the maximum of state funds for the troubled city. Baltimore's north–south light-rail line launched in 1988 and opened in 1992 ($379 million) from suburban Timonium to Glen Burnie in the south, an impressive 22.5 miles long. The MTA has since extended the line south to BWI Airport and north to Hunt Valley (now twenty-seven miles in total) at a completed cost of $680 million. Local and state money paid for the first phase while federal dollars paid for later additions.[177]

Outside the CBD, light-rail runs mostly in the abandoned right-of-way of a defunct railway. The light-rail trains, moreover, did not run close to where most existing or potential Black riders lived. The first section of the line served wealthier, whiter northern areas like Mount Washington that were served decades ago by commuter rail. Even so, one plush Baltimore County district, Ruxton-Riderwood, resisted having any stop because they believed it would "bring crime." This was typical coded racial language of the time employed by suburbs seeking to resist transit without appearing to be racist.[178] Nor did planners and city officials rezone stops for walkable higher-density development.[179] Weak planning led to low ridership. In 2015, light-rail had slipped to about twenty-three thousand riders per day on average. The light-rail is also deeply subsidized, with fares covering just 18 percent of operating costs (vs. 29 percent farebox recovery by buses and 23 percent by Metro).[180]

Baltimore's middling experience with light-rail is similar to Pittsburgh, Saint Louis, Denver, Charlotte, Houston, and so on. Train lines, absent a concerted effort to rezone areas around stations, improve bus service (including feeders to rail lines), restrict growth more generally, or reduce and tax auto infrastructure, will attract few Americans.

The Missing Buses

The MTA's investments in rail during the 1970s and 1980s overshadowed the continuing disinvestment in the dominant bus system. Public ownership, relying on a weak mix of state and federal funds (and exempting local governments from subsidies), was no cure for the long plagued bus service. In 1983, when the Metro opened, residents were already "fuming over a mediocre bus system."[181] Indeed, news from the front lines painted a "second tier" bus service portrait. Riders, in the swampy Baltimore summer, were "sweating, grouchy," and "using makeshift fans" because of broken air conditioning.[182] Dirty, late, or no-show buses were standard.[183]

Driving the decline in service was an aging, poorly maintained fleet. The *Baltimore Sun* provided extensive coverage of service problems, reporting that during the "depths that bus service reached in the 1970s and early 1980s . . . up to a quarter of the fleet would sometimes be out of commission." Federal grants for the renovation of buses had dried up, and the state required that the farebox cover 50 percent of operating costs. The MTA did not have enough money for sufficient skilled repair people and then paid out too much overtime to make up for the labor deficit. The total number of buses had fallen from over a thousand at its height in the late 1970s to nine hundred.[184]

The bus system lost riders in 1976, 1980, and 1981 thanks to fare increases and crummy service—undermining the potential ridership for the new rapid line. Revenue customers on the system between 1972 and 1981 did not break seventy-five million, except in 1980, although free or discounted fares for students and seniors brought total ridership to near one hundred million.[185] As ridership fell and subsidies lagged, MTA administrators took the same service reduction strategy their predecessors had pursued at the BTC: between 1980 and 1982, the MTA cut 2.8 million miles of service.[186] Poorly subsidized public ownership, thanks to limited state funding and no local subsidies, was no panacea. MTA buses remained crucial for mobility in the region, but the quality and ridership decline indicated that the system's financing was inadequate.

The MTA initiated "Project Quality" in 1982 to upgrade bus service.[187] The $29 million program, partly funded by a state gas tax, attempted to "stop the decline" by buying eighty buses a year for six years and initiating management and training reforms. New buses were less glamorous than futuristic rail lines, but investing in buses was an inexpensive way to improve mobility for most riders. The program also seemed to have been timed with the planned opening of the Metro in 1983, to assuage frustrated bus riders. Yet Project Quality, launched with fanfare, would barely be able to keep pace with higher labor costs, the Reagan era cuts to operating subsidies, and the state's limited subsidies.[188] The federal government had come through on massive capital grants for rapid transit development in the 1970s, but the Reagan administration started phasing out the small federal operating support the MTA depended upon.[189]

The *Sun* editorial page admitted in 1986 that relying on fares "has ill effects. It makes the MTA see itself as a business and not a public service."[190] In the search for business-like efficiency, the buses endured the worst of cuts and disinvestment during these crucial years, as they comprised about 80 percent of the MTA's total operating budgets. Damaging cuts to nighttime bus service in 1986, designed to help balance the budget, were ill timed with the suburban Owings Mills Metro station's planned opening in 1987.[191] And while Project Quality by 1986 had reduced the average age of the system's nine hundred buses from ten to six years, there were still lots of broken air conditioning systems, dirty buses, and scratched windows. The new head of the MTA acknowledged in 1986 that there had been too much focus on "new toys" (rail lines) even though "the bus side is carrying the majority of our customers." He also admitted that "some of our buses are an insult."[192]

Very little has changed for the better since the 1980s. The MTA's prospects are not bright, given the city's endless slide downward. Baltimore City is today (2021) down to 609,000 residents. The city remains highly segregated and hemmed in by more affluent suburban counties where many Black families have also moved. Baltimore's overall density has fallen significantly, declining from 11,153 in 1970 to 7,359 in 2019 (persons per square mile). Large sections of the once densely populated African American east and west sides are still more densely populated per square mile than suburban areas, but widespread abandonment of housing and persistently high unemployment has hurt potential ridership. The city and state have allowed abandoned or tax-delinquent properties to rot, at most stepping in to bulldoze crumbling housing. This slum clearance strategy, while understandable from a public health and safety basis, and now popular in many Rustbelt cities, permanently reduces density and potential ridership.[193]

With one in three Baltimoreans lacking cars, about one in five commutes on transit, and with 21 percent of the city's population living below the poverty line, transit remains essential to many families.[194] However, the MTA's decades of fixed-rail network is poorly located to best serve those who need transit most. Links to the suburbs remain weak despite population migration and jobs to the fringe. Charles Center has declined as an office center. The northwest, where the rapid transit runs, has lost population. Light-rail traverses low-density neighborhoods in the city and suburbs. The gentrified harbor front is either car dependent or walkable in a narrow area. Limited bus service thus remains the lifeline for regular MTA riders.

In October of 2019, MTA buses carried just over six million passengers or about 193,000 a day on average (counting each individual fare and transfer as a passenger). Thanks to urban decline, limited service, and transit abandonment, very few Baltimoreans ride unless they must. The MTA recently launched a major redesign of bus routes, to bring back riders, but it is hard to place faith in such management efforts.[195] The MTA's 2018 operating budget, comprised primarily of state funds, devoted just $305 million for moving 63.797 million Baltimore regional local bus riders versus $161 million spent on 9.3 million Maryland Area Rail Commuter (MARC) passengers traveling between Washington and Baltimore. Statistics like these reflect long-standing social and political priorities. The riders on MTA core bus services are 67 percent Black as contrasted with the 55 percent white ridership on MARC lines.[196]

It is telling that Black families, many of whom have now relocated to the surrounding counties, mostly drive if they can. In Baltimore County in 2013, for instance, the number of daily commuters using transit was about nineteen thousand persons, or 4.8 percent, even though the African American population is now 248,401 (2019). The large African American populations in auto-centric Anne Arundel (101,926) and Howard County (64,061) are also mostly living transit-free lives.[197] The higher incomes and low population density of these counties in 2019 remain a challenge for good transit service (1,382 persons per square mile in Baltimore County). Yet there are doubtless many more potential riders who might choose transit if the service were more reliable, and if neighborhoods were better designed for walkability. Decades of low-quality transit service that many families experienced in Baltimore City is also a deterrent to transit patronage.[198]

FIGURES 10A AND 10B. The thinning out of transit ridership in the Baltimore region between 1960 and 2000. Source: Transit Ridership 1960/2000, Social Explorer, accessed June 26, 2021.

The Baltimore case study offers insights into the real reasons for a century of transit decline in that city and many others. Baltimore city officials, powerful elites, planners, and voters encouraged accelerated streetcar substitution by BTC and NCL. Local leaders built a world-class highway and roadway network that siphoned off the most prosperous transit passengers. For decades, they failed to align zoning or planning with transit and resisted regional cooperation. Since the 1960s, the MTA has made other questionable decisions, including slow-walking public purchase, investing deeply in low-impact rail, and cutting back essential bus service. Decades of anti-transit actions like these took place in full view of a well-informed public, with blow-by-blow accounts of plans and policies featured on the front pages of the city's leading newspaper. The pattern of transit disinvestment in Baltimore was repeated, with variations, across the nation during the postwar decades.

Underlining Baltimore's anti-transit choices, as in other cities, were racist attitudes and policies that divided residents, neighborhoods, and governments. Highways smashed and divided neighborhoods where transit once thrived. City and state officials have left old neighborhoods to rot, accelerating customer losses for the MTA. A vast region of restrictive single-family zoning gave rise to low-density white-majority suburbs with minimal transit service. The population of Baltimore's now dominant suburbs has diversified, but the lack of density and minimum transit ridership remains. As in so many regions, there are potential transit customers in both suburbs and central cities, but the current MTA cannot deliver the service they need. Only a much more powerful and richly endowed MTA, aided by transit-friendly planning, could begin to balance the scales between autos and transit.

CHAPTER 5

Atlanta: Race, Transit, and the Sunbelt Boom

The loss of transit capacity in a Rustbelt city like Baltimore was a tragedy, especially given how city residents both then and now could have benefited from regional mobility. But the marginalization of transit in mushrooming Sunbelt cities like Atlanta, Charlotte, San Antonio, Houston, Miami, and Phoenix in the postwar years was an equally terrible transit disaster for the nation. These once small cities had modest private transit systems in 1945, extensive hinterlands ripe for development, and a robust tradition of laissez-faire government policies. As millions of Americans have packed into and around Sunbelt cities like these, in suburban-style environments, city leaders made auto-centric decisions that made it impossible for private and public transit companies to thrive.

Atlanta is a Sunbelt poster child for the missed opportunity of transit in an era of growth. For many decades, Atlanta had a high-performing private transit company and embarked on an ambitious rapid transit program in the 1960s and 1970s. But these efforts, as in so many other Sunbelt cities, were swamped by the car culture. In 2017, in the thirteen-county Atlanta region, just 4 percent of commuters used public transit, and 97 percent of households with workers own or have access to at least one car.[1] Drivers in 2014 logged an average of 143,994,000 vehicle miles *per day*. The 125 million annual passengers (2019) riding on a variety of regional transit systems, dominated by MARTA's rail and bus system, struggle to get where they need to go for work, education, or leisure.[2] The four MARTA rail lines—stretching east–west and north–south mainly in the city of Atlanta—often stop in car-centric office or shopping center environments with limited density and connecting service. Atlanta's transit system, like its neighborhoods, is also highly segregated, with about three of four MARTA riders nonwhite and making less than $75,000 per year.[3]

The same factors that ruined transit in declining Baltimore dominated in booming Atlanta: fiscal conservatism on the part of city leaders that delayed and limited public support for transit until after Atlanta had become a sprawling, multiethnic, regional giant; auto-centric planning including highways, urban renewal, and low-density zoning; and racial conflict that created hyper-segregated transit and neighborhoods that undermined attempts to build regional cooperation. As in most American cities, including Baltimore, government leaders made the critical decisions rather than the private transit company. The absence of NCL from Atlanta (and other fast-growing American cities where NCL did not operate, including Houston, San Antonio, New Orleans, Miami, Albuquerque, etc.) mattered little. It is uncomfortable to admit it, but Americans and their political representatives kneecapped mass transit.

The Divided Prewar City

Atlanta, as the south's railway hub, was potentially well positioned for leadership in mass transit. The city's business class and elite quickly adopted electric traction, with the first electric streetcars running in 1889. White families rode streetcars to live apart from industry, commerce, and the racially mixed neighborhoods in the center. They bought new homes in lushly planted, low-density, racially restricted residential neighborhoods on the north side like Ansley Park and Druid Hills. By the early twentieth century, most of the city's streetcar lines served the affluent and whiter northern half of the city because of the typically close connections between transit and suburban real-estate development. As in so many other American cities, elite neighborhoods like these were unlikely to remain sizable transit-oriented districts in the dawning auto age given their high incomes, low density, good roads and parkways, ample parking, and neighborhood commercial strips.[4]

As in all cities, competing lines at first cannibalized each other's service, but consolidation in 1902 eventually led to decades of comparative stability under what became the Georgia Power Company (GP). Atlanta's private transit operator, serving a city with only 200,616 residents in 1920, had not developed the dense web of streetcars or rapid lines as in industrial powerhouses in the North. Still, the city's system was well used for the size of the population. Atlanta streetcars, for instance, carried a respectable fifty-seven million riders total in 1913, and "at their peak in the 1920s, electric streetcars were carrying nearly 100 million passengers annually."[5] These ridership levels were only possible when nearly everyone walked or depended upon the streetcars. In a typical anti-traction stand, city officials allowed for a massive increase in private, competing bus jitney service as part of a strategy to drive the company into public ownership. The jitney strategy failed when the state legislature in 1919 rejected the mayor's push for municipal ownership.[6] The city, however, left the jitneys on the streets until 1925, thus undermining streetcar performance in terms of time and profits.[7]

City officials made important decisions before World War II that proved detrimental to the future of transit in the city. City leaders sharpened social dividing lines in 1922 through racially based zoning, effectively banning Black people from the higher-quality low-density areas and most of the city's land area. The courts rejected the city's racial zoning in 1924, but city leaders emphasized low-density living and racial segregation in their future zoning and planning decisions. The citywide zoning code, over time, kept new subdivisions and developing areas around them at artificially low-density levels by restricting multifamily housing despite active transit corridors and potential demand for apartments. Growing Black populations in the prewar city were thus limited to overcrowded neighborhoods in the west, east, and south on the edge of the CBD. Black people lived primarily in the shadow of the city's concentrated industrial and commercial districts and could not benefit from a transit system that allowed white families the luxury of suburban living.[8]

The city made transit as unpleasant as possible for Black riders by forcing Black citizens to follow humiliating Jim Crow rules. Segregation

FIGURE 11. Black domestic workers rode transit northward to the mostly white north side of Atlanta, 1939. Source: Marion Post Wolcott, Library of Congress.

on streetcars officially started in 1890, and according to historian Kevin Kruse, "conductors of streetcars had almost unlimited police powers." The company gave drivers "discretion" over seating and directed whites in front and Black people in back. As driving gained popularity among whites, some affluent white neighborhoods by the 1920s even asked the city to discontinue lines through their districts because the streetcars appeared to be filled with primarily Black riders. Most whites, however, "continued to ride, taking comfort in the knowledge that the racial code would be strictly enforced by the conductors."[9] Car ownership and jitney service provided some relief for Black riders in Atlanta and other cities. Historian Mia Bay, for instance, highlights the success of Atlanta's Black-owned Colored Jitney Bus Association (1922–25) that at its height operated sixteen buses on "the same routes as the streetcars until it was finally put out of business by the city council." Black riders were thus forced back on the segregated streetcars. Such sharply divided urban space would make it difficult for postwar leaders to create support for high-quality, broad-based systems.[10]

In the 1920s, the growing popularity of cars, notable in the city's downtown and leafy northern white suburbs, began showing up on the ridership tallies. GP started seeking alternatives that could better compete with cars and preserve their profits. The company, for instance, added bus routes in the 1920s to compete with emerging bus, auto, and jitney competition. "Shopper's Specials" from northern suburbs to the downtown with collector parking lots near subdivisions proved popular for ladies during the off-hours heading to Rich's and other downtown shopping emporiums. GP managers also saved money by switching to one-person streetcar operation on two hundred of its cars by 1930, a rare achievement for a prewar transit system, reflecting the comparative weakness of the labor movement in the South.[11]

The Depression accelerated modernization trends as ridership fell sharply during the crisis, but the net effect was mostly positive for riders. GP looked to the innovative technology of the electric trolley coach "to modernize the system, salvage the investment in electric power, and put an end to paving assessments." With the substitution of streetcars with trolley coaches, the company only planned to retain the heaviest trunk streetcar lines. The company even created an express trolley coach service to northern areas of the city, necessitating double sets of wires in the streets. Gas buses frequently served as feeders to trolley coach main lines. Ridership rebounded from Depression-era lows in the late 1930s even as the company began aggressively switching out streetcar lines, indicating both the popularity of the new trolley coach service as well as the recovering economy. Atlanta was not alone in discovering the charms of trolleybuses, but Atlanta developed the most extensive of the southern systems and one of the largest in the nation.[12]

Atlanta's wartime transit boom, requiring the dusting-off of old streetcar equipment to move citizens in a time of restrictions, set ridership records typical of other cities. Ridership hit 150 million riders in 1945. On just one express route, the popular Number 23 trolley coach express service to the north side, 5.8 million riders rode in one year. Yet even during the war years, it was clear that, as in other cities, political leaders were utterly uninterested in modernizing streetcar lines, much less getting into the transit business. On December 22, 1943, according to *Motor Coach Age*, "the Atlanta City Council adopted a resolution calling for the conversion of the rest of the system to trolley coaches and buses as soon as possible after the war." GP had no objections considering their positive experience with the trolley cars.[13]

The postwar years were a brief golden age of trolley coach service for the city. The company extended trolley car routes into new neighborhoods and out went eight streetcar lines, including popular runs on West Peachtree and Druid Hills. By 1946, of the 559 scheduled vehicles in the fleet, 62 percent were rubber-tired, and most of those were trolley coaches. The 153.8 million passengers who rode in 1946, about 450,000 per weekday, enjoyed excellent service.[14] The company, for instance, added 174 additional trips per day in 1947. In 1948, ten new trackless trolleys were arriving weekly, and it was clear that before long, "all remaining streetcars will be replaced by the modern, smooth-riding, silent, rubber-tired vehicles." The shift to trolley coaches required an $8 million capital investment, all privately financed, mostly with surplus cash GP generated in the boom years of 1943 to 1946. Indeed, Atlanta was getting the "most up-to-date public transportation to be found anywhere in the nation" without a dime of public money or financing. This self-financed renovation created unrealistic public expectations about the actual cost of high-quality transit in future years.[15]

According to the company executives, the streamlined trackless trolleys from Saint Louis Car Company allowed "more roominess inside, greater strength, and a smart appearance." The speed, fast acceleration on hilly streets, smoother ride, forced air ventilation (reliable air conditioning would take decades more innovation), and better insulation beat out the streetcars.[16] In 1948, there were only seventeen streetcar lines left, and the last streetcar line was gone by 1949. By that year, trolleybuses were 70 percent of the fleet and carried 80 percent of riders.[17] GP in 1950 supported thirty-one lines with 453 trolley coaches and 135 motor buses, a modernized system that, from many perspectives, exceeded the quality of the rail-based one it had replaced.[18]

Ridership did not, unfortunately, rise even with the modernization of the fleet. Quite the opposite. GP had invested millions in a system that the more affluent, white population of the city, living in northern areas where transit was most concentrated, was forsaking for autos. Between 1947 and 1952, for instance, Atlanta's car use increased by 195 percent; television watching reduced evening ridership to movie theaters and other live entertainment; auto-centric strip shopping centers drew customers away from downtown; and the five-day workweek reduced ridership.[19] The city was also rapidly expanding its highway network to make space for all those cars (see below). Ridership tanked. In 1947, there were 140 million riders,[20] but in 1948, just 110 million riders.[21] Riders chose to abandon a great transit system.

GP had done everything right—building a great transit system with excellent service—but it did not seem to matter. The company, losing riders but facing rising operating and capital costs, ran in the red during 1947 and 1948, which was unwelcome news for a profit-driven enterprise.[22] Executives had already considered selling in 1947 thanks to mounting red ink, declining market share, and the Securities and Exchange Commission's insistent demand that the company sell off its transit interests to satisfy long-standing antitrust goals. Nor could the company, thanks to federal antitrust restrictions, legally cover its transit losses from its power generation division. GP's transit operations in other Georgia cities like Macon were even bigger money losers. The company knew full well that automobiles were to blame. GP wanted out of transit, but there was little chance of finding a buyer for the system given the risk.[23]

During this era of rapid decline, the city and state could have provided subsidies or, at minimum, reduced the high taxes GP paid out of its fares. Another option would have been to raise fares. Mayor Hartsfield, however, was against raising the fare from 7.5 to ten cents in 1947 as was the regulator, PSC. City leaders and GP engaged in typical debates about reasonable returns for the firm. GP, for its part, pointed out that the fare had been the same since 1928 despite a tremendous rise in the cost of living and operations. The city maintained that the Atlanta operation was profitable from certain accounting standpoints.[24]

A series of damaging strikes settled the argument. A strike in 1949, as workers sought higher wages in an era of heightened expectations and declining fare collection, according to the *Atlanta Constitution*, drove commuters to "other means of transportation such as carpools and buying second-hand cars." Even after the strike ended, many were "still employing these facilities to a large extent."[25] During the strike, "scores of the city's merchants complained of serious decline in receipts."[26] When the dust settled, GP cut thirty-two trolley runs on the Monday after the strike, a 4.7 percent reduction, "laid to the loss of transit riders since the strike."[27] A much longer and even more damaging strike in 1950 brought down the curtain on GP operations in Atlanta. This strike lasted for thirty-nine days and convinced the GP that it was time to sell. The problem was that the company could attract no established buyers for their declining enterprise despite the high-quality system.[28]

The Atlanta Transit Company (ATC), organized rapidly during the strike by leading Atlanta citizens, would be led by Jackson Dicker, a retired GP executive. ATC bought the company at a reasonable price from a desperate GP and would resolve the strike by agreeing to generous pay and benefit increases. The new company thus preserved the for-profit model, which meant the city would still lack any responsibility for transit and transit managers would have few good options beyond service cuts and fare increases.[29] The ATC had initial advantages when it took ownership. The equipment was entirely new and energy efficient. Thanks to a fire-sale price offered by GP, the new company was able to use depreciation over three years to reduce total operating costs.[30] The new ATC management would desperately need those savings as ridership continued to drop throughout the 1950s.[31] These initial savings and opportunities proved fleeting.

Leveraging their power during the collapse of GP's operation, the employees had won major concessions despite trend lines that looked less than promising. In 1951, for instance, ridership was down to eighty-seven million, yet the company was still running just 5 percent fewer miles than it had in 1948.[32] The city's leadership continued to ignore tax relief or subsidy opportunities and only finally consented in 1951 to a fifteen-cent cash fare. Even so, customers could still save if they bought tokens in bulk, and students and midday shoppers still paid just a nickel! The company reminded riders that five-cent shoppers fares were the "same fare they paid to come to town on horse-drawn vehicles before the turn-of-the-century."[33]

Despite the fare increase, the company was predictably operating in the red again by 1953.[34] Ridership was still in decline "due to increased use of automobiles" while costs were up, including salaries and the 3 percent sales tax the company had to pay on fares.[35] By this time, "the present owners, who bought the system on credit, are making very little out of it other than their salaries." The ATC in 1953 and 1954 also resorted to "financial wizardry ... to squeeze some juice out of the lemon." To summarize what was a complex financing scheme, ATC created a separate company, sold half its buses to it, then leased them back.[36] Atlanta's private transit was operating on precarious ground. In 1955, the fare would rise to twenty cents, just one of many future increases that placed the entire responsibility for transit on the riders.[37]

In 1954, Robert L. Somerville took over management of the company. According to the *Atlanta Constitution*, Somerville was a "London-born, Scot-reared newspaperman turned professor turned transit company president" that would be credited later for rescuing "a near-bankrupt transit system" and returning it to profitability.[38] While this might have been an overstatement, he did preserve the system's reputation for clean business operations until he died in 1968. Rebranding the company as

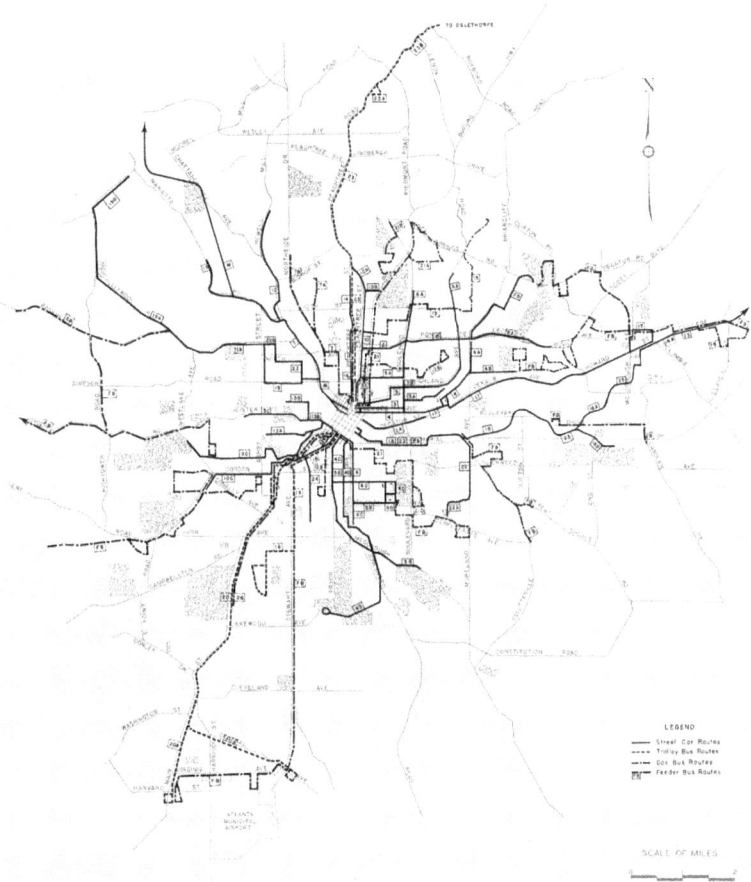

FIGURE 12. Atlanta's once-extensive streetcar system circa 1928. Map by Jordan Engel.

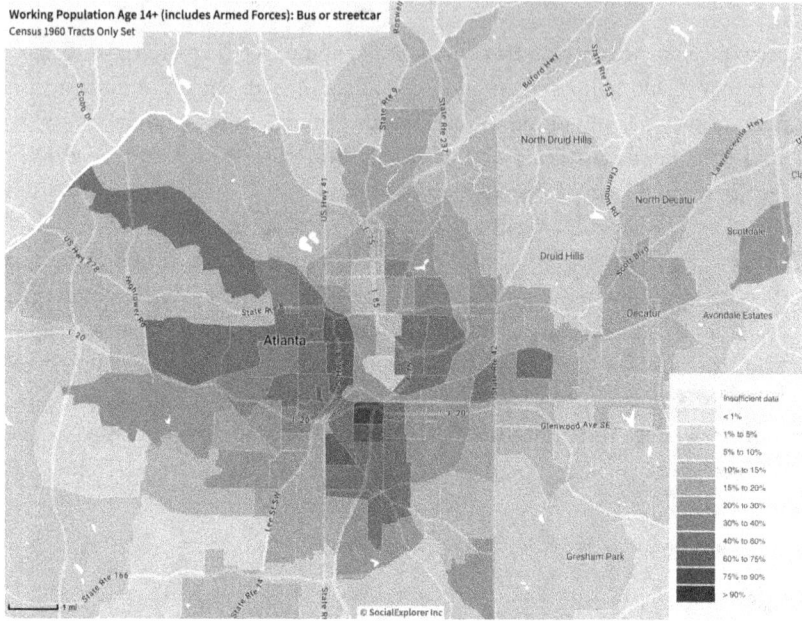

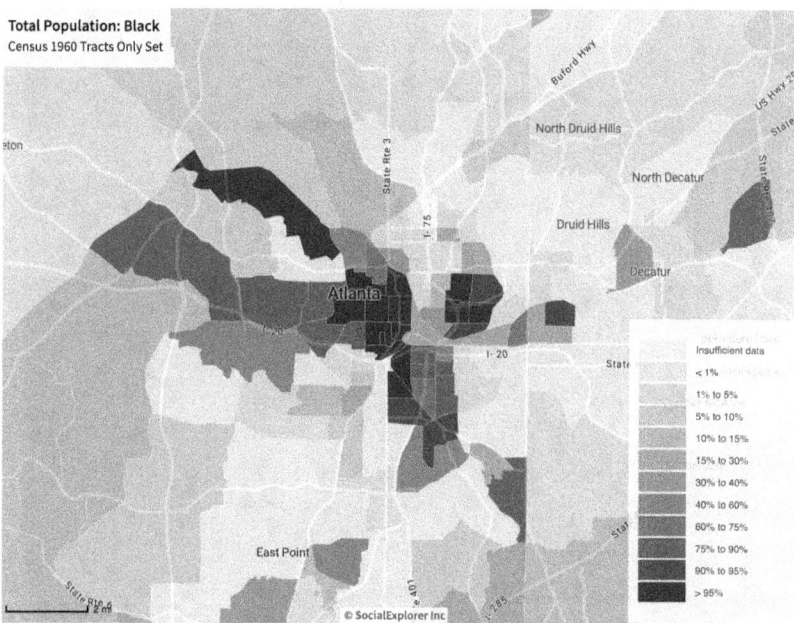

FIGURES 13A AND 13B. The transit network in 1960 still favored the affluent north side despite the clear predominance of Black riders from the near east, south, and west sides. The relationship between Black population density and transit is clear in these two maps. Source: Black, 1960/Atlanta Bus or Streetcar, Social Explorer, accessed June 26, 2021.

the Atlanta Transit System (ATS) in 1955, Sommerville hoped to stabilize the company's finances and ridership (then at seventy-two million).[39] He began investing in new diesel buses, thus reducing ATS's dependence on high-quality but also more infrastructure-intensive trolley coaches. ATS started "park and ride" in the suburban areas, including use of express buses on expressways.[40] The company also expanded bus service to the isolated Perry Homes public housing project and surrounding area in 1955 (converted to trolley coaches in 1956 after demonstrated popularity). Black areas, however, remained underserved despite higher demand.[41]

Limited service in many of their neighborhoods was just one of many problems for Black Atlanta transit riders. Jim Crow segregation continued to make life untenable for Black riders. According to historian Kevin M. Kruse, by the 1940s, "all Atlanta motormen were deputized and armed with revolvers," and some motormen had shot passengers without penalty. The city under William B. Hartsfield had toned down violence by the 1950s, but the humiliation continued. Leading Atlanta ministers in 1956, inspired by Dr. Martin Luther King's bus boycott in Montgomery and the Supreme Court's 1956 order ending segregation there, initiated civil disobedience to desegregate buses in Atlanta. The ministers notified city officials in advance of the protest, which took the form of ministers riding and exiting in front to initiate an arrest and subsequent court challenge. In the meantime, "segregationists . . . urged whites to abandon mass transit," which they believed would drive companies "out of business." The legal challenge took two years for a decision, during which time Jim Crow on transit continued. In 1959, with a decision in favor of the ministers, the bus system was officially integrated. The decision may have led to further declines in white ridership, but it is hard to say given the long-standing downward trend. By 1960, Black people composed one-third of the city population but were "59 percent of the rush patronage during the rush period."[42] In a sign of the times, ATS in 1961 finally hired its first two Black drivers.[43]

Redevelopment, Density, and Auto-Centric Planning

Declining ridership, transit financial problems, and racial conflict on buses is best viewed from a broader context of a changing city and region. Postwar city and regional leaders embraced a decentralized, lower-density model of urban development. Historian Carlton Wade Basmajian describes how "single-family neighborhoods of inexpensive Cape Cod cottages and ranches on quarter- and half-acre lots began filling in the empty land in the western and southern extents of the city.

Suburban development spilled over into unincorporated areas in Fulton, Clayton, DeKalb, Gwinnett, and Cobb Counties." The new subdivisions benefited from strip commercial districts, making downtown shopping less crucial. In 1952, a massive annexation that added 118 square miles of Fulton County to Atlanta boosted the city's population to 428,000. The Plan of Improvement, as the annexation was known, looked to efficiencies in regional services. Yet, city officials' choice to zone most of the annexed areas as low-density residential limited potential ridership in growing areas.[44]

It was understood at the time that annexation extended white control of the city government by diluting the growing Black vote with new white voters. Through their remaining political power, white leaders did everything to restrict Black expansion into desirable new subdivisions. There was, for instance, no public housing on the city's north side at all. White and Black people negotiated narrow "expansion areas" for Blacks to reduce overcrowding, mainly on the south and west sides of town.[45] City officials got very creative when it came to segregation. In Blandtown, for instance, the city used industrial zoning to push out Black families. The back-alley dwelling law of 1955 cleared out Black people from white areas where many had lived for decades in alley dwellings convenient to transit, as in Macedonia Park on the north side. Local officials encouraged or tolerated discriminatory mortgage practices in both urban and suburban locales.[46]

The Black middle class would eventually challenge many of these lines and expand their territory as whites fled to the suburbs, but the longer-term impact of zoning of this type has had a lasting impact on transit. Zoning was difficult to change because once residents moved in, white or Black, they believed neighborhoods should be unchanged, even when high-quality rail transit was eventually extended.[47] By 1982 in Atlanta, single-family zoning dominated about 60 percent of the entire city. This emphasis on freestanding housing was bad for both fair housing and future transit development. Most Atlanta suburbs went even further, combining low-density zoning with limits on multifamily housing, large lot size requirements, and even minimum apartment-size restrictions.[48]

The roadway and highway links between the expanded suburban-style environment and the growing suburbs outside the city line received the lion's share of public funding and attention during these years—again putting self-supporting private transit at a disadvantage. Drivers got the best of new transport technology, not only in the cars they paid for but the new highways and widened streets upon which they traveled. As a result, drivers enjoyed a growing network of roads by the 1960s that outcompeted mass transit.

The influential and precedent-setting Lochner Report (1946) recommended a regional high-speed network.[49] Many roadways also doubled as racial dividing lines, such as I-20 West, between white and Black areas.[50] A successful postwar Greater Metropolitan Bond program helped pay for a pioneering generation of expressways before the Interstate Highway Act.[51] Planners enthusiastic about highways were trying to bring order to a flow of about "150,000 cars daily into downtown Atlanta." Using typical biological metaphors, one 1952 article in the *Atlanta Constitution* claimed the "arteries aren't large enough; they may one day choke the city to death." The author demanded that "the Expressways must be finished, more parking spaces provided, and new streets built to provide free circulation for the lifeblood of a city, traffic."[52]

By 1956, city leaders could claim that "progress has been made in providing greater downtown parking space. The unfinished expressway system has speeded up access and departure." But they felt the city still needed more bypasses for "through traffic," "perimeter parking," and "better use of public transit.[53] The head of MARTA, Richard Rich, scion of the department store family, argued in the late 1960s that not only did the city need rapid transit but "the leadership of our city ... must press for speed in the completion of the perimeter expressway, I-485, the Northside Parkway, the widening of the North Expressway, the completion of the Stone Mountain Expressway, as well as improvement of surface streets." Atlanta needed these roads to "'keep even' with our present inadequate thoroughfares." Rich was calling for the completion of a highway system that would be far better than anything he could develop at MARTA.[54]

The impact of roads on transit was sometimes even more direct. As in other cities, some highway programs directly and negatively impacted the quality of service that ATS could offer. Highway rebuilding in 1952, for instance, hurt the trolley coach service by cutting off access to a "short and exclusive trolley coach underpass under the railroad tracks" in 1952. Changes in roadways, such as one-way streets, road widenings, and other route alterations, required rerouting trolley coach lines at a prohibitive cost to the company. The cost of maintaining the overhead electrical lines in the face of a constantly changing city road pattern encouraged the shift to diesel buses.[55] Even more destructive to transit ridership was the loss of the city's most densely populated districts close to the downtown. According to historian Ronald Bayor, "the east/west and north/south expressways (I-20 and I-75/85 respectively) were completed by the mid-to-late 1960s and resulted in the removal of many low-income Blacks in or near the CBD." These were the neighborhoods that provided the city with its most significant share of riders by this time.[56]

The city's devotion to redevelopment compounded the transit company's problems. Destruction of densely developed Black areas, most of which remained highly dependent on transit, accelerated with the urban renewal programs and low-density zoning that reshaped central city neighborhoods. In the late 1930s, the Atlanta Housing Authority pictured "the shadows of Georgia's domed Capital and Atlanta's handsome City Hall" falling "across a broad area of shacks and shanties." Downtown elites viewed the mostly Black low-income areas as a threat to the downtown's image and attractiveness. However, they often used the language of humanitarian concern to justify their ulterior motives of gentrifying downtown and its surroundings.[57] A 1945 Housing Authority map showed large areas of so-called substandard residential blocks around the CBD, west, north, south, and east—much of it also labeled as Black housing.

After redevelopment, large sections of once dense neighborhoods near the CBD reemerged as much lower-density garden apartment housing projects with mostly extremely poor people in them. The transit riders were often still there, as some displaced residents only moved nearby into overcrowded units. Due to displacement and discrimination in the 1960s, about 40 percent of inhabitants in these close-in neighborhoods lived in overcrowded units.[58] Eventually, however, density declined in the central neighborhoods as they became less attractive places to live, and new housing opportunities finally opened further out. Gone too with redevelopment were most commercial enterprises that once attracted visitors to the neighborhoods on transit lines, and federal officials refused to subsidize new retail districts even in extensive housing projects.[59] In the case of Techwood Homes near Georgia Tech, according to historian Lawrence Vale, city leaders intentionally wiped out a Black community to make way for an all-white housing project.[60] Public transit to new peripheral projects and older Black communities in the city and region was often slow, crowded, "remote or unavailable."[61]

Planners deployed a language of urban uplift long after it was clear that the program primarily targeted poor, Black areas for redevelopment. A 1949 analysis supporting urban renewal condemned the "poor platting, mixed land uses, poor zoning, congested streets, and narrow lots" of Black neighborhoods like Buttermilk Bottom near the downtown. Such areas would be rationalized in a modern manner at lower densities, separated functions, and faster roads.[62] The 1952 report *Up Ahead: A Regional Land-Use Plan for Metropolitan Atlanta* called for "artificial" reductions in density "to reduce existing densities, wipe out blighted areas, improve the racial pattern of population distribution."[63] Postwar Black leaders, according to Bayor, "could not prevent the destruction of large parts of its eastern and southern neighborhoods for commercial and civic redevelopment and the subsequent relocation of many displaced citizens." The city relocated many thousands of people (95 percent of whom were Black) to make way for civic priorities such as the expressways, a stadium, and a civic center.[64]

As in Baltimore and Chicago, by removing so many Black people from the center the leaders damaged the commercial centers of Black life where transit had been so crucial. Atlanta's legendary east side Auburn Avenue business district lost its importance as new highways, public housing, and other redevelopment undermined the district's attractiveness and scattered its consumer base. Redlining prevented new investment in these neighborhoods that might have led to higher-quality housing. The CBD attracted new towers, hotels, and single-purpose facilities like stadiums but lost everyday vitality as city leaders pushed out people of color who had lived, worked, and shopped in and around the older downtown.[65]

ATS in Decline in the 1960s

The city's redevelopment policies, and the general white flight to suburbia, undermined the transit company's ridership and established routes during the 1950s and 1960s.[66] The company, with no hope of public support, undertook additional economizing. The city traffic engineers' preference for one-way streets required rewiring the trolley coach lines, souring the company's leadership on this otherwise great technology. In the late 1950s, the company added to its diesel fleet but did not regularly renew its trolley coaches. By the early 1960s, the trolleys were from fifteen to eighteen years old and had not been produced domestically since 1952. Such challenges could have been overcome through renovation or equipment orders from abroad, as in San Francisco or Boston. Yet, renewal in these cities was made possible with strong public support and subsidies. ATS was not so lucky to have subsidies.[67]

In late 1962, the company announced that the trolley coaches would be gone by the end of 1963. In one fell swoop, the company would replace 270 electric trolleys with 213 new diesel buses at the cost of $6 million. Replacement reduced maintenance costs, and the smaller number of replacement vehicles reflected both declining ridership and lower maintenance needs of new buses.[68] New buses were undoubtedly welcome, and ATS branded their GM New Looks as "City Slickers," a strange choice in an anti-urban region. However, the buses were not air-conditioned when chilled air had become increasingly common. The new buses also were louder and more polluting in neighborhoods than electric trolleybuses.[69]

Company officials highlighted the benefits of removal to urban beautification, downplaying the negative dimensions of the change. They called the 560 miles of overhead electric wires "cobwebs from the ceilings of Atlanta's city streets," forming an "ugly canopy" that, once removed, would create a more beautiful environment.[70] ATS was determined to "take down hundreds of miles of wire, and hundreds of poles, many of them in downtown Atlanta" not only to beautify the city and save money on future maintenance but also because they planned to sell the copper in the wires for a million dollars. The ATS was down to scrap metal financing. There was nothing that the city could do about it because the company did not need "approval of Atlanta city government for the conversion"; instead, the company simply "informed" city officials of the change.[71] However, it appears to be the case that politicians supported the change as the PSC approved the company taking out a loan in 1963 for 213 new buses.

Even economies wrung from the rapid switch to diesel buses would not be sufficient to restore the company's bottom line. During the 1950s, attention had turned to the ridiculousness of a public-serving utility paying state and local sales taxes and registration fees. The head of the PSC admitted that "it appears unfair that the urban bus rider must pay substantial taxes for the improvements of highways they do not use." ATS paid these taxes even though the buses saved space on roads and remained essential for "low-income groups, aged persons and the disabled."[72] The *Atlanta Constitution* grudgingly admitted that some government help was in order: "Tax relief would be better than subsidies and ever-higher rates, which the public would have to pay anyway. Atlanta must always have a transit system."[73] Rural legislators, however, had killed the bill in 1958 to give urban transit tax relief on fares. The high taxes forced the company back to the dangerous game of farebox returns.[74]

Ridership was down from postwar heights, making fare hikes a risky method of financial improvement.[75] ATS carried fifty-two million riders in 1966,[76] fifty-one million riders in 1969,[77] and sixty-five million in 1970.[78] Even the best of the years were much reduced from seventy-two million in 1955 or 140 million in 1947.[79] The ridership numbers were particularly disappointing because by 1970 Atlanta's regional population was 1.76 million and the city alone was 496,973. The company claimed it had "kept pace with the city's astounding growth," but the mediocre ridership numbers spoke otherwise. In 1954, for instance, the company offered service on 364 miles of routes but by 1964 boasted that its routes now covered 826 miles, a 127 percent increase. However, many of these increased route miles were long express routes to the suburban edge that did not necessarily reflect improvements in service quality.[80]

City and state officials, resistant to public subsidy, played along with fare increases knowing full well that higher fares would lead to either ridership decline or stagnation. ATS, for instance, sought and received a fare increase from twenty to twenty-five cents in 1963.[81] Yet by 1967, the company was losing $2,150 a day, so demanded higher fares for school kids, midday shopper specials, and a five-cent transfer fee.[82] The PSC granted all increases except for school kids, thus leaving the company with a $115,000 annual gap.[83] ATS in 1968 received an increase to thirty cents per ride to address a predicted $450,000 deficit in the coming year,[84] and promptly returned in 1969 for a thirty-five-cent fare to address a looming $1.5 million annual deficit. A major factor was its $1.8 million tax bill.[85] The company was devoting five cents per fare to taxes.[86] Fares rose to forty cents in 1971 to address an expected deficit of $1 million.[87] The company got some tax breaks here and there, but there was reportedly only one other major transit system paying sales tax by this time. PSC signed off on these fare increases but also declared that "the time has come for a change in the concept of Atlanta's transit operation from private enterprise to some form of public ownership or for subsidization of the operations either direct or through tax relief."[88]

The lack of public support for public transit looked different at the end of the 1960s than it had decades before. Public transit was recast as an aspect of social welfare for the poor rather than serving as a public utility that potentially helped improve the lives of all Atlanta residents. According to the powerful editor of the *Atlanta Constitution*, Jack Spalding, transit was "a social necessity. We've walled off enough people in modern ghettos, in some cases insulating these areas with uncrossable freeways." Spalding proclaimed that transit was not a general utility but "for the disadvantaged portion of the public which can't afford autos." And the only way to provide that service was through public subsidy or ownership. This analysis was well-meaning but overlooked how transit could improve the environmental and social health of the city's *entire population*. But the *Constitution*, like many elected officials who read it, only thought rapid transit would be sufficiently modern and fast for the middle and upper classes.[89]

The social welfare viewpoint on transit was widely shared in the city among activists concerned about rising fares and crummy service. For instance, during debates on fare increases, "numerous witnesses indicated the bulk of transit riders are the poor." Mrs. Dorothy Bolden of the National Domestic Workers Union and Mrs. Ethel Mae Mathews of the Welfare Rights Organization rejected fare increases, "stressing the use by low-income maids, hospital and cafeteria workers of the buses, and the high proportion of their income that go to transport themselves and their children."[90] They called for a bus boycott by "students, maids and retired persons" that they hoped would lead to free bus service. An Economic Opportunity Atlanta Worker stated, "They say a nickel ain't nothing, but to us it's the same as $100 to them."[91] These social concerns do not seem to have moved the majority of the white electorate to support what many of them already viewed as a second-tier mobility option.

The social issues of Atlanta's poor communities directly impacted riders' experience daily, further damaging the reputation and reality of bus riding. Robberies went up rapidly during the 1960s.[92] The company in 1968 switched to exact fare collection, eliminating the need for drivers carrying change, in response to fifty-four holdups that year.[93] From what can be gleaned, everyday riding was unpleasant. One regular rider was exasperated: "The Buses do not run fast enough. Buses should come at least ten minutes apart.... Sometimes the buses are so crowded that they pass on by and this makes us late for school or work."[94] A worker from R. J. Reynolds Foods in Forest Park had no bench to sit on during his evening commute and sharply criticized service quality: "The bus seldom picks us up on time, and yesterday we waited forever. How could we get a bench at the bus stop?"[95] The bus system had, indeed, become a typical second-tier service thanks to the lack of subsidies.

MARTA

The push for rapid transit in Atlanta, which gained momentum in the 1960s and 1970s, looks different when viewed through the filter of a declining bus system. During the two postwar decades leading up to the launching of MARTA, the quality and volume of surface transit service declined precipitously. Yet the power structure mostly worked against everyday bus service improvement by failing to aid or buy the private company and engaging in auto-centric planning policies. While the operating bus transit system fell behind regional needs during the postwar period, a higher-status, cutting-edge hypothetical rapid transit concept filled the civic space where actual transit should have been.

As debates over rapid transit developed, the bus company and bus riders influenced the final plans so that everyday riders might benefit more from such a significant investment. Advocates scored a major short-term success in demonstrating the ridership possibilities of high-quality, deeply subsidized bus service. However, the rapid system that emerged followed the plans laid down by city leaders and powerful interests. As in Baltimore, downtown interests were in charge for decades in Atlanta's rapid transit planning and development. The first head of MARTA, Richard Rich, owned the city's famous downtown department store, Rich's. He and many others, who viewed themselves as progressive on planning issues, dreamed of building a transit system that would affirm the CBD's centrality and "big city" status and at the same time dramatically reduce regional congestion by getting drivers to switch out cars for trains. Like many other local observers, planner Larry Keating believes city leaders designed MARTA "to enhance the city's image" rather than seeking "a realistic solution to the region's transportation needs."[96]

Rapid transit was a staple of postwar Atlanta planning, although it is often difficult to understand why that was given the decentralized nature of the city. Planners looking at the growing automobile traffic and outward spread predicted multiple times that only a rapid transit system could prevent looming regional gridlock. The MPC, designated to develop (but not implement) plans for regional development, in 1952 envisioned a more structured and carefully designed region. They promoted a "planned population and geographic limit," a greenbelt, neighborhood unit plans, limited Black areas of expansion, slum clearance, and a "modest-sized heavy-rail system." In sum, a completely unrealistic plan for an American city, northern or southern, in this era.[97] A 1954 plan revision by the MPC embraced a more pro-growth outlook, but their idealistic vision, still including rail, manifestly failed to capture political support. The MPC's report, *Now for Tomorrow*, in 1955 also proposed a downtown station for both rapid commuters and intercity rail.[98]

In the late 1950s, the *Atlanta Constitution*, reflecting the enduring power of the downtown elites, predicted ominously that without rapid transit, by 1970, the city might need "36 lanes on the expressway, 28 lanes on a downtown connector and 120 lanes radiating out from the city on interstate systems."[99] Editorialists believed that without rapid transit, the central city might have to be "abandoned": "Without a central city to hold the region together, there would be less attraction for many of the industrial and commercial firms now seeking homes in the South."[100] This fearmongering was typical of the time and overblown given Atlanta's enduring growth to the present even with limited transit service. Still, the rhetoric kept the rapid agenda in play.

The Atlanta Regional Metropolitan Planning Commission (ARMPC), the successor to the MPC, in 1961 unveiled a $200 million rapid transit system. Such a system would serve downtown and knit Atlanta's five urbanizing counties together.[101] Ambitiously targeted to open between 1966 and 1969, the entire system would include sixty miles of rapid line, mainly using existing freight rail corridors and thirty-two stations. The design of the initial plan had major lines reaching out to three fast-growing northern destinations with growing subdivisions, employment, and commerce: Marietta in Cobb County; Norcross in Gwinnett County; and North Druid Hills and Emory University. The two other radials served the east side of Atlanta and Decatur and the airport in the south. Notably absent was a rapid line to the increasingly Black west side of Atlanta where many bus riders lived.[102]

The promotional materials for the plan released in 1962 by Parsons Brinckerhoff envisioned a sixty-six-mile total system, with forty-two stations, still relying on existing rail corridors. The plan now included a short west side line, but the suburban-style north side of town still had three lines and most of the system's trackage. Large, paved lots at major stops would offer free parking to suburbanites, and modern aluminum cars on the system would carry them downtown at an average of forty-five miles per hour. At the Transit Center—the meeting place of the north–south and east–west lines—the planners believed that 120,000 passengers would pass daily. The staging plan for development reflected the priorities of the civic leadership.[103]

The first rapid transit phase to open by 1971 was the first north–south segment, running twenty-two miles from Oglethorpe (wealthy areas on the north) to the airport on the south. Primarily African American east and west lines would have to wait for their sections until 1975, a long way off from 1962. The complete sixty-six-mile system was not to be in place until 1980. The plan had ignored the transit reality by prioritizing whiter and more affluent patronage of the future. Planners and civic leaders also sounded defensive as they tried to justify the lack of attention to the bus system. While losing bus service in 1962 would "endanger the economy of the Atlanta Metropolitan Region," as one-third of riders to the CBD at rush hour were still bus riders, buses were fatally "enmeshed in the same highway congestion" as cars. Rapid transit would be the best chance of building a better region.[104]

As in Baltimore, the push for rapid transit in Atlanta required federal funds. Longtime mayor William Hartsfield (1937–41 and 1942–62), a rapid transit supporter, asked HUD Secretary Robert C. Weaver to fund a transit study.[105] Ivan Allen Jr., president of the Atlanta Chamber of Commerce, threw in for rapid transit, and as mayor (1962–70), he prioritized the effort.[106] Governor Ernest Vandiver (1959–63) believed "our capital city has too much promise ... for us to sit by and see it stifled and choked by a traffic situation" and wanted to see rapid transit in place by 1970.[107] These political figures supported rapid transit development but ignored the declining situation for existing ATS bus riders.

Despite elite support, the complex challenge was securing broader electoral support among both urban and suburban votes while at the same time getting necessary state permission for what many rural legislators viewed as an urban priority. All that talk about transit as a social service for poor people and the racial integration of buses impacted white support. Statewide voters in 1962, for instance, rejected a constitutional amendment that would have allowed the formation of multicounty transit authorities.[108] A more restricted version of the legislation exclusively for the Atlanta region finally passed in 1964 thanks to a Rapid Transit Committee of One Hundred led by former Governor Vandiver.[109] But even in victory, fault lines emerged. Fulton, DeKalb, Gwinnett, and Clayton County voters formally endorsed the new MARTA in 1965, but Cobb County voters rejected it—a clear sign of growing suburban resistance to regional collaboration with a central city focus. To this day, Cobb remains outside of the MARTA system.[110]

Sufficient regional support materialized in 1965 to approve MARTA, but the authority was underfunded and underpowered from the beginning. According to the *Constitution*, the new authority lacked any steady tax revenue: "Rapid transit in Atlanta is stalled before reaching the tracks. It hasn't any fuel. The fuel it needs is cash. Without it, nothing can be done. And nothing has been."[111] A 1966 state referendum authorized 10 percent state aid to rapid transit. While hailed as a victory, in practice the small amount of potential funding limited the scale of the system by setting a low bar for state aid compared to the federal government.[112] State officials in 1967, for instance, were "cool" to a large state share of the funds.[113] Nor did MARTA have the power to control zoning or roadways around its stations, a significant issue in future years as streamlined rail cars pulled up to vast parking areas and sprawling suburban edge cities.

The notion of a fully funded federal transit system for the Atlanta region was attractive as an economic development proposition. Still, it did not align with contracting costs for transit in states like New York and California. Modern fixed-rail transit systems in an era of labor unions and expensive engineering far exceeded what federal officials alone were willing to fund (outside the national capital). Transit advocates in these states thus leaned on state and local taxes and various financing schemes to support transit development. The limited support in Georgia for transit from local and state officials was a liability for those dreaming of

Atlanta developing an actual rapid transit network. Parsons Brinckerhoff, in 1962, had estimated that the system would cost $292 million.[114] But MARTA planners by 1967 penciled out the system (now sixty-six miles) at the cost of $437 million. One casualty was service planned for Gwinnett and Cobb Counties. Nor were these 1967 figures the final word on MARTA costs.[115]

The planning for MARTA, including vast sums for the rail-based systems, was annoying to Robert Somerville at ATS. Somerville, with city help, had implemented the first bus-only lanes downtown in 1958, speeding up trolley coaches on Peachtree to 15.8 miles an hour, demonstrating the possibilities of rubber-wheeled vehicles to move fast with priority.[116] Somerville in 1960 even proposed to convert his company into a Metropolitan Transit District that would develop and build a rapid system for just $59 million. City leaders, however, had ignored him.[117] Somerville, in 1967, now invited himself back into the planning process. ATS planned "secretly" for an extensive system of "rapid busways," mostly running along the city's many existing rail rights-of-way. Somerville believed this system could be built for "thousands, not millions." Somerville derided "MARTA's costly and 'futuristic' plans which he charged can't be implemented for 'another 20 years.'"[118]

Simpson and Curtin, nationally famous transit engineers, developed a detailed consultant busway plan that included five major lines reaching destinations familiar to MARTA riders today (the airport on the south, Lenox Square on the north, Decatur on the east, Hightower Road on the west). The system relied upon 32.3 miles of trunk busways along existing but underutilized rail corridors linked to 750 route miles of rapid bus service. Buses would collect passengers in neighborhoods and then enter and run express on busways to downtown, where they would circle on an exclusive loop for picking up and dropping off passengers. The build-out would cost $22 million for roads, bridges, and ramps, and $30 million for rights-of-way, for a respectable total of $52 million, a fraction of the rapid transit plan.[119]

Busways were having a moment, with planning and development underway for limited systems in Los Angeles and Pittsburgh. GM understandably promoted the concept as an alternative to fixed-rail service. The US Department of Transportation, for its part, viewed bus-only lanes as a cost-effective option during the Vietnam War. A mass transit expert from Harvard thought the busways in Atlanta merited serious consideration as "the region should question seriously the need for a fixed rail facility."[120] Atlanta in 1967 had 3,800 persons per square mile versus eleven thousand in an older industrial city like Cleveland.[121] It is worth noting that the busway concept, while considered by Atlanta leaders and many transit experts of the time as an inferior option, has been repackaged today as bus rapid transit thanks to great success abroad.

First greeted by the *Atlanta Constitution* as a "stopgap measure," the busway concept eventually received full consideration in its pages. The notion of busways had genuine traction because the city was already sprawling out, the existing ATS system relied on buses, busways were cheaper, and they could be quickly built.[122] A highly featured editorial by staff journalist Bruce Galpin laid out the plan in detail, including an appealing map, and pointed to the social benefits of a bus-based system. Such a system of "busways would vastly improve public transit service for Atlanta's urban poor, especially in the Negro community. It would provide the first single-vehicle crosstown route linking the West Side . . . to the East Side. . . . It would serve the heavy flow of domestics from the West Side to the Lenox areas," and generally link the unemployed to booming suburbs.[123]

MARTA's Richard Rich made noises about the complementary aspect of bus service, but he commissioned a quickie report by the professional staff that attempted to deep-six the concept. MARTA staff "concluded that even the suggested abbreviated 'experimental busways route' would be a waste of public money." MARTA claimed real costs would be three to four times the $55 million bus company estimate (which was still much less than rail!), and ATS had failed to account for difficulties in developing the rights-of-way. Analysts could support an east–west busway route before MARTA eventually took over with rail, but that was it.

Somerville, for his part, believed that MARTA "kissed it off in two weeks,"[124] and went on the warpath. He pointed out that "there are no statistics to support" the idea that drivers would leave their cars behind for rail. New rail lines, he believed, would compete with his buses, and "so will draw riders off buses, not out of cars." He asked voters a provocative question: "Are you really prepared to put up the money to buy a new system to give people an alternative method of travel?" He also pointed out that the MARTA system failed to offer service to the "largest growing areas," would have only three downtown stations (vs. fourteen in Montreal), and in any case, "there's no point in going 70 miles an hour under Peachtree Street."[125]

The plan for busways made political trouble for MARTA. The city council members demanded that ARMPC study the options to resolve issues, and state officials were concerned enough to hold back rapid transit funding until the issue was resolved.[126] Rich secretly approached Sommerville and proposed to buy the bus system to help resolve the issue in December of 1967. The sale did not fly, but Rich co-opted Somerville. He appointed him to a Transportation Policy Committee to help MARTA determine strategy in February 1968. Sommerville seems to have become more muted, now seeking "balanced transportation" with "buses in high priority," but still believed that busways might serve "burgeoning suburbs" outside MARTA's rail network.[127]

Somerville died in 1968, and so did the real push for busways. MARTA deployed the busway concept in the following years as a rhetorical strategy to mollify Black residents concerned about lack of future rail service to their neighborhoods. MARTA never built a single busway even though the logic of busways continued to reassert itself. National consultants A. M. Voorhees and Associates, in a 1968–69 study commissioned by regional governments, "recommended a plan providing for only 10 miles of Rail Transit and 54 Miles of Rapid Busways."[128] The firm "argued that the constraints of a fixed-rail system did not make it the best transportation solution for a city like Atlanta" with such low density.[129] Despite significant public and expert support for busways, MARTA had successfully resisted a bus-based system.

The possibility of busways did not answer the downtown elite's felt need for a big-city rail system and central station. Rich remained devoted to rail because he believed that the "highly centralized business district" needed "rapid transit and convenient access" to maintain its role as "transportation hub, distribution center, headquarters for regional offices of most of the county's larger businesses and industries." Unlike those on legacy systems in cities like New York and Chicago, the advanced cars on the Atlanta system would be "air-conditioned, light-weight, spacious, rubber-cushioned, fast and comfortable." He believed a "better" system "WILL attract many thousands of motorists off our crowded expressways and city streets to ride rapid transit." He held up Toronto as "a living example of what rapid transit can do for a city . . . leading to a 10 BILLION dollar development explosion." And Toronto's subway was the magnet: "TWO-THIRDS of this construction was within five minutes' walk of a rapid transit station." This downtown-centric rhetoric was typical of the business elites who favored rail-based transit during these years.[130] The optimism was bolstered by architect-developer John Portman's wildly successful Merchandise Mart and Peachtree Center office and hotel complex in the CBD.[131]

MARTA's leadership, however, had dramatically underestimated the opposition. The busway option disturbed the fragile consensus the elite had been cultivating. Most Atlanta and suburban residents were already drivers who were not excited about a new property tax, projected construction costs were rising, and the Black community felt planners had ignored their real needs. MARTA scurried to make changes in preparation for a ballot measure.

Rushed, updated plans in 1967 gave new priority to the east–west rail line, connecting Black communities, because MARTA leadership admitted that "We've finally accepted the reality that this is where most of our riders are." A complete east–west route had, in fact, only been planned for a second phase because of the emphasis on diverting northern suburban drivers to rail rather than serving "captive" bus riders. It helped that HUD, in the context of growing urban unrest, was now "pressing for service to poorer sections" as an aid to "decaying areas."[132] The city received funding in 1968 for an impact study, hoping for a reset with federal officials who felt the city was "more concerned with moving trains than people."[133] Consultants for the study spun out alluring visions of rebuilt districts sprouting up around train stops that would connect rail to where the poor live and work. A major station near Clark Atlanta University and other historically Black colleges and universities, according to the consultants, would become a "melting pot . . . where the university complex could meet the poor, who in turn could be housed in high rise developments above the underground tracks." Building over tracks would "help solve housing problems . . . without Negro removal."[134]

As the vote neared in the fall of 1968, Black leaders had noticed just how little transit they were going to get for their tax dollar. The sugar-coating of a new urban vision and last-minute east–west rail priority promises failed. One group of leaders favored more rapid transit to low-density Black areas, including Perry Homes, Thomasville, Poole Creek, and Hapeville. Leaders also wanted their share of good jobs in the new system.[135] The Black community's support for transit had been taken for granted because a higher proportion of Black individuals still rode transit. But they turned against MARTA because "the proposed system ignores the city's disadvantaged areas" and, in their opinion, overwhelmingly focused on "lily-white" areas. As one activist explained: "You folks really messed this thing up by excluding Negroes. We're going to do what we can to defeat it on November 5."[136]

The Black establishment also opposed the MARTA plan. "Jesse Hill, CEO of the Black-owned Atlanta Life Insurance Company, was a leading critic, stating, '. . . of the 36 miles of transit system to be opened by 1975 only 4.3 miles have been earmarked to serve the large Negro west side population, and this . . . is totally unacceptable, inadequate and unrealistic as a westward limit.'"[137] MARTA stubbornly refused to budge on the demand for more specific lines to isolated, low-density Black neighborhoods. The planners believed, with some justification, that the $50 to $60 million for a line to Perry Homes had little merit: "You can't justify spending this much in a limited growth area." The city, of course, could have worked with MARTA to rezone the area for growth, but as in Baltimore, regional transit administrators were on their own and powerless on crucial questions of land-use and transit-oriented development.[138]

Nor were the suburbs thrilled about the spiraling cost of the system. MARTA was now projected to cost $750 million, with a local share of property taxes of $377 million, 10 percent from the state, and the rest from the federal government. Defenders tried to deflect criticism by pointing out that 70 percent of the local share would come from downtown property owners.[139] The MARTA proposal suffered further because the bond issue vote included the total interest costs in the proposal, an additional $615.4 million, adding a great deal to the $377 million baseline cost. These kinds of numbers certainly scared off a lot of voters, very few of whom were transit users at this period or would plan to ride. The bond issue failed in Atlanta, Fulton, and DeKalb Counties in late 1968.[140]

MARTA's powerful and determined supporters quickly regrouped. Richard Rich resigned, and MARTA and rapid rail supporters, including Mayor Sam Massell, the "John Lindsay of the South," redesigned the proposal and approach.[141] While sidelined in the initial planning, buses and existing transit gained new importance. ARMPC, still in favor of rapid transit, now strongly supported taking over ATS to stop fare increases and improve service more generally.[142] The federal government also endorsed the purchase of ATS and was willing to pay two-thirds of the cost. Mayor Massell, showing just how much he wanted rapid transit and Black votes, proposed a free fare system in 1970 to be supported by a half-cent rise in sales tax.[143] The fare had recently risen to forty cents, so an offer of this type was understandably attractive to the majority Black, low-income ridership in the city.[144]

A new planning spirit also emerged. The planners and city officials held listening events throughout the city and set up a citizen advisory group. East side Black residents remained concerned that the sales tax would mean that "they were bearing the cost of a system that would serve primarily suburban whites." But MARTA planners promised that the reduction in cost to ride, under a free or low fare model, "would show up for poor people as a net savings."[145] In a bid to address social issues, MARTA leadership promised that public ownership of ATS would lead to "extending lines into new suburban areas where jobs are, and where public transportation isn't and probably won't be under present management." MARTA promised a bus network "second to none." An integrated rail and bus system would make "all sections accessible . . . at a price the poorest worker can pay."[146] The rapid plan now included an expanded ATS system with new buses and routes, although buses would primarily serve as feeders to the rail system.[147]

The new and improved MARTA plan, now projected to cover the period from 1972 to 1982, was a $1 billion project for a seventy-mile combined bus and rail network. Instead of relying entirely on rail, the new plan divided express service between 52.09 miles of rapid rail and 17.6 miles of rapid busways. Service was much more evenly spread around the region, including the west and south sides. MARTA planners remained adamant, however, that on the west side, Perry Homes did not merit a rail line, but the area would be served by a rapid busway, as would some sections of east Atlanta. Nor would citizens have to wait long for a new rapid system. The east–west line would open in four to five years and north–south a year later. The most notable short-term change in planning was a promise to expand bus service immediately throughout the city. MARTA would add 430 buses to the 501 buses already in use by the ATS system with the aim of serving eight new crosstown routes. The new buses and routes, and one hundred new bus shelters, would mean shorter and more comfortable waits. A revolutionized bus system would offer much better service: "90 percent of those within the perimeter highway will be within walking distance of a bus route and all bus routes will connect to rapid transit stations."[148]

MARTA had also redesigned its financing plan considering homeowner resistance and a potential $1 billion cost for the system. They abandoned the original idea of an ad valorem property tax, which would have reliably generated a larger and more secure source of funding on a progressive basis, to a more regressive but more politically palatable sales tax.[149] At least at the beginning, there seemed to be broader support for the sales tax. Leaders in Atlanta, Fulton, Clayton, DeKalb, and Gwinnett Counties proposed a 0.75 percent sales tax matched to a long-term fifteen-cent fare. Given local political support and the application of the tax to only the areas to be served, the Georgia House in March of 1970 approved a one-cent regional sales tax for rapid transit. Governor Jimmy Carter's support was crucial, as was the federal government's promise to fully cover two-thirds of the total construction costs.[150] The tax, while small, was projected to raise about $49.5 million per year.[151]

Mayor Massell wanted a low fare as a critical factor of the final plan because he understood how important low fares were to Black civic leadership, but the MARTA board refused to commit to a fixed ten-year fare. They were willing to start with a fifteen-cent fare,[152] but with the cost of the rapid system now rising to $1.2 billion total, the board could not commit long term to low fares.[153] Newly elected African American leader vice mayor Maynard Jackson also wanted more for the Black community, including the fifteen-cent fare and a Perry Homes line.[154] The question of a busway or rail for Perry Homes remained in play. But Terrell Hill, MARTA's deputy general manager, still believed that northwest Perry was too "dispersed for rail" and the lack of "large industrial or commercial employment centers" made a rail investment there unwise. Plus, a Perry Homes busway that MARTA favored would cost $20 million versus $50 million for rapid.[155]

MARTA compromised and promised a fifteen-cent fare for seven years but made clear the fare would go up after that point. They also agreed, in theory, to a rail line to Perry Homes.[156] ATS would be purchased for $12.9 million, and a major expansion in bus service would follow. Given these significant concessions, Black leaders were on board by the fall of 1971, led by Leroy Johnson and Maynard Jackson.[157] Mayor Massell mixed hopes of $4 billion in total economic impact with a promise to offer "mobility for the community unequalled anywhere in United States," thanks to low fares and extensive new service.[158] Without public support for mass transit, the mayor warned ominously, "the young, poor, aged and handicapped would lose jobs and go on welfare."[159] The advertising pitch to communities also looked better than before leading up to the vote. Atlanta was now getting a $1.4 billion system, of which $947 million was from the federal government and one-third from a sales tax that would be applied only in Fulton, DeKalb, Clayton, and Gwinnett Counties. Thanks to the sales tax, most of which would come from the more densely populated and developed Fulton County, MARTA would save $150 million in interest charges by not selling long-term bonds.[160]

City leaders and MARTA had produced several compromises that assured wavering Black voters in Atlanta. But there was nothing that MARTA could really do to assuage white fears. Some residents in Gwinnett and Clayton, for instance, claimed to object most to the limited service they would get in the new proposal.[161] But other vocal opponents openly warned that "MARTA will relocate inner-city people in the suburbs" despite MARTA's denial of any such plan.[162] Misinformation was abundant, including "untruths" such as MARTA having the power of condemnation, taxation, and zoning. MARTA affirmed that it "must go to local governments for these powers to be exercised" and had "no power to build public housing." But the rumors were more powerful than reality.[163] MARTA barely passed with wins in Atlanta, Fulton, and DeKalb Counties, but the proposal failed in almost entirely white Gwinnett and Clayton Counties. According to Maynard Jackson, losses in Gwinnett could be traced to an "insidious racist campaign on an issue that should not have involved race." People in Clayton and Gwinnett were "misguided... about blacks moving to the suburbs" because of MARTA.[164]

The racist component of the rejection continued after the voting ended. The losing side did not go quietly, including demands for a recount by segregationist former lieutenant governor Lester Maddox. Fulton had gone for MARTA by just 462 out of one hundred thousand votes.[165] But the recount failed to change the outcome. The racial lines for and against transit and the marginal status of transit were evident even within Atlanta city limits. A sample of white areas in Atlanta found that they rejected MARTA by 54 percent.[166] Black leadership claimed, with justification, that "the black community is responsible for the MARTA victory." Indeed, citywide, 55.3 percent of the Black vote supported MARTA.[167]

Mayor Massell in 1972 looked past the animosity and envisioned a new society transit development would bring: "This system of maximum mobility will provide man's fifth freedom and health insurance for our economy far into the future."[168] MARTA, as promised, purchased the ATS for $12.9 million. MARTA had to buy secondhand buses for promised expansion on fifteen new lines and would order hundreds of new buses in the first years of public takeover. By 1973, the bus division of MARTA was running 603 buses on ninety-five lines, a significant increase in service. The lowering of the fare from forty to fifteen cents, and new service, drove the most robust ridership growth in years. In 1972, ATS had carried just 54 million riders, but by the end of MARTA's first year of bus operation, ridership had hit 65.5 million. The sustained service and ridership gains indicate the potential of deeply subsidized, very cheap, good quality bus service to succeed in an American city of low density. By 1978, MARTA's 830 buses carried 81.9 million riders on 130 routes—and these improvements took place before a single rail line opened.[169]

Low fares, which helped drive ridership, did not last. MARTA stuck to its promise and raised fares in 1979 to twenty-five cents, as the sales tax had failed to keep pace with rising costs. Without operating subsidies from somewhere else, there was nothing to be done.[170] By 1980 the fare had jumped to fifty cents; in 1988 the cash fare was eighty-five cents; and by 1996 the fare was up to $1.25.[171] Thus ended one of the most successful long-term experiments postwar in using buses and low-cost fares to develop a top-quality regional transit system.

MARTA's leadership added bus service under pressure in the 1970s but focused on rapid transit with the groundbreaking for an east–west line in 1975. MARTA, as promised, started construction first through the

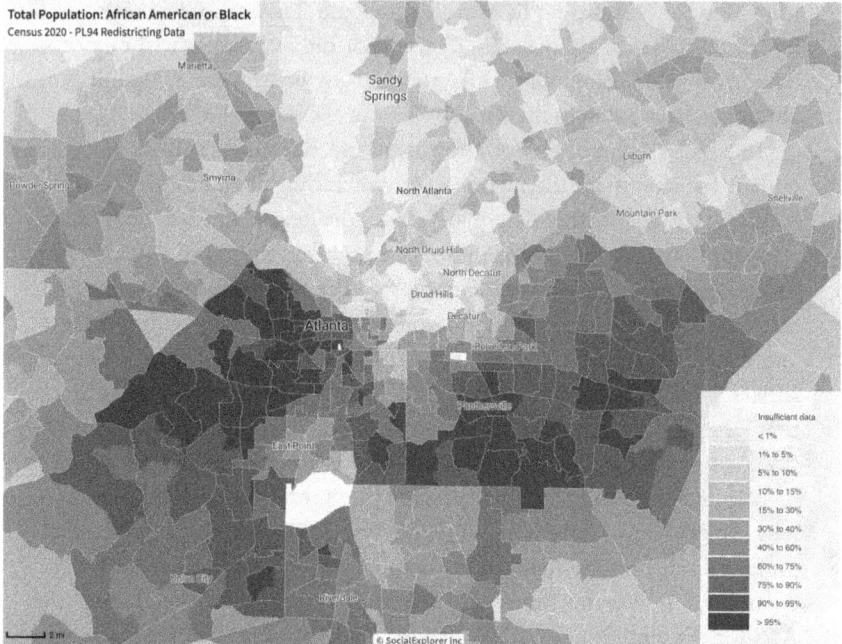

FIGURE 14. The rapidly suburbanizing Black population of Atlanta, spreading out to the south, southwest, and east of the city, would have been better served long term with a high-quality bus system. Source: Black, 2020/Atlanta, Social Explorer, accessed June 26, 2021.

majority west and east sides where most transit riders still lived. The first section of the MARTA lines opened for service in 1979, significantly later than initially promised, and was now supported by feeder buses rather than complemented by high-speed busways. The west side line was short compared to those in other directions. MARTA, moreover, dropped the Perry Homes rail and bus lines on the west side, despite expected objections from Black leaders, to devote more money to northward line extensions. MARTA, under pressure, eventually built a short western extension, of 1.4 miles. The plan for busways dropped from sight.[172]

The first section of the north–south line finally opened in 1982, decades after initial planning. The northern lines predictably underperformed given the affluent white population that had abandoned transit decades in the past. Many "northside whites largely declined to use" MARTA, and the system among many whites "was perceived as crime-ridden and used only by poor Blacks—a 1984 study found that its ridership was under half of the original projections and that 4-out-of-5 riders were transit-dependent."[173] Nor did the system reach the booming primarily white suburbs in Cobb and Gwinnett Counties. The chairman of MARTA in 1987 believed that "the development of a regional transit system in the Atlanta area is being held hostage to race." Ridership in 1987 on what was now billed as a $3.3 billion system only attracted about 240,000 daily riders. The ridership was much lower than the original planners had promised.[174]

Even after expansion in preparation for the 1996 Olympics, including a link to the airport, the combined bus and rail system in 1995 carried just 475,000 weekday passengers, about the same number who rode daily in 1946 when Atlanta was a small city. Figures 15a and 15b clearly illustrate the loss of the once-thriving transit districts near the CBD and a general dispersion of riders across the region—most of whom now live far from the fixed-rail investments. The underutilization of the rapid system became apparent during the Olympics as regional officials strongly encouraged transit use. With some additional buses in place, the rail and bus system carried a stunning 1.353 million riders on the peak day of the games. The city also saw a significant drop in air pollution during the games. Maybe more widely used mass transit might have benefited more than the poorest Atlantans.[175]

The Sunbelt Pattern

Atlanta is today a multicultural region that sprawls over many counties. The 2010 census included 2,645 square miles in Metro Atlanta's urbanized area, the second largest in the nation.[176] The metro population, estimated at six million people, enjoys low-density living and mostly resides outside the city and the neighborhoods with the high-speed MARTA rail lines. Almost all commuting takes place in cars, usually with a single driver.[177] Attempts to artificially enhance downtown, such as Underground Atlanta, the Atlanta Civic Center, World of Coca-Cola, stadiums, and so on have failed to generate the vitality promised by their promoters. Rich's downtown emporiums closed in 1991 thanks to declining trade and the bankruptcy of its new owner, Federated Stores.[178] Downtown Atlanta retail today accounts for a fraction of regional retail sales due to the proliferation of suburban shopping malls. Thanks to delays and low ridership, a hyped downtown streetcar route has been an embarrassment to city leaders.[179] The CBD has also failed to keep pace with business growth despite serving as the hub for rapid transit. Sprawling peripheral auto-centric office parks are poorly integrated with MARTA service.[180]

Transit development has had a minor impact on this regional pattern. Buckhead and Midtown within the city limits have developed as mixed-

FIGURES 15A AND 15B. The loss of ridership in Black neighborhoods close to the CBD is clearly indicated on these maps from 1960 and 2000. Source: Atlanta Mass Transportation 1960/2020, Social Explorer, accessed June 26, 2021.

use areas on the city's north side, and MARTA has been a positive contributor to these trends. Yet the northern sections of the city and region, including areas like Buckhead, remain sharply divided despite the hope that trains would help integrate public life. According to Larry Keating, "many whites do not have to go to the city to work, shop, or play; they can stay in the racially homogenous north side."[181] Even within the city, most neighborhoods have also become less transit friendly over time despite the investment in rapid transit thanks to excessive surface parking, widened roads, and the atrophying of older houses and stores.[182] The density of the city of Atlanta is just 3,154 persons per square mile (2010), despite a new era of multifamily housing rising in some neighborhoods.[183]

There are optimistic transit trends, at least before COVID-19 hit transit hard. Surrounding counties have increased bus service, and Clayton County, which has become majority Black, finally joined MARTA in 2014 after the failure of its own county-funded bus system. Regional voters approved additional sales taxes to upgrade transit service. But the challenge remains daunting, according to transit activists: "Nationally, Atlanta ranks 91st out of 100 of the largest metro regions for job access via public transportation, with only 3.4 percent of jobs accessible by a 45-minute public transit commute or less."[184] Rapid transit has also failed to reverse the image of mass transit. The region's large and primarily prosperous Black and Hispanic communities are as avid drivers as their white counterparts, even though three of four MARTA riders are nonwhite.[185] Given the frustration of relying on transit for most trips, this preference for cars among "choice" riders of all ethnicities is to be expected.

Atlanta's transit history is similar to many other cities with long-term private operations. Atlanta's private transit operators, independent of NCL, switched out streetcars for trolley coaches and buses. The city and state refused to aid the private companies, leaving managers free to reduce quality by ripping out the trolley coaches and relentlessly reducing bus service. As in other cities, politicians gave the successor public agency insufficient resources to make up for decades of disinvestment. MARTA, by design, lacks the funds, power, and reach to provide Atlanta transit customers with a competitive mobility choice. National planning trends—highways, redevelopment, zoning—undermined both the private transit companies and MARTA. As in Baltimore, the downtown regime's preference for rapid rail undermined more cost-effective and relevant options like busways and better bus service that might have better served those who still rode transit.

City and state leaders in Atlanta, as elsewhere, allowed white racial resentment to play out in low-density, segregated suburbanization and attendant political balkanization that made regional transit cooperation halfhearted, partial, and poorly funded. Sunbelt cities like Atlanta created a model of auto-based sprawl that now, due to rapid growth and suburban diversification, negatively impacts the mobility choices of tens of millions more Americans. Transit's marginal role in Sunbelt cities like Atlanta, Charlotte, Houston, Dallas, Miami, Phoenix, and Las Vegas undermines state and federal attempts to fund transit better. Such small numbers of riders count for little in political terms. There are still plenty of potential transit customers in Sunbelt metros like Atlanta, but to serve them well would require many changes in politics, funding, zoning, and race relations.

PART III

"Pay as You Go" Public Transit

The transition to publicly owned mass transit offered a promising alternative to systemic private-sector collapse. The systems in Detroit (1922), Seattle (1929), Cleveland (1942), and Chicago (1947) came under public control while they retained functioning systems and solid ridership. However, civic leaders forced the companies to rely entirely on fares despite early public takeovers. They denied the public companies substantial local, regional, or state subsidies until the 1960s and 1970s. This delay meant that they did not have financial support when they needed it most: the unrelenting ridership losses and wrenching urban changes during the postwar decades (ca. 1945–65).

Public systems like Chicago and Detroit admittedly had certain advantages over their private-sector counterparts, such as tax relief. Public ownership also created opportunities and distinctions from their private-sector counterparts that mattered to riders. The public companies in Chicago and Cleveland, for instance, sustained high-quality bus service longer in public systems even as the number of riders thinned out. Managers experimented with modern equipment such as quieter and cleaner-burning propane-powered buses and high-quality, electric trolleybus systems. Cities under public ownership usually maintained, upgraded, and sometimes modestly expanded the legacy rapid transit systems where they existed. Cities like Chicago and Cleveland would put federal capital grants to good use for modernization from the 1960s onward.

However, unsubsidized public transit was particularly vulnerable to declining urban conditions and regional inequality. Fewer residents showed up for any transit in neighborhoods politicians left to rot thanks to a combination of redlining, housing exploitation, and deindustrialization. Suburban residents, and those with money living within cities, rode transit at low levels thanks to spacious subdivisions, deeply subsidized arterials and highways, and racial hatred. In a classic example of resource hoarding, suburbanites resisted regional public transit operation and subsidies until systems had lost much of their appeal and ridership. It was clear that "pay you go" had become "pay as you cut" by the 1950s and 1960s.

Public transit managers of the unsubsidized kind, for instance, were just as devoted to bus substitution in Chicago, Detroit, Cleveland, and Seattle as NCL managers in cities like Baltimore, Saint Louis, and Los Angeles. Elected officials and most public managers believed buses represented the best solution to create self-supporting public companies under a "pay as you go" model. Unsubsidized public operators, in sum, did not maintain streetcars in any more significant number than NCL and other private-sector transit companies. In Chicago, for instance, public managers with broad political support dismantled the nation's largest single-managed streetcar system rather than modernizing the highest capacity, and often still well utilized, streetcar trunk routes. Public transit survived, but absent subsidies and transit-friendly planning, did not prosper for long.

CHAPTER 6

Chicago: The Failure of "Pay as You Go" Public Transit

Chicago squandered a tremendous opportunity at the end of World War II. The city had the nation's second most extensive rapid transit system in place, the nation's largest unified streetcar system, and an extensive commuter rail network. Its downtown Loop remained the center of regional business, wartime industries throughout the city boomed, and linear neighborhood commercial districts still benefited from the interaction of transit and pedestrians. The neighborhoods served by transit throughout the city remained densely populated to the edges of the city line.

Underneath the glamour of national unity and postwar bonhomie, the interwar factors of austerity, auto-centric planning, and racial conflict would undermine service and public ownership in America's second transit city. A CTA rider like David Catinella, interviewed in 1950, already had his doubts about transit's value: "I ride a streetcar to work, and it's not worth 20 cents. Now I am thinking of buying a car. Forty cents a day would about pay for the gasoline."[1] Riders like Catinella by the millions headed to the transit exits in the decades that followed. In 2018, for instance, transit accounted for just 13.2 percent of Chicago's regional mode share, while cars accounted for 77.4 percent.[2]

In Chicago, the streetcars and elevated lines gave their all for World War II, but they were run-down as were the tracks and infrastructure. CSL had won a modest fare increase, rising from seven to eight cents, during the war, but was unable to achieve modernization given wartime military production.[3] CSL managers in 1944 believed, moreover, that the ridership boom was temporary: "with the removal of restrictions on travel in private vehicles and the end of war production . . . [u]nless an effective effort is made to retain a part of the new riding that has come during the war period, the renewed competition of the private auto will force the industry back to its unenviable status of the 1930s."[4] CSL's "effective effort" included the nation's largest order for new equipment in 1945, with more PCC streetcars than buses. However, the company only sought to modernize the busiest streetcar lines with PCCs and convert twenty-two others to bus service. CSL also demanded a fare increase from eight to ten cents, a profoundly unpopular move despite the demonstrated need for modernization funds.[5]

Chicago's and Illinois's leaders had a stark choice in 1945: take over CSL and CRT or allow them to cease operations or, at best, raise fares, cut service, and grind downward. CSL was scratching by and had no hope of attracting private investors to renovate the aging fleet and rails; meanwhile, CRT could barely meet payrolls.[6] Mayor Edward Kelly, a Democratic Party machine politician who championed 1930s subway projects, and Governor Dwight Green, a liberal Republican and strong advocate of infrastructure upgrades, supported CTA's creation. Kelly had in the past opposed public ownership, but by 1945 he finally acknowledged that public transit was the "only way" to preserve and modernize transit. Public ownership of transit also finally gained the support it needed from civic, business, and community leaders. The future of CBD real estate was on the line if the rapid and surface systems failed as the density of office spaces required transit to prosper.[7]

Under pressure from a unified local front, the state government finally passed legislation to create a publicly owned CTA in 1945 to run the surface and elevated system as a unified operation. The sponsor of the Metropolitan Transit Authority Act in 1945 in the state senate was a young Richard J. Daley, who as mayor (1955–76) later became the force for the city's highway median rapid transit program.[8] Chicago voters endorsed the legislation and a fifty-year franchise in 1945.[9] CTA's debut, a moment of unity in city and state interests, was a watershed in city transit long imagined by transit advocates and many riders. After two decades of receivership, city and state leaders had finally come together to save and improve mass transit in what was then America's second-largest city. Even though the systems had been running on fumes for decades, it was not too late for a turnaround given strong wartime and immediate postwar ridership.[10]

The public buyout in Chicago took place decades before public ownership in Baltimore and most other American cities with private operators. It was only five years after New York had taken full city ownership of its subway system. The City of Chicago also gained significant control over the CTA, with the mayor appointing four of seven CTA board members, including the chair. City control was notable given that the CTA had a semi-regional function because it served not only the city of Chicago, but all of vast suburban Cook County except for six townships.[11]

Real-estate expert Homer Hoyt was just one of many civic leaders who hailed the arrival of CTA. He believed that "the tremendously beneficial effects of this coordinated, regional mass transportation system on real estate values in the entire Chicago metropolitan area can scarcely be overestimated." He predicted that "congestion in the loop and neighborhood business centers will be lessened . . . and more vacant property will be made available for business and industry."[12] CTA was, at heart, a business-friendly proposition given the massive amount of investment in Loop real estate, the hundreds of thousands of commuters, and the dozens of commercial retail districts built around transit lines. Planners, city officials, and downtown interests disliked streetcars and looked to a bus future but realized that only rail rapid transit could manage the rush-hour crush into the core from the city and the suburbs.

The details in the founding documents of the CTA foreshadowed a turbulent future. CTA had the power to operate transit, issue revenue bonds, purchase and consolidate systems, and modernize its fleet, but public leaders gave CTA zero taxing authority in the city or region. This crucial omission, a blatant case of selective fiscal conservatism, required the CTA leadership to rely mostly on revenue bonds or operating revenues (from fares) for modernization during a coming era of unrelenting and massive ridership losses. The self-funding mechanism devised by state leaders avoided potentially crippling debates at the state level about regional responsibility for transit because suburban areas resisted joining in a regional transit taxing district.[13] The distrust of the city government, understandable given the history of local corruption, contributed to the limits on CTA's power. The *Chicago Tribune* editorial board believed, for instance, that "public ownership . . . will substitute political manipulation for economic judgement."[14]

The low opinion of transit as an enterprise or investment is reflected in the fact that it took two years (1945–47) to sell the $105 million in tax-exempt bonds needed for purchasing and partially modernizing CSL and CRT. Investors were naturally skeptical that public ownership without taxation, or a rock-solid promise of government backing, was sufficient to guarantee the bonds. The sale of CRT and CSL to CTA at such a low price had meant that "private investors in these two companies suffered losses totaling an estimated $250 million. Thus, in effect, the investors subsidized Chicago transit to the extent of a quarter of a billion dollars."[15] Investor skepticism was justified because CTA was selling revenue bonds "secured solely by earnings."[16] One group of dubious syndicators felt that CTA bonds "would be unsalable unless backed by the power of taxation."[17]

Investors eventually signed on to the CTA bond offering thanks to the lure of tax-exempt bonds, generous interest provisions, and extensive accounting rules for the CTA board, including the ability to raise fares "free of urban political influence."[18] The advocates of public ownership knew that the predecessor private "companies had repeatedly been denied permission to charge rates of fare sufficient to meet advancing operating costs and expenses of modernizing equipment."[19] CTA opened its operations, in fact, with a fare hike on public takeover from eight to ten cents on surface lines, just one of many rapid-fire fare increases in the first decade of public operations.[20] CTA also had to maintain a series of reserve funds from its operating revenues and, just in case anyone was still nervous, "after operating costs, the CTA first pays bondholders for their money."[21] The investment firm handling the bond sales admitted that "Chicago's name is attached to them in such a way that the city's financial reputation would be damaged if prompt payments were not made."[22] The fact that Cook County sacrificed $3.5 million in annual taxes through public ownership freed those funds for paying interest and other costs.[23]

CTA had to use the lion's share to buy out remaining investors when the funding was finally in place: $75 million for CSL and $12 million for CRT. One investor scoffed that such sums were "a lot to pay for bankrupt lines."[24] But the judge supervising the receivership quickly signed off on the sale after two decades of failed attempts. CTA did not overpay for the companies. The book value of the two companies was about $250 million, including all the assets. CTA also benefited from $25 million in cash available from the surface line accounts.[25] This cash and the remainder of the bond funds were small down payments on what would become a planned $150 million modernization plan. Financing the purchase of the systems and modernization through debt diverted significant future revenues from transit reinvestment to bondholder pockets.[26] The reliance on fares and debt for so much of CTA's future also meant CTA could not build a high-quality regional system linking the city and booming suburbs.

Public Streetcar Substitution

As it had in the interwar years, Chicago's elite strongly supported the end of streetcar service as a critical dimension of the new public management. The 3,270 streetcars inherited by CTA in 1947, carrying most riders in the system, were an average of thirty-two years old and even the trolleybuses were fifteen years old. Many of the streetcars were ancient and expensive-to-operate two-person cars. The track system was also due for significant and costly upgrading.[27] In 1947, the *Tribune* held up aggressive streetcar substitution in Manhattan as a model: "Here in Chicago our transit authorities and city planners are still living in the 19th century, when the trolley car was invented . . . they continue to cling to the notion that the streetcar must remain the principal public carrier of local passengers." The *Tribune* was impatient for substitution: "Promises have been made that streetcars on certain Chicago lines will be replaced by buses. What the city needs is promises that the streetcars on all lines will be replaced."[28] Three leading traffic engineers in Chicago, including one who served as a traffic engineer for the Chicago Motor Club, described "the streetcar as a dangerous impediment to traffic—an impediment that may be eliminated by substitution of motor or trolleybuses." These experts pulled out all the typical objections to streetcars: dangerous passenger loading in the street, traffic jams, and slippery tracks.[29]

CTA obliged the city's long-standing call for streetcar removal. The agency's $150 million modernization plan (1945–55) was simply a more aggressive version of the 1937 city plan developed by Philip Harrington (who now served as CTA's first chair). CTA hired Walter McCarter to manage the system because of his remarkable success in bus substitution in Cleveland. He promised that he would also "'rubberize' Chicago's traction operations," by which he meant shift the system to buses and electric trolleybuses.[30] McCarter solemnly promised that "as long as he holds his position he would not recommend the purchase of any more streetcars for Chicago. He is convinced the future of local surface transportation lies with rubber-tired vehicles." The size advantages of streetcars, he believed, were "temporary" and outweighed by the disadvantages, including "heavy investment in rails, inflexibility, noise, middle of the street loading, and interference with other traffic." McCarter predicted in 1947 that only eleven lines, the most heavily used ones, would remain. Like most postwar transit managers, he was opposed to streetcar modernization and never seriously considered the option of saving them long term. However, he was excited about the "potential capacity of the City's rapid transit system—the subway and elevated."[31]

CTA's postwar plan called for rapidly winding up streetcar service on all but the busiest routes. To do so would require buying "2725 buses which will replace the operation of streetcars on 700 miles of track with modern bus service, establish 150 miles of express bus service, and 220 round trip miles of extensions." In a time of dramatic losses, managers were enthusiastic that streetcar substitution "sharply reduced labor costs and eliminated costly maintenance of streetcar track and overhead power distribution facilities."[32] The bus modernization in the short term would cost CTA $39.5 million, a sizable sum but much less than streetcar modernization. Because buses of the time lacked sufficient capacity to handle streetcar-level volumes, CTA ordered eight hundred new streetcars ($18.9 million) for 310 miles of "heavy lines" to be retained "for an undetermined period." This was not a reassuring promise, and only 683 streetcars were ever delivered. Moreover, most of these modern streetcars would end up converted to rapid transit vehicles in the 1950s. Chicago's myopic leaders could not see any redeeming value in streetcars, even for much-needed crosstown routes not served by the rapid lines.[33]

CTA's long-term commitment to elevated and subway rapid transit reflected the vision of its leaders and transit experts at the time that rapid transit could deliver commuters downtown at speeds rivaling cars. Chicago's rapid system, however, desperately needed an overhaul. The 1,621 passenger cars in the elevated system were even older than the streetcars, with an average of forty-two years in service.[34] CTA managers ordered one thousand "modern type rapid transit cars" because administrators felt that the "L" would continue to serve both as an intracity transit system and a quasi-commuter railroad to the Loop for suburban and outer neighborhood residents.[35] CTA devoted $50 million to make the elevated and subway "truly 'rapid' transit and more effective in handling the 'long haul' riding public." The limited mileage of rapid lines compared to surface transit (about 170 miles of tracks) and their higher losses and greater capital needs meant that CTA leadership was betting big on a system serving a narrow slice of the city and just a few suburbs.[36]

Rapid transit could address the traffic headaches created by a 26 percent increase in automobiles downtown between 1946 and 1951. CTA achieved consistent and sustained reductions in running time for rapid transit with new express (skip-stop) service, strategic closure of neighboring stations (about one hundred out of 227), and new equipment. From 1950 to 1960, CTA added 770 new metal cars as part of "unquestionable commitment to renewing this high-capacity asset," many of them old or new PCC cars adapted from the shrinking surface streetcar system. CTA cut seven branch elevated lines, about one-quarter of the system, because ridership had declined beyond repair, significant projects like expressways required route changes, or because they no longer competed with surface lines. The Milwaukee Avenue Subway finally opened in 1951, speeding elevated riders through the downtown, and increased ridership on the Northwest Side. Work was also underway on additional tunnels to the West Side. CTA redesigned many bus routes as feeders to the rapid lines.[37] Modernization paid off: rapid transit ridership only fell from 137 to 115 million riders between 1948 and 1956. Its modest slippage from 2.95 to 2.61 passengers per revenue mile compared favorably to loss of rider density in surface transit.[38]

CTA saved the rapid transit but moved aggressively on its substitution plans during these years, impacting a much broader area of the city and many more riders. In 1948, CTA added 372 motor buses, 298 streetcars, and 210 trolleybuses.[39] The streetcars were on their way out as the number of buses grew as CTA scrapped lines. CTA did not hesitate to replace even heavily used streetcar routes, shorten others, and switch out buses for trams on weekends to save money.[40] CTA banged the drum for bus substitution for years claiming that "where modern buses were substituted for streetcars on two routes revenues went up while operating costs remained about the same or decreased."[41] Another public relations release claimed that "studies recently completed by the Chicago Transit Authority disclose the substitution of buses for streetcars on Devon Ave. . . . has resulted in a great improvement in regularity of service."[42] CTA selected propane for most of its motor buses, as it was a good value and burned more cleanly and quietly than gas or diesel buses of the time. CTA even bought CMC in 1952, including 172 miles of additional local and express bus routes, as CMC's fortunes declined postwar.[43]

In 1950, CTA ordered nine hundred buses and 349 trolley coaches. According to *Motor Coach Age*, the authoritative source on buses, "In many ways, this was a trail-blazing decision. They were to be CTA's first 40 foot and 102-inch wide buses, intended to kill off heavy streetcar routes. Upon delivery, they did just that."[44] By 1951, 55 percent of surface passengers traveled on motor buses or trolleybuses.[45] By the end of 1954, just 153 miles of streetcar routes remained with just 495 streetcars in service.[46] CTA, pleased with its progress, made plans in 1954 to remove all streetcars in three years.[47] In 1957, CTA was down to two streetcar lines, albeit very busy ones boasting PCC cars. By 1958, however, CTA had cut these as well, rather than upgrading them as trunk routes.

CTA, a public company, had removed the nation's largest single-ownership streetcar system in about a decade without any help from NCL. The Chicago streetcars were gone before anyone really realized what was lost, and even before NCL and BTC had ripped out all the lines in Baltimore. The speed of removal seems to have been part of the plan by the CTA leadership. Chicago's strategy of streetcar substitution is just another nail in the coffin of the NCL streetcar conspiracy. Local decision making, including anti-streetcar political pressure, mattered much more than ownership.[48]

Balancing the Books on the Backs of Riders

The optimistic revenue targets, which included extensive provisions for interest payments, modernization funds, and payments to the city for the use of streets, had proved elusive for the CTA from the start of operations. In 1947, CTA reported that due to declining ridership, "the established fares did not provide sufficient revenue for the required modernization and the cost of operation and maintenance."[49] CTA, empowered by its founding documents to set fares without political interference, duly increased fares 1 percent in 1948 to cover costs.[50] Managers also targeted "duplicate" service or areas where "traffic does not warrant maintaining present schedules." In 1949, however, CTA's revenue shortages still violated its trust agreement for bond underwriting.[51]

Postwar inflation, ridership loss, and new labor contracts undercut operating and infrastructure economies that CTA counted on to balance the books. Improved salaries and benefits, unavoidable in the postwar years, would have been less destructive in a subsidized system that shifted some costs away from riders. For instance, a generous new labor contract in 1949 meant that sixty-eight cents of every dollar collected for fares went to wages and benefits.[52] CTA announced in 1949 a 5 percent service cut on an 11 percent loss of riders that year.[53] The base fare for surface transit was thirteen cents for surface and fifteen cents for elevated lines by late 1949.[54] The Illinois Progressive Party in 1949 called for the state government to "shift part of CTA cost to the taxpayer," but their proposal went nowhere.[55] By 1951, thanks to additional fare hikes, Chicago transit fares were among the highest in the country, even though, as a small consolation, a universal fare "long demanded by riders" finally arrived.[56] The CTA also paid the city $1 million per year for snow removal and $2.6 million in city vehicle taxes and state motor fuel tax.[57]

CTA managers made every effort to control costs, sometimes at the expense of service quality. They used bus substitution to reduce head count, dropping from 22,407 employees in 1947 to 15,086 in 1955.[58] These reductions aided economies, but even these impressive personnel reductions did not compensate long term for continuing ridership losses, the modernization plan, and much better pay and benefits for those who stayed. In 1950, the American Federation of Labor (AFL) union representing CTA workers admitted they were "the highest paid in the nation."[59] In 1952, CTA's employees won a 6 percent raise,[60] another increase in 1955, and more raises in succeeding years.[61] A militant, primarily white, labor pool of transit workers used their political force and struck to win raises and benefits, much like their other peers in the public sector. Transit union leadership in Chicago and other cities focused exclusively on wages and benefits rather than pushing for subsidies or system investment.[62]

The CTA board had by this time lost its optimism about "pay as you go" transit in postwar America as "in all cities local transit is forced to operate on an uneconomic basis because of the loss of off-peak riding to the automobile."[63] A CTA board member pointed out that fares were lower in New York, Boston, and San Francisco because "there are tax subsidies for transit in those cities."[64] Self-supporting transit was only possible when most city dwellers rode, including off-peak. When those riders disappeared, companies needed help, and quickly. CTA was also quick to point out that transit was the only thing holding back gridlock; transit was a public service that mattered. Without CTA's North Side rapid system, the city would need "two more eight-lane, limited-access expressways" to carry the equivalent number of passengers. Commuters would have to buy an additional six hundred thousand cars to handle the million daily passengers then riding the CTA system daily: "Such a floodtide of automobiles would choke all of the city's traffic arteries" and render the CBD unworkable.[65]

A *Chicago Tribune* telephone rider survey in 1951 gauging opinion about a proposed fare increase to twenty cents revealed worrisome trends and attitudes: "In general, the comment was that fares under the proposals would be too high for service rendered." Mrs. Albert Ericson believed that "a person is better off buying a car instead of paying 20 cents." Mrs. Ruby Van Mol's family had voted with their wheels: "We drive our own car, so it doesn't bother us."[66] For many Chicagoans, it was "cheaper to get the jalopy out on Sunday than to pay carfare to take the whole family to a park or a museum."[67] A *Chicago Tribune* reporter in 1950 spent forty hours riding transit and admitted that while it might have been a "bargain" to cross the city for just fifteen cents, over a route covering about thirty miles, a rider would need four transfers and "three hours to spare to get his money's worth." Transit riding was a "weary, boring, and somewhat hazardous business."[68]

A Republican alderman revealed the contours of a new critique developing against publicly owned transit, even of the unsubsidized kind. CTA was "the best demonstration anyone should need about the difference between socialism and private industry.... The socialistic CTA always needs more and higher fares."[69] An alderman from the North Side accused CTA, more typically, of "mismanagement." Despite higher incomes, the suburbs showed growing resistance to increasing fares, including Evanston, Cicero, Wilmette, and Berwyn.[70] CTA raised fares anyway but kept the fare temporarily below twenty cents for city riders and hit the higher-income suburbs on the elevated lines (such as Evanston) for twenty-five cents.[71] The state legislature finally relieved the CTA of state motor fuel tax in 1955 as one of the few concessions the state made to the CTA during these years.[72]

According to CTA leadership in 1956, they were engaged in a "bitter struggle between the inexorable forces of inflation, loss of patronage due to automobile competition, and manpower shortages versus service improvements and increased operating efficiency."[73] CTA fares rose in 1957 to twenty-five cents in a desperate bid to win that battle. It was the seventh fare increase since CTA took over and yet would only yield 35 percent more revenue because of a projected 6.8 percent loss thanks to higher fares, or seventy thousand riders a day. This was unwelcome news for an agency already losing 2 percent of its ridership a year.[74] On the first day of the new fare in 1957, there were 112,254 fewer riders (and a new complicated token system). Surface lines lost the most, 94,125 riders, or 6.41 percent, but even the elevated and subway lost 5.23 percent.[75] The "pay as you go" model did not adequately consider the impact of high fares on ridership. The loss of the off-peak rider was terrible news for Chicago because of the high labor and capital costs required to serve the rush hour.

In the late 1950s, the system was different from the 1945 streetcar-dominated one, and the trend lines looked bad for ridership and revenue. Still, CTA remained temporarily impressive thanks to public ownership in terms of service density. In 1957, CTA had ten rapid routes and 138 bus lines, serving all of Cook County except for six townships.[76] CTA had used its modernization funds, about $127 million, to renovate rapid transit and purchase 4,256 buses and cars. Through these means, CTA renewed the fleet. The funds that did not come from bonds and equipment trust certificates came from depreciation and modernization reserves drawn from operating revenues. The authority was much smaller, with just 11,500 employees in 1957, roughly half as many employees from its peak, primarily thanks to one-person buses and elimination of electrical and track infrastructure maintenance teams. Consolidation of the three companies also saved a lot of money on administration.[77] CTA's operating costs were $35 million less in 1957 than in 1948, proof of major economies.[78]

Transit expert Andris Kristopans of *Motor Coach Age* believes that in 1958, despite the loss of the streetcar system and significant ridership, "CTA was at this point at its highest point in terms of service.... Some 2500 motor buses and trolley coaches brought service to the old Chicago Surface Lines and Chicago Motor Coach networks, and nearly 1200 metal cars plied the rapid transit lines." CTA was offering a reliable

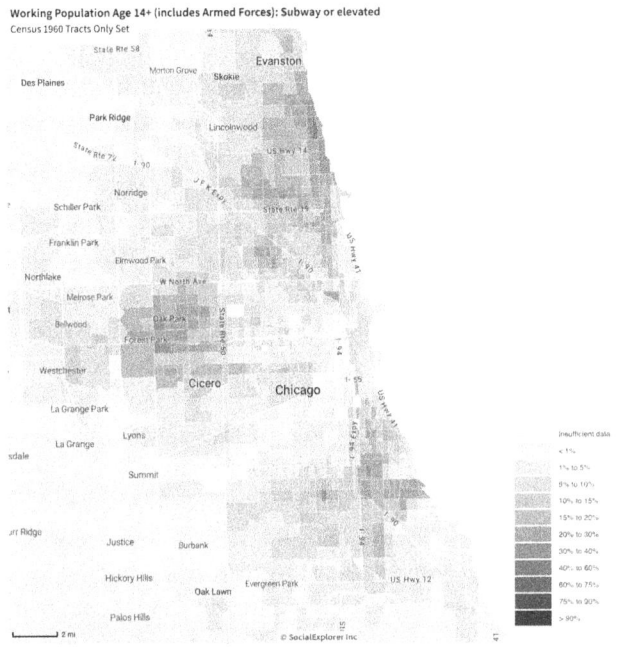

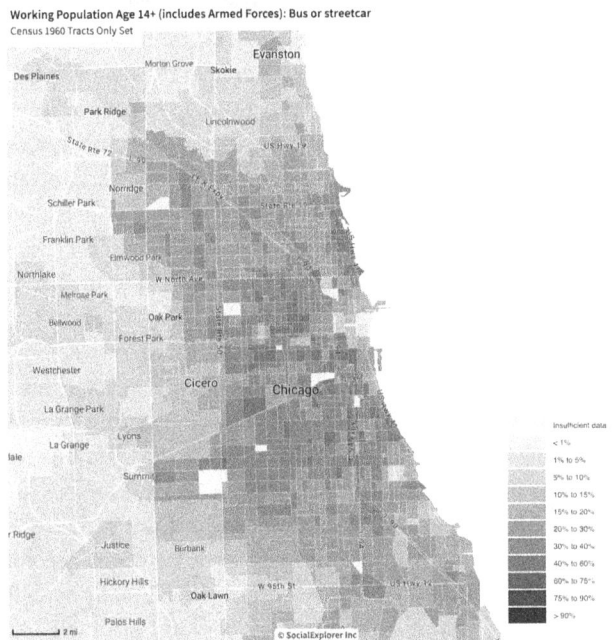

FIGURES 16A AND 16B. The more defined hubs of the elevated lines on the North, South, and West Sides (*upper map*) contrast with the comprehensive citywide service offered by bus and remaining trolley coaches across the city in 1960. Source: Bus or Streetcar/Subway or Elevated, 1960, Social Explorer, accessed June 26, 2021.

and comprehensive system: "just about any spot in the city was within a half-mile of a transit route, most were within two blocks. A majority of routes ran all night. . . . The fleet was maintained in good condition."[79] There were still about a one million daily users of CTA services.[80] A *Tribune* reporter in 1958 confirms Kristopan's analysis: "The transit authority, he found, is fast and efficient," and for his thirteen of fifteen transfers on his trial run, he waited less than five minutes. Reflecting the advantage of public ownership was service maintenance in the face of losses: "CTA has lost about 53 percent of its passengers without reducing its services."[81] From 1945 to 1956, ridership declined from 6.29 passengers per mile on surface lines to 4.28, reflecting lower density on a robust system.[82]

The ridership losses were staggering and would make the maintenance of this unique system challenging to justify politically. A crucial factor may have been the bus substitution program itself. The surface system still transported 426 million revenue riders in 1958, an impressive number for any extensive city system,[83] but the CTA failed to leverage or preserve the benefits of bus travel, thus leaving the new system behind the automobile in speed and comfort. CTA had ignored any contradictory evidence that would stand in the way of bus substitution, which they consistently promised would attract a new generation of riders with higher service. From the onset of substitution, riders in the neighborhoods did not agree that bus substitution necessarily brought improved service. The East Side Improvement Association in 1947 claimed that "substitution of buses for streetcars on three far southeast side routes has resulted in deterioration of service," including buses overflowing with students and workers.[84] Some riders interviewed believed that "the service under the management of the CTA has deteriorated as compared to that given by the old Chicago Surface Lines management."[85]

The city and CTA failed to work together to speed up bus service outside a few streets in the CBD, even though the tools to make buses move faster were well known to local officials. The CTA, with city assistance, had created a pioneering system of dedicated downtown bus lanes between Wacker and Michigan on Washington to increase bus speeds.[86] CTA's exclusive travel lane on Washington led to a 14.5 percent improvement during rush hours: "The savings in minutes through this relatively short section (7 blocks) show that were such traffic plans applied more generally, the savings in time to those who use mass transit would be considerable."[87] Unfortunately, CTA and the city did not build out a citywide bus rapid transit system despite the space on the city's broad and recently widened streets, thus leaving riders in the lurch.

CTA chairman Ralph Budd in 1951 admitted that buses were now just as bogged down as the streetcars they had replaced: "With all our new high speed equipment, our average speed is still much slower than it was years ago, because of the huge growth in vehicular traffic since 1946."[88] CTA stated flatly in 1957 that "the flexibility of buses is being progressively impaired by the increasing severity of traffic congestion and traffic delays." The authority's aggressive program of ripping out tracks and repaving roads had, the board now admitted, "attracted more motorists" who clogged roads and avoided transit. Local transit service was "no longer a lucrative monopoly" but a daily competition between cars and buses for riders and "street space." In 1957, CTA calculated that traffic delays to local service cost the authority a remarkable $117 million in losses per year.[89] The big bet on bus substitution, absent plans for exclusive bus lanes or other transit-friendly options, had not paid off in service quality. Buses needed transit planning too.

Auto-Centric Postwar Planning and Decentralization

Higher fares and sluggish bus service drove off riders, but underlying these losses were the private automobile's multiplying advantages. CTA leaders admitted in 1958 that "the private automobile is winning the competitive struggle with local transit."[90] It was not just suburbanites driving more. City residents also went nuts for cars as the number of registered automobiles rose from 131 to 242 per thousand persons between 1946 and 1958 despite plenty of transit still on offer.[91] The total population of Chicago increased from 3.661 to 3.8 million between 1948 and 1956, but transit rides per capita citywide dropped from 2.63 to 1.63 in the same period.[92]

CTA's transit modernization programs might have been far more successful if the region's leaders had not committed so fully during this period to making automobile driving much faster and often more reliable than transit.[93] Planners focused early on moving cars and trucks faster in and out of the downtown area, the area of most significant driver frustration. The city's creation of one-way streets in the CBD in 1951, a typical urban planning strategy for speeding up automobiles, required the rerouting of many surface streetcar routes.[94] Junking streetcars accelerated the transition sought by city officials by reducing the need for complex construction with rails in place. In 1957, CTA reported that "substitution of buses for streetcars also has been made easier, and in some instances has made possible, the establishment of one-way streets to expedite the flow of vehicular traffic. It has also simplified the task of the city, the county and the state in their extensive street resurfacing and repaving programs."[95] Bus substitution on the busy Western Avenue line, explained CTA officials, would help to "expedite the City's program of constructing through-lane overpasses at heavily used street intersections and of repaving the entire street."[96] CTA was a handmaiden of pro-automobile forces in the city government aiming to get the tracks and streetcars off the streets.

Chicago's political leaders planned for and funded a disruptive superhighway development program that would make riding transit much less competitive. The city council had green-lit a modest superhighway plan in 1939–40, but the war interfered. The 1946 Chicago Plan Commission's General Plan magnified the scale of the roads, proposing two hundred miles of highways stretching across the city and surrounding suburbs.[97] Fast crosstown routes as part of the highway plans would be a gamechanger as crosstown journeys by transit either required a trip to the center or a slower ride on a variety of streetcar and bus routes. The combined power of local, state, and federal funding—mostly unavailable to transit at the time—produced a superhighway revolution in just two decades. Planners bulldozed thousands of homes in white, Latino, and Black working-class neighborhoods to make way for mammoth roadways. For the West Side Congress Street Expressway alone, 1,575 families needed rehousing by 1952, with thousands of additional families in the way of future highways on the northwest side of the city. Politicians promoted public housing less out of humanitarian notions than the relocation demands of urban renewal and superhighway projects.[98]

The public sector had become the dominant force in developing a new generation of expensive automobile infrastructure through these autocentric policies while claiming that any transit subsidies were out of the question. The dream of high-speed mobility for a whole city was already within sight by 1960 according to the *Chicago Area Transportation Study*: "many of the routes outlined in the 1939 and 1946 plans have been built or are under construction. The Congress Street Expressway, the Northwest Expressway, the Edens and Kingery Expressways, and the Chicago Skyway have been completed. The Outer Drive has had successive improvements over the years. The Dan Ryan (South) Expressway is under construction. The Southwest Expressway is in an advanced stage of planning and should be completed by 1965. Clearly, the early plans have guided much construction to this date." The region's leaders committed to 288 miles of superhighways by 1960, with construction well underway. Thousands of additional supporting miles of wide, paved arterials in the city and the suburbs fed cars to the superhighways, representing an enormous local government commitment. Chicago did build new rapid rail transit lines along highway medians, described below, but these paled compared to the highway program.[99]

The contrast between the experience of transit riders and automobile drivers was stark by 1960, according to the *Chicago Area Transportation Study*, thanks to such extensive investment: "the average CTA rider pays 4.3 cents per mile, but spends an average of thirty-eight minutes in traveling from door to door. The automobile traveler pays from 4.5 to 6.4 cents per mile over a similar distance, but it takes him only twenty-two minutes."[100] This advantage of automobiles in an affluent society resulted from politicians' choices to prioritize superhighways over trams. The most considerable losses to transit were in the bus system because local drivers could expect to quit surface transit and operate their cars quickly for shopping or recreation trips. By contrast, downtown-focused rapid transit had the advantage of competition with high parking costs, more significant time to destinations, and crowded CBD roads. But all transit suffered in comparison to highways. One CTA study in 1963 attempted "to measure the devastating effect of automobile competition" on transit ridership in south Chicago. While context factors such as "population change and urban renewal" had to be taken into account, the opening of the Dan Ryan Expressway "leaves no doubt about the erosive influence of an Expressway on public transit patronage." Both rapid and surface lines adjoining the freeway experienced losses much higher than those experienced citywide.[101]

Auto-centric planning encouraged the mass movement of whites outward during this period as a car-based life became easier within the city limits. In the outer, white edge of the city of Chicago public transportation had become a minor factor in quality of life.[102] In the Bungalow Belt on the edge, only about one in four daily commuters used mass transit by 1960. The only higher regions of transit usage in the whiter areas of the town were on the North Side and a few neighborhoods on the far South Side near the lake that benefited from elevated or frequent electrified commuter rail service. These more prosperous center-city white populations, while a minority of inhabitants, were crucial to maintaining the rapid transit system from a political perspective. Yet, in general, the trend within the urbanized area was to cars.[103]

The far more critical movement postwar in the Chicago region was out of the city to all-white auto-centric suburbs. The encircling suburban towns not only resisted transit extensions and subsidies but by keeping zoning so restrictive, they made it impossible for transit to serve them efficiently on a "pay as you" go model. The new highways and arterials accelerated low-density growth in the suburbs. Decentralization of industry required car ownership for employees who now drove to single-story factories filling in suburban industrial parks.[104] Experts were aware of the problem decentralization posed to mass transit. Aside from older suburbs with elevated connections, Oak Park and Evanston most notably, where about one in four residents commuted by rail in 1960, most suburban areas notched ridership in the single digits, with just a few having higher commuter rail ridership straight to the business districts. The *Chicago Area Transportation Study* offered a succinct description of what would have to change to make transit work better:

> high densities and greater usage of mass transportation ... would require a reversal of current practices and policies in all or nearly all of the political jurisdictions in the Chicago area. Zoning regulations, road and parking programs, health and building codes, and assessment procedures might have to be changed. In addition, changes in lending policies, both by private institutions and government, would be required and private builders would have to be subject to additional controls.

However, the authors acknowledged that such changes were unlikely because "current popular demand, as expressed in thousands of daily decisions, has been predominantly towards low density use of the land."[105] Politicians believed, with some justification, that many transit-centric policies would hurt them with the suburban public.

Modernizing Transit for an Auto-Centric Region

In 1962, an experimental line known as the Skokie Swift uncovered latent demand for high-quality transit in close-in suburbs. The Swift was one of the first postwar federal transit projects, made possible thanks to a Housing and Home Financing Agency (HHFA) two-year demonstration grant. CTA officials won the grant by promising to use the funds "to determine the effectiveness and economic feasibility of linking a fast-growing, medium-density suburban area with the central city by means of a high-speed rail rapid transit extension coordinated with suburban buses and with the central city's extensive transit network."[106] This strategy pointed to a more transformational regional transit program with the ability to aid both affluent commuters and center-city job seekers.

Skokie, a northwest suburb, had grown 525 percent between 1940 and 1958,[107] housing 65,281 residents by 1962. Despite the population growth, the community had lost all its rail services. In the postwar decades, neither the CTA nor a dying interurban company could attract sufficient rail ridership on existing train service through the community due to low density and the car lifestyle. Driving, at first, was not much of a barrier to CBD commuting given the general affluence, new expressways, and downtown parking. The "mostly white-collar workers living in single-family homes" in Skokie, owning on average 1.4 cars per household, worked at high rates (56 percent) in Chicago's center city in 1960. Limited bus service—offered by private suburban bus companies and the CTA—was all that was left by the early 1960s.[108]

By the early 1960s, many city-bound commuters had tired of the crowded highways and irregular bus service. Skokie's town leaders, sensing the growing frustration, urged CTA to restart service on the abandoned five-mile rail track that had once served the community. CTA, with federal support, agreed to restart service as the Skokie Swift. The local political support for transit, including a promise "to pay part of the cost" (only about 7 percent local as it turned out), was a factor in CTA's commitment to the project.[109] The Swift boasted one-man-operated, high-speed, nonstop metal trains offering riders ten-minute headways during rush hours and a transfer to downtown-bound elevated CTA service at Howard. The reactivation of the five-mile interurban line, which required comparatively modest renovation, would provide express-only service between an expanded Dempster terminus in Skokie and the Howard elevated stop. Riders paid a premium fare of forty-five cents for the ride to the Loop (and paid a cashier before they boarded on weekdays to speed loading). The deliberately low twenty-five-cent parking fee made the Swift competitive with driving.[110]

The Skokie Swift service, thanks to these many attractive elements, was a hit from the start in 1964. CTA spent extensively on an advertising program in newspapers and on the radio that created positive brand awareness. The parking lots quickly filled with cars, and "kiss and ride" commuters filed into the Dempster terminal. Several surrounding towns also coordinated their bus service to Dempster. Managers had expected about one thousand riders a day, but 3,939 actually showed up on day one! CTA had to increase the number of trains to handle the crowds.[111] By summer of 1964 the Swift was carrying six thousand riders each weekday,[112] and in all of 1965 the Swift carried 1,848,000 total passengers.[113] Weekend ridership for recreation and game days also proved popular. Within two years of opening, the Swift handled 20 percent of Skokie-area commuters heading to the Loop, a robust percentage for the Chicago suburbs of the time. Twenty percent of the new Swift riders had switched from automobiles, and 86 percent came from houses with one or more autos. Many realtors reported a location near the Swift as "a positive factor in the renting of apartments," helping drive rental increases and a modest zoning change for a new apartment building.[114]

The Swift yielded unexpected social benefits because many of the new riders were city residents reverse commuting to suburban jobs. In the mid-1960s, Skokie and Morton Grove had grown aggressively to include 174 businesses with 12,524 employees, doubling its employment base from 1954. This boom resulted from "companies relocating from Chicago into single-story plants," a typical postwar trend that shifted taxes and jobs away from the urban, increasingly nonwhite, working class. Yet the Swift, a study found, had encouraged a significant growth in reverse commuters from Chicago, with 1,365 reverse commuters each day by 1968. Researchers found that for these workers from the city, the absence of the elevated and the Swift would mean their "journey would exceed two hours each way and this would undoubtedly preclude their working in Skokie." Most area firms reported that "at least one of four types of workers—women, nonwhite, skilled blue collar, and unskilled workers—had become more available to them a result of Skokie Swift." Nonwhite workers were cited as beneficiaries: "The new rapid transit service, it was found, had especially opened job opportunities to nonwhite workers living in Chicago." Employers sometimes provided shuttles to the Swift and frequently made mention of the Swift in both advertisements and interviews with potential staff.[115] The line's success suggested that more significant investment in limited-stop, high-speed transit in an auto-oriented location could work when a nearby rapid rail system offered links to a vital center city.

The reluctance to invest in similar express projects in the suburbs may have been rooted in the declining fortunes of suburban buses, privately run interurbans, and the commuter railroads. For instance, commuter rail ridership dropped massively, and the remaining private owners of the lines had started to cut service and close stations. Closures and less reliable service made suburban commutes to the CBD more complex and car dependent. The declining service severely impacted several city of Chicago neighborhoods that lacked or had lost extensive CTA service and relied on the local commuter stops.[116] Despite these losses, the enduring importance of the CBD to a remaining group of affluent regional commuters was the crucial factor to commuter rail's redemption, just as was the case with the creation of New York's MTA. The state government stepped in to save the commuter lines in the 1960s and 1970s, preferring at first to shore up the private companies rather than taking over direct management wherever possible (see below for the Regional Transit Authority [RTA] and Metra). But the state government had stepped in only after the region had lost many lines and stations, many riders had already shifted to cars, and the remaining equipment was often uncompetitive in comfort or speed with automobiles.

The CTA's development of rapid transit lines in the middle of new superhighways was the standout postwar success for the agency—and seemed to be a foolproof way of combining automobility with transit expansion. The building of these expressway rapid lines in Chicago was a watershed nationally. Detroit and Baltimore both flirted with the idea, and in New York, Robert Moses rejected solid proposals for transit extensions in highways. Yet only in Chicago did transit administrators develop significant rail lines in highway medians. Such lines, discussed as early as 1939, had some disadvantages because they did not run directly in high-density neighborhoods like streetcar and bus lines, requiring a walk or bus transfer to get to a station on the new lines. Riders also had to wait in the middle of noxious expressways. The CTA bet that the service quality (and feeder buses) would compensate for these obvious drawbacks. They were right.[117]

The median plan began moving ahead in the 1950s. A key supporter of these lines was Mayor Richard J. Daley, elected in 1955, ensuring that the city contributed to their creation.[118] The city issued bonds for the construction of these lines, about $25 million in total support, and only required CTA to cover the costs of the equipment in the medians.[119] CTA gave its valuable and wide transit right-of-way for constructing the Congress Street Superhighway (now the Eisenhower Expressway) on the West Side. The expressway median was reserved for rapid transit. By 1958, CTA had relocated the Garfield Park elevated service to the expressway median and connected it to the West Side subway tunnels.[120] According to the CTA, this nine-mile-long project was "America's first combined rapid transit railway and motor expressway."[121]

CTA's board rightly celebrated the median achievement in 1957 but was frustrated that they could not develop the "large-scale scale expansion of existing off-the-street, grade separated rapid transit facilities" that could compete with automobiles on a broader basis throughout the city. Thanks to the 1945 founding legislation, CTA was prevented "from obtaining the necessary funds by levying taxes."[122] It would not be until 1966 that Mayor Daley "proposed a public improvements bond" for median express routes in the already open Dan Ryan and Kennedy Expressways. Voters approved the $28 million bond by two to one, with the federal government picking up part of the tab. The total cost for these new extensions was about $4 million per lineal mile, a relative bargain and about half the cost of a subway of similar length.[123]

The extended Ryan/Kennedy rapid transit service (1969–70) added sixteen miles of combined service and fourteen new stations. Skidmore, Owings & Merrill created modern interiors with plate-glass windows, stainless steel trim, and terrazzo floors. Once aboard, riders enjoyed "smooth, comfortable rides" in "air-conditioned trains."[124] Key to the median express service was redesigning existing bus routes to bring riders to the new lines, including cuts to downtown sections of many existing crosstown bus routes. The expanding rapid system was based on the "obvious preference of the transit rider for rapid transit over bus." Riders, nonetheless, needed to be "won over from bus to rail for as much of their mileage as possible."[125] Managers figured that most riders would happily exchange a crosstown transfer to faster rapid routes in highways rather than endure a long and slow ride to downtown on a bus. Not that they gave riders a choice.[126]

CTA in 1970 offered an upbeat assessment of progress in ridership and service, but the figures presented also reflected the challenge for postwar managers when a highway was a neighbor. Ridership rose rapidly on the median lines, and CTA managers were rightly proud that "the majority" of passengers on the new rapid lines (about 782,000 total weekly) had simply shifted "from other CTA services," primarily buses. These veteran riders recognized "the greater speed and convenience which is offered" by the rapid lines. But even faster rail had trouble competing with expressways. The much smaller number of new CTA riders primarily came from other regional transit services rather than shifting from automobiles. At four stops on the Dan Ryan section, for instance, a survey "found that 27.5% of the passengers were not previously CTA patrons: 4% used suburban bus services, 10% suburban railroads, 8% used automobiles, and the remainder did not previously make the journey." In sum, most of the new customers, already small, were devoted transit riders trading regional transit for the CTA median service.[127]

Chicago's median transit might have gotten more drivers to switch if the lines had reached the suburbs or a connecting line (like the Skokie Swift). But these CTA median lines could not deliver substantial new service to the suburbs because of a lack of regional and state support for a complete rapid transit system in the highways. Suburbanites, for instance, rejected paying for large parking ramps that might have boosted ridership (as was the case in the Boston region). The median transit lines paled compared to the two-hundred-mile-plus highways being constructed during this period.

Transit Disoriented Development

City officials both endorsed highways and used planning tools to undermine traditional areas of dense ridership. The city government had created the Chicago Land Clearance Commission in 1947 to supercharge the redevelopment process by assembling and reselling the land. White city officials, planners, architects, and other civic leaders enthusiastically supported slum clearance, mainly of Black and Puerto Rican neighborhoods, replacing them with auto-centric "tower-in-the-park" projects or other low-density institutional uses. In 1955, for instance, Chicago's city planners believed that the city's blighted or near blighted areas "had increased to more than 50 square miles." Such inflated, fearmongering estimates counted as blighted tens of thousands of aging buildings that might have been overcrowded and run-down. Yet, these aging neighborhoods remained a crucial if unrecognized source of housing, employment, and transit riders. City leaders were unwilling to wait to see if what Jane Jacobs called "unslumming" could re-energize these areas through owner renovation and other market means.[128]

One example of the clearance process was the Lake Meadows (1955) project on the Near South Side of Chicago. The project, according to planners, "removed one of the worst blighted areas of the city." The towers in the park of Lake Meadows with sprawling lawns and parking areas reduced the neighborhood's density significantly and permanently despite the existence of convenient elevated service. The new public housing projects and institutional expansion programs (such as the Illinois Institute of Technology campus) developed nearby also dramatically reduced the density of the South Side areas well served by rapid transit. The rehoused population in middle-class projects was higher income compared to the original residents.[129] The felt success among city leaders of these master-planned projects, which we now look on with skepticism, led to citywide encouragement of planned district zoning that offered developers flexibility for larger-scale projects. Many projects were auto-centric with superblocks, limited neighborhood retail, and plenty of off-street parking.[130]

Despite targeted low-density redevelopment projects, city leaders and planners initially supported high-density zoning citywide postwar, reflected in a pro-growth zoning code revision in 1957. But bowing to an auto-centric age and the fashion of towers in the park, by 1953 planners had already increased on-site parking requirements for new apartment buildings—making even more space for the car in a city with extensive transit. Even more significant changes were in store. A collection of modern, privately owned high-rises sprouted postwar near or along Lake Shore Drive on the North Side. Targeted to professionals in the city's growing service sector, they generated sufficient density to help support the nearby elevated lines. Yet many neighborhood residents came to believe that these large buildings generated too much traffic and were out of place or unattractive. Quick-buck developers building barebones, medium-rise infill projects on small lots in popular neighborhoods was another sore point for neighbors. These infill buildings offered limited parking and lots of small efficiency apartments.[131]

With residents outraged over the traffic, aesthetics, and increased density of a few popular areas like the North Side, city officials in the 1970s amended zoning laws to downzone many neighborhoods (limiting highrises), increased on-site parking requirements, and limited the number of efficiency apartments. Limiting density in some of the few places with growth potential, when the city was losing hundreds of thousands of residents per decade, was politically popular but shortsighted. The downzoning and parking requirements encouraged automobile ownership that undermined future ridership in many neighborhoods. City officials also more aggressively terminated nonconforming uses (stores and factories) in residential areas. This practice created more monofunctional areas preferred by many residents, but these areas were now less likely to generate transit trips from workers or visitors.[132]

Just as consequential to density reduction long term near transit was private-sector disinvestment due to redlining, housing abandonment, and commercial decline. The city was slow to address fair housing. Pioneering neighborhood stabilization programs focused chiefly on whiter areas like Hyde Park near the University of Chicago. Older transit-rich shopping districts like Bronzeville lost many of their customers to slum clearance and migration of Black families away from these neighborhoods. The remaining housing stock in large sections of the South and West Sides fell into disrepair thanks to redlining and aligned disinvestment. Slum landlords took advantage of desperation to wring profits from substandard housing while the city stood by. Antidiscrimination housing laws finally passed in the state (1961) and city (1963) but, by design, were weak and difficult to enforce. Those minority families forced to relocate for highways, housing abandonment, or urban renewal often found betterquality housing in areas further out like Englewood as whites fled. But the once-thriving commercial districts in nonwhite expansion areas like Englewood often went into steep decline as whites abandoned houses, landlords milked the properties, and stores closed. Deindustrialization, decentralization, and discrimination continued to limit Black occupational horizons. Many of the expansion areas for Black families further south were also not as well served by rapid transit.[133]

Disinvestment and "slum clearance" in so many neighborhoods that once fed working-class riders into the transit system negatively impacted transit in multiple ways. CTA, for instance, abandoned a streetcar line that ran through an urban renewal area in Cottage Grove, replacing it with a bus route that "avoided the area of desolation."[134] According to *Motor Coach Age*, "another example of what CTA had to contend within the inner city was Ogden Avenue, much of which had become a string of abandoned buildings. Buses ran past them, sometimes nearly empty." CTA cut the line hard, including weekends and evenings. When the Dan Ryan rapid transit opened in 1969, CTA shifted the remaining buses to serve as "L" feeders.[135]

How well planning could have driven ridership was reflected in the transit-oriented location of the city's growing two-year community college system, postwar campuses, and many older universities. The chancellor of the community college system in 1977 explained that "when our new campuses were planned, we took into consideration 'high corridors of accessibility,' such as the Dan Ryan Expressway's rapid transit route and connecting bus routes." This transit-centered planning helped ridership as the approximately 107,000 students mostly used "CTA bus and rapid transit routes to get to our nine campuses and to their jobs." The community college system also reflected "the racial, ethnic and socio-economic distribution of the city's adult population, Spanish-speaking adults particularly." Students at the new Harry S. Truman College in densely developed Sheridan Park, for instance, enjoyed direct exits and entries to the CTA elevated line. The modernist University of Illinois at Chicago Circle (now the University of Illinois Chicago) and Illinois Institute of Technology campuses also benefited from nearby rapid transit access. The growing numbers of students at older but expanding city campuses like Loyola University of Chicago also benefited from rapid transit accessibility.[136]

Regional Resistance to Subsidies

In response to a changing city and staggering losses in patronage, CTA managers began cutting service quality in the 1960s.[137] The surface transit system suffered the most because it experienced considerable ridership losses. In 1961, for instance, CTA cut revenue bus miles by 1.25 percent to match a 1.15 percent loss in revenue ridership. CTA cut particularly hard on the weekend and non-rush hours: Sundays and holidays lost 4.18 percent. As cuts became the new normal, CTA would remain passable for daily commutes, particularly those living near rapid routes or feeder lines. Yet, the system would be less dependable for everyday living or as an actual car substitute. Rapid transit got a tiny 0.64 percent cut that year,

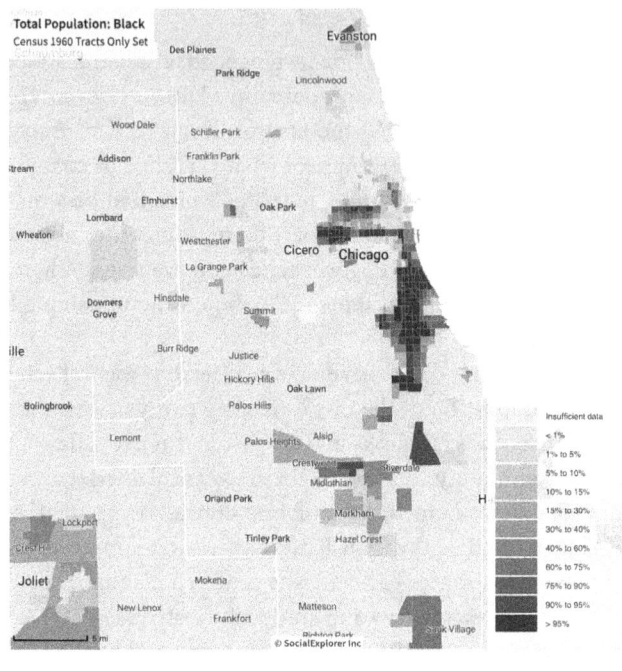

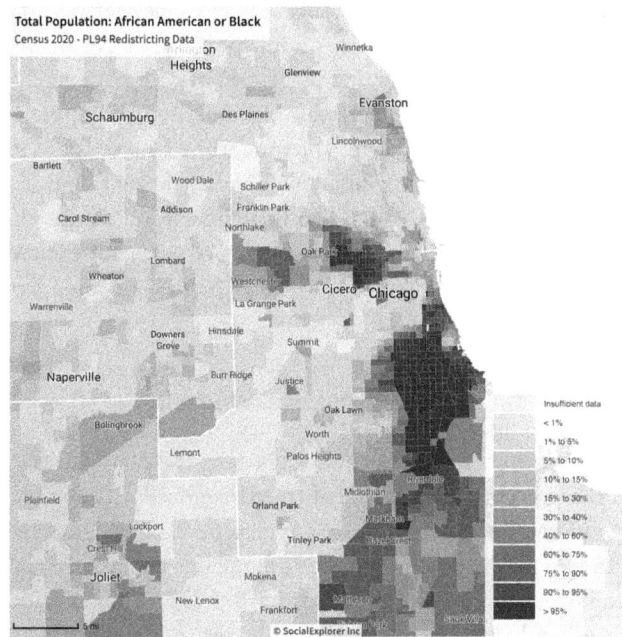

FIGURES 17A AND 17B. Many Black families found better housing by moving further south and west in Chicago, but on the South Side families often relocated to neighborhoods further away from the best elevated and bus lines. Source: Black, 1970/2020, Social Explorer, accessed June 26, 2021.

mostly from better utilization of existing lines. CTA was also pushing ahead on new rapid lines in the highway medians. Anyone with a calculator would have reached the same conclusion as CTA managers: the elevated system had a brighter future than buses.[138] Between 1948 and 1962, surface transit lost 52.65 percent of its ridership while rapid had lost only 17.11 percent.[139] Rapid transit even notched eight years of ridership gains between 1949 and 1966, while surface transit had just three positive years in the same period.[140]

CTA managers realized that public subsidy was essential to preserving service and tried to change public opinion by highlighting the broader social benefits of transit: "Providing these urgently needed traffic-free extensions of local transit services is just as much a community responsibility as providing highways, police and fire protection services, health and sanitation services, water-works, and parks and playgrounds."[141] Because transit was "no longer a lucrative monopoly," and fewer were riding, subsidies had to be provided to maintain service quality.[142] It wasn't just the city that benefited either, as CTA served twenty-eight suburbs. Managers pointed to the $2.8 billion total in public funds New York had committed to rapid transit as a precedent. In New York City, the only American system of equivalent scale, riders "finance only the day-to-day operating costs of the service."[143] Further improvements in Chicago, they believed, "cannot be financed by CTA riders," and "it is equally obvious that private capital cannot be persuaded to provide financing for sorely needed transit improvements and extensions."[144] CTA administrators and city officials began regular and frustrating journeys to Springfield for subsidies, but state legislators consistently rebuffed plans for transit support throughout the late 1950s and most of the 1960s.

Subsidy efforts in Springfield in 1957 revealed persistent fault lines. Downstate Republicans, for instance, believed CTA was a "'local responsibility'" and should be resolved "without state subsidy."[145] Chicago's suburban legislators "agreed to oppose the proposed subsidy on the grounds that it would be unfair to impose additional taxes on their areas" when their districts were unlikely to benefit in the short term from new service. A voice in the wilderness was a suburban Northbrook county commissioner who bravely announced: "I am in favor of CTA subsidy because if we don't have an extensive and efficient mass transportation system, it would be physically and financially impossible to build enough superhighways to accommodate all the motorists."[146] But the Republican state senate majority leader from suburban River Forest, a community served by CTA, was against the new tax because he was unsure if CTA would use the subsidies for "capital" needs instead of "big pay increases."[147] The

Chicago Motor Club president believed "any form of taxation to subsidize the CTA would be a dangerous precedent. Once a tax is imposed on the motorist for this purpose, it could become a never ending proposition."[148] The Chicago Real Estate Board came out against a property tax for transit.[149] Even some Democratic alderpersons in Chicago made their opposition known.[150] Legislators diverted the transit proposal to a special commission, where it died.[151]

Another state subsidy proposal in 1961, to be based on gas and real-estate taxes, seemed to be perfectly designed to attract suburban support. Not even expanded rapid transit in the highways, modernized signals on elevated lines, new subway cars, and parking garages at rapid terminals, all of which would favor suburban commuters, made a difference.[152] Chicago city interests again proved unreliable. The Chicago Association of Commerce, Chicago Real Estate Board, Central Area Committee, and Civic Federation came out against the plan and proposed a much smaller alternative.[153] The Chicago and North Western commuter railroad, still in private hands, also opposed the plan. CNW had invested $43 million into its system and viewed the proposed CTA Northwest Expressway median rapid transit as a blatant attempt to "put out of business and destroy what is regarded . . . as the world's finest commuter service—the five Chicago commuter railroads."[154] CTA would thus remain reliant on revenues as the effort failed in 1961.

Not only was CTA forced to cut service to stay solvent, but managers were also fighting growing social disorder that scared off many riders. Customers and bus drivers were at risk as the urban crime wave swelled due to the 1960s and 1970s urban crisis. Chicago and other cities responded as best they could with exact change provisions to protect staff from stickups. CTA claimed that the new rule, in place in 1968, "entirely halted robberies and assaults of bus drivers" by ending the practice of drivers carrying wallets full of change.[155]

A small note in the 1968 *CTA Annual Report* illustrates an additional social challenge many transit operators faced in postwar cities: "Contributing to an even greater loss in originating revenue passengers were the riots and fires . . . that erupted following the assassination of the Reverend Martin Luther King Jr. on April 4."[156] Surface transit ridership dropped to 346 million in 1968, a roughly forty million decline in one year. The rapid was also down by about ten million riders.[157] Typical CTA initiatives in the 1970s included outreach to minority groups and a zoo shuttle bus decorated with flora and fauna by participants from Model Cities youth groups on the South Side. Legendary ball player Ernie Banks, "one of the most popular civic heroes in Chicago's history," also served on the CTA board starting in 1969.[158]

CTA did what it could during the urban crisis to improve its image and attract riders, but attracting more passengers was simply too difficult. As a result, managers still relied upon fare increases and service cuts to balance budgets during the 1960s and 1970s. The basic fare had increased from twenty-five cents in 1962 to forty-five cents in 1971 (plus a ten-cent transfer).[159] Fare increases were a game of diminishing returns and alienated riders, an increasing proportion collected from poor and minority riders. Between 1964 and 1973, and despite numerous fare increases, CTA passenger revenues increased only from $131 to $172 million. Like most public transit companies, CTA was no match for its powerful unions, so even though the number of employees declined from 12,600 in 1964 to 12,100 in 1973, labor and benefit costs were way up.[160]

CTA fare increases, deferred maintenance, and service cuts had barely balanced budgets in the 1960s, but the formula failed entirely in 1971. The CTA began running deficits in 1971, a sobering $5 million,[161] and the reckoning was upon the managers as "costs soar out of proportion due to accelerating inflation, to the point where revenues were no longer sufficient to meet our daily expenses. It is regrettable that now, for the first time in its history, CTA must pin its only hopes for further improvements upon subsidies from governmental agencies."[162] The state finally provided $19 million in 1971, its first significant contribution to transit and one made grudgingly. The city and Cook County provided $9.5 million.[163] In 1972, CTA vice chairman James R. Quinn pleaded with city, state, and federal officials for financial help, threatening that "unless relief is afforded within a few week this public service cannot be given and other means of transportation would have to be found for about one million daily riders."[164] By 1973, the deficit had mushroomed to $34 million.[165] The situation was dire: "In 1973, CTA had to go on bended knee to the city and state begging for help." While CTA negotiated with the state, it had to cut service.[166] Grants from the state, city, and county for operating costs and debt service thankfully rose to $36.9 million in 1973.[167]

Had it not been for the federal government, CTA would have been unable to maintain its infrastructure. The days of using revenues to fund capital were coming to an end—forcing a new reliance on subsidies. CTA collected just $0.2 million in capital funds directly from CTA revenues.[168] The federal government became the principal patron of CTA capital programs, far exceeding the state and local governments. CTA initiated a $122 million capital program in 1971 with help from the US Department of Transportation, the Illinois DOT, and the City of Chicago; in fact, two-thirds of the money came from federal sources. CTA applied the funds to major station and signal upgrades, one thousand air-conditioned buses, and several new rapid transit terminals. Without federal funding, it is unclear if CTA could have invested in its plant at all.[169]

The era of declining service on the surface transit system, now all buses, would become an annual ritual.[170] In 1968, CTA implemented a 3.06 percent reduction in surface lines and a 1.15 percent reduction in rapid service as part of its cost-cutting measures.[171] Declining surface transit ridership justified cutting that system more dramatically. Ridership had dropped from 381 million riders on the surface lines in 1964 to just 272 million in 1973. Accordingly, CTA decreased the surface revenue vehicle miles from 108 million in 1964 to ninety million in 1973. Rapid transit ridership sank more modestly from 112 to 95 million during the same period. And vehicle miles offered on rapid had increased, up from 44 to 48 million, related both to the new extensions as well as the enduring faith of CTA leaders in the superiority of the rapid line.[172]

The remaining vitality in the compact Loop was a key factor in the comparatively robust ridership and sustained CTA investment on the elevated lines. Ridership had dropped on the public rapid and private commuter lines, but commuters from both city and suburbs, as in San Francisco, Boston, and New York, continued to ride transit to work downtown in large numbers. The Loop remained "the largest financial center in the U.S. outside Wall Street." The Chicago Board of Trade, the center of world commodities training, was a legacy of Chicago's long-standing role as a trade center for agricultural products. Distributed around the Loop's old and new skyscrapers were brokerage firms, accounting and legal firms, government offices, banks, traders, and the headquarters of large companies like Beatrice Foods. The Loop had thousands of hotel rooms, restaurants, and "the highest concentration of retail departments stores in the country."[173] At the new Sears Tower on weekdays, for instance, a survey of 5,673 workers found that "more than 37 percent of employees used CTA buses and rapid transit trains." Most of the other Sears workers traveled by various private commuter rail services, indicating the continuing connections of wealthy suburbs to the city center. Only 11 percent came by car—an impressive showing for a city in 1976.[174] In 1980, 23 percent of the region's total jobs were in the central city area, or 784,000 jobs.[175]

The Loop and rapid transit service was a bright spot in CTA service, but it was clear by the 1960s and 1970s that bus substitution, what they called "modernization," had still failed to deliver the speedier and better-quality service promised decades ago. But underperforming buses had little to do with the technology itself. CTA, for instance, kept buses in service longer to save money, raising the bus "retirement" age from twelve to sixteen years, and managers even kept some buses as old as twenty years on the road. Aging equipment undermined the comfort and reliability of buses, alienating many riders.[176]

City officials and CTA managers also failed to work together to create speedier bus service with dedicated lanes, left-turn priority, and other bus-friendly measures. Buses in 1973 moved on average at twelve miles per hour compared to rapid transit at twenty-seven miles per hour.[177] The late 1970s redesign of nine blocks of State Street into a transit mall for the exclusive use of buses and emergency vehicles was a rare effort where planning and transport worked together "to improve transportation and to minimize pedestrian-vehicle conflict." The effort demonstrated that buses could have moved faster citywide with good planning and civic support.[178]

Nor were buses, thanks to the gas crisis, the bargain to operate that they had been decades ago. In 1973, for instance, the mostly diesel fleet faced a 55.4 percent increase in energy costs. Slightly higher ridership during the gasoline crisis of 1973–74 did not compensate for these higher costs. The electric trolleybus service, which might have proved a hedge against high fuel costs, had already been eliminated as one of many short-term cost-cutting measures. To make matters worse, the GM diesel buses that CTA ordered in this period dreadfully underperformed in both power and air conditioning. The care, talent, and funding applied to rapid transit were sorely lacking in bus surface transit and helped reduce ridership.[179] Many CTA bus riders, more likely to be female than those on CBD-bound elevated lines, would shift to cars in the decades to come.[180]

RTA: A Regional Agency Only the Suburbs Could Love

As in Baltimore, Atlanta, Detroit, and so many other cities, regional transit faced an uphill battle given the deterioration of center-city economies and resource hoarding of whiter and more affluent suburbs. A good representation of the limitations of regional transit was the creation of Chicago's RTA in 1974. Designed primarily to save the CTA, it had the potential to aid the suburbs as well. The suburban bus and train companies were in serious trouble. While few suburban transit riders remained, better transit would benefit suburban employers who relied upon reverse-commuting city workers, workers and employers in blue-collar suburbs like Elgin, suburban seniors and those who could not drive for one reason or another, and the small number of wealthier suburban residents who rode commuter rail and the elevated lines.

However, undermining a true spirit of cooperation was the ever-widening gap between whiter, wealthier, auto-centric suburbs and Chicago, a municipality in crisis. The conventional image of transit as a service primarily used by low-income riders, often riding or waiting in disinvested neighborhoods or public housing, was no help politically. While still vibrant compared to most American downtowns, the Loop was losing ground to suburban edge cities, reducing commuter rail ridership. Many factories closed their doors across the city's mixed-use neighborhoods and relocated to one-story greenfield sites. In 1970, a narrow band of commuter rail suburbs still extended outward, but with daily ridership of only about 15–25 percent. Suburban towns like Evanston and Oak Park with direct elevated service also enjoyed rapid ridership. But most suburban counties had about 10 percent daily transit ridership or less, even with all modes (bus, elevated, and commuter rail) combined. For instance, in DuPage County, just 0.52 percent of commuters used buses, and just 10.23 percent used commuter rail.[181]

How the RTA in 1974 launched augured poorly for the future of regionalism. The CTA's growing financial problems finally led Mayor Richard J. Daley (1955–76) to seek suburban subsidies.[182] Republican state representatives made clear that any tax support for the CTA came with a requirement of a regional transit authority, what became the RTA, that included subsidies for the comparatively small number of remaining suburban riders.[183] With the support of the city's state representatives, the proposal for RTA came before regional voters in 1974. RTA triumphed narrowly and, despite the benefits to suburban areas represented by regional transit, only passed thanks to overwhelming city electoral support. The final vote count "showed the widening political rift between the city and the suburbs. The issue was carried by less than 1% of the vote, largely on its 71% majority in Chicago. Suburban Will, Kane, and McHenry Counties showed 9 in 10 voters opposed to the RTA."[184] These counties were primarily white, had limited transit of any kind, and were more uniformly middle or upper class than the city.

The suburbs lost the battle to stop the RTA, but suburban representatives had already won the war before the votes were counted. The state legislature had limited the reach of the new agency that ended up on the ballot. As a result, the approved RTA in 1974 was much less than might be hoped for: underfunded, divided, and toothless. RTA's governance, for instance, gave excessive weight to the suburbs given the low ridership and public support on the periphery: its board comprised six directors from the city and six from the suburbs, with city directors picking the executive director. This "balance" in practice led to paralysis, weak financial oversight, and "regional bickering" on crucial issues within the RTA. The RTA, for instance, lacked any control over land use near its constituent services, making it hard to imagine how ridership would grow. The suburban directors, according to the *Chicago Tribune*, mostly rejected any ambitious plans: "The fragmented and conservative political system in suburbia, which was opposed to the creation of a regional system in the first place, contributed to the problem by failing to formulate any strategic goals for its delegation to follow."[185]

RTA leadership (and state leaders) remained resistant to taxing at a level that would create transit excellence—despite RTA having been given authority to levy regional taxes of various kinds. RTA in 1976 collected just $15 for each registration fee per car in Chicago and three thirty-seconds of the state's sales tax in the Chicago region.[186] Suburban directors on the RTA board, for example, rejected a 1976 proposal by RTA staff to dramatically increase service by levying a regional gas tax. As one director pointedly asked, "Why should car drivers pay for CTA riders?"[187] Suburban RTA directors were unhappy that about three-quarters of what RTA collected annually went to CTA. In contrast, the remaining quarter went to RTA subsidized suburban bus routes (today's Pace bus system) and commuter rail (today's Metra). In 1975, for instance, public funds composed 33 percent of the CTA budget ($280.9 million), of which $91.238 million came from the RTA.[188] CTA's dominance of subsidies made perfect sense given the agency's much larger ridership, but the optics were terrible when the time came each year to dispense the funding. Many suburban representatives fumed that their constituents were getting the short end of the stick, even though some suburbs were usually getting far more transit than residents would ever use.[189]

Hurting the cause for regional cooperation was the devotion of Chicago RTA directors to low fares and high employee pay. Fares on the CTA, for instance, remained unchanged from 1970 to 1976, and only rose a nickel to fifty cents in 1976.[190] CTA budgets, meanwhile, had more than doubled from $188.7 million in 1970 to $446.1 million in 1979.[191] In the CTA budget of 1977, fares covered 63 percent of operating revenue.[192] The most significant factor in rising costs was personnel, who accounted for about 80 percent of operating expenses. CTA had unwisely inserted a ticking financial bomb by including cost of living adjustments into agreements.[193] Between 1967 and 1976 the cost to carry a typical passenger had skyrocketed from nineteen to 54.5 cents, primarily thanks to labor.

Thus, CTA might have been forced to charge a dollar ride without the additional RTA and federal subsidies.[194] CTA's budget deficits rose from $153 million in 1978 to $281.8 million in 1980.[195] Thankfully, the federal government was covering 80 percent of capital expenditures by 1980, without which managers would have deferred even more maintenance.[196]

Media attention remained focused on CTA bloat and failure to control costs, but at least CTA was moving millions of city and suburban residents. Unfortunately, RTA directors allowed for much less fiscal soundness in the suburbs, hurting the agency's reputation and helping to make a case for future cuts in state support. Suburban commuters, for instance, had about twice the income of CTA riders, but they were much more deeply subsidized. A ride on suburban commuter rail in 1980 was subsidized at seventy cents per ride and suburban bus rides at fifty-two cents; these ratios compared unfavorably to about thirty cents of subsidy for each CTA ride. In addition, many commuter rail routes were woefully underutilized as the locus of employment was shifting out of the CBD to edge cities, most of which were poorly located for train service. RTA had added 177 bus routes in the suburbs, primarily to justify the suburban role in RTA. Yet most were unprofitable because they aimed to service political requests and few suburbanites wanted to ride them. One notorious suburban RTA route between 1977 and 1980 had *zero* riders, and six other lines managed to attract only about two passengers a day. But the RTA was so politicized that RTA managers could not cut the lines without offending unions or key elected officials.[197]

The RTA system had been designed for failure and showed severe signs of strain by the late 1970s. In 1977, the RTA board finally passed a 5 percent gas tax on the region to prevent massive cuts. The tax added just 2.5 more cents per gallon, and yet many suburban directors still opposed it.[198] The state legislature and suburbanites did not forgive so easily. As the gas tax failed to relieve the RTA financing crisis, RTA asked for and received permission in 1979 from the state legislature for a new 1 percent regional sales tax. Unfortunately, the state legislature cut the gasoline tax in exchange. The regional sales tax, as a result, did not solve the financing problems, particularly for the CTA with its much larger budgets and low fares.[199]

The crisis deepened between 1980 and 1983. To address its growing deficit, RTA in 1980 raised the CTA fare to eighty cents, and CTA administrators slashed service.[200] Chicago now had the dubious distinction of charging the nation's highest fare.[201] However, the state government refused to bail out the RTA thanks to long-standing anti-urban and auto-centric biases. President Ronald Reagan's determination to slash subsidies upon which transit operators had budgeted and depended accelerated the crisis. Chicago mayor Jane Byrne in 1981 prepared for an emergency city takeover of the CTA rather than see the agency fail but did not act. With no better option, RTA in July 1981 raised the CTA base fare again, this time to ninety cents. CTA cut nine bus routes and slashed all-night service on twenty "owl service" routes.[202] CTA total ridership, highly sensitive to price and reduced service, fell from about 638 million in 1981 to 614 million in 1983.[203] More drivers seemed to be crowding the roads in the aftermath of fare increases.[204] The City of Chicago finally coughed up a $20 million loan, and, under pressure, the state provided a $100 million loan. Politicians, once again, damaged the system.[205]

The 1981 cuts to owl service reduced the utility of the CTA for some of the systems most "transit dependent" riders. As such, they provide a window into what Chicago was losing thanks to economies. The owl service in 1980, before the cuts, had been used by about thirty thousand loyal riders per night on sixty-three bus routes (166 buses) and four rail lines (45 train cars). Collectively, the ten million total annual riders on CTA owl routes was "greater than the total annual ridership of any one of about 57 percent of American transit systems." CTA had also preserved more owl service than most other cities, with some Chicago routes offering all-night service for seventy-five years. The primarily male patrons, riding to and from night shift work, usually walked just three blocks or fewer to their transit stops and once arrived, a maximum of three blocks to their destinations. The combination of short walks and transit ridership reflected the enduring ecology of transit-oriented development in Chicago. While some owl service remained after 1981, the cuts to this crucial network sent a strong anti-transit message to many longtime riders.[206]

The RTA reform package that finally emerged in 1983 had more bad news for the CTA and urban transit. The deal meant "political control has passed from the Chicago Democratic political machine, which generally favored a policy of high subsidies and low fares for social welfare reasons, to the more conservative Republican suburbs." A suburban executive director, who emphasized fiscal soundness, now ran RTA. With suburbanites in control, RTA's ambitions would remain modest. RTA had the power to impose several taxes ("a sales tax, a car rental tax, a motor fuel tax, an off-street parking tax, and a replacement vehicle tax"). However, in practice, RTA's fiscally conservative leadership relied upon fares, the regional sales tax, a tiny share of the state sales tax, and federal capital funding.[207]

The RTA in practice became a neutered "holding company" that handled financial oversight, regulation, regional planning, and service coordination for CTA and the now publicly run suburban buses (Pace) and commuter rail (Metra) systems. The state, reflecting suburban favoritism, mandated a CTA farebox minimum recovery ratio of 50 percent but not for the suburban transit operators. If CTA failed to hit the target, fares would rise automatically or force additional budget cuts to reestablish balance. Such an arrangement theoretically depoliticized fare increases, and fares rose rapidly in the 1980s; however, the higher cost discouraged transit use among the most price-sensitive, local riders. While RTA showed a sizable surplus by the end of 1984, it was primarily thanks to years of economies and much higher fares. According to many, RTA was "still underfunded," the state subsidy was only about $90 million annually in the first years, and reforms amounted to "playing with mirrors."[208] CTA only made it back to 1981 ridership levels in 1985, or about 638 million riders.[209]

Even though RTA subsidized the suburban bus and rail systems more deeply per ride than CTA, these systems still lacked adequate funding to service such a vast, low-density region. Pace bus service, for instance, served a six-county area as large as Connecticut (3,466 square miles). By 1985, for example, Chicago's suburban population was 4.29 million with a workforce of 1.948 million employees. The operators of the Pace suburban bus system admitted that decentralization created a "serious dilemma for mass transportation: the majority of the region's economic base has relocated to an area of lower population density without a central business district and is lacking in the capital infrastructure for transit." Since 1975, the region had added fifty-seven million square feet of suburban office space, "the majority of which is poorly accessible by transit patrons." The "suburb to suburb" commuter was "primarily served by the automobile."[210]

The number of Pace riders has declined steadily thanks to lack of comprehensive service, persistently high auto commuting rates, and deindustrialization. In 1989, using just 515 buses on fixed-route services, well-intentioned managers could sell only 3.4 million rides per month. Pace's fares covered only about one-third of its operating costs.[211] In 1999, the 601 Pace buses carried just 3.1 million riders per month. Employment and population losses in Chicago and the industrial suburbs with the highest Pace ridership, including Aurora, Elgin, Joliet, and Waukegan, were considered factors. Pace ridership, after all, was working class, with 45 percent of Pace riders lacking a car and 57 percent of suburb-to-suburb customers having no car.[212] Recent Pace bright spots include a limited bus rapid transit (BRT) initiative, some highway express lanes, and a more extensive fleet of 810 buses.[213] But Pace in 2019 carried just 26.2 million passenger trips at an average of speed of just 14.2 miles per hour. Pace lost an impressive $6.64 per passenger trip and had a fare recovery ratio of just 15.5 percent.[214]

The car-centric, low-density landscape of the region also presents a daunting challenge for Metra commuter rail. Metra service spreads widely and thinly over Chicagoland thanks to extensive commuter trackage inherited from private companies. Metra's commuter rail has hundreds of miles of lines and stations, but these impressive total figures obscured uneven service. Metra shares much trackage with active freight lines, leading to delays and limitations on service growth. Above all, Metra receives inadequate operating support from multiple levels of government to offer reliable, comprehensive service on its network. More popular routes such as the West Side Aurora branch and the South Side Electric District offered frequent service at peak times, but many others provided just a few runs each day.[215] Metra has boosted its fare recovery rate, now 46.8 percent, but focus on bottom-line thinking, as in other cities, contributes to minimum service. An additional factor in lost ridership may also be its aging fleet: 37.6 percent of vehicles are beyond their useful life. To bring the system up to a higher standard would require $12 billion in capital funding, yet Metra only spent $306 million in 2019, a typical level. The results show up in weak ridership returns. Metra counted only 61.5 million passenger trips in 2019, a minimal number given the region's total population of 9.459 million.[216]

Transit in a Changing City

RTA's weak funding structure not only proved unequal to drive growth in suburban ridership and service, but damaged the CTA. The CTA in 1986 remained well patronized with 2.1 million daily trips, split between 1.6 million on buses and five hundred thousand on rapid lines. CTA carried 87 percent of transit passengers in the region. CTA, however, faced an annual $300 million operating deficit and $280 million capital shortfall. Local or regional subsidies were in short supply, and the federal government's coverage of 78 percent of capital needs in 1987 was simply insufficient to make up for weak local and state support. The 60 percent of CTA buses already past their twelve-year life expectancy was one of many indicators of agency decline.[217]

Indeed, transit customers noticed the problems on their daily commutes. Passengers interviewed in a marketing study in 1989 gave CTA low ratings for comfort, cleanliness, and personal safety. The future looked bleak: "CTA bus and el . . . rated much lower than auto on all attributes

FIGURES 18A AND 18B. These maps show losses in total regional ridership from 1960 to 2000, with the exception of neighborhoods near North Side elevated lines. Source: Mass Transit, 1960 (combined streetcar, bus, subway, railroad, and elevated) and 2000 (all public transportation), Social Explorer, accessed June 26, 2021.

except 'inexpensive to use,' where they are rated only slightly lower than auto." The "average CTA ratings relative to auto raises broad concern about the perceived quality of CTA service."[218] The agency responded to budget shortfalls and declining ridership, as in decades past, with deeper cuts. A significant recalibration of the entire system, for instance, led to damaging bus cutbacks in 1997: "Since 1986, the CTA had lost 30% of its riders, but reduced service only 4%." As in the past, the ax fell hardest on the more extensive surface lines, with fifteen bus routes eliminated and cuts to off-peak bus service on twenty-four of the forty-six key bus routes. Riders complained, but they had no leverage except to stop by their local auto dealership, which many did.[219]

Preserving more service and upgrading quality were options worth considering had CTA possessed the funds. However, demographic changes out of CTA's hands accelerated the cutback strategy. In 2019, the city of Chicago housed just 2.7 million people, down from 3.6 million in 1950. Chicago's 25 percent population loss from 1980 to 2017 was particularly worrisome for ridership.[220] The city's Black population shrank 32.9 percent from 1980 to 2017, dropping from 1,187,905 persons in 1980 to 797,253 in 2017.[221] The steep decline in the city's Black population, and a resifting of where Black families choose to live, was sad news for CTA. In 1989, for instance, a marketing study found that "Blacks are much more likely to use CTA (especially bus) while Whites are much likely to use auto, especially as a driver."[222] The city's aggressive redevelopment of public housing, *The Plan for Transformation*, has played a role in reducing the number of transit-dependent Black families residing near rapid transit lines. The replacement New Urbanist housing developments are mostly market rate and include lots of parking.[223]

Many Black families who stayed in the city bought cars or moved beyond the rapid and most extensive bus networks. According to Chicago's DOT, the result today is that many "have long commute times to work, greater than 40 minutes—one way." Residents of these outer neighborhoods are also likely spending a larger share of their income on transportation than many other families more centrally located.[224] CTA closed underutilized stations on the elevated line in Englewood, which lost 59.1 percent of its Black population between 1980 and 2017.[225] The 79 bus route on the primarily African American South Side, the most popular in the CTA system, declined from "8.5 million riders ten years ago to 5.6 million in 2018." CTA total bus ridership declined 26 percent from 2008 to 2018, dropping from 245 to 180 million riders.[226] Riders are likely tired of moving so slowly. In 2019, the average bus speed was just 9.1 miles per hour (vs. rail of 18.1).[227] By 2018, 48 percent of CTA riders rode the elevated, up from 36 percent in 1999, primarily thanks to losses of bus riders.[228]

The movement of Black families to the suburbs has equally bad results for regional transit ridership. When Black families move to the suburbs, they overwhelmingly abandon transit, likely based on negative perceptions of the system they leave behind. In 2018, for instance, 22 percent of Black regional commuters rode transit.[229] These ridership levels are higher than most of their white suburban neighbors, but who can blame most Black families for changing modes? Between 1996 and 2015, for instance, the region added over one thousand miles of new expressways and arterials.[230]

Changing residential patterns of Latino families is another challenge for regional transit agencies. The growth of the city's Latino population on the West and Near North Sides backfilled some of the city's population and ridership losses since the 1950s. Newcomers from Puerto Rico and Mexico in the postwar decades established new social and cultural institutions, attempted to resist West Side urban renewal, and were willing to live in run-down housing because they had no better options. Neighborhoods like Pilsen and Humboldt Park benefited from the vitality of Latino migrants who often used transit.[231]

The Latino population in Chicago remains large in 2019 (776,000 persons), making up 28 percent of the city's residents. However, a recent Transit Center research project finds that in Chicago, "transit provides less access to opportunities for Black and Latinx residents than other residents. Transportation and development patterns create longer transit trips to healthcare and food. Expensive fares put opportunity out of reach for some riders."[232] There are several factors behind these dreary facts. Gentrification of close-in areas like Humboldt Park, with good transit, has displaced many lower-income families. The rapid Latino migration from transit-rich central neighborhoods to outer city neighborhoods and suburbs like Cicero and Aurora will also create many more Latino drivers long term.[233] As in other cities like Atlanta and Los Angeles, many Latino families in the Chicago region have developed carpooling networks that efficiently service their specific travel needs.[234]

CTA has had some modest successes in the last few decades, such as the elevated southwest Orange Line (1997) to Midway airport, renovated rapid stations, new buses, and has expanded bus signal priority.[235] However, transit's overall share of city commuters between 1980 and 2018 sank from 32.4 to 26.1 percent, while city automobile commuters increased from 58.5 to 65.4 percent in the same period.[236] CTA has a limited ability to address these trend lines. Its mandatory high farebox recovery rate

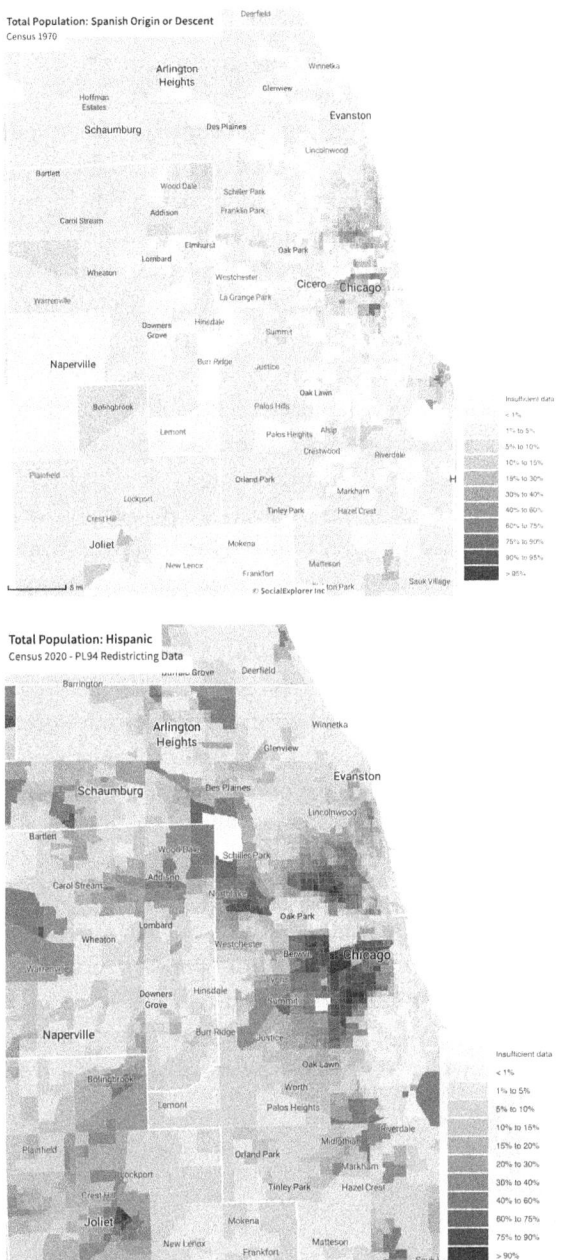

FIGURES 19A AND 19B. Latino immigrants were crucial to sustained CTA ridership in areas well served by transit on the Near West and North Sides (*upper map*). But the decentralization of the Latino population to areas barely served by transit threatens to undermine their ridership levels (*lower map*). Source: Hispanic or Latino, 1970/2020, Social Explorer, accessed June 26, 2021.

diverts most revenue to basic operations. In 2019, for instance, its rail farebox recovery of 49.6 percent was high compared to most peer agencies nationally. CTA is also dangerously underfunded on the capital side, with an estimated $18.9 billion in capital need. A considerable number of rail cars, for instance, have been kept in service beyond their projected lifespans. Complaints on both the bus and rail lines are up.[237]

The launching of the CTA in 1946 on a "pay as you go" model was widely praised at the time by fiscally conservative leaders. Yet CTA's self-supporting model, even with efficiencies from streetcar substitution, was unsustainable in an auto-centric, racially divided, and low-density region. Ridership fell but ultimately stabilized on modern elevated lines, but decades of fare increases and service cuts on the more comprehensive bus system accelerated ridership decline. Chicago demonstrated that American transit would fail to compete with cars absent deep subsidies.

The crucial role of density in transit operations also comes through powerfully in Chicago's story. The dispersed pattern of suburban living, where most Chicagoland residents, rich or poor, live today, makes it exceedingly difficult to provide transit outside the central city. In 2018, for instance, just 20 percent of regular commuters in the Chicago region living below the poverty line chose transit. If this growing working class in the suburbs lived and worked in suburban places better served and designed for transit efficiency, a large population might want to spend less on their automobiles.[238]

Chicago's transit history also points to the necessity of balancing transit and highway planning. Chicago was a leader in developing the country's first highway median rapid lines, but the experiment faltered thanks to lack of funding and suburban cooperation. CTA lost ridership for many reasons, but primarily because driving became a better option. City and state leaders who created an excellent highway network, lots of CBD parking, and widened streets knew exactly what they were doing.

CHAPTER 7

Detroit: Racism and America's Worst Big-City Transit

Detroit's terrifying urban decline has redefined the city's landscape, social structure, and image since the 1960s. The city has lost two-thirds of its population and most of its major industrial employers, the city government is in perpetual financial crisis, and nature has returned to abandoned neighborhoods. Living up to its reputation as the "Motor City," the city and region provide only limited mass transit service. In all of 2019, Detroit's public transit agency, the Detroit Department of Transportation (DDOT), carried just twenty-three million passengers; its suburban counterpart, Suburban Mobility Authority for Regional Transit (SMART), carried just 9.2 million passengers. These ridership numbers are no more than a rounding error in a region of four million people.[1] As a result, nearly everyone relies on private automobiles, regardless of social class or ethnic or racial identity. The remaining bus riders in Detroit, primarily people of color of limited means, struggle to get anywhere on what has been considered the worst of America's big-city public transit systems for decades.

What happened to Detroit's once-thriving public transit enterprise may be extreme. Yet there are striking parallels to service decline yesterday and today in other American cities.[2] The comprehensive shift nationally from private to public transit ownership in the 1960s and 1970s, associated with the beginning of federal transit funding, briefly raised hopes for a transit renaissance.[3] However, almost all cities ignored decades of funding and service problems in cities like Detroit and Chicago as they waded into public ownership. Detroit's public transit may be the worst in America, but not by much.

Progressive and Interwar Head Start

Detroit enjoyed many geographical attributes that might have worked to the advantage of both rail and automobiles in the long term. Detroit's five wide diagonal boulevards (Woodward, Michigan, Gratiot, Grand River, and Jefferson), central downtown, large industrial employers, a regular grid of compact homes, limited land regulation, and flat topography facilitated quick and inexpensive transit development. The growing streetcar network was vital to the city's growth, large factories, and the high quality of life of its emerging working and middle classes. Unfortunately for transit, many of the same factors that helped streetcars worked just as well for private automobiles. As local boy Henry Ford and other carmakers found ways to mass-produce cars for both the city and nation, the race was on for the future of the region's mobility.[4]

Detroit had a potential head start in creating a high-quality transit system that might have competed more effectively with motor cars. In the late nineteenth and early twentieth centuries, legendary Progressive-era reformer Hazen S. Pingree, first as Detroit's mayor (1890–97) then as governor (1897–1901), was a tireless advocate for publicly owned transit. He believed that municipal traction would free the city from the privately run Detroit City Railways (later Detroit United Railways, or DUR). Pingree thought that public transit was the natural extension of government from widely accepted public goods like parks and schools to "natural monopolies" such as waterworks, bridges, ports, and power generation. With the profit and corruption removed from street railways, and tax exemption granted to a new public operator, he believed that "public ownership of street railways would result in management at least as competent and efficient as private ownership." Instead of going into the pocket of investors or taxation, profits would be used to improve service and keep fares low for the city's working class.[5]

To finally gain acceptance of a municipal option took decades of activism. The state created the legal foundation for city-run transit in 1913, but a public system did not emerge until the 1920s. Mayor James J. Couzens, "the father of municipal ownership,"[6] a former auto executive turned municipal transit advocate, in 1921 put the DUR on the defensive with new municipal-owned lines, forced sales of DUR tracks, and onerous franchise restrictions and terminations. DUR investors in 1922 saw the handwriting on the wall and decided to sell their system to the city for $19.85 million.[7]

After the merger and purchase, the newly created Detroit Street Railway (DSR) of 1922 operated 1,457 streetcars on 363 miles of track with four thousand employees. Thanks to equipment orders previously placed by DUR, and new ones by DSR, Detroit residents enjoyed more modern streetcars in the 1920s than those living in many other cities that still lacked a public option.[8] Detroit's mayors controlled the DSR through the power to appoint members of the Detroit Street Railway Commission and the DSR general manager. The DSR raised fares modestly from five to six cents in 1923.[9] At this point, Detroit's modern public transit system had much in common with emerging public operations in San Francisco, New York, and Boston.

But there was a vital policy difference in Detroit that would lead to its departure from the top ranks of public transit. To gain broad voter and political support for public ownership, always a challenge in general ballot measures concerning transit, officials included a provision in the city charter banning any public subsidy of the new publicly owned DSR. As a result, all DSR's operations and capital funds had to be generated from the farebox. Nor was the DSR, as encouraged by early advocates like Pingree, tax exempt despite its public functions and regulations. Taxes diverted revenue from both operations and modernization financing. These poison pills, reflecting an extremely narrow view of the costs and benefits of transit to urban vitality, would do lasting damage to the long-term prospects of mass transit in Detroit. DSR, for instance, missed the city's major splurge on capital improvements in the 1920s and early 1930s. The City of Detroit ran up $299.9 million by 1933 in bond debt for various public improvements, just not a rapid or mass transit system.[10]

Detroit's working class continued to fill DSR streetcars in the 1920s despite the growing popularity of cars in the Motor City. Streetcars still delivered large numbers of workers rapidly to the large auto plants scattered around the city like the vertical Highland Park Ford Motor Company factory. The DSR would also provide massive amounts of streetcar service to Ford's new River Rouge complex where by 1930 DSR carried 110,000 workers daily on seven car lines, making 165 peak hour trips. DSR was saving these major manufacturers the cost of developing vast parking lots and reducing car congestion around the plants. The DSR in the 1920s added thirty-eight miles of streetcar lines citywide, focusing on unprofitable crosstown service lacking under DUR management. Most DSR route extensions of the time, according to *Motor Coach Age*, were "under 2 miles long . . . but they served a vital purpose—namely, to bring reliable transportation to developing districts and thus to help convince the public that the DSR was working in its best interest." In sum, DSR was still crucial to center-city industry, emerging suburban-style areas, and overcrowded central neighborhoods.[11]

DSR leadership and most politicians in the 1920s kept their distance from comprehensive plans initially developed by a Rapid Transit Commission in 1926. Detroit was fourth in population nationally, 1.242 million people, yet stood alone among big cities for the absence of rapid transit. The promoters of rapid lines sought a center-city subway and regional rapid transit "along the superhighways outside the congested City areas." The first four subways and rapid lines, 46.7 miles, designated for the "built up parts of the city," would run mostly in tunnels. The first phase would cost $187 million for construction (and $287 million for complete build), to be funded out of property taxes on owners near the new station (51 percent of the costs), direct city contributions (17 percent), and fares (32 percent). Fares, the plan promised, would cover operating and interest costs on equipment purchase, a key potential selling point to a skeptical public. Through these means, the commission envisioned a "pay as you go" method of financing a system to meet "the 15-mile city of the future." In 1924 and 1925, voters had already endorsed the outlines of the rapid transit financing plan.[12]

However, public support rapidly slipped away from the rapid transit plan, likely related to the accelerating 1920s decentralization trend. The *Detroit Free Press* in 1926 observed that the "sustained exodus to the suburbs . . . has been brought about through development of the automobile and the desire to get away from the congestion."[13] Suburban mayors theoretically desired subways to relieve traffic, but "they were almost unanimously opposed to the method of levying taxes and assessments to pay for the subway," calling planned taxes "excessive."[14] Detroit city councillors also disliked the taxation required, and even DSR "officials are understood to be opposed to subways" given their investments in streetcars.[15]

Objections multiplied, and the vote was delayed for years. Politicians predictably charged the commission with wasting public money on a plan "of which it cannot make any possible use at the present time."[16] Among those still supporting the subway plan's approval in a referendum in 1929 were Mayor John C. Lodge, good government advocates, and downtown interests like the department store Hudson's. It might surprise that the automobile industry was also pro-rapid transit. Rapid supporters Edsel B. Ford, president of Ford Motor; the president of Packard Motor Car; and the vice presidents of the Chrysler Corporation and Hudson Motor Car Company likely still saw many benefits to be had in rapid transit freeing up road space for cars and delivering workers to their massive factories.[17] The city's population in April of 1929 nevertheless voted 72 percent against a modified, more economical plan ($54 million).[18] "The people of this city," explained former mayor John W. Smith, rejected the "absurd" plan because they wanted "better transportation and they want it by rubber."[19]

During the lead-up to the vote, DSR managers set about speeding up streetcar service on major diagonal lines. Their effort aimed to discredit the subway plan by showing that faster streetcar lines, paired potentially with future short downtown tunnels ("dips"), would be more economical and equally effective as expensive and longer subways. Express streetcar service DSR added in 1927 on rebuilt tracks on Jefferson Avenue, for instance, ran faster than average thanks to many fewer stops. Buses waiting at key stops provided connecting local service. The streetcars under this system, which DSR officials promised would cut travel time from the far eastern sections by half, could now move sixteen to eighteen miles per hour. Early riders were two to one in favor, and one patron who missed his stop admitted: "that the car went so fast he had not realized that he had passed his street." The DSR manager promised that the arrangement made it possible "to maintain as speedy a service on the surface as that of a subway" with favorable average speeds to New York's local subway. The initial success of the new system made DSR consider extending "express service 10 miles past the city limits" per the city charter.[20]

The DSR express streetcar effort helped undermine support for rapid transit but proved fleeting. The unsubsidized DSR could not make express service pay at that time on Jefferson or Grand River Avenue routes and thus discontinued the service after just a few years. DSR's requirement to cover both its capital and operating costs limited long-term investment like this despite their inventiveness, popularity, and future promise. DSR more successfully adopted buses in the 1920s, with the first runs in 1925. Public bus service took advantage of paved streets and new automotive technology; DSR bus lines also competed well with jitneys and the privately run Detroit Motor Bus. But there were limits to maintaining even high-quality bus service. DSR added deluxe service on some routes like Woodward, but the Depression wiped out that service.[21]

As in so many other cities, elected officials worked at cross-purposes to the aims of mass transit. The city was awash in private jitneys by the 1920s, who openly stole riders from even the most popular streetcar routes. City officials, however, took their time in reigning in the service despite now running a public transit system dependent on fares. In 1921, for instance, there were 490 licensed jitneys on the Woodward route alone, the most popular streetcar route, and 1,424 in the city. City officials did not ban jitneys from the streets entirely until 1928, undercutting the effectiveness and revenue of the DSR service in the years that jitneys operated.[22]

Individual autos and taxis, in any case, were quickly becoming a much bigger threat than jitneys. A 1925 center-city traffic survey by the Rapid Transit Commission found that "passenger automobiles and taxicabs now constitute 92% of the vehicles engaged in passenger transportation" even though they carried "only 26% of the peak hour passengers." The "collective transportation facilities" (streetcars, buses, and jitneys) were only 8 percent of total vehicles but carried 74 percent of passengers. The commission warned that streets would be "utterly inadequate . . . if the majority of automobile owners chose to use them to travel to and from work during the rush hours."[23]

The city's leaders, despite these warnings, were more creative and proactive in dealing with the tidal wave of cars than adapting streetcar or transit service for the modern age. While the Rapid Transit Commission had envisioned median rapid transit in "super-highways," the city had already taken significant steps to upgrade the road network. Grand Boulevard, for instance, had been progressively developed as a "broad, landscaped avenue" running in a eleven-mile parkway belt around the city center. As a result, by the 1920s the boulevard had become "one of the most important traffic arteries of the city."[24] City and suburban leaders invested deeply and widely in paved surfaces and street widenings, like Michigan Avenue, to make automobiles work that much better for everyday life. The city was early to adopt traffic-control measures such as stop signs, streetlights, crosswalks, and one-way streets. Such upgrades aided the growing bus service but were negative factors for streetcars.[25]

DSR, like all transit companies, experienced significant losses in the Great Depression. In either cars or transit, fewer Detroit residents headed to the CBD during the Depression.[26] The way DSR managed its problems showed both the possibility and peril of the city's form of unsubsidized transit. Streetcar revenues cratered, dropping from $22 million in 1926 to $10 million in 1933. Because the city's charter prevented any transit subsidization, managers had to find economies and generate revenues. Fares in 1935, for instance, rose to ten cents, a questionable move during an economic crisis.[27]

The DSR, under the guidance of General Manager Fred A. Nolan (starting in 1935), aggressively pioneered public sector streetcar substitution by motor buses during the Great Depression. Nolan benefited from the talent in automotive design in the region. He worked with Ford Motor to develop a cheap, small gas bus with interchangeable parts to reduce maintenance costs. By 1938, DSR had 1,100 of these Fords in service and promptly ordered 1,100 more between 1939 and 1943. The small new buses delivered significant labor savings (one-person operation versus two for streetcars) and the typical reduction in streetcar capital costs.[28]

The success of the bus program in terms of economy encouraged rapid substitution but did not necessarily mean loss of service. DSR set a general policy in the late 1930s that buses replaced streetcars on nights and Sundays except for a few major routes and made some line conversions but maintained most of DSR's total mileage. By 1942, DSR had replaced twenty-five million miles of streetcar service with bus service and reduced streetcars from 1,600 (1934) to 908. Nolan planned to have all streetcars gone by 1953 and made no orders for new rail equipment.[29] Detroit's creation of a massive fleet of high-quality Ford buses was pioneering and demonstrated the possibility of high-quality, low-cost bus transit service.

DSR was innovative, but it was already clear that the challenges were more profound than just a national Depression. Decentralization by car, and loss of center-city vitality, dominated interwar development. Auto company headquarters left downtown during this period, and Detroit missed the typical 1920s downtown office boom. Between 1925 and 1940, the city experienced a 16 percent decline in CBD-bound traffic. And the traffic that remained was rapidly shifting to cars. By 1930, 33.8 percent of CBD traffic moved in automobiles versus 21.9 percent in Chicago.[30] Employers like Ford and GM sought out low taxes and cheap land for massive, one-story plants with free parking in the suburbs that could be better accessed by cars.[31] By 1944, about half of all of Detroit's manufacturing capacity had relocated beyond the city line. Due to changes in state law, Detroit failed to annex its booming suburbs after 1926.[32]

City and federal officials prioritized better roads that facilitated auto-based suburbanization overall. New Deal–era work projects, like the widening of Woodward Avenue, were undertaken without a vision for transit efficiency. According to *Motor Coach Age*, "No provision was made south of Six Mile ... to segregate the car tracks as had been done north of there, so that when private auto traffic later increased, congestion was just as bad as it had been before the street was widened." A 1938 WPA subway plan fell through.[33]

City leaders failed to use the emerging planning powers to help transit during the interwar decades. Dense neighborhoods with multifamily units in central city areas had developed near transit thanks to laissez-faire development, speculation, and overcrowding. The city during the interwar years continued to permit mostly unregulated sprawl within newly annexed areas. Developers focused on lower-density development popular with the automobile-owning public. Historian Thomas Sugrue writes that "the vast amount of open land available within the city's boundaries" reduced density citywide compared to many of its peers. By the 1940s, "there were many white Detroits," including lush neighborhoods of executives, "modest" neighborhoods for mid-level workers, and "innumerable blue-collar neighborhoods" filled with "small bungalows, most of frame construction, some of brick, crowded together" on small lots (twenty-five by one hundred feet).[34]

Detroit's zoning code, approved in 1941, underlined this existing and developing pattern of development in this self-styled "City of Homes." The ordinance allowed for only thin strips of businesses along active streetcar lines like Gratiot and Grand Avenues in the newly developed residential districts further out. Behind these stores were many square miles of lower-density residential neighborhoods, many with plenty of off-street parking. The zoning ordinance allocated "77.3 percent of the city's total area for residential use. Of the 67.58 square miles set aside for this purpose, 43.08 square miles are zoned for one-family dwellings, 19.55 square miles are zoned for two-family dwellings, and 4.94 square miles for multiple dwellings."[35] A Detroit of freestanding homes was not altogether unfit for transit, as density was much higher in Detroit's tightly packed working-class districts than in a typical American suburb today. But given the lower density levels now fixed by the government, the notion of "pay as you go" transit in the future, when wartime restrictions eased, was dubious.

Race was a crucial factor in decentralization both within the city and in its rapidly growing suburbs. The region's African American population mostly lived within the city of Detroit, 149,119 (9 percent of the city's total population) by 1940.[36] As a result of housing and employment discrimination, Detroit's rapidly growing African American population, crammed into areas north of the CBD and east of Woodward, endured overcrowded and substandard conditions. Racial conflict, much of it concerning the attempt by whites to stop Black migration from the worst ghettos, overflowed in a race riot in 1943 that led to the killing of twenty-nine African Americans. However, Mayor Edward Jeffries (1940–48) dragged his feet responding to the riot; city leaders continued to support segregated housing, most visibly in the public housing program then developing.[37]

The tensions on streetcars reached a crisis level during the war years and contributed to postwar white flight from transit. Historian Sarah Frohardt-Lane believes "contact between blacks and whites on public transit exacerbated existing racial tensions. . . . Passengers routinely interpreted unpleasant interactions on public transit in racialized ways, causing numerous fights between blacks and whites and negatively shaping their ideas about one another." DSR's hiring of Black operators during the war, out of necessity rather than an enlightened attitude, challenged racial dividing lines as "whites began to see the increasing presence of black operators and passengers as a sign that whites were losing control of public transportation." The number of conflicts increased during the war and became an everyday feature of police reports. During the war, a poll of white Detroiters found that, despite the northern location, "58 percent of white Detroiters surveyed wanted the city's buses and streetcars to be racially segregated."[38] Many whites would leave behind integrated city transit and neighborhoods as soon as possible.

The suburbs pursued segregation methods as they welcomed white ethnics fleeing diversifying neighborhoods. Dearborn, home to Ford's new headquarters and River Rouge plant, grew from just 2,470 inhabitants in 1920 to 63,589 in 1940, mostly in single-family homes.[39] The political leadership of Dearborn remained adamantly opposed to integrated housing and openly maintained the city as a "sundown" town. Almost no African American families moved into Dearborn at this time. Dearborn's segregationist suburban approach was typical in the region, with most suburbs housing less than 1 percent African American residents.[40] Extreme segregation would have dire consequences for the region's future and mass transit.

As in most American cities, the war was the last hurrah for mass transit. Wartime rubber, fuel, and vehicle production limits delayed additional substitution plans like the Grand River line. Streetcars were put back into full service and jammed with passengers. In 1945, DSR transported 493 million total riders on 900 streetcars over 426 miles of routes and on 1,900 buses over 990 route miles.[41] DSR was profitable from 1941 to 1944 thanks to the wartime boom. Yet losses that started in 1945 looked likely to increase in future years. DSR had financed its losses in the bad years using high-interest, short-term debt. Wages had also increased for workers. The streetcar fare, at six cents, had not changed since 1923. To lose money at the peak of ridership was an ominous sign. As in other cities, many worried that "there is a danger passenger volume may fall off when the automobile industry begins to satisfy its market."[42] The pessimists were right to be worried.

The Nowicki Wrecking Machine, 1948–61

Within Detroit's political class, there remained some support for retention and modernization of the remaining car lines in the postwar period.

However, rail supporters failed to comprehend that maintenance of lines required more than just farebox collections and strong words in a time of massive postwar ridership losses and low-density sprawl. The result of failing to subsidize transit was an overreliance on the belt-tightening approach of DSR general manager Leo Nowicki, who, in full view of the public and politicians, aggressively dissected and reduced the system to a fraction of its former glory during his long term in office.

In the immediate postwar years, buses replaced streetcars on nighttime routes again, larger buses entered service, and politicians made more concessions to cars. The City of Dearborn, for instance, had wanted streetcars off its streets in 1940, and by 1947 they were gone.[43] The ease with which the Detroit City Council acceded to replacing the Grand River streetcar line in 1947 reflects the shallowness of support for transit. At first, the council was skeptical about the benefits of bus substitution on such an essential diagonal route in the city. They permitted only a trial run of buses on Grand River to "give the DSR a chance to prove its claims that without streetcars it can provide faster, more comfortable and more economical service."[44] The council even insisted that safety zones and streetcar tracks had to stay until after the experiment.

However, as in so many other cities, powerful voices remained pro-substitution—even without NCL anywhere in sight. Mayor Edward Jeffries believed, for instance, that "after the busses have been running for 48 hours no one will want to return to the street cars."[45] The *Detroit Free Press* also believed the trial run would win "public support" and facilitate "switch-over on other lines."[46] The DSR replaced sixty-four streetcars with 125 new coaches,[47] and within a few months claimed that the Grand River experiment led to an eight-minute improvement on evening runs.[48] The council, which had no financial leverage over the DSR and a limited stomach for conflict, signed off on the permanent removal.

Councilman, and later mayor (1948–50), Eugene Van Antwerp was a rail supporter, including the possibility of rapid subway or elevated lines. Yet his influence was limited to his short term as mayor. His appointment of Leo Nowicki as DSR general manager in March of 1948 also reflected the weakness of even the strongest transit supporters like Van Antwerp. Nowicki, a city councilman, construction engineer, and a powerful former lieutenant governor who "never has been associated with a transportation company," was committed both to streetcar substitution and budget cutting.[49] So while Nowicki ordered 106 PCC cars, per Mayor Van Antwerp's direction, bus conversion continued apace for remaining lines like Michigan and Gratiot.[50] Nowicki endorsed wholeheartedly the notion that the DSR should pay its way, requiring that fares go up and service down to meet anticipated ridership losses and rising labor costs. In 1948, for instance, a fare increase to thirteen cents contributed to 2 to 6 percent losses of riders on routes, leading Nowicki to call for even more "economizing" to meet reduced demand. Nowicki led the DSR until 1961 and maintained an unswerving devotion to economizing, with devastating impacts on riders.[51]

Nowicki admittedly faced some unique challenges in maintaining an even financial keel and sustained ridership. The city was lower density than many others, and the city sprawled outward thanks to few geographical barriers. As the home of the American auto industry, the dominance of private cars was predictable. The average Detroiter rode transit just 213 times a year, fewer than in Chicago (270), Philadelphia (356), and Toronto (445).[52] Indeed, by 1948, there were "more people in Detroit who use their own cars than any other city in the United States" for commuting. However, Mayor Van Antwerp promised to "remove the stigma that we have the worst transportation system of any large city in the United States." Yet most riders had either resigned themselves to the increases or were planning to switch to autos. As one rider put it: "I don't care anyway. I'm getting a new car soon and it'll be cheaper to drive my own car than pay 13 cents for a bus ride." Maybe not, because drivers even today underestimate the total daily cost of relying on their cars, but that belief was typical.[53]

In 1948, Mayor Van Antwerp proposed a DSR subsidy to reduce the financial problems and maintain low fares but failed to gain broad support from the council. There were also the legal limits on subsidies that would have required a citywide vote on charter reform.[54] By 1948, the DSR had piled up $32 million in debt and had difficulty paying its electric and pension bills. Mayor Van Antwerp admitted that the system he inherited was "broke, head over heels in debt" and operating at a loss for more than a year. His inability to secure subsidies left DSR in Nowicki's hands.[55]

Nowicki initiated cuts to service in the fall of 1948 as part of a plan to find $1.8 million in savings. These cuts came in the shadow of a fare increase that managers knew would drive away riders even without service reduction. Buses replaced streetcars on five additional lines,[56] and riders had access to much less service at nonpeak times. The union reported that the system had lost 12–15 percent of service over the previous year.[57] Nowicki defended cutting service to match declining ridership even though a city councilman pointed out "that the decrease in service has driven passengers away and encouraged them to use their own cars."[58] Pressure for another fare increase due to financial stress was debated in 1950. A new mayor, Albert E. Cobo (1950–57), initially wanted "to see what these economies will do,"[59] but by April, signed off on a fare increase to fifteen cents.[60] Initial surplus revenue, thanks to higher fares and more economies,[61] could not prevent losses in the fiscal year 1950–51 of $2.7 million.[62]

Not only was the system rapidly losing riders, but like all postwar systems, its revenues failed to keep pace with generous labor deals. The labor problem had set in almost immediately at the war's end. A strike in April 1946 had the secondary effect of demonstrating the fragility of transit as former riders crowded into each other's cars. Some found that cars offered quicker and more comfortable commutes.[63] The high labor cost also incentivized the rapid removal of the streetcar lines as two-person cars remained a bulwark of union job protection, as was typical nationally.[64] In 1947, reflecting continuing conflict, 1,600 maintenance workers walked off their jobs.[65] Thanks to generous contracts designed to keep workers appeased, by 1950, sixty-eight cents of each dollar collected went to employees, 63.91 cents for current labor costs, and 4.25 cents for pensions.[66]

The relatively generous packages did not prevent a prolonged strike over wages in 1951 of 3,100 DSR employees, shutting the whole transit system down for fifty-nine days.[67] The settlement in June of 1951, according to the *Detroit Free Press*, probably came too late to help many who depended upon transit: "How much the stores and businesses of Detroit suffered, especially in the downtown area, is anybody's guess. And who can set a price on the inconvenience and tax costs to which thousands of people were put?"[68] The paper believed that DSR "may never recover completely from last week's strike" because, as was the case in earlier years, passengers "found other means of getting to work" and a "substantial number of them never will return to the streetcars and buses." Twenty-four hours into the strike, the worst auto traffic snarls had cleared as commuters adjusted their schedules and shared rides. They could look forward to even better driving in just a few years: "Once the expressways are opened up . . . Driving time, for many of them, will be cut in half. It will be safer, speedier and more comfortable to drive their own cars than to take a DSR bus or streetcar." DSR's staff were getting excellent wages, but at what price to riders and the prospects of transit as a whole?[69] The DSR, for instance, used the 1951 strike as another justification for labor cost reductions through the conversion of streetcars to larger buses now available from GM.[70]

Labor costs primarily continued to drive fare increases in the 1950s. In 1952, for instance, DSR raised the fare to twenty cents even though the company expected to lose fourteen million riders. This was the fifth increase since World War II.[71] In 1953, the DSR reported that "while income has risen, the number of people actually riding DSR buses and streetcars has declined." So, while the higher fares juiced annual reports, they also discouraged system use.[72] Between 1945 and 1954, DSR lost money annually seven times.[73] Nothing much had changed by 1959 at the DSR: "Being a publicly-owned utility, it has been subjected to many pressures for high wages and fringe benefits which have not always been economically justified." For example, by the late 1950s, DSR had as many pensioners as active workers.[74]

Economies, required by the lack of subsidies, were the death knell of streetcars. The plans for the final replacement of even the more popular streetcar lines reflect the thin support for quality service. In 1954, for instance, the *Detroit Free Press* reported that "some 39,000 daily riders on the Jefferson line have been getting exceptionally good and frequent service from the 40 modern streetcars now being used." Trams arrived every 1.5 minutes during peak hours, five minutes off-peak, and eight minutes in the evenings: "Few bus lines offer such fast service." Despite higher total operating costs than buses, "the Jefferson line is a moneymaker for the DSR. A large majority of the patrons, gathered from the relatively densely populated neighborhoods nearby, apparently are satisfied and fear that a change may bring less service." Yet Nowicki was eager for substitution of streetcars with larger GM coaches offering seats for fifty-one riders. Removing Jefferson's streetcars would enable easier turns for automobiles and a "speedup of general traffic" once the streetcars and safety islands were gone. DSR would also achieve long-term savings incurred by the "costly maintenance of overhead power lines and double tracks." DSR would have had to spend $1.6 million to repair the tracks on the line if streetcar service remained. Nowicki claimed that "the major factor is the huge cost of rebuilding the tracks and repairing the overhead. Many critics fail to take this into consideration." He countered that "riders on the Jefferson line are protesting something they haven't yet tried. Once they get used to these buses they'll never want streetcars back."[75]

While some Jefferson riders "objected to the substitution," Nowicki and city officials ignored them.[76] Mayor Cobo approved the plan on a trial basis.[77] Nowicki, in early 1954, took rapid action to substitute the buses on Jefferson and quickly branded the change a "success" with more customers riding buses in the first three weeks than once used streetcars. The initial robust bus service offered, while not maintained for long, was a factor in public acceptance.[78] Given the successful removal of the Jefferson line, Nowicki targeted the Gratiot and Woodward lines for removal; they too were gone by 1956. The DSR sold many of the still serviceable PCC streetcars to Mexico City, providing reliable service for many more decades. Had federal or state subsidies for transit arrived in the 1950s, it seems likely that these trunk lines would have been retained and upgraded.[79]

The declining position of the DSR and the loss of higher-quality streetcar service as one price of economy prompted debates about either tax relief or direct subsidy, but as in so many other cities, leaders and voters refused to take these steps to aid transit. Management failure was often cited as a reason to withhold support. In 1951, one DSR critic claimed, "there is something radically wrong with a big transit outfit like the DSR when it can't make money." DSR, after all, "has a ready market of twenty-five or thirty million assured customers a month. It has a low priced product to offer... and it has no organized competition." The "quality of management" was, therefore, to blame rather than the weak financial structure.[80] In one clever full-page photographic feature in the *Free Press*, reporters tried to deflect blame for the financial problems to leadership by highlighting DSR hypocrisy. Nowicki "took his warm comfortable drive from his Outer Drive home" on a fourteen-minute route to a parking spot just ten feet from his office door instead of a cold walk and two bus transfers taking thirty-one minutes.[81]

Tax exemption, which might have restored millions to the DSR's bottom line, was rejected based on concerns about mismanagement. In 1953, for instance, DSR paid $1.5 million in city and suburban taxes (where lines extended beyond the city line), but legislators refused to budge.[82] In 1957, the *Free Press* almost came out for subsidy and tax relief, as "transportation falls into the same category as community health service, water or any other vital utility." DSR, however, was then "among the fifteen largest taxpayers in the City of Detroit." If the city decreased the agency's taxes, "general taxpayers" would have to pick up the slack.[83] Editorialists also worried about "rank discrimination against the people of Detroit unless the suburbs also agreed to waive their taxes."[84] In 1958, an anti–tax relief advertisement reminded voters that "when the city took over private transit lines, it was clearly provided in the city charter that the DSR should pay its own way."[85] Voters rejected tax relief in 1958. There always seemed to be more reasons to resist subsidies or tax exemptions than to endorse them.[86]

The DSR's founding documents from 1921 had come to haunt it. Nowicki and other DSR officials "pretty well agreed that there is only one way to go—downward in already skeleton service, and upward in prices." Nowicki knew that either DSR had to collect "money out of the farebox to pay our way, or adjust service where patronage is lacking, or both." By the late 1950s, the impact was visible to observers. Reporters discovered that the DSR headquarters in 1958 looked "more like a morgue than the nerve center of a huge transit system." DSR had reduced the total head count by a third in just a few years. Remaining riders, now paying more per ride, were getting less: "Service schedules have been sliced so far on many lines that further economies would leave no coaches operating at all. Riding is way down." When buses finally showed up, they were usually "worn-out coaches" whose life was primarily extended for "bookkeeping purposes." One in four coaches was considered "worthless," and half of the 1,331 bus fleet "should be retired and replaced in the next year." But there was no funding to do so.[87]

DSR's numbers looked as bad as its offices and buses. Ridership in 1958–59 was down to 147.5 million, compared to 492 million in 1944–45.[88] Nowicki had reduced debt by more than half,[89] but DSR devoted 13 percent of its gross annual revenue for pensions for three thousand retired employees thanks to generous labor contracts typical in the public sector.[90] In 1959, responding to the continuing financial crisis, DSR raised the fare to twenty-five cents, drilling hard for gold into its remaining ridership.[91] DSR profits rose after the fare increase, but passenger volume sank 11 percent lower year over year thanks, in part, to the fare hike.[92]

Under Nowicki's leadership from 1948 to 1961, the system lost 75 percent of its ridership, dropping from 440 million (1947) to just 117 million (1961) revenue passengers. The amount of equipment also decreased from 847 streetcars and 2,272 buses in 1947 to just 1,153 buses and 54 trolley coaches in 1961.[93] In 1948, 435,000 residents came to the CBD on an average weekday, and two out of three did so on a DSR vehicle, then primarily streetcars. By 1960, just 343,000 made the same trip, and just one of three on DSR's bus fleet.[94] It was well known in 1961 that "DSR offers poor service."[95]

Nowicki's legacy looks even worse when viewed through the lens of race. Like all postwar transit managers in the north, Nowicki avoided discussing riders' changing racial identity, and DSR did not publish statistics by race. However, the 1960 census, which for the first time included mass transit ridership, makes clear that whites had mostly abandoned transit under his leadership. The neighborhoods with a higher African American population, primarily those with higher density, had much higher bus ridership. Some areas had as high as 40 percent of bus commuters.[96] Both the declining mass mobility within the city center and the lack of transit to suburban locations would negatively impact the occupational horizon of Detroit's growing nonwhite population. Nowicki also followed a pattern of hiring discrimination that limited African American workers to the lower rungs of the ladder. The total share of Black workers at the DSR

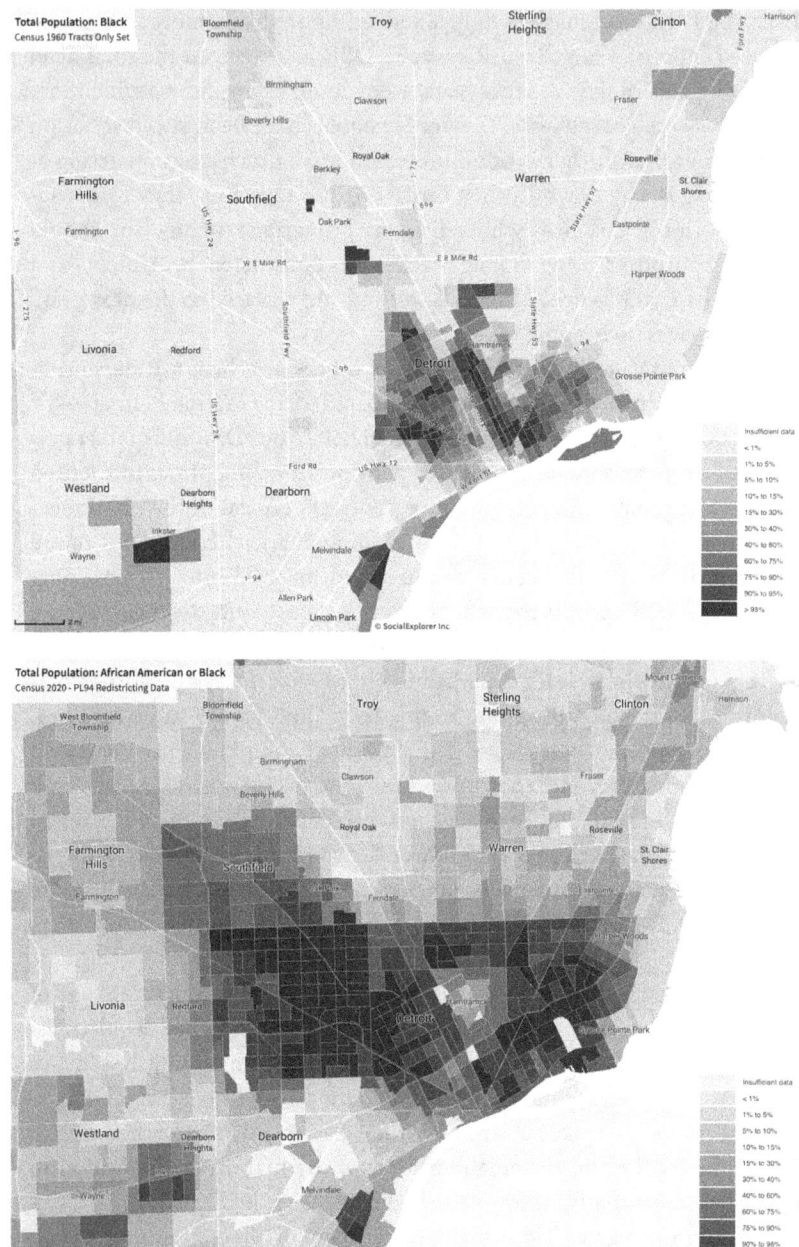

FIGURES 20A AND 20B. In 1960 the city's Black community was moving beyond the most restricted areas. Today, many Black families have left Detroit, and transit, for auto-centric suburbs. Source: Black, 1960/2020, Social Explorer, accessed June 26, 2021.

was much higher in Detroit than in Boston and many other cities, thanks to more desirable private-sector factory work. However, Black workers were stuck in place. In 1964, for instance, 51 percent of employees were Black, but only 3 percent of them worked in managerial roles.[97]

Postwar Planning: Highways, Urban Renewal, and Rapid Transit

The postwar troubles of transit cannot be blamed entirely on Nowicki. DSR subsisted on an unsustainable gruel of fares during Nowicki's years while Detroit's leaders simultaneously financed ambitious highway plans and destructive urban renewal programs. These projects robbed transit of riders, made the transit system slower than driving, and disrupted the areas best served by transit. Redevelopment of the downtown also ignored opportunities for leveraging the major transit routes for dense linear development. City leaders and powerful elites also spent years and much effort on "pie in the sky" rapid transit programs while neglecting to fund the existing mass transit in the city.

By 1947, the city had committed to plans for 107 miles of expressways that would supposedly end congestion.[98] For the first sections of the John C. Lodge and Edsel Ford Expressways, the city provided $5.6 million, Wayne County $5.6 million, the state $11.2 million, and the federal government $18.5 million. The two expressways became part of a twenty-seven-year build-out for a planned comprehensive "high-speed traffic" network that was a transit killer. The city even planned to build a parking garage for seven hundred cars under Washington Boulevard "to help solve Detroit's critical parking problem."[99]

Drivers benefited from much more than just highways and parking. The city by 1954 had added three miles of one-way streets and 120 traffic signals,[100] and found millions for grade separations, street widenings, and other roadway improvements. Mayor Albert Cobo, for instance, wanted $3.3 million in additional funds for street improvements in his 1954–55 budget.[101] Elected officials simply followed the trend lines of the people they represented. For instance, car registration in Wayne County increased 100.2 percent from 1945 to 1960.[102] Even DSR transit employees in 1954 wanted more parking space at the Gilbert Terminal for the cars they drove to work.[103] Highways drew away riders and sometimes directly undermined service for those transit riders who remained. The creation of the Edsel Ford Expressway required disruption in a streetcar line. DSR cited the lack of overpasses for streetcars over the Lodge Expressway as a factor in deciding for bus conversions.[104]

The city's fifteen-year urban highway plan by 1954 envisioned seven expressways of 105 miles, with the federal government expected to pay about half of the billion-dollar total. The City of Detroit, which often sold bonds to fund its share, would pay only one-eighth of the total bill after the state and county covered the rest. The local enthusiasm for highways can be explained, as in other cities, in part by such intergovernmental largess.[105] Even the *Detroit Free Press* in 1956 had to admit that "new expressways, street widenings, and the parking problem receive almost exclusive attention."[106]

The impact of highways on the city center and transit was profound, especially when combined with car-friendly urban renewal projects. Not only were neighborhoods subject to permanent noise, barriers, and pollution due to highways, but their construction led to community distress and, in some cases, greater isolation. By 1973, city officials and private interests had paved over 74 percent of Detroit's CBD to aid the movement and parking of cars. Detroit's freeway system had swallowed 2,600 acres of land by this point. Removing so much property from the rolls reduced tax revenues by $149 million in value, or $10 million in value per year.[107] The expressways also displaced about nine thousand primarily Black families.[108]

Car-centric urban renewal of the CBD and surrounding neighborhoods, some of the denser in the region, also cut into the potential ridership of DSR. Detroit was early to the urban redevelopment game with the Detroit Plan (1947) providing $1.5 million of its general funds for slum clearance. With the creation of a federal urban renewal program in 1949, costs for slum clearance shifted to the federal Title I program. As in other cities, the aim in Detroit was to answer suburban flight with pods of middle-income development that would draw people back to the center. City leaders, for instance, cleared a dense, mixed-use area of 129 acres in the Gratiot area in the early 1950s, including 1,950 African American families living in 910 structures. Overcrowded or dilapidated units may have offended reformers' sensibilities but were excellent for transit. The Lafayette Park (1959) development that replaced the neighborhood offered a car-friendly, low-density mix of towers, town houses, open fields, and parking areas—right next to downtown.[109] Displacement for urban renewal and highways hurt the city's higher-density, transit-riding areas and the African American population. Lafayette Park pioneered racial integration, but many more nonwhite families were removed than replaced.

In the decades that followed, many more disruptive redevelopment projects in or near the downtown, including expanding Wayne State University and the Detroit Medical Center, replaced comparatively dense, mixed-use Black areas near transit with single-use, car-centric environments. According to June Manning Thomas, nonwhite families bore 85 percent of the impact for postwar urban renewal; and many small businesses never recovered. The city built only a few public housing projects and provided inadequate relocation support. By 1962, she estimates that about 160,000 African Americans had been negatively impacted by the various redevelopment and highway projects. The areas targeted had higher proportions of riders, long-established lines, and greater population density. Between 1960 and 1967 alone, the city knocked down 25,927 dwellings as part of continuing clearance for urban renewal, highways, school development, and abandonment.[110] Detroit leaders were so devoted to these policies that they even cleared Poletown in 1981 to make way for a GM plant. The 465 acres cleared had "contained 1,500 homes, 144 businesses and 16 churches." A less dense city center, and one less favorable to transit, resulted from destructive multidecade public policy choices.[111]

The creation of a highway network that outperformed the streetcar and bus lines, and destructive downtown redevelopment, did not undermine the faith of all transit supporters. Unfortunately, as in other cities, civic leaders could never warm to buses and continued to dream of high-tech, heavy-rail solutions. Indeed, the dream of high-speed rail was an old one in the city. Like those in every American city, Detroit's leaders had devoted energy, if not resources, to plans for rapid transit in the early twentieth century.[112] City leaders ignored additional rapid transit plans created in 1923, 1924, 1926, 1929, 1932, 1941, and 1942. In 1944, for instance, transit consultants had made "a large, slick-paper report on an expressway and transit system." But the DSR promptly "threw this report out the window in 1945" and focused on bus substitution.[113]

Postwar, ambitious transit plans remained unmet. The influential Engineering Society of Detroit in 1946 came out against the DSR's postwar bus substitution plan. It recommended that the city and state reserve space inside expressways for "high-capacity, publicly operated rapid-transit rail service." They promised that a transit mall in expressways could carry five times the passengers as buses in regular lanes.[114] The city planning commission in 1947 also called for "center mall facilities for eventual rapid transit" in the Edsel Ford Expressway, as did Mayor Van Antwerp. Yet, the city council, state highway officials, and DSR rejected the proposal.[115] According to state highway officials, a sixty-foot center parkway for future rapid transit would delay construction and cost $1.3 million a mile to build.[116] The state highway commissioner reminded median transit supporters that "he knew of no way that State money for highways could be used to pay for a rapid-transit system for Detroit."[117]

DSR leadership consistently bad-mouthed rapid transit even though it could have complemented their bus system: "All previous reports submitted by the DSR have opposed rapid transportation."[118] DSR general manager Richard Sullivan believed that rail would prove "too costly for the DSR, and would require tax subsidies."[119]

Rapid transit, die-hard supporters believed, might be the key to getting back some of the shoppers and workers otherwise sticking to the suburbs. The *Detroit Free Press*, reflecting downtown interests, consistently endorsed high-speed rail over the years while resisting subsidies for bus and streetcar transit: "Rapid transit, in our opinion, is the desirable solution to Detroit's faltering public transportation system."[120] Detroit's Board of Commerce in 1956 highlighted the remaining strength in transit use in the CBD, with 50 percent of downtown workers and 70 percent of downtown shoppers still using mass transit.[121] Vitality in the CBD was reflected in hordes of shoppers at the city's flagship store: "Hudson's, at its height in the mid-1950s, served 100,000 customers per day; the store boasted its own telephone exchange."[122] But even a complete rapid transit system would have faced an uphill battle to divert shoppers back to the downtown. By 1954, according to June Manning Thomas, the downtown accounted for just 9.9 percent of regional retail sales as a ring of malls strangled the center city. And even Hudson's was aggressively expanding to the suburbs.[123]

A median rapid transit system, regional rail, or partial subway system reappeared in the years that followed but made no headway given the auto-centric path already well underway.[124] Expressway coordinator Glenn C. Richard pushed back on additional calls for a separate transit line within the expressways in the early 1950s. He pointed out that express DSR coaches on highways would work "as well as private automobiles" and was the option "which the people are willing to pay for." As he justifiably pointed out, "the people of Detroit have had plenty of opportunity to express themselves on subsidizing the transportation system, and they have always turned it down."[125] He cleverly argued that "the expressways will give Detroit a 'beautiful mass transit system.'"[126]

An ambitious monorail proposal in 1958 by the Detroit Rapid Transit Commission for a $225 million, 53.9-mile system with six lines brought out a similar analysis.[127] The director of the city Department of Streets and Traffic claimed that rapid transit could not work in Detroit because the city's population density was only 11,500 persons per square mile, quite different from the "large apartment districts" in Chicago and New York.[128] Indeed, the prospects for a heavy-rail system had much declined. DSR general manager Nowicki predictably claimed he "could find no merit in a monorail because with expressways and better highways, people prefer to drive their own cars." This from the head of the DSR![129] Rapid transit was a distraction from the DSR's mounting financial problems.

The 1960s Disaster

Detroit was bound to lose riders as many of its largest employers either closed or relocated to the suburbs, and white flight ensued. Yet, the complete loss of the system quality on such a scale had much more to do with the political economy than pure market response. After all, in 1960, Detroit had a total population of 1,670,144 inhabitants. There were plenty of potential riders (poor, working class, old, young, people with disabilities, etc.) if the City of Detroit, and other levels of government, had committed to sustaining a high-quality system. There were still plenty of moderate-density neighborhoods along the major transit corridors, even if there was not much transit left.[130]

The divide between suburbs and city widened in the 1960s and 1970s. Detroit's African American population rose to 482,223 residents in 1960 as southern workers continued to seek opportunity in the north. The city of Detroit, however, entered a period of industrial, commercial, and demographic decline while its segregated suburbs thrived.[131] Warren, Michigan, a typical suburban town on Detroit's northern boundary, mushroomed from just 727 people in 1950 to 89,246 residents in 1960 due to combined residential, commercial, and industrial growth. Thanks to discriminatory practices, just nineteen of Warren's inhabitants were African American in 1960.[132] While Warren census tracts on the Eight Mile Road boundary with Detroit had bus riding levels of 5 to 8 percent, tracts further north ranged from under 1 to 2 percent of daily bus riders. Ridership in all these tracts slipped even lower during the 1960s.[133] Warren was typical. Of the 178,000 new homes added in the region between 1950 and 1956, only 750 were open to nonwhites. Suburban towns like Dearborn, Royal Oak, and most others aggressively restricted multifamily housing through their zoning codes. Suburban transit ridership in the pristine white subdivisions was predictably minimal across the city line in every direction. The absence of a significant suburban commuter rail base limited any regional or state action for better transit as was the case in New York or Boston.[134]

Discrimination consistently disrupted life for African Americans within the city limits during the 1960s. June Manning Thomas explains that remaining Detroit white voters in 1964 voted by a majority to create a law that banned any fair housing restrictions on sales or rentals. The courts quickly rejected the policy, but as late as 1971 fifty-three tracts in the northeast part of the city were all white, and in these tracts, transit ridership was lower than citywide. A rising African American working and middle class moved into areas from which whites were leaving, but the progress was fleeting, with resegregation and disinvestment frequently following white flight. According to Manning, "Detroit's leaders could not or would not resist the tide of racial prejudice" and refused to pursue open housing laws and public housing desegregation well into the 1960s. Many neighborhoods lost density, and the 1967 riots decimated many commercial districts and accelerated white flight.[135]

A failed transit system was ideal for segregating neighborhoods; simply allowing the transit system to die restricted outer neighborhood and suburban access. The DSR in 1962 was losing money and passengers, according to the new manager James E. Bostick, because "a great many people have left for the suburbs, and industry relocated outside the central city. People don't have to rely on the DSR anymore."[136] A suburban Grosse Pointe Woods homemaker now had an expressway just a few blocks from home, "and 20 minutes later I'm downtown. How can a bus beat that?"[137] Certainly not the bus system left by the 1960s.

While the 1947 system had offered 102 million revenue miles annually for riders, by 1962–63 DSR miles on offer were down to just thirty-eight million.[138] On those remaining miles, DSR was having trouble gathering enough riders. In 1963, DSR's fifty passenger capacity buses carried thirty passengers 80 percent of the time. So, the DSR started looking at buying smaller buses to save money.[139] The DSR was also still paying more retirees in 1963 on pensions than it was employees to drive its buses. A remarkable 2,700 pensioners required DSR to set aside $3.9 million annually to the pension fund. DSR was also on the hook for reduced fares for seniors and school kids for $3 million per year,[140] and Detroit was the only city lacking state reimbursement for school fares.[141]

Mayor Jerome Cavanaugh supported a city subsidy of DSR in 1962 but failed to gain city council support. Another round of debate about the fairness of the tax requirements ensued.[142] The absurdity of the anti-exemption group was always easy to caricature, as the *Free Press* pointed out, "It would seem odd to have the Institute of Arts or the Public Library or the Department of Public Works pay taxes to the city. Yet, the DSR has been doing just that since its inception."[143] The council in 1964 finally approved a public vote on the issue. Why the change of heart? The city council realized that its intransigence prevented the DSR (and the city more broadly) from garnering emerging federal support for transit.

The Urban Mass Transportation Act of 1964 made available capital grants for mass transit, but only covered two-thirds of the cost; local or state funds had to make up the rest. In what was a watershed, voters finally approved DSR's exemption from most taxes in 1964 and authorized "the Common Council to appropriate from the city's general fund the required (one-third) matching monies needed for the DSR to obtain federal grants."[144] The Detroit Board of Education, fearing loss of tax revenue, fought the exemption but the Michigan Supreme Court ruled in 1966 that DSR could be exempted from city and school property taxes.[145] The DSR was, thanks to these efforts, able to take advantage of a $10 million federal grant in 1966, with the city providing $4.9 million—toward new buses and a planned terminal.[146] The state offered exemption from Wayne County property tax in 1965.[147]

Despite the exemption, the financial conditions at DSR further deteriorated. A 1968 fare increase from twenty-five to thirty cents had failed to dent the growing deficit. Then, in 1969, voters finally approved supporting the DSR out of general funds. This approval came a half-century after DSR had opened for business and after so much had already been lost. Why the dramatic change after so many decades of resistance? The DSR's deficit of $5.6 million in 1969 was an existential crisis, with just seventeen of sixty-three bus routes profitable and pensions absorbing 20 percent of revenue.[148] It was finally clear to the *Detroit Free Press* just who would suffer most with higher fare costs and reduced service: "Further increases would be a hardship to the very poor, the elderly and school children," most of whom were African American.[149] The editorial page had finally come around to subsidy many years too late because "there is a public interest in making it practicable for people to move about the city, even if they cannot afford to drive."[150]

In the postwar years, the failure to stabilize and expand the transit system to the suburbs was already a significant factor in high African American unemployment in the city during the 1960s. African Americans had done well gaining jobs in center-city plants. Yet, by the 1960s, high Black unemployment was linked to continuing discrimination and relocation of factories to suburbs with limited transit service. One-quarter of young African Americans were unemployed in Detroit. Lack of geographic mobility, in addition to employment discrimination, was a factor in the 1968 riots. Instead of aiding the populations left behind, the riots did even more damage to Detroit's denser, mixed-use areas that had risen around transit.[151] In a regional 1969 study, employers admitted that "those individuals with transportation problems are not generally hired," primarily those from the inner city.[152] Very little progress would be made in the decades that followed. By 1985, one study found 386,000 suburban jobs unreachable by mass transit.[153]

The arrival of subsidies at a modest level did not prevent a freefall in revenues and ridership in the system during the 1970s. In 1970, for instance, the city provided a $4.7 million subsidy to DSR, enough to prevent insolvency but not to develop a better system.[154] Nor would the city government be in a good position to make up for the losses or help rebuild a system. The post-riot city was hemorrhaging residents with a high proportion of the losses in the white middle class that possessed the funds to cover growing government costs. The city's total population dropped from 1,511,482 in 1970 to 1,203,339 in 1980, and the white population in that decade sank from 838,877 (55 percent) to 413,730 (34.38 percent). By 1980, African Americans comprised 63.07 percent of the city's population or 758,939 persons. Factories continued to abandon the city for the suburbs. Population and employment losses played out negatively for the DSR, including fewer riders and a limited appetite of city leaders for transit subsidies.[155]

The DSR in the 1970s cycled through a downward spiral of deficits, fare increases, service cuts, and ridership losses. The DSR in 1970, for instance, raised fares from thirty to forty cents while cutting more service.[156] The only good news was 117 new coaches delivered thanks to federal largess. But the bad news kept coming. In 1971–72, ridership had dropped to ninety-three million passengers, and the DSR projected a $15 million loss in fiscal year 1972–73. So up went the fare again in 1972, from forty to fifty cents, again paired with more service cuts, including all service after 2 a.m. The reductions might save $2.5 million total but would in no way offset the massive predicted deficit of $15 million.[157] The city, for its part, claimed that there was no slack in its $675 million budget to make up for such a significant loss.[158] By late 1972, modest city help, federal funds, layoffs of employees, and service reductions had cut the deficit.[159] Between 1966 and 1972, only 1966 was profitable at the DSR because of "the cumulative impact of the freeways, the growth of the suburbs and the removal of jobs from the city."[160]

DSR poorly served the remaining riders. Central neighborhoods still had sizable percentages of remaining riders (20–40 percent bus riders) in 1970. Higher transit ridership in these select areas was tied to the fact that 60 percent of central city residents lacked cars.[161] However, more successful whites and African Americans in Detroit neighborhoods within the city limits rode at 5–15 percent daily. There were almost no transit riders in the suburbs except for the remnant suburban bus service and connecting DSR lines.[162] The steep drop-off in ridership by location, reflecting declining interest and transit service availability, was a typical metropolitan pattern for American cities like Detroit that lacked legacy commuter rail. The failure to develop transit reduced the mobility of poor African Americans most directly, but there were also white people who might have been too old, poor, or young to own a car. In 1973, for instance, 26 percent of Detroiters in the region (including both suburbs and city) did not own cars.[163]

Yet attracting middle-class whites to a second-tier system was unlikely. Instead, lower-income people of color had become the primary customers for DSR. The protesters against service cuts at public meetings reflected the demographic shift. For instance, about 460 mostly elderly Black people protested cuts in June of 1973.[164] The remaining riders not only faced the prospect of reduced service during this era of disinvestment but had a terrifying ride in the 1970s: "Crime and vandalism on Detroit's buses increased more than 50 percent between 1970 and 1975." Ridership had dropped 25 percent in that period. It was clear that only the most desperate remained: "All those people who have some other logical choice have been driven away. You're down to what the transit industry refers to as a very 'captive ridership.'"[165]

Race and Regional Planning Failure

In the minds of many advocates, the only hope for creating a higher-quality system for a declining city like Detroit was a regional agreement that tapped the federal government and the wealthier suburbs. The *Detroit Free Press* believed that the solution to regional congestion was "obtaining a mass rapid transit system which will move people, not vehicles."[166] SEMTA (Southeastern Michigan Transportation Authority) emerged in 1967 as Detroit's underwhelming answer to regional transit planning.

The Detroit region had several strikes against it when developing and sustaining regional rapid transit. Downtown retail was a shell of its former glory, crime was high, and cultural institutions further out along Woodward dissipated the CBD's attractiveness. Cars had also compromised the attractiveness of the CBD to suburbanites for culture or urbanity. By 1975, parking lots, freeway ramps, and streets covered three-quarters of downtown.[167] The extensive electric interurban service, formerly linking cities and suburbs, was long gone. The remnant commuter rail service was minimal, eliminating the potential role of a suburban elite in transit advocacy, as was the case in New York, Boston, and Chicago. Private suburban bus lines were in crisis and failed to coordinate service with the

DSR despite carrying passengers into the CBD. The DSR had raised the regional transit challenge when it ripped out its legacy streetcar systems and failed to modernize them, including those formerly linking the suburbs. In 1969, there were fifty-three DSR bus lines with suburban links, but the company ran just 7 percent of its total mileage in the suburbs. Auto-centric planning and living remained dominant. New freeways were under construction, and there were now 2.8 million registered cars in the Detroit region.[168]

The emergence of the federal government as a funder of transit was the crucial turning point, in line with the city's decision to provide tax exemption to DSR, in developing an entity to manage regional mass transit. In 1964, local and state leaders authorized a multiple county transit authority to win federal funds. A multiyear, multimillion-dollar planning study effort known as TALUS (Transportation and Land Use Study) provided an analytical framework for the problems and opportunities on a regional basis. Mayor Cavanaugh favored city and DSR control of future transit, but suburban and state leaders saw things differently. The state created SEMTA in 1967 as a seven-county transport authority to purchase the DSR and remnant suburban bus systems. Suburban representatives dominated SEMTA even though DSR had the most transit riders. SEMTA, moreover, lacked any power over land use that might have created opportunities for transit-oriented development and thus boosted suburban ridership.

Without a massive federal infusion of funds, SEMTA never stood a chance of creating a high-quality regional system. Unfortunately, as with the creation of the DSR in 1921, a poison pill inserted in the legislation rendered SEMTA extraordinarily weak: the new agency lacked a taxing power.[169] SEMTA could rely only on federal funds, revenue bonds, and fares. SEMTA's primary role in the early years of operation was buying out failing suburban bus systems to run them as a transit operator and organizing local, state, and federal funds for regional bus purchases.[170] It was not until 1972 that the state's voters approved a slight diversion, half a cent, to transit from the state gas tax.[171] In 1974 and 1976, the state legislature approved some additional modest subsidies for transit, primarily to help the state qualify for hundreds of millions in federal transit funds. Yet, the state aid was not at a level, even with federal assistance, to rebuild a regional network.[172]

The long-standing financial problems of the DSR also proved to be a significant hindrance to the planned takeover of DSR by SEMTA in 1970. Without DSR under its control, SEMTA's claim to be a regional transit operator was meaningless. Suburbanites, however, balked at picking up the costs of DSR pensions and operations. Detroit leaders, for their part, were skeptical about SEMTA's commitment to DSR inner-city riders and workers. A former head of DSR, for instance, remained unconvinced: "Now when the poor are about to inherit the city, the one valuable thing remaining will be taken from them by people who are not elected by them or responsible to them."[173] The head of SEMTA, Thomas Lipscomb, assured city leaders that SEMTA would prioritize "the poor and working-class citizens who must rely on public transportation. Black citizens ... should have no fears that a regionalized DSR would not provide them top-notch service." Given the white hostility and flight that the city's Black population had experienced, it is not clear why they should have had faith in Lipscomb's promise.[174]

The negotiations over the SEMTA-DSR merger dragged on for years. Coleman Young in 1973 ran, in part, on a platform of keeping DSR under Detroit's control. Young, grappling with a city in steep decline,[175] aimed to turn the DSR into a regional system rather than selling to SEMTA. As he explained, "We service the region with water and sewers already, so why not with buses?"[176] As newly elected mayor in 1974, Young was "cool" to the sale of the DSR to SEMTA and had an extensive list of demands for any purchase or merger: a vote by Detroit citizens, reasonable fares in Detroit, a higher price for the purchase, and protection of DSR employee rights. Moreover, he refused cooperation with the suburbs if it involved "any move that would rob the city, which now has a Black majority, of its power and influence." He claimed whites aimed to "'castrate Black political power' by advocating regionalism or state action to deprive cities of home rule."[177] His concerns had some validity, given Detroit's growing role in paying the bill for transit from general revenues. DSR (renamed DDOT in 1974) never did join SEMTA despite years and years of debate.[178] Young had reason to doubt the ability of SEMTA to deliver on upgrading regional transit given its lack of funding and ridership from the suburbs.[179]

The Detroit region ended up with just another poorly funded transit agency. SEMTA, for instance, cut 35 percent of service in 1983 thanks to federal budget cuts.[180] By 1985, SEMTA was running deficits on a total budget of just $69.2 million, and most of the funds it collected were sent to the DDOT.[181] After all, DDOT carried 240,000 riders versus thirty-three thousand on SEMTA's 203 active buses during peak hours.[182] SEMTA was barely serving a massive suburban region with millions of residents. SEMTA, when it participated in center-city issues, also poorly managed the development of rapid transit, the only outcome of which was the embarrassing People Mover project (see below).[183] The state reorganized SEMTA in 1988 as SMART, covering just three counties (Wayne, Macomb, and Oakland), further undermining its ability to design or operate metropolitan-scale systems. Today, the agency receives limited regional tax support, and its 255 fixed-route buses typically carry only about twenty-nine thousand passengers per day in a region of approximately four million people.[184]

Rapid Transit Illusion

Despite his early anti-suburban rhetoric, Mayor Coleman Young (1974–94) looked to rebuild downtown in partnership with the region's white business elite. Rapid lines, including a Woodward subway, remained a long-standing priority because many civic leaders still believed such a line could help restore city-suburban connections and the CBD's lost popularity.[185] Eager for federal funding and bullish on trains, many SEMTA officials shared Young's priorities. SEMTA's chair in 1974 cited the impact of Toronto's subway on central city health as a model for Detroit: "office buildings sprang up, new ones, apartment buildings. The Toronto system is beautiful."[186]

Repeatedly, however, the devil was in the details when it came to even the most basic cooperative efforts in the Detroit region, much less a regional rapid transit system to match Toronto. In 1969, a TALUS study recommended 118 miles of high-speed transit,[187] but SEMTA declined the proposal. Then, in 1969, the city floated the Woodward subway idea again, but SEMTA claimed to be holding out for a proper regional plan.[188] In 1974, executives at GM and Ford supported a $5 billion SEMTA mass transit plan that would include seventy-five miles of rail to bolster their downtown Detroit Renaissance project,[189] but federal officials remained dubious.[190] Even though federal officials were skeptical about the demand for the rapid system in 1976, SEMTA claimed there were still enough riders left "to warrant a heavy rail subway" on Woodward and Gratiot. As some pockets of density remained, that might have been true, but the logic of rapid development was stronger decades past.[191]

Lacking a regionally accepted rail project, Detroit was losing out to other cities in the race to secure federal funds that might improve transit and create jobs desperately needed in an era of deindustrialization. In 1976, for instance, Buffalo expected to rake in thirty-seven dollars per person in transit funding over the next four years, and Cleveland expected twenty-eight dollars, but Detroit was on track for just $3.50 per person. Bickering among city, regional, and state politicians was at the heart of the problem. As a result, federal officials had become skeptical that the region was a wise transit investment.[192] In 1977, for instance, federal officials told Detroit officials to scale back plans for rapid transit to $600 million maximum, a level of funding that would not have covered a plan then circulating for a thirty-eight-mile light-rail system, with underground sections on Woodward and Gratiot.[193]

Suburbanites, for their part, remained even more hostile to rapid transit; in particular, they disliked the subway Mayor Young and many others favored on Woodward Avenue. As the cost of the Woodward line mounted to $830 million in 1977, one suburban representative complained, "I find the use of over three-quarters of a billion dollars to build a mini-subway an unwise expenditure of tax dollars." Moreover, such an expensive line would "deprive areas not along that small stretch of Woodward of their fair share of transit dollars."[194] In 1977, Macomb County officials opposed SEMTA's rapid transit plans, and one promised, "if all that money is dumped into a subway, I wouldn't doubt that we would pull out" of the regional agency. Politicians in Macomb were responding to their most energized constituents: "At every public hearing in Macomb on an issue of this kind, the anti-regionalists are out in force, dominating the meeting with their angry, emotional rhetoric." One speaker promised a subway would "provide inner-city criminals with access to the suburbs in barely coded racial rhetoric. She, too, got a thunderous ovation." Macomb, according to the *Free Press*, "bore the full brunt of the great migration out of the ethnic neighborhoods of Detroit's east side." The whites arriving "tended to be hardworking, ethnically clannish, conservative in social attitudes," and seeking "refuge" from the big city.[195] SEMTA and city officials continued to push rapid transit,[196] but the 1970s and early 1980s plans for a mix of subways and light-rail on Woodward and Gratiot also flopped.[197]

Unable to gather sufficient support for regional rapid transit systems, Detroit and SEMTA ended up with a money-losing downtown elevated circulator known as the People Mover. Detroit had been selected by federal officials in a national competition among cities in 1976 for the system, then projected as a 2.3-mile system that would link the planned waterfront Renaissance Center with downtown on an elevated loop. Initially, the People Mover was not supposed to be a stand-alone system; instead, it would have linked the CBD riders to regional rapid. But since SEMTA and the city never built that regional system, it would become an orphan.[198]

The best that could be said about the People Mover was that it would link the shiny new Renaissance Center and convention center with the rest of downtown. But, unfortunately, SEMTA bungled the development, and by 1985 the system was $72 million over budget with a total $210 million cost.[199] *Mass Transit* magazine pointed out that the circulator would do little for a blighted downtown with few residents. Nor would commuters get many benefits. Of the 102,928 CBD workers, 72 percent drove a car, and most of the rest, 25 percent, rode a bus. The People Mover had little to offer either group.[200] The 2.9-mile system finally opened in 1987 to much fanfare, but it was all show. A 1985 study had predicted thirty-seven to forty-three thousand riders a day,[201] but by 1989, there were just eleven thousand daily riders, and it was losing millions.[202] Nearly 65 percent of People Mover riders in a 1988 survey were sightseers from conventions riding for a lark.[203]

Detroit had spent millions of mostly federal dollars on the People Mover while its regular bus riders had been getting even less service. An early order SEMTA placed for new GM buses in 1978 revealed a growing divide: "The suburban buses have large, cushioned seats, while Detroit's coaches have fiberglass seats built to withstand vandalism." Detroit's fleet was already "badly scarred by vandals who slash seats and scribble graffiti."[204] Riders cannot have been too pleased. In 1978, five hundred DDOT buses were ten years old or older, and one-quarter were out for service daily. The humiliation of being reliant on DDOT had multiple dimensions. Long waits, dirty buses, and limited routes were just part of the problem. SEMTA suburban bus service, with about thirty thousand riders per day, whisked its passengers on "express service to downtown Detroit past waiting DDOT riders."[205]

To experience the system firsthand, the *Detroit Free Press* in 1979 sent one hundred of its employees out on the system, and 41 percent of them arrived late. The test found that "buses were dirty, schedules were meaningless," and drivers showed riders a general lack of courtesy.[206] In 1979, six hundred people turned out to "to protest the city's bus service, which many describe as dirty, slow and, above all, mismanaged" in front of a Detroit City Council hearing.[207] No one was listening. Despite offering minimum service, Detroit raised fares from fifty to sixty cents per ride in 1980.[208] By 1983, the fare was a dollar, and riders showed their appreciation by showing up less.[209] Just one-third of the remaining riders paid the full adult fare, half of the riders counted were transfers or students, and many others were seniors. DDOT only kept going thanks to city, state, and federal subsidies. In 1982–83, for instance, DDOT collected $13 million from the city. Subsidies helped cover the growing deficits but combined were not able to sustain a quality system.[210]

On a typical Monday in 1985, the DDOT had just 280 buses in daily

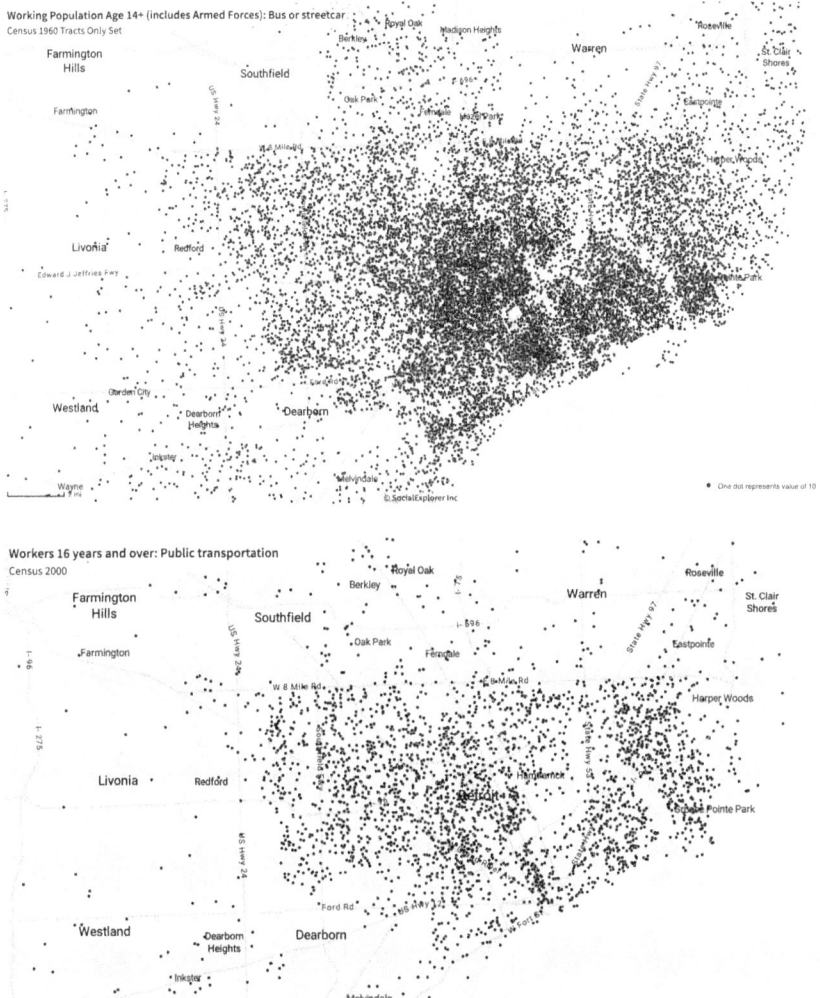

FIGURES 21A AND 21B. This map pair illustrates the massive losses in ridership between 1960 and 2000. Source: Public Transportation, 1960/2000, Social Explorer, accessed June 26, 2021.

service for a system that needed five to six hundred buses to serve the sixty-three remaining routes. So few buses were in service because three hundred of DDOT's 747 buses were twelve to seventeen years old and unreliable.[211] By 1986, the system was down to just 180,000 total passengers per day (including transfers, single ride in each direction, etc.).[212] The agency was cycling through managers, a clear sign of institutional collapse, and the new head of DDOT admitted, "We are serving our passengers, overall, very poorly."[213] There remained many potential riders in 1985, as one in four Detroit households had no car, but the price would have had to be lower and quality higher to attract more ridership. A reporter spent eighteen hours on buses, interviewed fifty riders, and rode ten routes to test the system. Sadly, no buses followed the printed schedule, "and, at one downtown stop, more than 100 riders waited—some more than 45 minutes—for three buses that never came." The reporter found that "riding a DSR bus is like visiting a broken-down world."[214]

The history of transit and neighborhood disinvestment continues to hold Detroit back today. City, state, and federal leaders have refused to intervene for decades in a growing plague of abandoned housing citywide. Vast areas of the city have depopulated, and the city's policy of clearing rotting housing will accelerate losses. The loss of population, compounded by decades of service cuts, shows up on transit statistics. DDOT carried just 1.839 million passengers in December of 2019, or about sixty thousand passengers per day on average; in November of 2021, the monthly ridership figure had dropped to 755,230, or about thirty to thirty-five thousand per day.[215]

The loss of feeder bus service and neighborhood density have also undermined the new 3.3-mile Q Line streetcar, built for $187 million, along a section of Woodward. In 2018, for instance, the line attracted just 3,376 riders a day versus five to eight thousand riders estimated by transit consultants. The Q Line shares much with the slow and tiny downtown "streetcar" systems recently opened in cities like Milwaukee, Atlanta, and Kansas City. These are most often urbanistic showpieces, designed to enhance a city's image and CBD land values rather than meeting actual transit demand.[216]

Detroit's Enduring Challenges

Detroit offers mostly cautionary lessons for transit. Detroit, like Chicago, demonstrated that both unsubsidized and minimally subsidized transit withered in the low-density, auto-centric American urban context. Tax exemption and a publicly appointed manager were insufficient to achieve competitive service. At many points in the past century, city, suburban, regional, and state leaders could have developed financial supports (taxes, fees, etc.) that would have helped sustain service and ridership. The cost to taxpayers, if spread widely, would have been modest compared to the benefits to equity, the environment, and traffic congestion.

Admittedly, even a deeply subsidized system would have faced many challenges in Detroit. It was unfair to expect DSR or DDOT to thrive when restrictive zoning, highway construction, and redevelopment policies militated against transit. As in Detroit, policies that damage dense neighborhoods or have let them rot also took their toll on the transit agency. The development of rapid transit, absent regional rezoning, or more substantive neighborhood stabilization, would have been unlikely to generate much additional investment within the city limits. Detroit's history demonstrates that transit, while often planned or operated in a vacuum, responds to factors such as zoning, race relations, redevelopment, disinvestment, and highway plans.

Detroit's extreme racial divides foreground the typical damage of segregation and suburban resource hoarding to transit. Transit could not thrive in the Detroit region or most other American cities because of sharp social divisions that developed among city neighborhoods and between central cities and suburbs. The provision of higher-quality suburban bus service designated for white CBD-bound passengers in Detroit is similar to quality differences between city buses and suburban-oriented commuter rail or light-rail in nearly every American city. Transit customers received the message. In Detroit, as elsewhere, nonwhite riders abandoned buses as soon as they moved to the suburbs or could afford to buy cars. American transit lines will face enduring problems if the neighborhoods and regions through which they run are so deeply divided.

PART IV

Public Transit That Worked Better

In the annals of American mass transit, just a few cities stand out for the extent to which they retained and modernized better-quality mass transit systems in the postwar years. Preservation and modernization of more systems might have gone better with an early commitment to public support like that developed in Boston, New York, and San Francisco. These systems were by no means perfect, then or now, but they were notable for sustaining an enviable level of daily service, thanks to subsidies, even in the worst of times. This reliability, regardless of mode, is most important to regular riders going to and from work, school, and play. The combined impact of *timing, subsidies, density,* and *demographics* was key to relative success in better-performing systems.

The *timing* of public ownership was crucial: the earlier the public sector got involved, the better for transit. San Francisco created Muni in 1904. In the early twentieth century, New York launched its municipal subway as a private-partnership, opened its first municipal-owned and -operated line in 1932, and bought out the last private operators of subways in 1940. Boston started subsidizing private transit in 1918 and took full ownership, with subsidies, in 1947. Public ownership and subsidies in these cities emerged from the demands of urban majorities, still mostly white, for improvement in systems upon which the entire city and some affluent suburbs still relied. Ridership and operating losses remained modest at the point of the takeover, and few could imagine the kinds of subsidies that would be required in the future when ridership went over a cliff. Promises of significant service improvements also appealed to many voters.

The willingness of politicians, the public, and the media to support *subsidies* for these public companies was essential to success. Subsidies ballooned in the postwar years as rising fares and falling ridership covered a declining percentage of operating and capital costs. Subsidies came from massive public bond issues for capital projects, designated taxes or tolls, direct cash infusions from city and state taxes and treasuries, and the federal government.[1] Subsidies plus tax exemption enabled the preservation of lower fares, more service, and modest expansion despite much-reduced ridership. State and federal subsidies from the 1960s onward complemented existing local support, creating new opportunities for modernization and expansion.

Urban density mattered. Postwar San Francisco, Boston, and New York were American cities with dense downtowns and neighborhoods. Downtown business interests, the media, and neighborhood pressure shaped pro-transit local political cultures. Almost all of America's older industrial cities also once boasted crowded downtowns and thriving center-city neighborhoods. Cities like Baltimore, Cleveland, and Saint Louis lost far more of their downtown vitality than a city like New York thanks to capitalist restructuring including deindustrialization and loss of regional headquarters. However, these cities' misguided policies (highways, restrictive zoning, urban renewal, public housing, and housing exploitation) destroyed vulnerable neighborhoods at a scale that reduced density and potential ridership.

Cities like New York, Boston, and San Francisco endured a typical era of destructive public policy like urban renewal and highways, but the overall effect was muted. Their diverse economies better weathered deindustrialization, including large and powerful universities, cultural institutions, banks, and corporate headquarters that retained a more extensive employment base in or near city centers. Urban redevelopment programs frequently yielded successful new downtown offices, apartment buildings (market and subsidized), campuses, regional hospital complexes, and entertainment complexes. Many citizens fought successfully against the worst redevelopment policies, leaving large neighborhoods relatively untouched by postwar slum clearance. These cities also benefited by having dense neighboring suburbs and cities, linked by rails, such as Hoboken, Brookline, and Oakland. Density preserved complementary transit.

The fourth and related factor in the relative success was the city's *demographics*. In Boston, San Francisco, and New York, a vocal and substantial portion of the city's white elite lived in areas where transit was an integrated, visible, and valuable dimension of neighborhood life. Boston's Back Bay and neighboring Brookline, Manhattan's Upper West and East Sides, and Pacific Heights in San Francisco created well-heeled transit defenders. The white straphanger was more typical in San Francisco, New York, or Boston than Baltimore or Cleveland postwar. Cities that retained significant white, elite suburban transit ridership, or added riders thanks to gentrification, gained powerful advocates for regional taxation or state government action. As suburban commuter rail failed, state leaders finally got busy creating regional transit authorities and taxation so that wealthy suburbanites could still ride trains.

The percentage of the nonwhite population as a total share of the city's population, while still substantial in these cities and crucial for sustained ridership and pro-transit activism, was also smaller than cities like Chicago, Detroit, Baltimore, and Atlanta. White leaders encouraged highly segregated, exploitative neighborhoods in Boston, New York, and San Francisco for decades. But public policy changes in these cities, related to neighborhood resistance, prioritized neighborhood stabilization, infill, and affordable housing. Efforts like these helped retain customers near transit lines. African Americans and post-1965 immigrants often located to these older neighborhoods, creating new generations of transit customers. Where and who transit served mattered, given the political and social nature of the institution.

CHAPTER 8

Boston Pioneers Public Regional Transit

The Boston region saved and expanded its transit system in the postwar period despite experiencing typical American suburbanization. Bostonians had been moving outward for decades, but the trend accelerated during the postwar years thanks to a mix of public and private action. The city of Boston's population dropped from 801,000 in 1950 to 562,000 in 1980,[1] while the metropolitan area thrived.[2] In 1963, an impressive 85 percent of all trips in the Boston region took place in cars.[3] If the Boston region was going to have mass transit and a system that at least aspired to serve more people in the communities where they lived, it would have to be even more closely tied to regional rather than urban fortunes. Boston fell short of its most ambitious suburban transit expansion plans. However, it still had the essential elements in place postwar to preserve and sustain a modestly successful system of regional mass transit: *timing, subsidies, density,* and *demographics.*

Timing. The Elevated Trusteeship (1919) and MTA (1947) launched before the most significant ridership losses or subsidies needed were fully comprehended. Public ownership and regional subsidies, once in place, led to more ambitious city-suburban transit planning.

Subsidies. Often grudgingly, local and state leaders expanded the depth and type of subsidies available for transit, as reflected in the MBTA (1963) that replaced the MTA.

Density. City officials destroyed many old neighborhoods with highways or urban renewal programs, but citizens revolted early and successfully against many projects. Boston and some of its transit-served neighbors such as Cambridge and Brookline maintained enough density for an active and latent transit customer base.

Demographics. The sizable white population that still lived near transit, including influential elites and college students, created a different image, experience, and political base for transit that helped preserve and expand the system for the more diverse MBTA ridership today.

The long-deferred push for public ownership, delayed for decades by the public-private trusteeship arrangement, finally succeeded in 1947. After two decades of transit assessments, the fourteen towns' representatives were eager to end what many considered to be subsidies to the company shareholders rather than to riders. Advocates of what became the MTA optimistically promised that buying the elevated would "lead to elimination of the annual deficit assessed against" the fourteen towns.[4] Excitement ran high even though the promises of deficit elimination proved to be a dream. No matter. In 1947, "virtually every seat in the large Gardner Auditorium was filled" as "a parade of Greater Boston officials and legislators placed themselves in favor of public management." The regional endorsement was vital.[5] Boston also had a modest transit system, so many advocates thought that public ownership would be manageable. In 1947, Boston boasted just 288 miles of surface streetcar track, 52 miles of rapid transit, 170 miles of bus service, and 31 miles of trackless trolley service. Ridership was robust, with 388 million annual passengers in 1947, and was another cause for optimism.[6]

Boston's tradition of well-run regional systems—parks, sewers, and water—supported by taxation remained a model for the new MTA, according to the *Globe*: "because Greater Boston is an economic unit, the state has been compelled to take over many of its functions. The result is that the people of the area have lost control of their water supply, their sewers, many of their parks, and their street railway system. For all these they are taxed."[7] The state government had already established its agencies and authorities as a quasi-metropolitan government for the populous Eastern Massachusetts region. Another factor in securing approval was the legendary Edward Dana, a revered figure whose devotion to transit put a competent, consistent face on the transit issue. After graduating from Harvard, Dana joined the elevated in 1907. He worked his way up from the bottom and served as general manager from 1919 to 1959. His long tenure was a remarkable achievement in the transit industry, where the churn of leadership often became a political distraction.[8]

The new MTA opened for business in 1947 with a name and mission attuned to addressing the decentralized character of the region.[9] The commonwealth paid $22.4 million to purchase the shares of the Boston Elevated and assumed $75 million of its debt, thus ending the controversial dividend payments, but not necessarily profits for investors.[10] A New York syndicate eagerly bought new MTA bonds for the purchase given the continuing responsibility of the fourteen towns, affirmed in the new public ownership legislation, to make up the deficits. The willingness of private finance to cover Boston transit debts, because regional taxation guaranteed payment, stands in contrast to Chicago, where it took two years to secure bond financing for the purchase of the private transit companies because of fears of CTA default.[11]

During the planning phases of the legislation, both a state-appointed Metropolitan Rapid Transit Commission and the MTA planning staff after the agency started operating in 1947 made many ambitious promises about the future of regional transit under public ownership. Rapid transit to the suburbs was needed, according to managers, "to serve those people who, since 1920, have moved beyond the five-mile area now served by the rapid transit lines." Only a system competitive with automobiles in terms of time and cost could be expected to attract and retain suburban riders.[12] A $100 million plan would pay for "speedy electric-train service" to twenty-nine cities and towns in the Boston region with up to ten rapid transit routes. Among the suburban towns to receive planned rapid transit terminals were Waltham, Lexington, Needham, East Dedham, North Woburn, Reading, and Lynn.[13]

The expansion plan made sense because the distances to these towns from downtown Boston were not that great. Yet the difference in service quality and ticket price paid by suburban rail transit riders at the time was enormous. Moreover, electric rapid transit, mostly built along existing rights-of-way, would replace faltering diesel private commuter rail service. The 2.5 million residents of Greater Boston, the boosters promised, would "have one of the most modern, self-supporting, unified transit systems in America." Advocates assured the skeptical that "the system is not being forced on any community" and taxes would be levied only as the MTA added rapid transit service. These plans were ambitious and have not been realized today. Still, they were an important statement of principle for the region.[14]

In the first postwar decade, MTA staff focused on more realistic expansion plans: building out or updating existing rapid transit routes, rather than the ten new regional rapid lines. The postwar rapid transit plans included extending the Cambridge and Boston/Dorchester subway line (today's Red Line) southward to Quincy and Braintree and northward to Alewife and Arlington. A new subway line under Massachusetts Avenue in Cambridge as part of the extension to Alewife would remove streetcars and thus "release the full width of Massachusetts avenue for automobile traffic." Extension of rail to Revere (Blue Line) from East Boston built on subway construction already underway. The MTA also planned to replace the main elevated line running between Charlestown and Forest Hills (Orange Line) with subway service. The MTA management claimed that the older elevated structures posed "serious obstruction to vehicular traffic" and were a "detriment to the development of the communities" thanks to noise and shadows.[15] Regional commuters and shoppers would also benefit from plentiful free parking at planned rapid transit stations.[16] The MTA made a point of providing ample space for car parking at rapid transit both to encourage ridership and as a way to cement political support from suburban leaders.

The only streetcar service designated for long-term preservation was today's Green Line, linking the west side of the city (sections of Boston, Brookline, and Newton) with downtown. More ridership persisted in these neighborhoods thanks to reliable streetcar service and sufficient density of CBD-bound workers in the contributing neighborhoods. While many stately homes were near the routes, more important were the many multifamily buildings along or near the lines, many still filled with commuters and college students. Separated streetcar rights-of-way speeded service to the downtown subway tunnels. The design of the lines and downtown congestion made for competitive commuting despite aging PCC trolley cars.

MTA managers planned to convert other remaining streetcar lines, most of which lacked their exclusive rights-of-way, to bus or trackless trolleys to economize and speed up auto traffic. As in Chicago, Detroit, Cleveland, San Francisco, and New York, public ownership and management did not guarantee a pro-streetcar policy. Car drivers certainly had a lot to cheer for as lumbering streetcars, tracks, and safety islands disappeared from city streets. Without any prodding from nefarious NCL, and little evident resistance from city residents (who could read about and experience the changes firsthand), MTA managers had by 1951 reduced streetcar surface lines to 188 miles while raising the miles of bus routes to 179 and trackless trolleys to 78.[17] The old Boston Elevated had 3,372 streetcars for service in 1918 but just 609 left in 1952.[18] The MTA had replaced streetcars on thirty routes by 1958, mostly since World War II, with a mix of gas, diesel, and trackless equipment. Only today's Green Line and the short line from Ashmont to Mattapan on the south side survived postwar streetcar substitution.[19]

The complexity of public opinion concerning streetcars is reflected in the MBTA plans to remove an outer section of the streetcar (Green) lines known as the Arborway. In 1962, for instance, the MTA managers got an earful in interviews with business owners and residents of the neighborhood over the future of remaining surface streetcars. Pro-streetcar resident sentiment ultimately stalled the MTA's aggressive substitution plan for this line, but the business community in the area at the time mostly demanded bus substitution. The owner of Karsh Jewelers on Centre Street, along which streetcars ran, was "100% in favor of buses" and called for the MTA to "eliminate street cars." In agreement for bus substitution were the owners of a camera shop, a laundromat, a variety store, Carroll Cosmetics ("it would help the merchants"), and Harvey's Hardware (who called streetcars "passé"). Citizen resistance stalled the termination of the Green Arborway line until 1985, but the sense of MTA streetcar service as outdated was a factor in the push for substitution citywide.[20]

The MTA was moving ahead on bus modernization, but like its peers had to grapple with a postwar financial crisis thanks to declining ridership and higher costs.[21] The MTA already overran its budget by $2.7 million in 1947; the rosy financial predictions of public ownership were off base. The new MTA, for instance, was still paying fixed changes of $9.5 million a year, including interest on bonds, property taxes, and rental fees for subways.[22] The MTA had terrible news for the fourteen towns: "We wish we could say that your ownership of the railway ends all financial worries connected with public transportation in this area. But that is not so." The tax assessments on the towns resumed. The Somerville Board of Alderman in 1948 demanded a strike against the higher taxation,[23] and some legislators aimed to add eighteen fringe communities to the tax base for the MTA, but their un-assessed neighbors were not interested in paying for theoretical mass transit of the future. As one skeptic remarked, "I certainly don't see why towns that don't use the MTA should pay for it."[24]

Democrat Paul A. Dever ran for governor on a strong MTA reform program in 1948, indicating that it had not taken long to shift public opinion against public ownership.[25] Dever was critical of the MTA and Republican-led management. As governor-elect he proposed a ten-point plan including the notion "that MTA subways and rapid transit lines were 'highways'" and "maintenance of such highways [would] be paid for out of the state's receipts from gasoline and other automotive taxes." He also wanted to exempt the MTA from taxation, end the requirement of higher fares to cover operating costs, and transfer subway ownership to the MTA. Dever claimed his plan would save the MTA $8.175 million per year.[26] Most of Dever's visionary funding proposals failed to receive support, but the governor in 1949 did succeed in the refinancing of MTA debts, thus reducing the annual fixed charges to $4.8 million per year. He had also put some fairly radical subsidy ideas into circulation.[27] In 1950, the annual assessable deficit on the towns was down to only $539,000, thanks to refinancing economies and higher fares, but deficit reduction proved fleeting.[28] Dever scolded the legislature for failing to adopt his full MTA program, forcing him to accept MTA fare increases,[29] in 1950, to fifteen cents for combined surface and rapid and ten cents for surface.[30]

Labor was the most challenging factor for the MTA to control, just as it was in every American city. Thanks primarily to bus substitution of two-person streetcars, the MTA consistently cut head count, but there was strong political resistance to cutting feeder bus lines with weak ridership. One MTA official observed that "the average legislator is more interested in keeping bus service on Sunday, no matter how skimpy the patronage, than in the deficit." Lower head counts, moreover, did not necessarily compensate for much richer rewards. MTA was a pioneer in offering its workers collective bargaining rights.[31] The MTA managers had to deal with navigating eighteen different labor contracts and twenty-seven different unions.[32] By 1956, 85.2 cents of each dollar in revenue went to direct wages, retirement funds, and payroll taxes.[33] In 1960, 94 percent of the operating cost increase was driven by raises in wages, retirement, or health.[34] It should not surprise that Boston had only one major strike between 1919 and 1960. MTA workers ranked fifth out of nineteen leading public and private transit systems in compensation. The mostly white workforce used transit employment to join the middle class.[35]

Workers' high wages and benefits were entirely out of line with system revenue, forcing cuts worrisomely like those in other cities. Between 1948 and 1950, for instance, ridership dropped from 381 to 307 million and then kept on dropping year over year.[36] By 1954 MTA ridership had slipped to 244 million.[37] Rush hours remained full, but service off-peak and weekends, crucial to profitable operations, consistently dropped thanks to the "increased number of automobiles."[38] As early as 1949, MTA managers started to cut what they called "unnecessary mileage."[39] In the early 1950s, managers started cutting on weekends, holidays, and off-peak hours more aggressively. In total, they chopped two million miles of service between 1950 and 1951,[40] cut service system-wide by 4 percent in 1952,[41] and in 1953 terminated runs with fewer than ten passengers a trip. The aim, according to managers, was to create "a frequency of service commensurate with the possibilities of remunerative patronage." The MTA targeted owl, off-peak, and weekend service because "the inroads which the family automobile has made into patronage of public transportation lines all over the county can never be entirely reversed."[42] There would be more cuts to service in 1955, and the MTA even began closing subways during the early morning hours.[43]

Fare increases often accompanied service cuts. Harvard researchers in 1953 predicted that higher fares "will only drive more patronage away," but fares rose anyway.[44] When the MTA received permission in 1954 to raise fares to twenty cents, they lost 9 percent of passengers.[45] By 1956, ridership had shrunk to 219 million.[46] With further losses of 3 percent in 1957,[47] and a 2.6 percent reduction in 1958. The declining loss rate indicated to optimistic MTA officials that ridership was "nearing a 'hard core' minimum point."[48] Yet it still was not the bottom. By 1959, the system was down to 202 million riders.[49]

Managers targeted bus and trackless systems to preserve the more popular rapid lines for the most significant cuts. In 1960, for instance, the 4 percent system-wide service cut primarily impacted feeder lines to rapid transit.[50] In 1960, the MTA eliminated most owl overnight service for surface lines.[51] Between 1948 and 1960, managers had slashed total mileage in service from 54.7 million miles to 38.6 million, or nearly 30 percent.[52] Even rapid customers could sense the change. A 1961 rider, for instance, complained about the "inadequate, inefficient and discourteous service" on the subway lines, remarking that "if there was some other way for me to travel to and from work I would, however, you have me . . . trapped." She felt "like a sardine in a can" at rush hours and decried "the frequent breakdowns, or tie-ups." Indeed, the 1960s looked grim for the MTA's future.[53] It did not help that the crowded and less frequent ride now cost more. Fares in Boston remained low by national standards, but they still rose 124 percent total between 1948 and 1963.[54]

The Suburban Imperative

Longtime MTA general manager Edward Dana could see clearly by 1956 that "our indispensable mass transportation has been allowed to wither on the vine in our zeal to satisfy the needs of automobile traffic."[55] As in other cities, postwar suburbanization was the root of these ridership losses. The city and suburbs doubled down on a massive highway program funded by a mix of local, state, and federal funds in the postwar decades.

City and state officials worked closely to move automobiles through the region at a speed that few transit systems anywhere could match. For example, Route 128 encircling cities and suburbs was upgraded to a four- to eight-lane superhighway during the 1950s, opening new areas for development. The 1948 State Highway Master Plan included a new series of expressway radials connecting downtown to Route 128, the Central Artery (cutting through downtown), and a potentially destructive new interior beltway. Some of the more ambitious roadways failed to reach fruition in close-in neighborhoods, like the interior beltway and South-

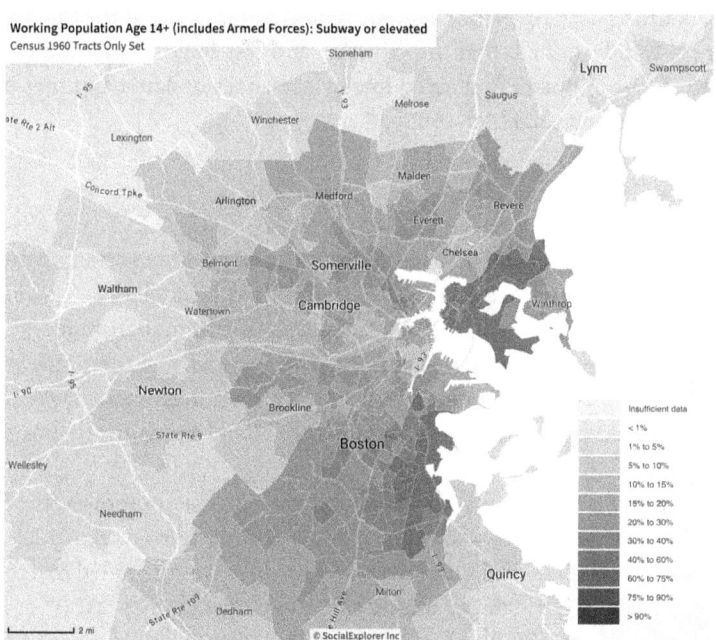

FIGURES 22A AND 22B. The elevated lines (*lower map*) encouraged and grew to serve dense development around stations. Bus and streetcar ridership (*upper map*) remained more widely distributed across the region. Source: Bus or Streetcar, 1960/Elevated or Subway, 1960/Social Explorer, accessed June 26, 2021.

west Expressway (see below), helping keep transit a strong competitor for some riders. But William Callahan, the Boston region's Robert Moses, successfully promoted and built out most of this outer regional road network that put existing transit to shame.[56] Driving was not just prevalent in outer suburbs either. In the fourteen towns of the MTA, where transit was more accessible, vehicle registrations increased 74 percent between 1946 and 1955.[57]

The Route 128 corridor suburbs in the 1950s, thanks to the highway programs, rising prosperity, and federal mortgage support, experienced growth rates of 36.4 percent. City residents, according to historian James C. O'Connell, were eager for auto-centric, low-density living, especially if subsidized by local, state, and federal policies: "Postwar middle-class and lower-middle-class families were tired of living in five-story walk-up blocks in the North and West Ends, the decaying row houses of the South End, and the three-deckers and old fashioned single- and two-families on tiny lots in Cambridge, Dorchester, and Somerville." Suburban towns zoned out most multifamily housing and created minimum lot sizes that preserved a country feeling even as the number of residents skyrocketed.[58] In 1970, when the dust of the postwar boom had settled, suburban Middlesex County had a density of just 1,648 residents per square mile (pop. 1.39 million) despite the inclusion of densely developed areas like Cambridge and Somerville. Norfolk County was even lower, 1,478 residents per square mile (pop. 605,000). By way of contrast, Suffolk County's density, including Boston, was 12,177 residents per square mile (pop. 735,190).[59]

Compounding the MTA's obstacles to regional service, commercial suburban districts rarely developed adjacent to transit. Shopping centers clustered around 128 exits while restaurants and stores boomed along suburban strips like Route 9 and US 1. According to Horace Schermerhorn, a member of the MTA Board of Trustees, suburbanites often "found it unnecessary to use public transportation . . . every one of the cities and towns are developing parking areas in their business section making it easier and easier for the public to drive to them and shop."[60] Industrial parks blossomed along Route 128 to tap the growing populations for an emerging generation of high-technology firms like defense contractor Raytheon, spun out from MIT. Most of these industrial parks were poorly located for transit, usually on vast greenfield sites near highways, as towns sought property tax without redeveloping their older village main streets for higher-density offices or retail operations.[61] Only about 15 percent of daily MTA riders in 1960 came from outside the fourteen-town MTA district, indicating the declining importance of transit to most Boston regional residents.[62]

To MTA managers and other transit boosters, rapid transit still seemed like the best hope for adding suburban riders, at least the small numbers still heading downtown for work, shopping, or leisure. MTA leaders believed that the "chaos of traffic" at rush hours gave separated transit a unique advantage: "We believe there is considerable doubt as to whether superhighways leading in and out of Boston will do other than attract more automobiles into this daily chaos." In 1954, for instance, the MTA opened rapid transit to Beachmont, Revere, and Wonderland in the north by using existing, abandoned surface rail rights-of-way.[63] And while legislators rejected Callahan's call for median public transit on Route 128,[64] the MTA was far advanced in a "rubber to rail" policy reflected in fifteen parking areas near rapid transit with moderate cost to park and ride.[65] By 1959, 826,000 cars used MTA lots, but the MTA only made $121,000 in fee revenue from them. The aim was to maintain the suburban-city connection regarding ridership and political support for transit subsidies rather than use parking as a significant contributor to the MTA's bottom line. There was much more revenue to be had in future taxes.[66]

Edward Dana in 1956 was among many of those disappointed that, while some modest postwar extensions had opened, "Boston's rapid transit had stalled at about the eight-mile radius. It should have been extended long ago to nearly twice that distance, in coordination, of course, with federal and state highways and large parking areas."[67] As approximately 82 percent of MTA riders used the rapid lines versus 18 percent for solely local travel, indicating their attractiveness, Dana was right about a missed opportunity.[68] Experts agreed, given the outward migration, "that the major hope for MTA's future lies in extending new rapid transit fingers to the suburbs."[69]

A visionary regional project of the era, similar to the Skokie Swift in Chicago, was refitting a former suburban commuter rail line for limited-stop streetcar subways. The approach promised faster service at a modest price. The state legislature in 1957 approved a new line from western Newton (near the rapidly expanding Route 128 state highway) that traveled on an existing ten-mile private right-of-way, primarily through lush Newton and Brookline suburbs, to a downtown Park Street subway connection. The project cost just $9.2 million, modest for its length, by retrofitting the abandoned Highland branch of the shuttered Boston and Albany commuter line. The MTA saved additional funds by reusing PCC streetcars from discontinued streetcar lines elsewhere in the system.[70] The line terminated 11.69 miles from Park Street, making its reach "twice as far as any other . . . rapid transit line," opening a new era of suburban semi-rapid transit.[71]

Suburban commuters flooded into the new service when it opened in 1959 despite the old equipment. A massive, two-thousand-car lot at the final station, and a few smaller lots closer in, were crucial to success.[72] In that first year, the Highlands (now Riverside Green Line) branch carried on average twenty-six thousand commuters a workday, making 134 round trips. The failed private commuter line it replaced had only taken 3,140 riders in sixteen trips in its last era of service.[73] MTA's leaders admitted in 1960 that, despite this ridership success, the new line lost $803,874 in 1960. The MTA general manager, recently relocated from New York, dismissed such losses because "true, economical, mass transportation must be subsidized one way or another." The service's ability to free "the equivalent of one traffic lane in the highway system during the peak hours" by cutting about 1,300 cars from nearby highways at peak times had to be considered in any accounting of transit extensions.[74] Approximately 35 percent of Riverside riders switched from driving to transit, a high figure in this era, and quite a few others had switched from higher-priced, slower, privately run suburban bus service.[75] Unlike many light-rail systems that followed, the Riverside line had many unique advantages as it connected to subway tunnels and other lines downtown. It helped that Boston's traffic was already horrendous.

The number of riders mattered, but *who* was riding the line promised a renewed suburban market for mass transit. Ridership surveys indicated high incomes; half of the riders surveyed were managers or professionals. According to the *Boston Herald*, the elite customers indicated that "the assumption that the middle and upper-income groups will scorn rapid transit is shown to be wrong."[76] A letter to the MTA from a vice president of State Street Bank, with suggestions for improvements in the new line, indicates the high status of many riders. Another gentleman from Wellesley, who worked for investment house Merrill Lynch, had similar ideas for service upgrades that would reduce crowding and speed service. He mentioned that "with slight improvements I feel that I could be encouraged to use your much publicized Riverside branch probably 100% of the time."[77] In 1960, realtors claimed that the Riverside line improved property values in western suburbs such as Wellesley, even if these towns did not directly benefit from a local stop. The option of cutting "a drive to Boston to work has resulted in a group of prospects from a wider area who are interested in owning homes in this area." About 40 percent of new riders came from beyond the MTA district.[78] The MTA boosted service on the Riverside line in 1961 in response to delays and numerous complaints about crowding. Popularity represented its own challenge.[79]

Not all was rosy in regional cooperation under the MTA. For example, the New Haven Railroad began moving to end its New Colony commuter rail service on the south shore as early as 1948. Some called again to extend MTA rapid transit to Quincy and Braintree to connect these towns to the rapid lines (Red Line) running through the Cambridge-Dorchester tunnel.[80] Yet Braintree and Quincy, in a nonbinding referendum, overwhelmingly voted against the extension of MTA rapid transit in 1948. The Chamber of Commerce and business groups feared "increased tax rates."[81] The MTA deficit was a significant problem, according to the *Boston Globe*, for "winning assent of the suburbanites to such new MTA extensions."[82] The state delayed acting and decided in 1958 to subsidize the Old Colony railroad to remain in service rather than force a new rapid system on the towns. The Massachusetts House of Representatives rejected another Old Colony MTA takeover in 1960. With daily commuting in most outer suburbs in the low single digits, gaining political support regionally would be challenging.[83]

MTA to MBTA

Rising deficits set in motion significant increases in the assessed regional deficits during both the 1950s and 1960s. Even though the MTA tax counted for only 14 percent of the total real-estate tax increases (between 1950 and 1960) in the city of Boston, the total sums collected made good headlines.[84] The assessable fourteen-town deficit was $7.8 million in 1952,[85] and a whopping $18 million in 1959.[86] MTA managers even admitted that the annual deficit was "becoming a negative state of mind."[87] The MTA's manager in 1961 may have predicted "an end to the operating deficit itself in three or four years,"[88] but only a few million came off the top. Like a fare increase in 1961, some deficit solutions had hurt ridership.[89] Fares still covered 69 percent of operating costs in 1963, and while high compared to today, this was much reduced from 81 percent in 1948.[90]

As in other cities, the deficits contributed to public and journalistic criticism of transit management. A walkout in 1961 stranded 350,000 commuters on a "bitter January morning."[91] To onlookers, the MTA was the most "politically-hamstrung street railway agency in any big American city." The governor appointed the trustees, the legislature "[froze] into law so many restrictions," and an Advisory Board (1952) from the towns policed expansions and assessments. An arbitration board appointed by the state controlled wages and fringe benefits.[92] Governor John A. Volpe, in 1961 thought, "it is little wonder that in this climate no community beyond the immediate limits of MTA service desires to become part of it."[93] A Democratic push in early 1962 gave the MTA Advisory Board, composed of representatives from the fourteen cities and towns, greater control over MTA budgets, a clear sign of growing political dissatisfaction.[94] A stunning $21 million town assessment in 1963 led to local taxpayer revolt.[95]

While understandably favored by the rest of the state, the heavy burden of the transit taxes on just fourteen towns was unfair because many citizens in Eastern Massachusetts indirectly benefited from the system through reduced traffic and transit connections. Governor Volpe, for instance, strongly supported spreading deficits to "fringe" communities in early 1962,[96] because "for a healthy future for all, MTA must break the bonds of its present legal prison and tap the populous suburbs."[97] The fourteen towns had been understandably "reluctant to approve various needed rapid transit extensions" because of fear of additional taxes.[98]

Several factors coalesced to push the state legislature to rethink the structure of the MTA, leading to today's MBTA. City life was changing in the 1960s, bringing new relevance to mass transit. The bloom had come off the full-throttle development of highways. The 1948 State Highway Master Plan, launched with a $100 million bond, had led to destructive projects: the Central Artery that wiped out great swaths of the downtown, Storrow Drive that paved over valuable sections of parkland on the Charles, and the various radial expressways requiring extensive clearance and displacement. While regional planners had predicted that highways would fail to manage traffic unless there were "complementary plans ... for extensions and betterments of the rapid transit system,"[99] those plans had not been realized.[100]

Nor were the completed highway networks always dependable. On December 30, 1963, "an immovable mass of automobiles clogged downtown streets and the expressway for hours. That was the nightmare when an estimated 100,000 vehicles—many of them single occupant—tried to squeeze into roads designed to carry perhaps half the number." It was noted that "at the same times, MTA's rapid transit lines operated without interruption."[101] Boston's antique downtown street network had proved "entirely inadequate for any large volumes of automotive traffic." The successful freeway revolt in Boston took place primarily after the passing of the MBTA in 1964 (see below), but general dissatisfaction with highways was already widely felt in the early 1960s and would be key to lobbying for greater state support.[102]

The reemerging downtown growth regime was another force for state-subsidized transit. The dense downtown needed transit to thrive. In the late 1940s, Boston enjoyed twice the rate of service jobs as the rest of New England, with continuing strengths in finance, insurance, and law. By 1963, reflecting this strength and the growing white-collar sector, 242,000 workers crowded daily into downtown Boston, or about 20 percent of Eastern Massachusetts employment. Development-friendly policies included clearing old commercial areas like Scollay Square and lifting downtown building height limitations. Under the leadership of Mayor Collins and planning entrepreneurs such as Ed Logue at the Boston Redevelopment Authority, new complexes such as the Prudential Center and Government Center redefined downtown as a place for modern businessmen. By the mid-1960s, several bank buildings had sprouted, including State Street Bank's high rise. Successful CBD renewal was crucial to transit's continuing relevance and broader political support for renovation and expansion.[103]

The immediate catalyst for MTA reform, and the creation of the MBTA in 1964, was the imminent collapse of surviving commuter rail service to the various suburbs and towns surrounding the core. Regional suburban concerns continued to drive statewide transit policy in Boston, as in New York and Philadelphia. A combined federal and state grant in 1962 for commuter rail support in Eastern Massachusetts, for instance, had attracted many riders back to the rails through more service and lower fares. But when the temporary funds ran out, so did the additional service.[104] In 1963, thanks to continuing losses, two dominant private railroad carriers (the Boston and Maine and New Haven) asked permission to drop commuter service along the north and southwest suburban routes. MTA reported that it could not "on its own, act to help these people. The MTA can only suggest, or prod or urge," because most of the affected areas were outside the fourteen core towns.[105]

As in New York, the power of the suburbanites was the key to unlocking long-standing plans for metropolitan systems like the MBTA.[106] The residual Boston regional commuter riders, usually well under 10 percent of daily commuters in any towns, belied their political and economic power; wealthy areas such as Beverly and Concord hit above their weight. As a result, many politicians began to support suburban transit improvement, even if the likelihood of immediate service improvements remained distant. "The gnawing horrors of congestion and accidents on the expressways," according to the *Globe*, "have impressed some key suburbanite leaders that rail as well as rubber must be part of a balanced transportation system."[107] Suburbanites also stood to benefit from future federal transit subsidies with public ownership.[108] The transit managers were ready: "The basic strategy of the MTA is to enlarge the spider's web, out to the periphery of Rte. 128" where suburbanites would park and ride to downtown Boston.[109]

The inability of Boston's MTA to reach the regional transit goals set a decade or more in the past was an underlying factor in organizational reform. Beyond limited extensions on the Blue Line and the new Riverside line, the MTA's ambitious plans for expansion had made no headway.[110] All the three rapid lines remained distinct, linked only by passages through stations, and each had distinctive equipment. There were just forty-three rapid stations total. The Everett–Forest Hills line (today's Orange Line) had relatively new cars but stretched just eight miles (fifteen stations) and remained on its clanky old, elevated structure for almost the whole route, except for 1.23 miles downtown under Washington Street. The Cambridge-Dorchester line (today's Red Line) had new cars but was just nine miles long. The East Boston line (today's Blue Line) stretched just six miles from Bowdoin to Wonderland. Today's Green Line streetcar subways remained popular on the west side and Brookline but were still running older PCC cars, built between 1941 and 1951. Preservation of the rapid and streetcar subway lines was a victory over abandonment, but the system was not keeping pace with the region's growth.[111]

A state-authorized Mass Transportation Commission in December 1963 called for the MBTA, which would "own and operate or control virtually all commuter rail, bus and rapid transit service within a 40-mile radius of Downtown Boston." The MTA staff created a detailed MBTA plan with the help of a federal grant. The proposed MBTA was championed by a powerful state legislator, Mario Umana of Boston.[112] Umana supported an extensive expansion program, including seventy-eight towns, commuter subsidies, and rapid transit extensions.[113] Democratic governor Endicott Peabody in 1964 endorsed the expansion to seventy-eight cities, rapid transit expansion programs, commuter rail subsidies, and bailouts for suburban bus companies.[114] The MBTA emerged as a compromise between suburban political leaders who "recognized the need to improve service outside the core area" and inner-city representatives seeking "to distribute the cost of the system more widely."[115] Many believed, as well, that Edward Dana was the true "father" of the MBTA, lending his considerable prestige to the effort.[116]

The MBTA, expanded to include seventy-eight communities, would spread the burden more equitably on a regional basis long term. However, the sixty-four added towns would pay much less than the original fourteen towns directly served by rapid lines. The new towns also benefited from a schedule of slow, planned increases in their share into the 1970s. MBTA reports were filled for years with attempts to provide transparency to the assessment calculations, but even one analyst admitted that the "complex assessment formula" was challenging to follow. In sum, however, "each MBTA community paid for its specific services, while the entire region shared the cost of general benefits." The state also gave the MBTA the power to raise fares without Department of Public Utilities (DPU) approval, a nod to "pay as you go" budgeting that, while perhaps fiscally responsible, could have threatened Boston's successful retention of riders thanks to its comparatively low fares. The political price of integrating the skeptical suburbs into a notoriously costly assessment scheme was a promise to control local assessments.[117]

The plan as passed included $225 million in state-secured bonds for capital investment, funded partially by an innovative statewide two-cent-per-pack tax on cigarettes. The commonwealth would assume millions in MBTA costs annually, including 90 percent of the debt service cost for rapid transit extensions and 50 percent for commuter rail continuation. These priorities directly addressed sticking points in service expansion and assured suburbanites they would get a hefty share of the new funding.[118] The MBTA launched in 1965 with promises that riders would benefit from faster commutes, air conditioning, quieter cars, and soft seats in just a few years. Peter Chermayeff's T graphic system, including color-coded rail lines (Red, Blue, Green, and Orange) papered over the distinct nature of the lines and their varying states of repair, making it appear to be a more unified system than it was.[119] By 1967, the MBTA was counting on millions annually from a mix of state tax breaks (on fuel), assistance on its general debt service, commuter rail subsidies, and interest payments on new bonds.[120]

Multiyear subsidy agreements with the Boston and Maine and New Haven Railroads were finally signed in 1968 to continue service for just sixteen thousand remaining commuters in forty-seven communities, at the cost of $4.6 million, who were "saved from the bleak prospect of a cessation of railroad commuter service."[121] The MBTA subsidized commuter rail routes with diesel services such as those to Concord on the west and Beverly in the north as part of the regional bargain, despite the highly restricted zoning and an auto-centric lifestyle.[122] The mayor of Boston, John F. Collins, responsible for 56 percent of MBTA subsidies, was understandably upset in 1967 that "the public subsidy cost for railroad commuter service is exceedingly high," with fifty-two cents of required subsidy per trip on commuter rail versus four cents on rapid transit.[123] However, the subsidies would continue with strong support from influential political and business leaders in the wealthy suburban areas served by commuter rail.[124]

The MBTA's 1966 expansion plan included just five rapid transit extensions running twenty-nine miles, a more realistic program than in past years.[125] MBTA officials believed that "rail transit beyond a densely settled core city is unlikely to be economical."[126] Managers thus promised to plan a new system "upon the present one, which provides an excellent base for expansion and modernization." So even though "the scope of the system must include all 78 communities," the MBTA's standard that "every rapid transit line must be a self-supporting operation" tempered the visionary elements.[127] The MBTA priority projects were, therefore, familiar: the Red Line extended to both North Braintree–Quincy and Alewife, and a southwest (Orange) corridor project to replace the elevated and extend the line to Melrose.[128] The Orange Line Southwest Expressway (I-95) median rail project, modeled on Chicago, would be a "dramatic first for this section of the country" and would ultimately include "future extensions farther into the Southwest suburbs."[129] The MBTA also planned for twenty-five thousand parking spaces near transit stops so that suburbanites could benefit from rail transit.[130]

The expansion plan encouraged bus feeder routes to rapid transit and lots of parking, but the managers of the new MBTA showed much less faith in buses. In Toronto, by way of contrast, managers used an expanded, extensive, and dependable bus system to link the suburbs firmly to the city and mass transit. Boston focused mostly on rail in the years that followed. Despite their many advantages in terms of noise and pollution, even the trackless trolley routes mostly turned out to be temporary expedients. In 1952, the MTA had 440 trackless trolleys,[131] but by 1966 the peak of MBTA rush-hour trolley service included just forty-seven trackless trolleys.[132] Over time, most of the remaining diesel bus lines became "feeder" routes to rapid transit routes. So, while riding an MBTA bus in 1966 was still a bargain, just ten cents, it did not buy access to a high-quality regional bus network. Moreover, even in 1966, most bus routes were still within six miles of downtown, and the average route was just 3.5 miles long. The peak MBTA bus routes used just 669 buses spread thinly across a vast region.[133] The lopsided rail versus bus funding remained constant over time.

The rail + parking lot formula, typical in the United States, undermined the reputation of an excellent transit technology like buses suited to highly decentralized regions. Had suburbanites understood the potential of bus service, allowing them to leave their cars at home entirely rather than paying for parking at stations, the history of the MBTA might have been different. New investments in regional buses in Boston looked mostly to high-speed express bus service along highways, a typical strategy in postwar cities, leveraging highway infrastructure. Express bus service initiated in 1967 on the Massachusetts Turnpike attracted over three thousand riders a day from Watertown-Newton to Boston. It proved to managers that "public acceptance of a fast, clean and comfortable trip into the core city" was attractive.[134] But express service like this, as in other cities, had limited potential to reshape suburban travel patterns.

MBTA planning for new rapid transit service took place in the context of typical challenges to daily operations. The MBTA, for instance, absorbed most of the costs of failing suburban commuter rail and bus lines, further ballooning its deficits. Much of the equipment and infrastructure was old. According to internal records, the PCC cars on the Green Line were showing their age with frequent derailments and collisions. The MBTA had problems finding enough PCCs to maintain service on its lines.[135] The deputy general manager claimed that while the new rapid transit cars were "one of the best fleets in the county," the Green Line PCCs were "the one sore point in MBTA equipment" because "breakdown daily is much higher than any other type of equipment."[136]

As in other American cities, managers in the late 1960s and early 1970s also had to contend with growing disorder on mass transit including antiwar protests, vandalism, and various forms of violent crime, perpetrated on both riders and MBTA staff. Between January 1 and June 30 in 1966, there were 1,424 incidents on the system, including vandalism, assault, pickpockets, and so on, and 171 arrests by MBTA police.[137] By 1969, the MBTA was spending $750,000 per year on its police force.[138] In 1968, in response to the "discontent and unrest that has scarred the urban scene in summers past," managers ran an "Employment Express" bus to booming Route 128 office and industrial parks from Roxbury.[139]

The MBTA, in an era of riots and civil rights, finally reckoned with its own sins of human resources. Out of six thousand MBTA employees in 1966, only approximately one hundred were nonwhite.[140] A 1968 memo from the manager of labor relations on the plans for a new cohort of apprentices reflects the external pressure for equity: "As you no doubt know, apprenticeship is a very sensitive area and a matter of great concern among minority groups." He believed there should be "an opportunity for the Authority to continue to make available for members of such groups employment opportunities in the Machinist Apprentice area."[141] An outreach program in 1968 to prepare potential pre-apprentice trainees for the hiring exam in Roxbury was "Drive Your Troubles Away." The MBTA *Commuter* newsletter targeted at current employees nevertheless felt it had to point out that attendance in the pre-apprentice program did not guarantee "a position with the Authority. They will be required to take the same examination as any other applicant."[142] It was hard to hide in the newsletters, however, just how white the MBTA staff was at the time. The affirmative action programs have slowly diversified the MBTA's staff (see below), but it has taken decades of outreach and efforts.[143]

Even More Subsidies

Without the new financing provided by the MBTA, Boston's regional transit system would have been in permanent crisis mode, as was the case in Chicago. Mayor Collins, in 1966, had brushed off the concerns about MBTA assessments because even though he was not "completely happy" about the situation, he also assumed "that the directors are spending money carefully, because it is public money." This equanimity about transit spending was rare for a postwar American mayor and would not be sustained.[144] The MBTA leadership, for its part, admitted enduring problems of inflation and fixed costs but also cited the requirement that "we operate routes that do not make a profit, that do not break even, that lose money. And we must."[145]

Labor costs had increased for multiple reasons. Thanks to shorter days, holidays, coffee breaks, vacations, and other benefits, managers in engineering and maintenance, for instance, calculated that the productivity per employee dropped 31 percent between 1946 and 1968. Yet the challenge of maintenance was greater than ever thanks to rapid transit vehicles that were "vastly more sophisticated and complex." The multiplying diesel buses rapidly replacing the trackless trolleys also required 28 percent more person-hours per mile. The growing army of private autos on the roads not only stole fares but increased operating costs: "Today, the rate and extent of collision damage being suffered by our bus and PCC car fleet has soared to disconcerting heights." In 1969, for instance, the management counted thirty-four buses, nine PCC cars, five rapid cars, and two trackless trolleys "held-in for major repairs necessitated by collision." And these were just the worst cases. Managers calculated that 40 percent of trades' time had to be devoted to collision damage; these were hours lost to regular maintenance. Pensions, vacations, and higher wages across the board drove costs up despite reduced head counts from postwar highs.[146]

Higher costs, absent extensive operating subsidies, meant higher fares. A fare increase in 1968, for instance, increased revenue per ride even though it discouraged ridership.[147] Assessments also went up. In 1969 the

MBTA assessed the communities $31 million,[148] $61.5 million in 1971,[149] and a startling $74.5 million in 1972.[150] Such high deficits and modestly declining ridership (in 1971, 149 million passengers)[151] provoked a predictable backlash from the towns. The increasingly vocal MBTA Advisory Board, reflecting the political leadership of all the MBTA towns, highlighted rising wages and pension costs. They began to use their final budget approval power to get the attention of the governor and state legislature. In 1970, for instance, they recommended a $10 million cut to demonstrate the "critical and urgent need for additional state financial assistance."[152] With Boston mayor Kevin White at the lead, the Advisory Board demanded a summit with the governor, legislative leaders, and MBTA managers. Like other board members, Mayor White felt that overreliance on property taxes had led to the "threadbare facility that now exists." The board restored the cut, but the issues remained unresolved.[153]

The long-term aim of members was now to extend the financing beyond the seventy-nine MBTA cities and towns.[154] Mayor White reasoned that the eastern region "generates over one hundred million dollars in gasoline taxes every year—money that is used to build highways throughout the state." Yet the state legislature refused to spend money "to provide an alternative to highways in this region." White, who reported that Boston's share of the assessment would be $33 million in 1972, had prepared legislation "that requires the state to take over the entire deficit, lock, stock, and barrel."[155] Even towns with modest payments were outraged. For instance, according to local officials, the town of "Wayland paid hundreds of thousands of dollars in MBTA assessments for practically nothing in the way of transit service."[156]

The Advisory Board went to the brink in 1972. The board that year highlighted what they considered to be the inequity in the MBTA budget: 49.5 percent came from property tax assessment, 39.6 percent from fares and various revenue, and just 11 percent from state aid.[157] In 1972, the board demanded state legislators "approve no highway appropriation except as part of a balanced transportation package."[158] The Advisory Board, led by White, effectively zeroed out the MBTA's essential supplementary funding request in the summer of 1972,[159] in order "to force state takeover of the deficit."[160] The board eventually approved the supplement but had nearly forced a crisis in operations.[161]

The year 1973, like 1918, 1947, and 1964 before it, was another "historic departure" for Boston's mass transit system. The state in 1973 made an aggressive move to right the ship by approving unparalleled transit support from general revenues—a step long demanded by the Advisory Board. In a rare move nationally, "the Highway Trust Fund will be opened up for mass transit projects—fifty percent of the MBTA's net cost of service will be assumed by the Commonwealth."[162] Among the elements assumed by the state included debt service, commuter railroad subsidies, unreimbursed depreciation, amortization, and an additional payment that year of $35 million from general revenues.[163] Governor Francis Sargent admitted that the "maximum use of federal and state assistance" was required because "local property taxes, already overburdened, cannot bear the strain of more and more assessments and expenditures."[164] The Boston region had come a long way since the modest subsidies of the elevated.

Direct state contributions to reducing the annual deficit became part of the MBTA formula for retaining service in the face of record national inflation. In 1975, for instance, the seventy-eight towns would have been stuck with a $125 million bill had the state legislature not approved a $52 million subsidy. The MBTA raised bus fares to twenty-five cents and rapid to fifty cents in 1975 in response to "interests of the taxpayer" and rampant inflation.[165] The towns, despite state aid, remained in the crosshairs at assessment time in the late 1970s. There were plenty of aggrieved drivers who rejected arguments about transit taxes' social and economic importance. Organized as Citizens for Limited Taxation, they succeeded in getting a ballot initiative passed in 1980, Proposition 2.5, that set an "outer limit on how much revenue could be collected from real estate" from district communities.[166] Managers, under pressure, cut service 9.5 percent in 1981,[167] and raised fares again, this time from fifty to seventy-five cents for rapid fare, while bus fares doubled to fifty cents—a significant blow to local riders.[168]

The MBTA was only able to avoid the relentless cutting and fare increases required in Chicago and other cities during this time because of blank checks from the state. The new law in the Boston region, for instance, capped local assessment at $95 million in 1982,[169] a limit that could have generated mammoth deficits and widespread service reductions. Yet, in practice, the state simply made up the growing difference between lost tax assessment and the growing cost of operations with "state-collected funds."[170] So, even though the total deficit was $370 million in 1985, for instance, commonwealth and other assistance covered most of it because the state only charged the towns $104 million of the deficit. The state government dutifully covered the remainder.[171] The towns, and the remaining MBTA riders, had successfully slipped the bill to the whole state population rather than just the most urbanized eastern half. The mood at the statehouse in the late 1980s, according to MBTA managers, remained surprisingly tolerant: "there is a sense that key policymakers are concerned not only about a negative reaction from the public but are convinced, on philosophical grounds, that relatively low fares are optimal."[172]

The pattern set in 1918 has held to the present. Despite a 634 percent increase in the deficit between 1965 and 1991, the agency continued to operate at a high level of service, at modest cost to consumers, largely thanks to state support. Economist José Ibanez-Gomez calculated that, in 1970 constant dollars, the cost to ride "per linked passenger trip fell from 27 cents in 1965 to 21 cents in 1991, a reduction of 27 percent." Low fares, he believes, were key to ridership growth in the 1970s and 1980s. The number of subsidies to keep the system moving would shock the earliest supporters of regional transit, but the fact of state support would not.[173]

After decades of making up annual deficits year over year, the commonwealth in 2000 substituted this makeshift tradition with Future Funding, "which among other things dedicated 20 percent of the state sales tax to the MBTA." Future Funding has grown into one of the nation's most effective pro-transit state financing programs.[174] Transit generosity does have limits in the Boston region. In 2015, thanks to questions about MBTA budgets and management, the commonwealth created a Fiscal and Management Control Board. But the subsidies continued to flow despite the state oversight. For instance, in 2019 alone, the dedicated sales tax to the MBTA came to $1.032 billion, which, when combined with the local assessments of $170 million, comprised more than half of MBTA's total annual budget of $2.057 billion. Extraordinarily little transit would run in Boston without these subsidies.[175]

Regional Transit after the Highways

The ongoing financial troubles of the MBTA in the 1960s and 1970s might have led to the abandonment of long-held dreams. But in Boston, thanks to preserved density, citizen pressure, a booming economy—and the mix of fares and local, state, and federal support—MBTA managers moved ahead with expensive but significant line extensions. If the accomplishment was much less than the earlier plans had envisioned, it was more than might be justified by ridership alone.

The resistance to urban renewal had helped preserve more density than might have survived otherwise. The General Plan for Boston (1950), for instance, envisioned clearing 20 percent (2,700 acres) of the central city. Leaders eventually removed one-third of the historic core for urban renewal or highway projects.[176] Yet, Boston's emerging historic preservation movement, supported by wealthy, white urbanites in transit-rich areas such as Beacon Hill and the South End, rallied in the 1950s and 1960s to defend neighborhoods threatened by urban renewal and highways.[177] The West End neighborhood clearance tragedy inspired white ethnics to fight major planning initiatives in districts such as Charlestown and East Boston in the 1960s. The BRA's executive director, Ed Logue, compromised in Charlestown, agreeing to 90 percent rehab in 1965.[178]

The high homeownership rates in the towns served by the MBTA, such as Cambridge and Sommerville, dominated by whites who owned houses or two- and three-flats, were crucial in preserving moderate density more broadly. Residents helped stop highway plans from smashing through many more of these areas. In addition, the massive postwar expansion in the major universities in Cambridge, MIT and Harvard, created significant demand for close-in apartments and convenient transit. The expanding megastructure campus of the University of Massachusetts Boston was an essential new destination on the Red Line to the south of the CBD.

Resistance to slum clearance also grew in minority neighborhoods. The city experienced a significant increase in its Black population: growing from 23,679 in 1940 to 104,707 in 1970 (from 3 to 16 percent). Black families remained highly segregated even as they broke out of the most crowded areas. For example, Washington Park in Roxbury was 70 percent white in 1950, but 70 percent Black in 1960. The Jewish population of Dorchester and Upper Roxbury dropped from seventy thousand in 1950 to sixteen thousand in 1970. Black families who rented and bought many whites' former houses helped preserve both density and transit ridership.[179]

City officials in the postwar years counterproductively targeted Black sections of Roxbury, the South End, and Dorchester for urban renewal, including clearance and highways. The BRA's Ed Logue, under pressure, finally backed off the most damaging clearance programs in the 1960s. For instance, Logue emphasized rehabilitation (75 percent) in Roxbury. Thanks to density, transit ridership remained consistent in Roxbury between 1960 and 1970, with ridership rates of about 40–50 percent in both censuses.[180]

The city's comparatively aggressive program of subsidized housing, as in New York City, has likely contributed to sustained ridership in many neighborhoods. Many of these public and affordable housing projects are transit accessible and, because of the low or moderate income level of the residents, more likely to produce riders. Boston, for instance, has mostly preserved and renovated its public housing despite social and management issues. Starting in 1983, the city also required subsidized housing in market-rate buildings and added inclusionary zoning in 2000. According to Harvard's Gerald Frug, "almost 20 percent" of Boston "housing stock (in some neighborhoods, over 40 percent) was subsidized in 2000." Who lives near transit matters.[181]

State highway planners still had plans in the 1960s to crisscross much of the metro area with highways. But Robert Davidson, a transportation consultant in tune with the changing zeitgeist, reminded readers in a 1963 *Globe* editorial that while "billions of dollars have been invested in streets, highways, and broad expressways," the "'captive passengers' without cars" were "left with limited mobility because no automobile is available." Transit, he argued, was "for the less fortunate non-automobile user; the student, the elderly, the secretary."[182] Citizen resistance began in earnest in the mid-1960s when, according to the MBTA, the "bulldozers began clearing land for a new expressway that would connect interstate I-95 with the center of Boston." The destructive highway development phase, and the prospect of even more disruption in surrounding towns and cities, led to widespread displacement and citizen revolt. Under enormous activist pressure, Governor Sargent finally declared a moratorium on additional highway construction in 1970 within the Route 128 corridor.[183]

The cancellation undermined the entire planned regional highway network. Planners cut several superhighways: the Inner Belt (designed to cut through sections of Boston, Cambridge, and Somerville), the connecting section of the Northwest Expressway through Cambridge and Sommerville, and I-95 highways both on the north shore and in the southwest. As a result, even today, only the north–south I-93 highway and east–west Mass Turnpike make uninterrupted journeys from the suburbs to the city center. Cancellation on such a massive scale improved prospects for future transit thanks to a much less efficient and more crowded highway network. Equivalent cancellations to highways from the period were rare and took place in San Francisco and New York with similar benefits for transit competitiveness.[184]

In 1974, the federal government permitted a diversion of funds originally promised for highways to mass transit. These funds and growing federal capital support for transit, more generally, proved crucial to maintaining MBTA's rapidly inflating capital plans.[185] The staff revised the MBTA's master plan in 1966, 1968, 1969, and 1971, each time with a higher price tag on the planned improvements.[186] In 1966, for instance, the MBTA announced a capital plan of $346 million, with the federal government promising to cover $126 million of the total.[187] An advertising firm hired by the MBTA in 1967 encouraged leaders to rebrand the T as a "progressive public transportation system" on the mend whose high costs were "simply the price that must be paid for progress."[188] The managers seemed to heed the advice. In 1968 the MBTA floated a trial balloon for $500–$700 million in capital funds, including rapid extensions.[189] The MBTA began borrowing more money, $250 million, against promised federal funds for what was now definitely a $700 million capital program.[190] Between 1965 and 1973, the MBTA hoovered up $294 million in federal grants and claimed the nation's greatest percentage of federal grants in a capital plan. For 1974–83, an additional Transit Capital Program projected spending $605 million, split equally between federal and local funding (bonds).[191]

MBTA's expansion and modernization programs funded from these plans benefited from good timing. The 1970s were grim in the city of Boston, with high unemployment, deindustrialization, fights over school integration, and the city's population dropping from 641,000 to 562,000.[192] However, at the regional and CBD level, the story was brighter. The Massachusetts Miracle of the 1970s and 1980s in academe, high technology, hospitals, design, and finance helped pay for the state-level subsidies. Tech workers in Cambridge and white-collar employees on their way to the CBD also helped fill trains and buses.[193] In the 1970s, the Rouse Company's Faneuil Hall "festival marketplace" project and the pedestrianization of the Downtown Crossing shopping area leveraged nearby transit lines. The MBTA accordingly counted modest ridership increases in the 1980s, growing from 153 million T riders in 1983[194] to 164 million riders in 1985.[195]

MBTA made effective use of federal and other capital subsidies to rebuild and modestly expand its service. The MBTA, for instance, reinvested in the Green Line streetcar subways. The excellent quality of the West End streetcar system's original design, including so many exclusive rights-of-way and direct access to downtown subway tunnels, helped advocates defend them. While there had been talk in the 1960s of "replacing all the trolleys" with diesel buses, such a move was quashed. According to *Mass Transit* magazine, "protests from environmentalists, a vocal segment of Boston's large academic community, coupled with Massachusetts's decision to scrap plans for a cross-town expressway that would have intercepted the trolley tracks," saved the streetcar lines.[196] In partnership with San Francisco, the MBTA ordered new Boeing Vertol streetcars in the early 1970s, primarily thanks to federal funds. The first cars arrived in Boston in 1975 and featured an articulated midsection, smoother ride, less noise, and better lighting, heat, and air conditioning. The revamped lines demonstrated that city leaders elsewhere could have modernized more streetcar systems in the postwar years.[197]

By 1985, the MBTA's bus routes had also made a modest comeback, carrying 365,000 riders per day on an improved and expanded fleet of 1,162 buses. Yet buses in Boston, as in so many other cities, remained a lower priority for the agency despite their potential for comprehensive service over large, low-density areas.[198] According to Gomez-Ibanez, under the MBTA, "bus, streetcar, and trolley bus mileage increased by 11 percent between 1965 and 1990," a fraction of the increased mileage on rapid transit of 107 percent. The MBTA, responding to longtime concerns about bus service quality, has a well-advanced program today to upgrade service, including new buses and a rapidly expanding network of exclusive lanes.[199]

Rapid transit modernization and expansion proved complicated and expensive on the Orange and Red rapid lines. However, unlike Baltimore or Atlanta, the extensions attracted more riders once completed because they developed from an intact legacy system with surrounding density. After decades of development, the MBTA finally opened the aboveground Red Line extension to Quincy in 1971, stretching just 6.35 miles. The line offered a one-seat rapid connection directly on the Red Line to downtown Boston and Cambridge and tapped an area of sizable population with terrible car traffic. From September to December 1971, the extension carried 1.9 million riders, or about twenty-two thousand passengers a day.[200] The Braintree stop (1,322 parking spaces) opened in 1981, and the Quincy Adams station finally opened in 1983 with a mammoth two-thousand-car garage. The extension to these communities, competing effectively with crowded highways, was part of Boston's long-term strategy of moving suburban drivers to transit and delivering service to regional assessment payers.[201]

The northern Red Line subway extension from Harvard Square to Alewife took much longer than intended (1978–85) and was extraordinarily expensive for just 3.2 miles ($547 million, or $1.3 billion in 2020 dollars). Cambridge's emergence as an edge city, including the growing campuses and related research enterprises for Harvard and MIT, was crucial to ridership, as was the rebounding Boston downtown. The neighborhoods around the new Red Line extension stations by 1987 boasted 1.4 million square feet in new commercial space with another 2.3 million square feet planned. As on the south shore, park-and-ride lots were crucial, with about a third of the new riders leaving their cars behind at the vast Alewife parking structure.[202]

Exclusive suburbs limited the Red Line expansion plans on both ends of the line. Suburban Arlington residents, for instance, successfully fought off extensions beyond Alewife, which is at the Cambridge-Arlington border, on a typical suburban not-in-my-backyard basis.[203] The prosperous residents of Milton on the south side of the Red Line stopped the conversion of the Ashmont-Mattapan PCC line to rapid transit, including a new repair yard at the end of the line. The Milton Board of Selectman in 1968 came out against the high cost, low ridership (three thousand people per day on the PCC line), loss of PCC local stops, an ugly elevated track structure, lack of parking, and projected congestion. The charming PCCs still run on the line to this day.[204]

The Orange Line modernization, adopted in the spirit of 1960s advocacy planning, brought MBTA managers together with citizens in the late 1970s to develop a community-friendly plan to replace the canceled Southwest Expressway project. Planners moved sections of the entire elevated line away from its traditional Washington Street elevated route, surrounded by nonwhite, densely built-up neighborhoods, to the nearby open cut made by the planned highway and additional rights-of-way purchased from railroads. The relocated line impacted an area of up to four miles wide, holding about 25 percent of the city population, including much of the city's nonwhite residents, a higher percentage of whom still used mass transit.[205]

Thanks to years of community advocacy above ground on the Orange Line, a revitalized corridor included a fifty-two-acre linear park with bicycle paths, ball courts, gardens, landscaped walkways, and new auto crossings to reknit areas destroyed by the road clearance.[206] The planned open spaces, new housing, rapid transit stops, new high schools, and a community college came at a high price. The main segment opened in 1987,[207] at $743 million ($1.6 billion in 2020 dollars).[208] While some questioned the shifting of the elevated line from its traditional route, and the MBTA eventually provided the Silver Line semi-BRT as partial compensation to Roxbury residents, the Orange Line has grown in popularity thanks to rising density along its route.

The MBTA, as part of the continuing regional bargain, also saved and helped update the region's commuter system that might have disappeared entirely. Given the crucial role played by the seventy-eight towns in creating the MBTA, attention had to be paid to the small but politically essential riders in far-flung suburban towns. Suburban commuters are still waiting for high-speed electrified trains (developed over time in much of the New York and Philadelphia commuter rail systems). Yet, the MBTA's mix of subsidy and direct management of commuter rail had demonstrable success in staving off in the 1960s a complete collapse of the commuter rail system. The MBTA opted for a mix of direct management and contracts with private operators to meet the needs of suburbanites rather than complete public management (an arrangement that persists today). By 1981, the combined commuter lines hit an annual ridership of ten million passengers, the highest until then in Boston-area commuter rail history. Revenues covered 25 percent of operations, up from 22 percent, which can be read as either success or failure from a financial point of view.[209]

The investment in saving the commuter rail system paid off—at least for the remaining, often affluent, riders. Between 1979 and 1983, commuter rail ridership increased 34 percent, reflecting the growing strength of the downtown financial sector.[210] In 1985, the commuter rail system's eight lines served eighty-five stations along 244 route miles. Today's twelve commuter lines serve 137 stops on 388 route miles, including a distant city like Worcester in Western Massachusetts. Sizable ridership (about 121,000 daily riders in 2019) has proved the value of rescuing the system. Extension of commuter rail service has been key to expanding the number of MBTA towns to 176.[211]

The commuter rail success is notable, but the dividends to regional congestion are limited by exclusive suburban zoning. The Lincoln Land Institute estimates that "if land near Greater Boston's transit stations averaged 10 units per acre instead of 6.4," builders could add another 253,000 housing units to the region. Many commuter rail stops lack sufficient density despite the subsidized transit on offer. Hopefully, this will change in future years.[212] At the time of this writing (2022), the state was rolling out new statewide rules requiring a minimum percentage of multifamily zoning in MBTA towns near rapid and commuter rail transit stops. The new guidelines responded to long-standing pressure from organizations like the Citizens' Housing and Planning Association, the Livable Streets Alliance, and the Metropolitan Area Planning Council.[213]

The built achievement under MBTA control was costly and remains expensive to maintain today. In recent years, growing numbers of derailments on the T system have highlighted the challenge and spurred action. The MBTA-DOT five-year capital plan (2020–24) approved in 2019, for instance, totals $18.3 billion for a mix of rail projects, including modernization of the rapid lines, Green Line extension and modernization, and commuter rail upgrades.[214] It is fair to say that, despite the episodic maintenance issues common to all aging transit systems, Boston today has a better integrated rapid system, with bus feeder lines and abundant terminal car parking, than most American cities. If derailment is less common in other cities, it is because they have no rapid transit to speak of.

The region's relative transit success was not predetermined or guaranteed. The MTA and MBTA faced similar trend lines to nearly every American city. Boston lost over 50 percent of its transit ridership in the

FIGURES 23A AND 23B. The comparative consistency in the Boston region between 1960 and 2000. Source: Elevated/Subway/Bus/Railroad Combined, 1960; Combined Public Transportation, 2000, Social Explorer, accessed June 26, 2021.

first postwar decade, and transit has not kept pace with cars, population growth, or regional sprawl. Only 34 percent (2014) of city of Boston commuters rode transit daily,[215] and in the Greater Boston Area it was just 14 percent (2016).[216] Yet quality service is still there for those who need or want it. In 2019, before pandemic losses, the MBTA carried 362 million passengers on its vehicles (1.2 million daily trips), not much different from postwar highs. An impressive 86 percent of low-income residents (and 80 percent of all residents) in its service area lived within a half mile of service. The less reliable bus service is being upgraded through a Better Bus initiative, including exclusive lanes, route redesign, and better shelters.[217]

Politicians prioritized transit in the Boston region, in part, because of the many benefits that the majority white population still derived from transit in the postwar years. But it would be a mistake to think that the affluent or even white population are the primary beneficiaries of transit preservation today. Because the Boston region has diversified significantly, so has transit that runs through changing neighborhoods. The city of Boston, for instance, in 2019 housed 25 percent Black, 19.8 percent Hispanic or Latino, and 9.7 percent Asian residents, thus giving a nonwhite majority access to decades of system preservation and modest expansion. Some surrounding towns with extensive transit service, much of which was saved during the era of white working-class dominance, have also diversified.[218] The MBTA is also a path to social mobility and stability for a large nonwhite workforce. In 2020, for instance, MBTA operators, drivers, and affiliated workers were 36.9 percent white and 60.1 percent nonwhite (of whom 49.1 percent were Black). Decades of affirmative action have improved equity, as in other cities.[219]

The practical lessons from Boston are numerous and contrast sharply with the preceding stories from Baltimore, Atlanta, Chicago, and Detroit. Regularly expanding regional subsidies have been the key to low fares, stable and comprehensive service, and modest service expansion. Regional political leadership's insistence on state legislative support for transit, encouraged by voters in the powerful urbanized eastern section of the state, was crucial to gaining those subsidies. What is most heartening from Boston's transit century is the widespread belief in transit's contribution to creating a livable and equitable city region combined with the willingness to pay for these ideals. Political leaders, under pressure, paid more than lip service to transit as a social value.

Boston's experience illustrates that transit ridership can remain an essential element of city life when powerful elites, average citizens, and elected leaders encourage dense development and scale back highways.

The successful highway revolt that stopped major programs like the Inner Belt helped transit remain more competitive with cars in central urbanized areas. Citizen resistance to urban renewal and clearance, and more tolerance for density in places like Cambridge and Boston, added to the potential number of riders near the lines. Had Boston and surrounding towns been redeveloped at even greater densities, the picture would be even brighter today.

CHAPTER 9

San Francisco: Deeply Subsidized Public Transit

> San Francisco's municipally owned transit system operates under a clear-cut philosophy that sets it distinctly apart from privately owned traction companies. Nobody would object to seeing the Muni make a profit, but the people have made it pretty plain that profit is not the motive for running this particular system.
> *San Francisco Examiner*, 1957[1]

During the first postwar decades, mass transit declined rapidly in the San Francisco Bay Area as in the rest of America. Despite the dense, transit-rich area that comprised the city of San Francisco, auto registration in San Francisco County (comprising the central city only) increased 48.8 percent between 1945 and 1950.[2] Like its peers elsewhere, San Francisco's postwar political leadership devoted itself to expressways, downtown parking ramps, slum clearance and urban redevelopment, and streetcar substitution with buses and electric trolleybuses. These projects, to varying degrees, disrupted transit-centric neighborhoods and patterns of travel. The number of Muni passengers declined in San Francisco from 332 million in 1945 to 197 million in 1965. This steep decline in ridership was typical for cities nationally and may surprise those who mistakenly believe that San Francisco inevitably succeeded in the postwar transit business.[3]

San Francisco was also part of a sprawling region that transitioned to pervasive automobility, adding additional threats to the viability of mass transit to the postwar metropolis. The changes beyond the city limits were dramatic, including booming subdivisions south toward today's Silicon Valley in San Jose and north across the bridge to Marin County. Leaders in Oakland across the bay allowed an NCL subsidiary, Western Transit, to rip out all the streetcars. NCL not only severed the rail link between

Oakland and San Francisco but left Oakland residents entirely dependent on shrinking diesel bus networks and higher fares. Loss of suburban transit riders reduced connecting ridership in the city of San Francisco. The combined impact of decentralization and transit disinvestment was raging car use and declining transit ridership.[4]

Yet, crucial differences distinguished San Francisco's twentieth-century transit history from many other American cities. At many points, San Francisco could have ended up with much less transit, zero rail service, many more highways, more destructive urban renewal, and as a combined result, even fewer transit riders and less service. San Francisco, for instance, refused to sell to Western Transit, associated with NCL, even if it meant accepting the idea of long-term public subsidies. In San Francisco, citizen resistance to redevelopment and highways, public support for transit, and elite devotion to the center city helped balance the scales between automobiles and mass transit. More broadly, the combination of timing, subsidies, density, and demographics proved crucial to leaving more transit in place in San Francisco, and thus sustaining more ridership and political support, than a typical American city. San Francisco has much to teach Americans looking to dig their way out of a deep transit deficit.

An Early Public Advantage

San Francisco was one of the first cities in the nation to authorize municipality-owned transit. Yet, as in Boston and New York, the full development of a subsidized public transit system took decades to realize. A progressive city charter in 1900 authorized public transit operations that could compete with reviled private traction operators consolidated as the United Railroads (later Market Street Railway Co.). However, voters only approved bonds in 1909, and the first section of the municipal Geary Street Railway did not open until 1912.[5] In 1913, the voters approved a $3.5 million bond helping Muni to add a host of new lines in the 1910s and 1920s. The modest annual payment of $100,000 on the 1913 bonds, made possible with low-interest, long-term bond financing secured by the city, was key to expansion.[6] By 1932, the city had, in total, also provided $999,938 from general taxes primarily for interest payments and bond redemptions. Muni ran a "surplus" from 1913 to 1926 thanks to factors such as attractive bond financing, direct government subsidies, growing ridership, and minimum taxation. While modest compared to postwar subsidies, direct public support established an essential precedent for later government action.[7]

The pace of Municipal Railway line development picked up after demonstrating the benefits of new equipment and service. The 1930s public system was small compared to its rival Market Street, serving only about one-quarter of the city's riders with just eighty-two single-track miles in place by 1933. Yet, the public managers accomplished what Boston and New York—and few other cities—could claim during the interwar years. Muni, thanks in part to the bold vision of city engineer Michael M. O'Shaughnessy, pioneered a high-quality generation of new mass transit that sharply contrasted with the declining legacy service of Market Street. Muni, drawing on property assessments placed on areas enhanced by extensions, built projects like the Twin Peaks (1923) and Sunset (1928) tunnels that provided rapid service through steep hills to mostly undeveloped western and southwestern areas of the city. Muni extensions like these created profits for real-estate speculators and thus "contributed to the rapid development of San Francisco and a large increase in the taxable value of the districts into which the railway has pioneered."[8]

Unlike the situation in most American cities, Muni benefited from but was not entirely at the mercy of land development interests. Decoupling transit service from real estate in San Francisco was a major advantage because the public made a long-term commitment to serve new neighborhoods even after the initial real estate profits had been realized. A leading transit expert in 1931 claimed that "the transportation service rendered by the Municipal Railway is found to be of very good quality" and predicted correctly that San Francisco "will be one of the last cities in America to witness the disappearance" of streetcars.[9] Looking back on this era, the *Examiner* could claim that "for more than thirty years prior to unification [1944] the old Muni Railway operated at a profit under superb management."[10]

Muni benefited from a zoning code that permitted high residential density in many areas where streetcar lines, often under political pressure from residents, had extended. The dense zoning contrasted strongly with more typical cities like Baltimore and Detroit that set stringent limits on residential and commercial development further out to the detriment of the transit operator. San Francisco's 1921 zoning code, according to the city's official planning history, "largely reproduced the City's existing development patterns. The zoning ordinance contained no height limits and only limited residential density in the 1st Residential District while most of the City's neighborhoods were designated 2nd Residential." Large second residential districts, including those further out in still-developing areas like Richmond and Sunset, allowed for a mix of single-family and multifamily dwellings. The 1921 code also encouraged continuous commercial uses along the entire streetcar lines running through these neighborhoods. In sum, the 1921 zoning code, in force until 1961 with some amendments, was generally transit friendly. San Francisco in these respects shared much with Chicago and New York.[11]

The city's families, crowded tightly into aging wooden walk-ups in the city's close-in neighborhoods, now used the Muni lines to ride to new and more spacious housing in areas such as the sprawling Richmond and Sunset Districts. As families moved into the mix of housing developing along the lines, density rapidly increased. In 1940, there were still some partly developed distant census tracts in the Sunset District with just four thousand persons per square mile, but closer-in Sunset census tracts already boasted fifteen to twenty-five thousand persons per square mile. Those native-born whites who retreated to First Residential District tracts developing in the southwest were certainly driving cars more by the 1920s thanks to larger lots, off-street parking, parkways, and wider streets. But even the tony residents of an esteemed enclave like Olmsted-designed Saint Francis Wood (1912) were promised and then enjoyed a quick ride downtown through the Twin Peaks tunnel when it opened in 1923.

Elite areas like Saint Francis Wood and middle-class areas like Sunset and Richmond would remain crucial in future decades to sustain Muni's ridership and broader political support. The demographics of these growing Muni districts on the city's western side mattered. They were almost entirely white and would remain so for decades; as a result, transit service remained a mostly segregated experience (even without Jim Crow) and a majoritarian political concern. For instance, in 1930s redlining maps, the Sunset and Richmond Districts rated Blue and Green, indicating the high degree of racial exclusivity and single-family homes. Wealthy suburbs like Saint Francis Wood included covenants to maintain racial purity. White real-estate interests and politicians, reflecting broad racist sentiment, restricted the small Asian and Black populations to close-in, overcrowded areas such as Chinatown for decades. The Asian population of San Francisco was just 4.37 percent, or 27,700 persons out of 634,394 city residents. In 1930, the Black population of San Francisco was just 0.6 percent of the total population, or 3,803 individuals. As a result of segregation and these low numbers, both native-born and immigrant whites predominated in all areas served by the expanding Muni and Market streetcar lines. Most whites faced little prospect of sharing transit, schools, or housing. San Francisco's ethnic profile in the interwar period differed from Baltimore, for instance, and was more like Boston.[12]

When combined with growing auto popularity, the Depression had the potential to undermine the growing system's progress. Yet Muni's status as a municipally owned utility, by then part of the Public Utilities Commission (PUC), put it in the more stable category of municipal services such as water, electric power (sold by the PUC at cost to Muni), and the airport. The decision to count transit as a municipal service mattered. The system had suffered some loss to cars in the late 1920s, but the Depression hit ridership just as hard in San Francisco as other cities. Muni managers cut back service, wages, and hours across the system in the early 1930s but avoided the dramatic service cutbacks or damaging receivership experienced in most other American cities.[13]

With subsidies, deficits blossomed into modest surpluses. For instance, in the fiscal year 1933–34, were it not for Muni's exemption from $5.369 million in city, county, and state taxes, the company would never have run a $165,000 surplus.[14] These surpluses helped cover the "large losses by reason of the operation of lines into sparsely settled districts."[15] Muni in 1938, for instance, used part of the surplus to cover "feeder bus routes to districts of the city now badly in need of transportation." Muni had a keen interest in developing crosstown service to make transit more practical for those trying to avoid the time-consuming task of going to the CBD for any significant trip outside the radial lines of the streetcars. Such feeder routes were crucial to keeping political support from the middle class living in districts further out, but the lines were usually expensive to run because of low ridership. The company also kept all fares low, charging just five cents a ride (vs. seven cents for Market Street rides) and offered free transfers when average street railway fares nationwide were 8.33 cents. Low fares would become an article of faith in San Francisco, as in Boston and New York, and helped keep transit competitive with car ownership despite the greater time and social discomfort of catching trains and buses.[16]

Political leaders nurtured Muni, but at the same time, they fanned public anger at the Market Street Railway, leading to anti–private transit policies that helped to run the company into the ground. In this respect, San Francisco's leaders were as shortsighted as those in any other American city. Market Street entered receivership in 1919, leading to its reorganization under the Standard Power and Light Company. Private transit managers, stuck with a low fare, jitney (unlicensed taxi) competitors, high taxes, a growing public competitor, and serious discussion of a public buyout, refused to invest in their tracks or lines during the interwar years. Voters, suspicious of rewarding company owners and angry about crummy service, rejected bond offerings to buy the company in 1925, leaving company managers to their own devices and riders at their mercy.[17]

In 1931, a desperate Market Street gave up control of its franchises to the city in exchange for a twenty-five-year operating permit, leaving the future of private mass transit in doubt. Market Street streetcar ridership dropped from 198 million in 1925 to 112 million in 1938, thanks to the Depression and the negative factors described above. Voters rejected another bond offering in 1938 to purchase the system. Managers milked whatever last profits they could from aging equipment; riders avoided the Market lines if they could.[18] Muni during the war years carried 53 percent of the city's passengers on just one-third of the city's equipment and one-quarter of the tracks of the Market Street company. Riders were voting with their fares and enjoyed a discount of two cents by choosing Muni over Market Street. Voters rejected buying the company out, once again, in 1943.[19]

The interwar years cemented Muni's emerging role in city transit, but regional leaders and the federal work programs laid the groundwork for future trouble. The Golden Gate (1936) and Oakland–San Francisco Bay (1937) Bridges, New Deal–era work projects, offered high-speed routes to drivers looking to escape crowded housing, slow ferries, and transit riding. The Bay Bridge included streetcar service (until 1958), but after the war, once linked to growing interstates, the bridges mostly encouraged additional car commuting by those seeking to live in lower-density neighborhoods outside the city limits. The bridges also funneled millions more cars and trucks onto city streets, slowing down mass transit and creating demand for new parking garages.

The bridge development and general street improvement of the era aligned with the auto-centric consensus. The San Francisco Planning and Housing Association, which played a significant role in promoting postwar redevelopment, in 1942 argued that "the automobile has created problems which force us to re-shape our city." According to historian William Issel, "the war also intensified the commitment among private and public activists to improve streets and boulevards within the city, build better highway connections between the city and the region, and create an efficient balance between highway building and transit modernization and expansion."[20] The tension between auto-centric planning and neighborhood resistance would dominate postwar planning, leading to a different outcome in San Francisco than in most other cities.

Better versus Worse Substitution

Muni's wartime surpluses broke the logjam over the consolidation of Market Street and Muni in 1944: $2 million of which the city used to buy out Market Street investors for $7.5 million.[21] The remainder of the purchase was funded from future earnings, and Muni raised fares to seven cents with the merger. This financing strategy would divert revenues from modernization, but using surplus earnings for the purchase, approved by voters in 1944, was politically essential given the Market Street animus in the general population.[22] At the time of the merger in 1944, the combined count of the fleet, most of which were older Market Street equipment, was 899 vehicles: 678 electric streetcars, 38 cable cars, 165 motor coaches, and 18 trolley coaches.[23] Most of the Market line vehicles, 440 in total, were old and in poor condition, and 79 were inoperable.[24] Dramatic changes were in store for the combined system.

The *San Francisco Examiner* believed that the city had paid a "blackmail price for the Market Street Railway's pile of junk," but as in Chicago and New York, consolidation under one public owner was an essential step in developing a more integrated transit system.[25] In the first years of merged service in San Francisco, moreover, riders enjoyed an enlarged service area because consolidation brought mostly minor, if numerous, route redesigns. Changes that were made primarily impacted duplicate, money-losing services that developed in the era of competition.[26]

Consolidation could not have come a moment sooner. Muni ridership in 1945–46 remained at an "abnormal" level of 326 million, as few options existed for the record 827,400 residents jammed into the city (a 30.4 percent increase from 1940). However, managers knew full well that the end of gasoline and tire rationing and wartime industries spelled trouble. Labor costs were also rising rapidly thanks to a successful strike and generous new contract (1946). Muni was forced at the time to use the bulk of its profits for financing the remainder of the Market Street purchase.[27] Managers raised fares to ten cents in 1946 to address these issues, but the future looked bleak.[28]

Despite the merged company's faltering condition and the prospect of deep and endless subsidies, the city resisted the siren song of selling to those associated with the NCL concerns. In 1947, Jesse L. Haugh of Western Transit Company in neighboring Oakland announced that he wanted to lease and operate Muni. Haugh was a significant force in Western Transit, Pacific City Lines, and NCL—all institutions devoted to bus substitution as the basis for postwar transit profits. Haugh dangled an annual lease payment of $700,000 a year in front of public officials in San Francisco,[29] who otherwise faced the prospect of rising deficits and tax support under continuing public Muni management. As did many transit executives of the time, Haugh held up New York's streetcar substitution as a model to emulate. Manhattan, he claimed, seemed to have adjusted fine to losing its streetcars despite being "more densely populated than San Francisco." Of course, such an analysis of bus superiority in New York conveniently overlooked the hundreds of miles of subway lines underground as the critical element in New York's transit success even when the streetcars were gone.[30]

Haugh's bus substitution arguments had either won over or steamrolled transit politics in most of California. The various GM-supported entities (NCL, Pacific City Lines, Western Transit, etc.) succeeded in removing almost all streetcar services in California, including whole systems in Los Angeles, Oakland, and San Diego. After substitution, they proceeded to "right size" bus systems with declining ridership, as was the case in Baltimore and Saint Louis, where NCL also dominated. When it came to postwar transit, it was own it or lose it. The differences in San Francisco public opinion concerning the role of transit are striking and speak eloquently to an alternative path other cities might have followed. NCL's wrecking ball was stoppable.

The PUC, of which Muni was part, believed that the "lease of the MR to private interests would raise taxes and reduce service to the riding public" because an "all-gasoline bus system . . . is highly undesirable and cannot render satisfactory service." The system would also eliminate the demand for "part of its market for Hetch Hetchy" (hydroelectric power plant) as the PUC could not, by law, sell electric power to private interests. Worst of all, "there is no guarantee whatsoever that the extensive city coverage and frequency of service now being given by the MR would be continued" by Haugh. The PUC made clear the difference: "A public utility of the MR exists for the sole good of the people. In private hands it exists primarily for private profit and gain. Consequently, the only way Western Transit could stay in business would be to reduce service and eliminate lines until revenues exceeded operating expenses." Looking at the destruction of rail and bus transit in cities like Baltimore and Oakland illustrates the wisdom of this analysis of private-sector methods and aims.[31]

The emphasis on the advantages of public ownership was widespread. The influential *San Francisco Examiner*, for instance, did not bite on Haugh's offer: "It is quite possible that in twenty years the people would again be forced to buy another pile of junk in order to get rid of Haugh."[32] The Board of Supervisors rejected the plan in 1947.[33] The supervisors rebuffed Haugh in 1952 when brought back by an anti-transit supervisor, even though Haugh was offering over a million dollars a year to lease the system. Haugh saw dollar signs when looking at the money to be made running buses through San Francisco's densely populated hills and valleys—at least in the short term. City leaders elsewhere chose to collaborate with NCL rather than pursue public ownership that carried more political and financial risk.[34]

City officials rejected selling the system outright, but the various consultants hired by Muni, the PUC, and the city in the 1940s shared NCL substitution goals in the late 1940s. Consultants consistently recommended Muni reduce the streetcar system to a minimum, saving only those routes that traveled through the tunnels and down Market Street, and rely instead on a robust network of trolleybuses or diesel buses everywhere else.[35] The PUC throughout the postwar decades, according to longtime Muni watchers, "followed its own precepts of cost cutting and supposed modernization, with no consideration of what the people wanted, what costs they would support, and what form of transit would service the City best." The PUC, city politicians, and managers ignored, for instance, a 1945 plan they had commissioned from a former Market Street executive that would have preserved a "strong core of basic radial streetcar lines."[36] A major citywide planning effort in 1947 pushed by Mayor Roger Lapham (1944–48) referred to streetcars as "a heritage from the past." It concluded that the streetcars did not justify the $51 million price tag for total rehabilitation.[37]

Stiffening the spine of leaders in San Francisco for both public ownership and streetcar substitution was voter endorsement of a sizable bond offering for transit modernization in late 1947. System managers desperately needed the $20 million provided for modernization and new transit vehicles given the decades of deferred Market Street maintenance. Under the plan, the city would use its sales tax to cover the cost of bond financing of the railway, thus diverting general taxation to support transit.[38] The bonds could be sold at an extremely attractive 1 percent interest level because of the city's excellent credit rating.[39] So far, so good for transit.

The 1947 bond effort made clear to the public and all politicians that funds would overwhelmingly go to streetcar removal and substitution. Transit managers envisioned a future system that would include 922 vehicles. Most of the system would be rubber-tired, thus clearing more streets for autos and trucks and reducing labor and capital costs. A renewed system would include just 256 streetcars compared to 399 trolley coaches and 267 motor coaches. To get to this future, managers planned to buy only fifty-five new streetcars compared to 361 trolley coaches and buses.[40] So few streetcars were needed because the bonds would help get streetcars off the roads: $22.85 million of the bond was designated to remove 160 miles of street railway track and subsequent repaving. The massive sum indicates the requisite spending required for ripping out such an essential piece of urban infrastructure. Voters also approved $5 million for parking structures "with the view of making possible the maximum use of downtown streets by auto traffic and mass transit."[41] Without any prodding from NCL, Muni managers and allied city officials—with the voters' full consent and knowledge—attacked the streetcar system to speed up auto traffic in the city. The benefits to drivers in the program were crucial to its passage when many other bonds had failed.

The auto-centric bonds complemented the general direction of postwar policy.[42] Postwar, San Francisco officials, with state and growing federal aid, initially did everything they could to make driving much more efficient.[43] Postwar plans for highways in the city envisioned a network of high-speed expressways and freeways crisscrossing and ringing the city, smashing through many of the city's most dense neighborhoods, and undermining the competitive advantages of mass transit. Some dreamed how cars in the future would circle "the city on a freeway along the Embarcadero" or traverse "the new Panhandle Freeway, which connects with the Golden Gate Bridge via Park-Presidio Drive."[44] City officials never built the ambitious 1948 plan for encircling and crossing the city with highways (see below for more on the freeway revolt). Still, sections of I-280 and I-80 within the city limits did move ahead and would eventually encourage suburban dispersal with help from the bridges and connecting roadways. The cars and trucks piling into the city slowed up surface transit, including the new buses and trolley coaches, which proponents had selected because of their higher speed.

Auto-centric planning directly influenced streetcar operations and competitiveness within the city limits. A 1949 editorial in the *Examiner* identified auto-centric city policy as a hindrance to transit's progress: "Every time the city improves a street, builds freeways, sets up garages, it is, in effect, competing with the streetcar and bus system. Yet the cars and buses are needed."[45] For instance, in the densely packed Western Addition near downtown, redevelopment plans from 1947 envisioned traffic moving "smoothly along a few broad, scientifically engineered motorways, such as Geary and McAllister Boulevards."[46] City leaders targeted Geary streetcars for removal, and by 1956, the streetcars were gone on the street despite the line's crucial east–west route. The removal of streetcars set the stage for auto improvements: "Geary Street this year will be the scene of a vast widening project in the Western Addition from Franklin St. to St. Joseph's Avenue."[47] Growing resistance to highways in the early 1950s did not stop city officials from making a more car-friendly city.

Plans for slum clearance complemented auto-centric planning. The city's official planning history has acknowledged the damage done in this era by "aggressive forms of urban planning," including "proposals for large-scale super-block developments" and "preferences for suburban-style amenities over the older urban fabric."[48] In the massive Western Addition plans from 1947 (and subsequent amended plans for the area through the 1950s and 1960s), city planners targeted a transit-rich neighborhood right next to downtown for clearance and gentrification. City officials had stigmatized the Western Addition (including much of the Filmore area) for a long time as a "blighted" area of substandard housing and worrisome social ills.[49] In 1950, the census tracts in the Western Addition ranged from forty-one to sixty-five thousand persons per square mile, many of whom were nonwhite city residents with few other housing options.[50]

Planners promised that they could eliminate "the dilapidation and disorder of more than half a century" in the Western Addition with clearance. Gone too would be "the indiscriminate mixing of commercial, industrial, and residential structures."[51] The accent of the planning was on higher-income white residents gentrifying the city. The Jefferson Square section of the project alone targeted thirty-six blocks for clearance, making way for a lifestyle "associated with suburban communities." Planned towers in the park allowed for a reduction in the district's population from eight-five to seventy-five thousand inhabitants.[52] Planners and the Board of Supervisors openly rejected community resistance to displacement of Asian and Black families and businesses for this upper-income vision.[53] Thanks to a host of delays, the Western Addition redevelopment project did not begin until the second half of the 1950s. The Redevelopment Agency ultimately displaced twenty thousand families for Geary Street widening, the Japan Trade Center, and new housing and commercial projects.[54]

Both the Western Addition and Mission redevelopment projects would be scaled back significantly thanks to successful citizen resistance in the 1960s. Still, city officials had already damaged neighborhood life and density with slum clearance and road expansion. Planners of the time ignored the role played by diversity of uses, small businesses, and concentration of people in making livable places and supporting successful transit operations. An unintended bright side of the urban renewal story in San Francisco was that the few redevelopment projects on the books moved at such a glacial pace that activists had time to develop organizations to resist them.

A 1947 city charter amendment to retain cable cars was another early, if incomplete, milestone of postwar citizen revolt against the dominant ideology of car-centric planning. A few cable car lines had escaped modernization to streetcars or buses in San Francisco after the 1904 earthquake and fire because they performed well on steep hills compared to streetcars. In the interwar years, the Market Street Railway delayed removing the final cable lines under its control during World War II because it lacked the buses to replace them.[55] Articulate, well-funded, professional white supporters, primarily women, loved them both as local transit options (serving wealthy Nob Hill, for instance) and for their unique style. Activists saved them postwar through charter amendments and strategic organizing even though they were expensive to operate and served only a tiny portion of the city.[56] Voters were "committed to support of the cable cars with their traditions that identify them with San Francisco."[57] City leaders and transit managers, despite these amendments, still did everything they could in the 1950s and 1960s to reduce the cable car system to a couple of fun tourist lines.[58] While important as an early salvo against the dominant auto-centric society at the time, the cable car preservation effort failed to protect the more numerous and practical streetcars upon which many more citizens depended. Streetcars lacked the charm of the cable cars. They also blocked a lot more of the roadways.

The seismic shift in policy came in 1948 when city leaders hired Colonel Sidney Bingham, a key architect of the destruction of New York's streetcar lines, to plan for Muni's future. Bingham quickly developed an "emergency plan" of rapid conversion of fifteen streetcar lines to motor coach, emphasizing buses over trolleybuses. Only eight streetcar lines would remain in his plan, and even on these legacy lines, buses would replace rail service on evenings and weekends.[59] Despite the massive cuts to streetcars, Mayor Elmer Robinson (1948–56) "remained enthusiastic about Bingham's report."[60] In the succeeding years, Muni followed through on Bingham's plan, replacing nine of the fifteen streetcar lines by 1951 with rubber-wheeled vehicles.[61] Bingham did endorse a fairly ambitious subway system, including the future Market Street lines, as planners at the time believed rapid transit could compete better than surface lines. His recommendation was crucial to preserving the last few streetcar lines through the tunnels and on Market Street.[62] The absence of NCL in San Francisco did not, however, mean preserving a robust streetcar network.

Such aggressive streetcar replacement plans responded both to declining ridership and the typical fears of key business groups and political leaders concerned about the liabilities of transit taxation. The San Francisco Real Estate Board in 1948, for instance, "called on the board of supervisors to force the Municipal Railway to pay its own way without tax support."[63] Had the Department of City Planning in 1950 not commissioned a long-term plan for rapid transit underneath Market Street, Muni might have cut the last of San Francisco's streetcar lines. The replacement of the bulk of the streetcars took place with little to no public consultation as the deputy city attorney believed that only line abandonment, rather than mode shift, required public input. When a court finally called this reasoning into question, the tracks and streetcars were gone.[64] Not everyone was pleased, but critics were ignored and failed to coalesce into powerful opposition. A letter to the *Examiner*, among quite a few of this type, described riding buses and trolley coaches as worse than streetcars and encouraged voters to reject "every bond issue to improve the Muni with stinky General Motors diesel buses."[65]

The substitution process continued with the city's hiring in 1950 of Colonel Marmion D. Mills as transit expediter. A former GM Yellow Coach and National City Line executive, Mills had been a key force for bus substitution in twelve cities.[66] Mills remained predictably gung ho on substitution in his 1951 report on San Francisco: "The bond issue had made clear to the public that the city was intent on using the funds for a fleet of modern vehicles composed of street cars, trolley coaches and motor coaches."[67] Indeed, by the time of Mills's 1951 report, Muni was already operating 493 motor coaches and 398 trolley coaches versus just 210 electric streetcars and 27 cable cars. Muni had already disposed of 417 electric streetcars under public leadership,[68] and had permanently removed one hundred miles of rails.[69] This accelerated process led to a "reduction in streetcar operation" from 16.9 million miles in 1947 to just 5.2 million in 1950, a 69 percent reduction.[70]

Mills, for all his pro-bus bravado, acknowledged that the city was weathering the mode shift differently than other Pacific coast rivals. In his opinion, this upbeat prognosis was "due to greater public approval of the Muni as the conversion program is pressed and service improved; the parking problem here; economic conditions, and the compact city which increases the public transit riding habit."[71] Mills was a strong supporter of the trolley coach for San Francisco despite the electric overhead wire maintenance and the lack of GM electric production vehicles. Mills believed that "trolley coach lines provide better transit service at lower operating costs than the present Muni streetcars."[72] Muni bought 380 trolley coaches between 1947 and 1952 compared to just twenty-five PCC streetcars.[73]

The case for trolleybuses was helped by their quiet and fast operation (on steep hills), low maintenance costs, and the low-cost power provided by the PUC: Muni just paid the "wheelage" for the power from Hetch Hetchy. So attractive was the trolleybus from a financial and operational perspective that fourteen converted streetcar routes had spent only about a year as motor coaches before being changed to trolley coach lines. This shift from motor bus to trolley coaches happened almost nowhere else in the United States. Mills also endorsed retaining the Twin Peaks streetcars as part of the emerging subway consensus, another departure from most NCL-related consulting that looked to complete substitution.[74]

Public pressure was a factor in saving a few streetcar lines, elevating the trolleybuses, and making them a long-term service. Mayor Robinson almost lost reelection in 1952, according to the *Examiner*, "because the people don't like buses. Nobody criticized the streetcars or trolley coaches but there was a general dislike of the buses. The mayor had to bear the burden of that feeling against the jolting rides, lack of ventilation and bunched service which are inseparable from the buses."[75] Some voters, for instance, rejected additional bonds for Muni in 1953 not because they were against mass transit but because they found more buses distasteful.[76] As one letter writer commented, he had "interviewed scores of voters" and found "the people do not want 108 gasoline buses, and they do not want to spend more money on track removal. What they want is more PCC type streamlined street cars and trolley coaches."[77] The writer positively equated streetcars and trolley coaches, indicating a felt difference between trolley coaches and buses even though both ran on rubber wheels.

As a result of this type of pressure, Muni riders enjoyed more service in 1950 than 1947, with managers adding 0.64 percent of service while ridership dropped 17 percent in the same years.[78] By 1950 trolleybuses traveled a much increased 6.6 million miles and gas buses 17.9 million miles, largely compensating for the significant cuts to the streetcars.[79] The entire network of routes citywide remained in place because the substitutions impacted the mode rather than the quality of service.[80] A Muni advertisement in 1950 claimed that service "now runs within two blocks or less of most San Francisco residences."[81] There was no temporary service stability, as was typical in most American cities during this time, but a long-term commitment to quality. In 1955, for instance, Muni collected twenty-nine million fewer fares than 1950–51 but was still "operating its vehicles as many miles and as many hours as in 1950–51."[82] This consistency of service remained even a decade later: the total miles operated in 1945 was twenty-nine million and in 1963 still a robust twenty-six million miles despite massive ridership losses.[83] The city lost streetcars and riders but not service.

Devoted riders did not endure the constant cuts and route changes that characterized almost all postwar systems. In the still densely populated Western Addition in 1960 (twenty-three to forty-seven thousand persons per square mile), not yet fully cleared and more ethnically and racially mixed than most of the city, about 42–50 percent of daily commuters still used transit—very high for postwar neighborhoods anywhere. But transit ridership could also be comparatively robust further out. For instance, in the Sunset District, an almost entirely white, middle-class area in 1960, density ranged from seven to fifteen thousand persons per square mile, and daily working ridership in the census tracts ranged from 29 to 42 percent, with many tracts in the 30 percent range. The failure to build highways contributed to high ridership in areas like these. San Francisco's white riders also spent most of their rides in primarily white spaces. The city's segregation remained the norm, and the total percentage of Black residents remained low.[84]

The remaining riders benefited from abundant service and a diversity of good quality, if heavily used, equipment. In 1956, Muni's 2,800 employees guided 179 electric streetcars, 47 cable cars, 389 trolley coaches, and 537 motor coaches up and down the city's hilly streets on 63 different lines. That year, streetcars accounted for just 14.6 percent of miles operated compared to 34.0 percent trolley coaches, 49.7 percent buses, and 1.7 percent cable cars.[85] Muni took advantage of substitution in other cities to buy older equipment at bargain prices. Managers, for instance, in 1957–58 leased sixty-six used PCC streetcars from Saint Louis. Maintaining a diverse equipment base was more expensive and complicated for managers and repair workers, but Muni's riders benefited from so much service at such a low price.[86] Buses and trolley coaches in other cities would have had a much brighter future if they had been subsidized at a comparable level to San Francisco.[87]

Subsidies = Service

San Francisco ridership trends looked better than most other American cities. Yet, as in every other American city, the general preference for cars, particularly in off-peak hours, robbed Muni of its former surpluses. The system, after all, lost 42 percent of its ridership in the first postwar decade.[88] Because Muni maintained service as ridership fell, and because ridership fell so quickly and deeply, even the aggressive substitution that reduced total employment and saved on capital costs did not prevent significant deficits.[89] Low fares and high labor costs created growing deficits in a time of declining ridership.

The widespread sentiment among political leaders that the fare had to stay low to encourage ridership had many positive effects even though the principle helped drive up deficits. San Francisco's political leadership and citizens resisted dramatic cuts to all lines, accepting subsidies as a permanent situation. Mayor Robinson in 1949, for instance, may have been pro–bus substitution, but he "set his foot down firmly yesterday on further cuts in services or additional fare increases" proposed by Muni managers. Unlike the case in most cities, the mayor had the financial tools to back up his resistance. Robinson acknowledged that if Muni "must run a deficit to provide adequate service, then the Muni will have to be provided with a tax subsidy."[90] The PUC, reminded of its public role and subsidies, thus pledged to Robinson that "there will be no curtailment in MR service and no fare increase."[91]

Managers seemed to have understood that ridership had to remain high to sustain political support for a comprehensive system. They also knew that other cities were already shedding riders faster than necessary, thanks to frequent fare increases. Muni built on the city's long-standing tradition of low fares, as in New York and Boston. San Francisco maintained a five-cent flat fare for thirty-two years, only raising it to seven cents in 1944, ten cents in 1946, and fifteen cents in 1952. The twenty-cent flat fare would only be implemented in the fiscal year 1969–70.[92] By 1958, twenty-seven American cities already required a twenty-cent fare, often with additional transfer or zone charges.[93]

A social value system concerning the proper role of the farebox in transit service remained dominant in San Francisco. A 1958 debate about fares, for instance, brought an estimate that a fare increase would raise $4 million dollars but also cut ridership by nine million. City leaders in 1958 agreed that it was "not time" to raise fares that would "accelerate the trend away from the use of transit."[94] Managers of transit certainly knew well the relationship between fares and ridership. In 1956, the PUC had reported that in cities over five hundred thousand, a 1 percent increase in fares typically led to a 0.26 percent decrease in passengers.[95] In San Francisco, the city paid to support its principles. There was grumbling as the subsidies rose, and Muni managers and the PUC often favored fare increases, but city leaders refused to agree to them. San Francisco riders, therefore, had a riding bargain on their hands for decades.

The fight to reduce labor costs and thus reduce deficits first focused on the streetcar replacement program. Like all transit managers, Marmion Mills despised the two-person streetcar rule put in place for an earlier era of equipment, calling it "feather-bedding, pure and simple." He called for its repeal, "as an initiative ordinance only the voters could repeal it."[96] Voters finally approved the repeal in 1954 only after many other streetcar lines had already been removed, in part, to save on the high labor costs of two men per car.[97] One estimate in 1956 found that the switch to one-person crews saved Muni $4.5 million annually.[98] In 1958, the last two-person streetcar crews were gone.[99]

Maintaining excessive off-peak service in San Francisco was another red ink machine required by labor contracts, although the additional service helped many off-peak riders and Muni driver salaries. Muni's buses and streetcars carried most riders two hours a day, but union rules treasured by the AFL kept them moving even when mostly empty. Mills estimated that some "200 vehicles are shuttling around uselessly every day."[100] Muni's head count may have dropped between 1945 and 1957 by 1,729 jobs, but higher wages and benefits ate into much of the savings.[101] Like many others in the state, Muni unions had their pay pegged to wage rates in distant and tiny Torrance, California. With just nineteen drivers left in 1954, managers in Torrance could raise pay more generously than in big cities. This questionable practice generated substantial raises that added up to millions on Muni's books.[102]

Public subsidies, as in Boston, were the key factor in maintaining service in the face of consistently low fares, high labor costs, and falling ridership. In 1949, for instance, 21.5 cents of every $6.09 of city property tax collected, or $1.776 million, was diverted to support Muni. The city provided another $700,000 of sales tax for funding the bonds that year. These were relatively small budget line items for the city but crucial to the survival of Muni—and rarely duplicated outside of San Francisco.[103] Between 1946 and 1956, Muni received a total of $11 million in property taxes.[104] In 1956–57, for instance, city residents learned that "it will cost San Francisco taxpayers 40 cents per $100 property valuation to subsidize" Muni.[105] By 1959–60, the net loss was up to $4.6 million, yet tax contributions of $4.457 million and additional funds from the city's Capital Improvement Fund of $894,000 covered the losses. Muni would claim a $1.1 million budget "surplus" that fiscal year thanks to city support. Another hidden public subsidy was the low-cost power the Hetch Hetchy Power System hydroelectric plant "delivered to the Railway at a lower cost than if purchased from a private company."[106]

The Muni subsidy became a regular part of the annual cycle of news and taxes. Dollar amounts expanded to cover the growing deficits, allowing for the maintenance of a comprehensive, reliable system serving a dramatically smaller ridership. One analyst in 1956 believed it was "common knowledge that for many years the Municipal Railway has been receiving a substantial tax subsidy from the people of San Francisco, and there appears little, if any, likelihood that this situation will change in the foreseeable future."[107] Indeed, the real-estate developers pushing for giant new towers in the CBD benefited as much as riders. The Downtown Association of Business in 1958 believed that "transit is the life blood of the business life of the city.... We have supported the subsidy idea and will no doubt continue to do so."[108] This was a rare statement by business elites in this era. Thanks partly to subsidies, service retention, and more dramatic losses in most American cities, by 1958, Muni had the highest per capita riding in the country and was running the nation's fourth-largest system. Subsidies were a key to this relative success.[109]

Inventing Un-American Urbanism

Even with low fares and comprehensive service, San Francisco did not reverse the massive ridership losses of the postwar decades in the 1960s and 1970s. Muni was down to 138 million passengers by 1969–70, a long way from inflated wartime highs of over three hundred million.[110] The city and region had changed in ways that made the recovery of lost riders a challenging prospect. Not only had the city's population declined to 715,000 residents in 1970, but car ownership and use within the city had become commonplace.[111]

The city's Planning Department did not help sustain Muni, often working at cross-purposes. Planners emphasized urban renewal and slum clearance in the center that frequently reduced density. Further out they preferred a suburban-style environment, including single-family homes, larger lots, and off-street parking, resulting in neighborhoods less likely to generate riders.[112] A transit-oriented lifestyle had become atypical for the 2.5 million residents in the metropolitan area. Even urban areas lost their transit-centric flavor. NCL and city officials wrecked transit in Oakland, and the last tram traveled the Bay Bridge to San Francisco in 1958. Given these local and regional challenges, Muni was lucky to stabilize service quality and ridership in the 1960s and 1970s. This stabilization, moreover, set the stage for renewal of systems with federal funds, new rapid transit thanks to BART, and new immigrant riders.

An essential factor in Muni's long-term stability was the collapse of highway development within the city itself. City leaders in the 1940s and 1950s had planned a dense network of city highways that would have wiped out or ruined large sections of neighborhoods had they been built. The "freeway revolt" politics of 1950s San Francisco started early compared to other cities, was far more successful than any other city except Boston and New York, and tilted the transportation scales in Muni's direction. The *San Francisco Chronicle* began criticizing highways in 1954, as did groups of wealthy white residents and minority citizens whose neighborhoods lay in the target of the roads. The lost homes, noise, additional traffic, and ugly roadbeds from planned highways would have impacted extensive sections of Telegraph Hill and waterfront neighborhoods in the east, the Fillmore and Western Addition, and middle-class blocks in the Sunset District.[113]

Elected officials eventually understood the political liability of auto-centric policies and joined the movement to tame the highways. Historian Issel nicely understates the dramatic change in public policy: "In January 1959 neighborhood preservationists and environmental activists convinced the San Francisco Board of Supervisors to rescind its approval of seven of nine freeways scheduled for construction by the state highway."[114] The *San Francisco Chronicle* celebrated halting of construction in 1959 on the waterfront Embarcadero Freeway: "We oppose and have consistently opposed the hideous monstrosity which the State Highway Commission built along the Embarcadero in front of the Ferry Building."[115]

Moreover, the Board of Supervisors remained steadfast in its resistance in the decades to come, canceling modified expressway plans in 1966 for the Golden Gate and Panhandle Freeways. Without the revolt, according to the Department of City Planning, "San Francisco's cityscape may well have included a freeway through the Sunset, an additional freeway through the Mission, a freeway through the Panhandle and Golden Gate Park, bridges to Alameda and Angel Island, and a continuous stretch of the freeway along the entire northwest waterfront from the Bay Bridge to the Golden Gate." Given the city's small size, these highways would have had a dramatic impact on both neighborhood ambiance and mobility.[116] Widenings of some key streets like Geary took place, but Muni remained a decent option for traveling in the city compared to slow auto movement on surface streets. The failure to build so many highways also made the city and its neighborhoods a more pleasant and livable place to live, work, and shop. Transit in Boston and New York yielded similar benefits from extensive cancellation.

The rising towers in the CBD in the 1960s and 1970s were excellent for transit ridership and city tax revenues. According to planner Chester Hartman, Skidmore, Owings & Merrill's sleek Crown Zellerbach building (1959) was the first major office tower built in the city since 1930. Dozens of large contemporary office towers would follow its lead.[117] San Francisco's dense and growing downtown in 1962, according to the *Examiner*, stood in "marked contrast" to many "comparable metropolitan areas—Los Angeles, Oakland among them—where the traffic blight turns downtown blocks into gap-tooth parking lots. Property values decline, tax resources dwindle." Nor could cars, highways, and garages manage all the workers in these buildings, cementing the transit-CBD relationship. The symbiotic interrelationship between transit and real estate was crucial: "San Francisco has a virile downtown in good part because of the Muni system. The convenient transit facilities give thousands of people efficient daily transportation."[118]

Skyscrapers bloomed from the 1960s onward on both sides of Market Street, reinforcing the city's role as an essential outpost in an emerging global city network of finance and corporate services. Later projects like the Embarcadero Center (1971) and the Transamerica Pyramid (1972) built on 1960s success. Taxes on the millions of square feet of new space contributed to city coffers supporting mass transit. The proliferation of skyscrapers raised concerns among environmentalists about urban scale, but antigrowth propositions had limited success at the ballot box until the 1980s.[119]

The Department of City Planning responded to growing dissent with initiatives like the Urban Design Plan (1971), designed "to protect its existing fabric and essential physical characteristics . . . to cultivate human-scale amenities; and to provide landscaping along streets for livability." Yet so desirable was center-city office space, and so powerful was downtown interests, that growth continued. According to Hartman, many planners worried that Muni had an insufficient peak capacity to handle all the projected CBD-bound workers during rush hour by the early 1980s. Pressure for better service from affluent workers in the city's outer reaches and downtown real-estate interests helped retain political support for subsidies.[120]

Muni's downtown service, in the long term, also got a boost from the planning and building of the BART lines that eventually linked the San Francisco, Berkeley, and Oakland business districts with a variety of fast-growing suburbs. High-speed regional transit had come into focus as a possibility during the 1940s, with early solid advocacy by military planners during the war years. Instead of just building on the tradition of interurbans and the Bay Bridge trams, planners and a growing number of enthusiasts in the 1940s and 1950s envisioned something altogether more daring, including high-speed service and a long, underwater tunnel under the Bay.

San Francisco's financial and political leadership postwar eventually viewed high-speed BART service as a key dimension of maintaining downtown property values. Highway cancellation on such a large scale made powerful figures such as Mayor George Christopher (1956–64) and business interests take rapid transit more seriously than they might have otherwise.[121] Moreover, the opportunity to build a Market Street subway to speed trains would free the downtown surface streets of the last trolleys. In 1960, for instance, Muni officials were happy to report that "the Mayor's Transportation Council adopted a plan for rapid transit routes which would include a double-deck subway under Market Street." The old streetcars would run on the top tunnel deck and rapid transit on the bottom. Muni stood to gain directly by linking directly to a new regional system while rubber tires would finally own Market Street on the surface.[122]

BART, first approved by regional voters in 1962, grew slowly in the 1960s and 1970s thanks to typical regional squabbles and cost overruns.[123] By 1966, the total cost of the first phase had inflated to $1.2 billion. Despite voters having been promised the "finest rapid transit system in the world," the first section of the system that opened in 1972 was comparatively small.[124] From a critical perspective, Muni ended up on the wrong side of the regional bargain. Neither Muni nor BART passengers could freely transfer between systems, and the number of stops in the city was limited. BART and Muni also remained distinct systems with separate fares.

From a more positive perspective, BART helped sustain San Francisco's CBD as a growing business center from the 1970s onward as developers planned large buildings in expectation of world-class regional transit. In 1981, Muni finally started service in the double-deck subway tunnel on Market Street by modernizing the city's remaining streetcar lines, speeding up service significantly. Unlike Baltimore's isolated subway, BART and Muni complemented each other in the long term. Muni was an intact, dense urban system, providing extensive opportunities for connecting passengers within the city limits; BART provided the basis for selected convenient regional connections including Berkeley and Oakland.

Muni also benefited from the collapse of the urban renewal consensus. The city's emerging historic preservation and environmental movements in the 1950s and 1960s were vital to protecting neighborhoods from clearance for urban renewal. The slow pace of redevelopment meant that little in the way of official renewal had been accomplished compared to Chicago or New York, where large sections of the city fell to the bulldozer and wrecking ball—and often in areas well served by transit. The largest project indicates how badly things might have gone in San Francisco. The Western Addition–Fillmore project negatively impacted sixty blocks of homes, and a thriving Black business community lay in ruin.[125] The density of the Western Addition fell in the 1960s, but thanks to more moderate clearance, historic rehabilitation, and new construction, population density in Western Addition census tracts in 1970 ranged from nineteen to fifty thousand persons per square mile, still dense enough for transit. Of course, it helped that the cleared sections of the Western Addition redeveloped in a reasonable amount of time, including less alienating, low-rise, mixed-income, high-density housing developments on the remaining grid of streets.

San Francisco's unique demographic profile benefited Muni. The extreme racial conflict and segregation of Chicago, Detroit, and Baltimore undermined the quality of all public services within these cities as whites abandoned and then refused to support or use critical public services like public education, public housing, and public transit. San Francisco was also highly segregated but, like Boston and New York, had an atypically low ratio of African American residents for a big American city, even compared to other cities in the region like Oakland. In 1970, San Francisco was just 13.39 percent Black. Most Black families lived in the highly segregated Western Addition or in Bayview–Hunters Point, but San Francisco lacked the vast, decimated, and segregated districts of Baltimore, Detroit, and Cleveland. As a result, the small number of Black families in San Francisco benefited from more transit and neighborhood vitality than was typically offered in Rustbelt American cities.

San Francisco and Muni also benefited as a gateway city for immigration, particularly post-1965. Like New York's MTA, Muni benefited from a large, lower-income, international working class living in center-city neighborhoods, many of whom came directly from societies where mass transit was held in higher regard. San Francisco in the 1960s already had a much higher share than typical, for its time, of Latino residents (Spanish origin, 14.24 percent in 1970), many living in crowded, highly segregated neighborhoods such as the Mission, well served by transit. By 1980, the city was also 21.71 percent Asian, attracted by the mutual support and networks of long-standing Asian communities, the city's reputation for tolerance, and the Pacific Rim location. The Asian population grew rapidly in middle-class areas like Richmond and Sunset, helping sustain density and ridership. In 1980, Sunset still had thirteen to twenty-eight thousand persons per square mile. Transit ridership in 1980 in districts like these was still 30–40 percent of daily commuters on average. Like New York and Boston, San Francisco became a diverse, globalized city with transit as a crucial component. Densely populated immigrant areas, with high concentrations of workers in the service industry, are suitable for transit ridership.[126]

Mixed in with the growing minority population of the city during the 1950s, 1960s, and 1970s was a much higher than typical number of white residents, including a remaining white middle class in areas like the

Sunset and Richmond Districts and in much of the southwest districts; a sizable white elite in Pacific Heights and similar enclaves; LGBTQ pioneers in the Castro; and the thriving beatnik and counterculture of the 1950s and 1960s in North Beach and Haight-Ashbury. Many subcultures frowned upon highways, cars, split levels, and everything else that defined mainstream suburban America. As many white residents continued to live in the central city and ride Muni, they used their political and social clout to support transit as indicated, for instance, in the retention of cable cars and streetcars, and the tolerance of politicians for growing subsidies. In addition, quirky San Francisco attracted millions of prosperous vacationers. Some of them rode Muni services to Haight-Ashbury and other neighborhoods, and others jumped on cable cars (and more recently reintroduced antique streetcars) for journeys to renovated Ghirardelli Square, Fisherman's Wharf, and Chinatown. The net result of citizen activism and demographic change in San Francisco was much lower population loss, a booming downtown, livelier public spaces, more mixed-use districts, and higher density than typically found in an American city. All these factors built a fertile ground for transit.

More Subsidies and Reinvesting in Muni

Muni could only profit from and encourage urban vitality, tourism, and density because the system remained in place in the 1960s and 1970s for the remaining residents to ride. In 1963, due to density and the simple fact that Muni had preserved service, managers could still boast that "nearly nine out of ten people live within two blocks of one of the 61 convenient MUNI lines." San Francisco still had "nearly the highest per capita riding habit in the United States."[127] The comprehensiveness of service, according to Muni historians John McKane and Anthony Perles, was crucial for long-term ridership: "By 1967, by holding fares down, keeping a large volume of service on the street and subsidizing operations from ad valorem taxes, the Railway's patronage had returned to the levels of 1955, a remarkable feat among North American transit systems."[128] In 1967–68, the annual ridership was 148 million passengers.[129]

Low fares and deepening subsidies remained the key to service preservation because, despite the city's manifest advantages, transit still faced competition from cars and decentralization of work and living. The fifteen-cent flat fare and free transfers remained in 1963 a relative bargain as San Francisco had the second-lowest fare in the nation, the same as New York, and only New Orleans was lower priced (and with much less service).[130] As in the past, Muni officials could maintain the low fare due to "San Francisco's policy to give tax support to public transit as a necessary and essential public service" linking downtown and the far-flung neighborhoods.[131] The annual Muni city subsidy was up to $9.7 million in the 1967–68 fiscal year, just another sign both of the declining state of the system's finances and the civic commitment to maintaining service in the face of persistently low ridership.[132]

As deficits rose, both PUC administrators and some business leaders in 1965—including the Downtown Association, Real Estate Board, and Chamber of Commerce—occasionally complained about Muni subsidies.[133] But politicians held out for as long as they could. Mayor John F. Shelley in 1966, for instance, defended low fares and demanded that the PUC move beyond "mere financial analysis" because bottom-line thinking was "misleading." Instead, PUC administrators should consider the "desirable economic effect of leaving fares at their present low rate" and place more emphasis on how fare hikes would negatively impact "the business community, the outlying residential areas, and particularly individual costs to the riders." It was the riders, after all, who "have given the city the third highest and nearly the second highest per capita riding habit of any city in the United States."[134] A predicted $14.2 million deficit in 1968–69 led the Apartment House Association to urge a fare increase to "ease the taxpayer burden."[135] The PUC that year was ready for a fare increase that might have raised an additional $5.6 million,[136] but the Board of Supervisors rejected the increase by ten to one.[137]

Eventually, fares had to go up simply to keep the deficit from reaching embarrassing levels. The sensitivity of ridership to fares, as true in San Francisco as most other cities, was confirmed in 1969–70 when the PUC finally raised fares to twenty cents. One estimate attributed a 5.2 percent loss of ridership to the increase.[138] Additional ridership losses were related to another fare increase in 1970–71, this time from twenty to twenty-five cents.[139] Not only did the fare increases fail to stop deficits, but in 1972 Muni still lost $24 million.[140] However, Muni reminded irritated city residents that the twenty-five-cent unlimited-transfer fare remained one of the great transit bargains in the nation. By 1972, the basic fare in Chicago was forty-five cents plus transfers. Given the bargain San Francisco riders had enjoyed, it is hard to believe that these explanations mollified many riders.[141] Fare increases contributed to a decline to 122 million revenue passengers in 1971–72.[142]

Powerful voices called for more investment, not less, in Muni. In 1972, for instance, the Local 240A of the Transport Workers Union joined neighborhood activists and the Sierra Club in protesting major service cuts. Mayor Joseph Alioto felt enough pressure to request the PUC "dig

FIGURES 24A AND 24B. *Top*, Muni maintained an extensive trolley coach system long after most American cities had abandoned them. *Bottom*, Modern Muni Metro streetcar subway, 2017, on its way through the Parkside and Sunset Districts. Source: Eric Fischer, wikimedia creative commons.

a little deeper to find funds to run the service at normal levels."[143] The influential, business-friendly San Francisco Planning and Urban Renewal Association's report, *Building a New Muni* (1973), investigated Muni and found "unacceptable transit service." Their solution was even more subsidies because "everyone must recognize that transit is an essential public service just like schools, streets, and fire protection." The report argued that "referring to a 'deficit' is nonsense" and dismissed politicians that thought this way.[144] City officials seemed to agree and slowed the increases compared to their peers in other cities. After all, "the City seems resigned to its continuing need to underwrite the Muni's operations and has not attempted to force the railway to make any unusual or severe cuts in service."[145]

A reflection of the solidity of public support, and the lengths the leaders would go to attract riders, was Muni's creation of a pioneering monthly pass system initiated in 1973, costing riders just $11 monthly for unlimited rides, liberal transfers, and an even cheaper senior pass of $2.50 (the base monthly Muni Clipper Card, at just $81 per month, remains a great value in 2022).[146] Such municipal extravagance was only possible when individual fares mattered much less than before. By 1974–75, general city taxes of $29.2 million made up 41 percent of Muni revenues, and fares just 33 percent, with general revenue sharing 17 percent. Deep subsidies had simply become the way Muni did business and has remained the model to the present. Had other cities pursued lower farebox ratios earlier, rather than cutting as ridership fell, there would be more transit that survived to the present.[147] The State of California in 1971 also started providing annual operating support for mass transit derived from the state sales tax on diesel fuel.[148]

Muni engaged in a great deal of renovation and long-term planning for an organization running a chronic and rising deficit. Subsidies—PUC, city, state, and federal—were crucial for imagining a modern, higher-quality future for transit. Muni desperately needed investment after decades of hard use and limited capital funding. Experts in 1966 called Muni "obsolete" and all of its running fleet "outmoded." In the repair yards, mechanics struggled to find replacement parts, forcing them to "cannibalize" older equipment. Tracks and stations were also in poor condition. Muni managers proposed a massive renovation program in 1966, combining local bonds and future federal funding. Muni managers also proposed to scrap the last streetcars and replace them with a combination of buses and hypothetical service from a planned city subway and rapid transit system of four new lines and two rapid bus corridors.[149] The Muni improvement program failed to garner the two-thirds vote needed in 1966.

Another attempt to gain voter approval for transit bonds failed in 1968.[150] Muni bonds were never popular with the public, many of whom already drove, and the two-thirds majority required to get the bond issue passed was difficult to muster on any issue. Voters and politicians were also likely leery of giving Muni managers too much money by this time because of the bus-centric approach many disliked; Black leaders were also upset that Muni was still so white dominated as an institution.[151]

San Francisco riders enjoyed a range of service options that few other cities in the United States had maintained by this era, but electric vehicles still faced an uncertain future. In 1969–70, Muni carried twenty million electric streetcar riders, eleven million cable car riders, forty-five million trolley coach riders, and sixty-one million motor coach riders.[152] In the late 1960s, Muni leadership, influenced by industry practices still favoring buses, actively sought a "massive reduction in trolley coach operation through dieselization, truncation, or elimination of lines." General manager John Woods, a big fan of diesel, would have moved forward with reductions in electric service but discovered that the public remained fans of streetcars and trolley coaches.[153]

Citizens stood up for the remaining streetcars and the electric trolley coaches in the late 1960s.[154] Muni, as a result, placed an order in 1973 for 343 new trolley coaches from Canadian builder Flyer Industries, delivered in the late 1970s. Trolley coaches were no longer produced in the United States as almost all other cities had cut the high-quality service.[155] The case for electric transport grew stronger with the development of BART, increasing fuel prices, and a new electricity subsidy from Hetch Hetchy. The PUC manager of utilities, who was already selling electric power at cost to Muni, transferred the maintenance of supporting electric power infrastructure for its fleet to Hetch Hetchy from the Municipal Railway. Muni now had to spend less to maintain their trolley coach and electrical streetcar systems.[156]

Even after losing bond offerings for additional substitution, managers and city officials quickly found a partial workaround in 1968 from both anti-bus sentiment and the need for more general Muni renovation: the Municipal Railway Improvement Corporation (MRIC). The MRIC was a nonprofit that could sell city-backed bonds, the proceeds of which would be used to buy new equipment without the public securing the debt.[157] For instance, with these funds, Muni bought four hundred new and improved diesel GM New Look buses between 1968 and 1970, even without voter approval.[158] In San Francisco, even pro-bus sentiment in management had ended up creating a new form of subsidy. As a result, in the mid-1970s, Muni pursued a $290 million modernization program

FIGURES 25A AND 25B. San Francisco has maintained its ridership better than most American cities. Source: Bus or Streetcar, 1960/2000, Social Explorer, accessed June 26, 2021.

funded by a blend of MRIC funds, state funds from the gas tax, PUC support, and the federal government (UMTA), which covered 75 percent of the program.[159]

The renewed Muni in the 1980s attracted both city and suburban commuters, raising worries that as "the concentration of downtown high-rise office building development continues, the pressure on Muni Metro can only increase."[160] Density citywide remained high enough to make transit work, feeding workers into CBD-bound trams. In 1980, for instance, the overall density of San Francisco was 14,344 persons per square mile. Post-1965 immigration was crucial to sustaining this density and transit service. Asian American activists in the 1970s and 1980s fought successfully to improve bus service between thriving Chinese American neighborhoods such as Richmond with the cultural and social hub of Chinatown. The activists also successfully pushed for the substitution of diesel buses with faster and more powerful electric trolley coaches on a popular line. A new generation had discovered the value of good transit.[161]

Muni was on an upswing in the 1970s and 1980s, but city planners were still actively working against the density that made transit run better. Responding to pressure from anti-development neighborhood activists, city planners created a residential rezoning in 1978 that "resulted in tighter controls on residential density through the use of a 40' height limit, rear-yard and front-setback requirements."[162] Only in the last two decades, with the department's "Better Neighborhoods" orientation, has city planning "shifted the focus to finding more space for housing in new mid-rise, transit-oriented mixed-use neighborhoods, recognizing the need to accommodate housing demand in a thoughtful, sustainable way."[163] This transit-friendly approach comes only after decades of city planning policy attempts to reduce or curtail density, policies that encouraged many residents to fight any increases in construction. "Better Neighborhoods" is simply a return to the model of living enshrined in the 1921 zoning and the streetcar city.

Learning from San Francisco

San Francisco's hills, isolation, and compactness aided transit development and patronage. Today's San Francisco continues to have key advantages for transit including high population density (in 2019, 18,666 persons per square mile), ethnic diversity, and a thriving technology and financial sector. Deindustrialized cities like Detroit, Chicago, and Baltimore have a harder uphill battle than San Francisco to restore the transit habit. Many Americans look at San Francisco and believe that, because of the city's unique attributes, they have nothing to learn. They should look more closely.

San Francisco, like Boston, demonstrates that consistency in service matters more than a particular style of mass transportation. The key to making rubber-wheeled vehicles work at Muni (now San Francisco Municipal Transportation Agency) was a large fleet, consistent service, regular modernization, low fares, and deep subsidies. For instance, in 2018–19, the City of San Francisco provided SFMTA General Fund support of $413 million and parking and traffic fees of $291 million. The State of California also provided operating support of $181 million. Fares provided only $197 million of the $1.190 billion in SFMTA revenue.[164] *Mass Transit* summarized the pattern succinctly when analyzing the 2021 budget: "SFMTA has four main sources of revenue: general fund (34 percent), parking and traffic fees and fines (31 percent), transit fares (18 percent) and operating grants (17 percent)." Muni has ongoing deficits related to the pandemic, and deep ridership losses during peak hours, but the deep subsidies promise a brighter future than most agencies. Thanks to subventions, managers have developed an aggressive social equity agenda including free fares for low-income youth. In 2019, voters even passed a tax on ride share companies about half of which will go to transit.[165]

Most Muni riders travel on seventy conveniently located bus and trolley coach routes (served by 333 electric trolley coaches and 477 motor coaches). These rubber-tired vehicles—aided by a small light-rail and subway system, cable cars, and historical trams—transported an average of over seven hundred thousand passengers per day pre-COVID-19, about 225 million riders a year, a significant improvement from postwar lows. Muni is wrapping up a new 1.7-mile Center Subway project linking South of Market, Union Square, and Chinatown, thus better serving some of the "city's busiest, most densely populated areas," but buses remain central. In addition, a growing number of riders benefit from BRT enhancements on major streets like Geary and Van Ness; plans are also underway for switching out electric trolley coaches with battery-powered buses. Buses make great transit with the right planning and investment.[166]

San Francisco, like Boston, also illustrates the importance of the interrelationship of highway planning and mass transit. By building so few highways in the first place, thanks to a successful freeway revolt, the city of San Francisco was a natural experiment in the benefits to transit of limited highway service. Had San Francisco built more highways decades ago, many fewer would ride transit today despite the extensive, low-cost service on offer.

CONCLUSION

Beyond Transit Fatalism

Twentieth-century Americans were not likely candidates for building world-class transit, given the popularity of cars and mass suburbia. However, it is reasonable to think, given the relative success of cities such as San Francisco and Boston, that civic leaders and voters in cities elsewhere could have struck a better balance between mass transit and private automobiles. Unfortunately, the case-study narratives from Baltimore, Atlanta, Chicago, and Detroit reflect more typical choices and outcomes for American mass transit. Thanks to the century of anti-transit decisions, a mobility renaissance in most American cities will take more than a new light-rail line or bus lane to get customers back.

The case studies amply demonstrate the price of failing to subsidize transit in periods of the greatest crisis. Transit agencies in cities like Boston and San Francisco would have cut their systems more sharply postwar, like those in Baltimore and Detroit (and hundreds of other cities) had it not been for predictable forms of local and state direct support. No substitute has ever been found for dependable local and state transit-oriented taxation. The reviving fortunes of transit in Los Angeles, Portland, and Seattle show that even cities that once ripped out most of their rail systems can re-add quality transit thanks to consistent local or state subsidies. Transit agencies will have to do a better job controlling operating and capital costs, but what passes for government transit funding at all levels in the United States has been insufficient to create or maintain excellent systems.

As the preceding examples of local anti-transit decisions illustrate, the federal government did not single-handedly destroy American transit. Yet, national policy could have been more transit friendly. The relative success of federally subsidized rapid transit development in Washington, DC, funded at an extremely high level for reasons of national pride, indicates the missed opportunity. For instance, in a typical year such as 2020, the federal government provided about $2.6 billion for transit at a 50/50 percent split of national and local funding. Road infrastructure, however, received about $45 billion annually and an 80/20 percent split of federal and local project costs.[1] The massive 2021 infrastructure bill that provided $39 billion in additional capital funding for mass transit might signal a new era. However, it seems unlikely that the federal government in the long term will dedicate the hundreds of billions in needed capital funding for mass transit modernization, system expansion, or operations. The constituency for transit has grown small, and electric vehicles have replaced transit as today's environmental priority.

Given the low priority of transit in national policy, local and state governments, which already provide most transit operating subsidies nationally, will have to dig deeper. Demonstrating local and state government commitment to quality transit is the most feasible way to build sound systems and, longer-term, a national pro-transit movement. State governments are the most likely source of significant new transit support given their resources, regional reach, and taxing power. In Boston, San Francisco, and New York, the relative success of transit was related to state funding and financing. State leaders have options, including gas taxes, general revenues for transit, and transit financing (such as state-secured bonds). States and related authorities can also adopt demand-management techniques such as congestion pricing and tolling that can generate consistent transit funding. Both state legislatures and the federal government should also reform environmental review requirements for mass transit that often stall projects and raise construction costs.[2]

Transit funding alone will not build ridership: transit-oriented development and transit-centered planning are crucial to building cities that work better for transit. The case studies in this collection contribute to decades of transit analysis that document the essential role residential and commercial density plays in transit performance. Cities like Boston, San Francisco, and Chicago that maintained urban density better supported transit than sustained anti-density policies in Baltimore, Detroit, and Atlanta. The lesson from transportation studies and these case studies is clear: no new fixed-rail system or extension should be built without a plan for rezoning for higher-density development near stations. Zoning reform in Minneapolis, Portland, and other cities offers additional hope for greater density near transit.[3]

Incremental changes to zoning law could benefit transit. Legalization of accessory dwelling units (ADUs), for instance, permits small new apartments and cottages in neighborhoods at affordable rents. The passing of legislation in states like California and Connecticut legalizing ADUs more broadly is promising for increasing density. Cities like Los Angeles and San Diego are already experiencing booms in ADU development. The end of minimum parking requirements for new development may also aid transit ridership. Developers are eager to reduce on-site parking when given the opportunity, as demonstrated in downtown Los Angeles and sections of New York.[4]

Curbing auto-centric planning and spending at the local, state, and federal levels is another indirect means of making transit more attractive. The case studies in the book illustrate that politicians, engineers, and planners did everything they could to build or rebuild their towns for the auto age, even before the federal government created the interstate system. The auto-centric bias remains. Between 2009 and 2017, for instance, the government added 223,494 lane miles to public roads.[5] The federal government paid for most interstate program construction, but as the case studies have shown, local and state governments have been significant promoters and underwriters of highways, arterials, and other roads. Today, state and local governments combined spend more on maintaining road infrastructure than the federal government.[6]

The efficiency of roadway networks creates significant obstacles to transit service today and commits the nation to automobility for decades into the future. Highway cancellation and removal could help tip the balance in transit's favor by making transit-served areas both healthier places to live and harder to cross by car. Cities like Rochester and Syracuse have projects underway, and there are proposals in other cities.[7] Overly wide arterials could also be narrowed as "complete streets" with space for transit, walkers, and bikers.[8] However, highway removal and street redesign will only impact transit if road networks lose much of their everyday speed and convenience; minor or temporary efforts will change very little. Driving must be slower, more expensive, and more agonizing than sitting on a train or bus.

Streets that include exclusive transit lanes are slowly catching on after decades of experiments here and abroad. Popularized in Brazil and Columbia as bus rapid transit (BRT), American BRT options now include exclusive and painted bus lines, priority signals, and high-quality shelters. Pioneering projects include Cleveland's Health Line, Boston's Silver Line, New York's (semi-BRT) Select Bus Service, and San Francisco's growing exclusive bus lane network.[9] Agencies are also experimenting with "Better Bus" strategies including frequent grid-based bus service, additional buses, fast transfers, fewer stops, and signal priority. Rethinking archaic hub-and-spoke routes, many little changed since the streetcar- and CBD-dominant era is one way to better serve riders who today travel in many directions.[10]

Better funded, planned, and operating transit has the potential to address a persistent defect in the American urban scene: the lack of excellent quality transit for those that need it most. Transit cannot alone undo decades of discrimination, but it is unrealistic to imagine rapid social progress where automobiles are a prerequisite for a decent quality of life. The case studies from Baltimore, Atlanta, Detroit, and Chicago illustrated the cost to people of color when transit declined. Where and when transit runs matters for access to employment, education, and housing. Unfortunately, transit riding is so difficult in most cities that it is punitive. It does not have to be that way.

Multiple examples from the historical case studies show that well-conceived, sustained transit service pays social equity dividends. The better buses and rapid transit in 1970s Atlanta, the upgraded Orange Line in Roxbury, and comprehensive bus service in San Francisco are examples of how transit can increase access to the best of what a region offers. In the suburbs, too, low-cost suburban buses could help integrate suburban workforces and make residential relocation of low-income residents to areas of "opportunity" more practical. While sparse nationally, commuter rail systems can enhance equity with more stops and low-cost service in working-class areas once overlooked in these suburb and CBD networks.

Some transit agencies, even with their limited funds, are taking short-term, substantive action. The growing popularity of free or reduced-fare programs indicates new interest in social equity. New York's MTA, San Francisco's SFMTA, and Boston's MBTA, among others, now offer income-eligible fare reductions. Given the small percentage of farebox returns in many cities, and the reliance on public subsidies, such programs make sense to grow ridership and promote equity. However, it is worth remembering that more equitable transit can only sustain itself in the long term in the context of a deeply subsidized transit agency.[11]

The renewed focus on housing equity and fair housing may benefit transit. Investing in transit-rich center-city neighborhoods through additional mortgage lending and multifamily housing sponsorship can add and keep riders where transit already exists. Nonwhite districts with legacy transit, such as West Philadelphia or Chicago's South Side, desperately need more investment in quality affordable housing to stem decades of abandonment. Allowing gentrification to be the significant force for growth and renovation, as is the case in most cities, will often yield few riders per new resident thanks to the parking garages often built as part of market-rate housing. In the suburbs, tools like enhanced vouchers,

ADUs, zoning reform, low-income housing tax credits, and fair housing enforcement can increase the number of low-income transit customers. Such city and suburban measures would potentially drive up regional ridership and balance access for those that need it.[12]

Transit can help the country meet social justice and environmental goals, but a century of anti-transit decisions raises the challenge. Low-income people of color are more likely to ride transit, but their patronage should not be taken for granted. Transit customers, just like everyone else, want to be dependable workers, friends, students, and parents without struggling every day for a ride. They deserve service as dependable, respectful, and convenient as that enjoyed by drivers. If transit agencies fail to provide that quality, they will find whatever automotive options they can.

Acknowledgments

Family members Leanne, Roxie, Ron, Naomi, Rachel, Scott, Zoe, Zach, and Eliana have been a great comfort during these remarkable years. Hats off to the staff of Metro North's Hudson Line and New York City Transit for maintaining excellent transit service throughout the pandemic. Let us all make sure transit agencies get the operating and capital funds they need to thrive in coming years.

Thanks to the volunteers who opened the doors to the Motor Bus Archive in Trenton, New Jersey, and provided primary documents and back issues of the indispensable *Motor Coach Age*. Librarians aided my research at the Institute of Transportation Studies Library at the University of California, Berkeley; the Massachusetts State Archive; the New York Public Library's Forty-Second Street Research Library; and the legendary Maryland Room at Baltimore's Enoch Pratt Free Library. A heartfelt thank-you to the staff of Social Explorer and all those who have scanned a century or more of transit-oriented documents.

University of Chicago executive editor Timothy Mennel and Historical Studies of Urban America series editor Amanda Seligman provided direction on the draft manuscript in multiple dimensions. The anonymous reviewers provided insights that improved the final manuscript. Thanks as well to the Press's Susannah Engstrom and Mark Reschke for their guidance during the review and production process. Detailed comments by Yonah Freemark at the Urban Institute and Zachary M. Schrag of George Mason University helped sharpen the text. Thanks to Hunter College students Emily Froome-Kuntz and Turquoise Martin for assisting in the initial scan for relevant articles.

I am grateful to Professors Joseph Viteritti, John Chin, Matthew Lasner, Owen Gutfreund, Laura Wolf-Powers, Jill Simone Gross, Mehdi Heris, Lili Baum Pollans, Sigmund Shipp, Victoria Johnson, Vivian Louie, and Edwin Melendez for making space for me in Hunter College's renowned Department of Urban Policy and Planning. Hunter College president Jennifer Raab has built a world-class urban university in which the department thrives. Marisol Otero-Morales and Miriam Galindez have been great company these last few years. The engaged graduate students in the Hunter planning programs have sharpened my transit-oriented thinking.

Notes

Introduction

1. Among the many recent studies that consider the impact of roads on urban neighborhoods are Angie Schmitt, *Right of Way: Race, Class and the Silent Epidemic of Pedestrian Deaths in America* (Washington, DC: Island Press, 2020); Kristen Day, "Active Living and Social Justice: Planning for Physical Activity in Low-Income, Black, and Latino Communities," *Journal of the American Planning Association* 72, no. 1 (Winter 2006); Chia-Yuan Yu1, Xuemei Zhu, and Chanam Lee, "Income and Racial Disparity and the Role of the Built Environment in Pedestrian Injuries," *Journal of Planning Education and Research*, 2018. See also Reid Ewing, *Costs of Sprawl* (New York: Routledge, 2017).

2. The relationship between transit and urban form from a global or comparative perspective is explored in the planning literature in books such as Glenn Yago, *The Decline of Transit: Urban Transportation in German and U.S. Cities, 1900–1970* (Cambridge: Cambridge University Press, 1984); Jan Logemann, *Trams or Tailfins: Public and Private Prosperity in Postwar West Germany and the United States* (Chicago: University of Chicago Press, 2012); and Robert Cervero, Erick Guerra, and Stefan Al, *Beyond Mobility: Planning Cities for People and Places* (Washington, DC: Island Press, 2017). Global perspectives on social and other dimensions of transit include Ralph Buehler, "Transport Policies, Automobile Use, and Sustainable Transport: A Comparison of Germany and the United States," *Journal of Planning Education and Research* 30, no. 1 (2010): 76–93; D. Gilbert and C. Poitras, "'Subways Are Not Outdated': Debating the Montreal Metro, 1940–60," *Journal of Transport History* 36, no. 2 (2015): 209–27; J. Young, "Searching for a Better Way: Subway Life and Metropolitan Growth in Toronto, 1942–78," unpublished PhD diss. (history), York University, 2012; J. English, "The Better Way: Transit Service and Demand in Metropolitan Toronto, 1953–1990," PhD diss., Columbia University, 2021; D. Bownes, O. Green, and S. Mullins, eds., *Underground: How the Tube Shaped London* (London: Allen Lane, 2012). Toronto's transit story is also told in Chris Prentice, "Buses in Toronto," *Motor Coach Age* 21, no. 5 (May 1969): 4–25; and Chris Prentice, "Toronto Update," *Motor Coach Age*, 32, no. 6 (June 1980): 4–11.

3. The government settled the anti-trust case against GM and NCL in 1951, but the conspiracy gained broader attention in the energy and environmental conscious 1970s. See Bradford Snell, "Proposal for Restructuring Automobile, Truck, Bus, and Rail Industries, Presented to Subcommittee on Antitrust and Monopoly," Febru-

ary 26, 1974 (US Government Printing Office, 1974), quotations from p. 3. Cinematic treatments that have popularized the conspiracy include *Who Framed Roger Rabbit?* (1988) and the documentary *Taken for a Ride* (New Day Films, 1996).

4. Scott Bottles, *Los Angeles and the Automobile: The Making of the Modern City* (Berkeley: University of California Press, 1987), 3. Other works that address the broader context of the turn to cars include D. Brodsely, *L.A. Freeway* (Berkeley: University of California Press, 1981); James Wolfinger, *Running the Rails: Capital and Labor in the Philadelphia Transit Industry* (Ithaca, NY: Cornell University Press, 2016); Paul Barrett, *The Automobile and Urban Transit: The Formation of Public Policy in Chicago, 1900–1930* (Philadelphia: Temple University Press, 1983); Sy Adler, "The Transformation of the Pacific Electric Railway: Bradford Snell, Roger Rabbit, and the Politics of Transportation in Los Angeles," *Urban Affairs Quarterly* 27, no. 1 (September 1991): 51–86.

5. Bottles, *Los Angeles and the Automobile*, 49.

6. See, for instance, Carl Abbott, *Greater Portland: Urban Life and Landscape in the Pacific Northwest* (Philadelphia: University of Pennsylvania Press, 2001).

7. Among the academic histories of American mass transit are Mark S. Foster, *From Streetcar to Superhighways: American City Planners and Urban Transportation, 1900–1940* (Philadelphia: Temple University Press, 1981); Charles Cheape, *Moving the Masses: Urban Public Transportation in New York, Boston, and Philadelphia* (Cambridge, MA: Harvard University Press, 1980); David W. Jones, *Mass Motorization and Mass Transit: An American History and Policy Analysis* (Bloomington: Indiana University Press, 2008); Brian Cudahy, *Cash, Tokens, and Transfers: A History of Urban Mass Transit in North America* (New York: Fordham University Press, 2001); Martha Bianco, "Technological Innovation and the Rise and Fall of Urban Mass Transit," *Journal of Urban History* 25, no. 3 (1999): 348–78; and George Smerk, *The Federal Role in Urban Mass Transportation* (Bloomington: Indiana University Press, 1991).

There are excellent chapters or sections on transit in important works of urban history, including Sam Bass Warner, *Streetcar Suburbs: The Process of Growth in Boston, 1870–1900* (Cambridge, MA: Harvard University Press, 1962); Kenneth T. Jackson, *Crabgrass Frontier* (New York: Oxford University Press, 1985); John Teaford, *The Unheralded Triumph* (Baltimore: Johns Hopkins University Press, 2019); Robert M. Fogelson, *The Fragmented Metropolis: Los Angeles, 1850–1930* (Berkeley: University of California Press, 1967); Clay McShane and Joel A. Tarr, *The Horse in the City: Living Machines in the Nineteenth Century* (Baltimore: Johns Hopkins University Press, 2007); Clay McShane, *Technology and Reform: Street Railways and the Growth of Milwaukee, 1887–1900* (Madison: State Historical Society of Wisconsin, 1974); Mark S. Foster, *From Streetcar to Superhighway: American City Planners and Urban Transportation, 1900–1940* (Philadelphia: Temple University Press, 1981); Paul Barrett, *The Automobile and Urban Transit: The Formation of Public Policy in Chicago, 1900–1930* (Philadelphia: Temple University Press, 1983); Owen Gutfreund, *Twentieth Century Sprawl* (New York: Oxford University Press, 2004); Peter D. Norton, *Fighting Traffic: The Dawn of the Motor Age in the American City* (Cambridge, MA: MIT Press, 2008); J. Mark Souther, *Believing in Cleveland: Managing Decline in "The Best Location in the Nation"* (Philadelphia: Temple University Press, 2017); and Peter Hall, *Great Planning Disasters* (Berkeley: University of California Press, 1980).

For individual cities, New York's massive system is understandably the most popular with historians, including Clifton Hood, *722 Miles: The Building of the Subways and*

How They Transformed New York (Baltimore: Johns Hopkins University Press, 2004), and more recently, Philip Plotch, *The Last Subway: The Long Wait for the Next Train in New York City* (Cornell, NY: Ithaca University Press, 2020). There are very few non–New York social-minded urban transit histories, but an excellent one that considers planning, policy, and transit development is Zachary M. Schrag, *The Great Society Subway: A History of the Washington Metro* (Baltimore: Johns Hopkins University Press, 2006).

Many urban history articles situate transit in wider trends, social patterns, culture, etc. See Zachary M. Schrag, "The Bus Is Young and Honest: Transportation Politics, Technical Choice, and the Manhattanization of Manhattan Surface Transit, 1919–1936," *Technology and Culture* 41, no. 1 (January 2000): 51–79; Sarah Frohardt-Lane, "Close Encounters: Interracial Contact and Conflict on Detroit's Public Transit in World War II," *Journal of Transport History* 33, no. 2 (2012): 212–27; D. Scott, "When the Motorman Mayor Met the Cable Car Ladies: Engendering Transit in the City That Knows How," *Journal of Urban History* 40, no. 1 (2014): 65–96; Jonathan English, "Derailed: The Postwar End of New York City Subway Expansion," *Journal of Urban History* (December 2019); M. Foster, "City Planners and Urban Transportation: The American Response, 1900–1940," *Journal of Urban History* 5, no. 3 (1979): 365–96; J. B. C. Axelrod, "'Keep The "L" Out of Los Angeles': Race, Discourse, and Urban Modernity in 1920s Southern California," *Journal of Urban History* 34, no. 1 (2007): 3–37; Karen W. Moore, "State Impediments to Transit-Centered Planning in Milwaukee, Wisconsin, 1916–1928," *Journal of Urban History* 40, no. 2 (2014): 318–44.

8. The number of transit enthusiast books is enormous and valuable for the quantity of data about agencies, changes in operations, and challenges over time. Among the best is the entire run of *Motor Coach Age*, published since 1950 by the Motor Coach Society, http://www.motorbussociety.org/mca/. I found the following institutional histories extremely helpful: Michael R. Farrell, *The History of Baltimore Streetcars* (Baltimore: Greenberg, 1992); Herbert Harwood, *Baltimore Streetcars: The Postwar Years* (Baltimore: Johns Hopkins University Press, 2003); John McKane and Anthony Perles, *Inside MUNI: The Properties and Operations of the Municipal Railway of San Francisco* (Glendale, CA: Interurban, 1982); George Krambles and Arthur Peterson, *CTA at 45* (Chicago: George Krambles Transit Scholarship Fund, 1993); and Alan Lind, *Chicago Surface Lines: An Illustrated History* (Park Forest, IL: Transport History Press, 1974).

9. See Moore, "State Impediments to Transit-Centered Planning in Milwaukee, Wisconsin, 1916–1928."

10. Martin V. Melosi, *The Sanitary City: Urban Infrastructure in America from Colonial Times to the Present* (Baltimore: Johns Hopkins University Press, 2000), 122–23. Morton Keller argues powerful streetcar companies operated in a "cozy relationship with the utilities under their surveillance." See Morton Keller, *Regulating a New Economy: Public Policy and Economic Change in America, 1900–1933* (Cambridge, MA: Harvard University Press, 1990), 60.

11. Teaford, *The Unheralded Triumph*, 234–40.

12. Foster, *From Streetcar to Superhighways*, 14.

13. Glenn Yago confirms that "if municipalization occurred when transit was a popular issue in local politics, as in the Populist era, a tradition of transit service was institutionalized locally." In systems that shifted to public control pre-1945, including San Francisco, New York, Cleveland, and Detroit, "mass transit declined less than the mean of other large American cities." See Yago, *The Decline of Transit*, 25.

14. A recent study finds that "spending on one transit mode is, in general, positively associated with spending on other modes." See Jonathan Levine, "Is Bus versus Rail Investment a Zero-Sum Game?," *Journal of the American Planning Association* 79, no. 1 (2013): 5–15.

15. See the extensive discussion of the planning profession's role in favoring roads over transit in Foster, *From Streetcar to Superhighway*.

16. The literature on freeways, automobiles, and urban development has developed a cohesive environmental, social, and physical viewpoint that has also played an essential role in public debates about the future of highways. See Robert Caro's *The Power Broker* (New York: Knopf, 1974); Kenneth T. Jackson, *Crabgrass Frontier* (New York: Oxford University Press, 1985); Clay McShane, *Down the Asphalt Path* (New York: Columbia, 1995); Mark H. Rose and Raymond Mohl, *Interstate: Highway Politics and Policy since 1939* (Knoxville: University of Tennessee Press, 2012); Bruce E. Seely, *Building the American Highway System: Engineers as Policy Makers* (Philadelphia: Temple University Press, 1987); John Jakle and Keith Scully, *Lots of Parking* (Charlottesville: University of Virginia Press, 2004); Joseph F. C. DiMento and Cliff Ellis, eds., *Changing Lanes: Visions and Histories of Urban Freeways* (Cambridge, MA: MIT Press, 2013); Christopher W. Wells, *Car Country: An Environmental History* (Seattle: University of Washington Press, 2012).

17. Garrett Power, "The Unwisdom of Allowing City Growth to Work Out Its Own Destiny," *Maryland Law Review* 625 (1988): 626–74, 626.

18. Sonia Hirt, *Zoned in the USA: The Origins and Implications of American Land-Use Regulation* (Ithaca, NY: Cornell University Press, 2014). Also of interest on the sociocultural dimensions of zoning are the following: Paige Glotzer, *How the Suburbs Were Segregated: Developers and the Business of Exclusionary Housing, 1890–1960* (New York: Columbia, 2020); David M. Freund, *Colored Property: State Policy and White Racial Politics in Suburban America* (Chicago: University of Chicago Press, 2007); John Mangin, "Ethnic Enclaves and the Zoning Game," *Yale Law and Policy Review* 36 (2018): 419.

19. An example, from many, of the weakness of American regional planning: Gian-Claudia Sciara, "Metropolitan Transportation Planning: Lessons from the Past, Institutions for the Future," *Journal of the American Planning Association* 83, no. 3 (2017): 262–76.

20. For recent work on urban renewal, see Sarah Stevens, *Developing Expertise: Architecture and Real Estate in Metropolitan America* (New Haven, CT: Yale University Press, 2016); Lizabeth Cohen, *Saving America's Cities: Ed Logue and the Struggle to Renew Urban America in a Suburban Age* (New York: Farrar, Straus, and Giroud, 2019); Kenneth T. Jackson and Hilary Ballon, eds., *Robert Moses and the Modern City: The Transformation of New York* (New York: Norton, 2007); Francesca Ammon, *Bulldozer: Demolition and the Clearance of the Postwar Landscape* (New Haven, CT: Yale University Press, 2016); Alison Isenberg, *Designing San Francisco: Art, Land, and Urban Renewal in the City by the Bay* (Princeton, NJ: Princeton University Press, 2017). Older classics include Arnold Hirsch, *Making the Second Ghetto: Race and Housing in Chicago, 1940–1960* (Cambridge: Cambridge University Press, 1983), and Mindy Fullilove, *Root Shock: How Tearing Up City Neighborhoods Hurts America, and What We Can Do about It* (New York: Ballantine, 2004).

21. Among the many works of recent interest addressing local highway resistance are Karilyn Crockett, *People before Highways: Boston Activists, Urban Planners,*

and a New Movement for Citymaking (Amherst: University of Massachusetts Press, 2018); Roger Biles, "Expressways before the Interstates: The Case of Detroit, 1945–1956," *Journal of Urban History* 40, no. 5 (2014): 843–54; Raymond A. Mohl, "Stop the Road: Freeway Revolts in American Cities," *Journal of Urban History* 30, no. 5 (2004): 674–706; Hilary Moss, Yinan Zhang, and Andy Anderson, "Assessing the Impact of the Inner Belt: MIT, Highways, and Housing in Cambridge, Massachusetts," *Journal of Urban History* 40, no. 6 (2014): 1054–78; Katherine M. Johnson, "Captain Blake versus the Highwaymen; or, How San Francisco Won the Freeway Revolt," *Journal of Planning History* 8, no. 1 (2009): 56–83; Jeffrey R. Brown, Eric A. Morris, and Brian D. Taylor, "Planning for Cars in Cities: Planners, Engineers, and Freeways in the 20th Century," *Journal of the American Planning Association* 75, no. 2 (2009).

22. Erick Guerra and Robert Cervero, "Cost of a Ride," *Journal of the American Planning Association* 77, no. 3 (2011): 267–90, quotation from p. 267.

23. George S. Smerk, *The Federal Role in Urban Mass Transportation* (Bloomington: Indiana University Press, 1991), 94, 118–20, 219.

24. Some federal transit operating funds also came online in 1974, but the Reagan administration cut these. David W. Jones in *Mass Motorization and Mass Transit* explored mode share in depth. For current mode share and the state of the industry, see American Public Transportation Association, "2020 Public Transportation Fact Book," March 2020, https://www.apta.com/wp-content/uploads/APTA-2020-Fact-Book.pdf. For recent analysis on trends, see https://www.urban.org/urban-wire/us-public-transit-has-struggled-retain-riders-over-past-half-century-reversing-trend-could-advance-equity-and-sustainability.

25. The NCL subsidiary in Montgomery never recovered from the bus boycott even though the company, eager to recoup its ridership, was openly pro-integration during the conflict. See Felicia McGhee, "The Montgomery Bus Boycott and the Fall of the Montgomery City Lines," *Alabama Review* 68, no. 3 (July 2015): 251–68. For descriptions of bus boycotts in Atlanta, see Ronald Bayor, *Race and the Shaping of Twentieth-Century Atlanta* (Chapel Hill: University of North Carolina Press, 1996), and Kevin M. Kruse, *White Flight: Atlanta and the Making of Modern Conservatism* (Princeton, NJ: Princeton University Press, 2005).

26. See the classic David Goldfield, *Cotton Fields and Skyscrapers: Southern City and Region, 1607–1980* (Baton Rouge: Louisiana State University Press, 1982).

27. Editorial, "Race Riots," *Chicago Tribune,* July 29, 1919, 8.

28. See, for instance, Lisa Schweitzer "Planning and Social Media: A Case Study of Public Transit and Stigma on Twitter," *Journal of the American Planning Association* 80, no. 3(2014): 218–38.

29. Sylvie Laurent, *King and the Other America: The Poor People's Campaign and the Quest for Economic Equality* (Berkeley: University of California Press, 2018), 227.

30. See, for instance, Evelyn Blumenberg and Gregory Pierce, "A Driving Factor in Mobility? Transportation's Role in Connecting Subsidized Housing and Employment Outcomes in the Moving to Opportunity (MTO) Program," *Journal of the American Planning Association* 80, no. 1 (2014): 52–66; Lingqian Hu, "Job Accessibility of the Poor in Los Angeles," *Journal of the American Planning Association* 81, no. 1 (2015): 30–45.

31. Laurent, *King and the Other America*, 227.

32. See chapter 6 of my *How States Shaped Postwar America: State Government*

and Urban Power (Chicago: University of Chicago Press, 2019), on the MTA during the Nelson Rockefeller administration.

Part One

1. Dean Locke, director of research, United Railways and Electric Company, "A Brief for the United Railways and Electric Company Presented to the Baltimore Traffic Committee," May 1934, Maryland Room, Enoch Pratt Free Library, EPFL, 10.
2. Foster, *From Streetcar to Superhighways*, 58.
3. Foster, 123–24.
4. Foster, 156.

Chapter One

1. Power, "The Unwisdom of Allowing City Growth to Work Out Its Own Destiny," 649.
2. Locke, "A Brief for the United Railways and Electric Company Presented to the Baltimore Traffic Committee," 8.
3. Harry Bennett Jr., "Baltimore MTA," *Motor Coach Age*, March–April 1989, 4–21.
4. William H. Surrat, Letter to the Editor, *Baltimore Sun*, January 12, 1920, 4.
5. "United Railways and Electric Company of Baltimore: An Analysis," by Mackubin, Goodrich and Company, February 16, 1931, Maryland Room, EPFL.
6. "Summary of Report on Transit Reorganization," *Baltimore Sun*, July 19, 1935, 4.
7. Power, "The Unwisdom of Allowing City Growth to Work Out Its Own Destiny," 641, 644.
8. Baltimore Urban Renewal and Housing Agency, "The Residents of Mount Royal-Fremont Urban Renewal Area," 1960, 3http://archives.ubalt.edu/burha/pdfs/R0019_BURHA_S10_B05_F029.pdf?.
9. "Historical Statistics on Population," Population Division Working Paper No. 76, February 2005, U.S. Census Bureau," https://www.census.gov/content/dam/Census/library/working-papers/2005/demo/POP-twps0076.pdf.
10. Hanson Baldwin, "Along the 'Avenue in Baltimore's Harlem," *Baltimore Sun*, May 11, 1928, 7.
11. Social Explorer, 1920 and 1940 Census, Race, County Level.
12. West side boundary used as North, Pratt, and Fulton Streets with the CBD as the eastern boundary. Total population of district was 137,847 in 1940. Baltimore Population Density per square mile, 1940, Social Explorer, accessed June 30, 2021. General population statistics from https://www.census.gov/content/dam/Census/library/working-papers/2005/demo/POP-twps0076.pdf.
13. "Baltimore Tries Drastic Plan of Race Segregation," *New York Times*, December 25, 1910, 34, 43.
14. Power, "The Unwisdom of Allowing City Growth to Work Out Its Own Destiny," 633, 626–74.
15. "North Baltimoreans Fear Negro Invasion," *Baltimore Sun*, January 21, 1921, 18.
16. Glotzer, *How the Suburbs Were Segregated*, 83–114.
17. Foster, *From Streetcar to Superhighways*, 65.
18. Henry A. Barnes, Commissioner/Baltimore Department of Transit and Traf-

fic, "Rapid Transit Possibilities for the Baltimore Metropolitan Area," November 1958, University of Baltimore Special Collections, Digital Resource, A-1.

19. Power, "The Unwisdom of Allowing City Growth to Work Out Its Own Destiny," 626–74.

20. "Commission on Zoning Urged for Baltimore," *Baltimore Sun*, August 20, 1920, 7.

21. "To Fix Residence Zones," *Baltimore Sun*, November 17, 1919, 18.

22. Power, "The Unwisdom of Allowing City Growth to Work Out Its Own Destiny," 633, 626–74.

23. Baltimore Population Density per square mile, 1940, Social Explorer, accessed June 30, 2021.

24. Black, 1920 and 1940, Social Explorer, accessed June 30, 2021.

25. Richard Rothstein, "From Ferguson to Baltimore," April 29, 2015, Working Economics Blog, Economic Policy Institute, https://www.epi.org/blog/from-ferguson-to-baltimore-the-fruits-of-government-sponsored-segregation/#:~:text=In%20Baltimore%20in%201910%2C%20a,African%20Americans%20to%20designated%20blocks.

26. "Would Put 'Jim Crow' Cars on Street Railways," *Baltimore Sun*, January 30, 1924, 6.

27. "'Jim Crow' Electric Car Bill Killed in House," *Baltimore Sun*, February 6, 1924, 4.

28. "Club Endorses 'Jim Crow' Bill, *Baltimore Sun*, February 3, 1924, 4.

29. Kelker, De Leuw and Company, "Routing of Street Railway Lines and Methods for the Improvement of Traffic Conditions in the City of Baltimore," 1926, Maryland Room, EPFL, 50.

30. "Summary of Report on Transit Reorganization," *Baltimore Sun*, July 19, 1935, 4.

31. Locke, "A Brief for the United Railways and Electric Company Presented to the Baltimore Traffic Committee," 9.

32. "Paying the Park Tax Was Easy When Service Wasn't Important," *Trolley News* (United Railways and Electric Co.), October 26, 1931, Pamphlet Collection, Maryland Room, EPFL, 3.

33. Foster, *From Streetcars to Superhighways*, 124–25.

34. Editorial, "Once Again the City Calls in Outsiders," *Baltimore Sun*, July 21, 1944, 10.

35. Locke, "A Brief for the United Railways and Electric Company Presented to the Baltimore Traffic Committee," 99, 10.

36. Andrew M. Giguere, "'. . . And Never the Twain Shall Meet': Baltimore's East–West Expressway and the Construction of the 'Highway to Nowhere,'" MA thesis, June 2009, 72.

37. Kelker, De Leuw and Company, "Routing of Street Railway Lines and Methods for the Improvement of Traffic Conditions in the City of Baltimore," 26.

38. "Tells Need for Subway," *Baltimore Sun*, March 5, 1920, 5.

39. "The Story of Baltimore's Street Cars," *Trolley News* (United Railways and Electric Co.), August 1, 1927, Pamphlet Collection, Maryland Room, EPFL, 3.

40. Harry Bennett Jr., "Baltimore MTA," *Motor Coach Age*, March–April 1989, 4–21.

41. "Summary of Report on Transit Reorganization," *Baltimore Sun*, July 19, 1935, 4.

42. United Railways and Electric Company of Baltimore: An Analysis by Mackubin, Goodrich and Company, February 16, 1931, Maryland Room, EPFL, 14.

43. Locke, "A Brief for the United Railways and Electric Company Presented to the Baltimore Traffic Committee," 11.

44. United Railways and Electric Company of Baltimore: An Analysis by Mackubin, Goodrich and Company, February 16, 1931, Maryland Room, EPFL, 6–7.

45. "Paying the Park Tax Was Easy When Service Wasn't Important," *Trolley News* (United Railways and Electric Co.), October 26, 1931, Pamphlet Collection, Maryland Room, EPFL, 1–3.

46. "Summary of Report on Transit Reorganization," *Baltimore Sun*, July 19, 1935, 4.

47. A 1935 federal ruling requiring the separation of power-generating divisions from transit companies did not impact Baltimore. This was another strike against transit in cities like Atlanta, where profitable power-generating divisions subsidized money-losing transit operations. Harry Bennett, "Baltimore, Part I, 1915–1945," *Motor Coach Age*, July–August 1988, 4–36.

48. "Summary of Report on Transit Reorganization," *Baltimore Sun*, July 19, 1935, 4.

49. Foster, *From Streetcars to Superhighways*, 121–23.

50. Harry Bennett, "Baltimore, Part I, 1915–1945," *Motor Coach Age*, July–August 1988, 4–36. PCC 1945 figures from Harry Bennett, "Baltimore Transit under NCL," *Motor Coach Age*, November–December 1988, 4–36.

Chapter Two

1. Chicago Surface Lines, "Seeing Greater Chicago: A Sightseeing and Route Guide," 1926, 23.

2. Carl Condit, *Chicago, 1910–1929, Building, Planning and Urban Technology* (Chicago: University of Chicago, 1973), 49.

3. Application for "The Chicago Park Boulevard System Historic District, National Register of Historic Places," Registration Form, National Park Service, 2012, 6–7, 142.

4. Hugo S. Grosser, "The Movement for Municipal Ownership in Chicago," *Annals of the American Academy of Political and Social Science* 27 (January 1906): 72; Also Samuel Wilber Norton, *Chicago Traction; A History, Legislative and Political* (Chicago: self-published, 1907).

5. *Encyclopedia of Chicago*, entries on Chicago Sanitary and Ship Canal and Schools and Education, http://www.encyclopedia.chicagohistory.org/pages/1124.html.

6. *Encyclopedia of Chicago*, 208–15.

7. Alan R. Lind, *Chicago Surface Lines: An Illustrated History* (Park Forest, IL: Transport History Press, 1974), 174.

8. Hugo S. Grosser, "The Movement for Municipal Ownership in Chicago," 72, 74, 82. https://www.jstor.org/stable/1010478.

9. https://www.chicago-l.org/history/; https://en.wikipedia.org/wiki/Chicago_Traction_Wars; https://www.google.com/books/edition/Chicago/wxJ9j6s_wRwC?hl=en&gbpv=1&pg=PA219&printsec=frontcover.

10. CTA, "Chicago's Mass Transportation System," February 15, 1957, 1–24.

11. Chicago Surface Lines, *Annual Report*, January 31, 1921, 23.

12. Chicago Surface Lines, *Annual Report*, January 31, 1926, 1–10.

13. "Zoning Gives City More Room," *Chicago Daily Tribune*, January 21, 1923, 17.

14. Dominic Pacyga, *Chicago: A Biography* (Chicago: University of Chicago Press, 2009) 219; University of Chicago, *Census Tracts of Chicago Grouped into 180 Areas Showing Population Density per Sq. Mile, 1930* (Chicago: University of Chicago Press, 1934).

15. Chicago Surface Lines, *Annual Report*, January 31, 1935, 1–9.

16. Chicago Surface Lines, *Annual Report*, January 31, 1935, 9.

17. CTA, "New Horizons for Chicago Metropolitan Area," 1958, 1–32.

18. Lind, *Chicago Surface Lines*, 201.

19. Christopher Robert Reed, "Beyond Chicago's Black Metropolis: A History of the West Side's First Century, 1837–1940," *Journal of the Illinois State Historical Society (1998–)* 92, no. 2 (1999): 119–49.

20. Editorial, "Race Riots," *Chicago Daily Tribune*, July 29, 1919, 8.

21. Reed, "Beyond Chicago's Black Metropolis: A History of the West Side's First Century, 1837–1940," 119–49.

22. http://www.gif-explode.com/?explode=http://i.imgur.com/xZoKnTa.gif.

23. Social Explorer, 1920 and 1940 Census figures by Census Place, accessed June 30, 2021.

24. Daniel Burnham, *Plan of Chicago*, http://livinghistoryofillinois.com/pdf_files/Plan%20of%20Chicago%20by%20Daniel%20H%20Burnham.pdf, 73–76. Foster also believes the plan emphasized an auto-centric vision; Foster, *From Streetcar to Superhighway*, 42.

25. Walter D. Moody, *Wacker's Manual of the Plan of Chicago*, Chicago Plan Commission, 1920, 87, 128, 155, 148, https://hdl.handle.net/2027/cool.ark:/13960/t6737bf5p.

26. Condit, *Chicago 1910–1929, Building, Planning, and Technology*, 236–39.

27. *Chicago Area Transportation Study*, Final Report, Volume 3, Transportation Plan, July 1960, State of Illinois, County of Cook, City of Chicago, 75.

28. Condit, *Chicago, 1910–1929*, 236–39.

29. *Chicago Area Transportation Study*, Final Report, Volume 3, Transportation Plan, July 1960, State of Illinois, County of Cook, City of Chicago, 48.

30. Application for the Chicago Park Boulevard System Historic District, National Register of Historic Places, Registration Form, National Park Service, 2012, 125, 141, 142.

31. Chicago Surface Lines, *Annual Report*, January 31, 1928, 1–12.

32. Chicago Surface Lines, *Annual Report*, January 31, 1928, 1–12.

33. Chicago Surface Lines, *Annual Report*, January 31, 1930, 7.

34. Chicago Surface Lines, *Annual Report*, January 31, 1931, 3.

35. Lind, *Chicago Surface Lines*, 383.

36. Allison Shertzer et. al, "Zoning and the Economic Geography of Cities," *Journal of Urban Economics* 105 (2018): 22.

37. Homer Hoyt, quoted in Allison Shertzer et. al, "Zoning and the Economic Geography of Cities," *Journal of Urban Economics* 105 (2018): 20.

38. Shertzer et. al, "Zoning and the Economic Geography of Cities," 20–39.

39. Joseph Schweiterman and Dana Caspall, *A History of Zoning in Chicago: The Politics of Place* (Chicago: Lake Claremont Press, 2006), 17–44.

40. Editorial, "The New Zoning Law," *Chicago Daily Tribune*, January 14, 1923, 8.

41. Michael Ebner, *Creating Chicago's North Shore: A Suburban History* (Chicago: University of Chicago Press, 1989).

42. Edward H. Bennett, *Plan of Winnetka* (1921), 43, 19, 45. Available as PDF at https://www.winnetkahistory.org/wp-content/uploads/2014/06/Plan-of-Winnetka-1921-resized.pdf.

43. Chicago Population Density per square mile, 1940, Social Explorer, accessed June 30, 2021.

44. Chicago Surface Lines, *Annual Report*, January 31, 1940, 1–18.

45. Chicago Surface Lines, *Annual Report*, January 31, 1924, 1–15.

46. Chicago Surface Lines, *Annual Report*, January 31, 1927, 11.

47. Chicago Surface Lines, *Annual Report*, January 31, 1928, 1–12.

48. Chicago Surface Lines, *Annual Report*, January 31, 1931, 11.

49. Chicago Surface Lines, *Annual Report*, January 31, 1942, 3.

50. Chicago Surface Lines, *Annual Report*, January 31, 1927, 1–11.

51. Chicago Surface Lines, *Annual Report*, January 31, 1933, 3.

52. "Good Will Great Asset," *Surface Service Magazine*, January 1932, No. 10, Northwestern University Transportation Library, NUTL Digital Collections, 10.

53. Chicago Surface Lines, *Annual Report*, January 31, 1937, 1–11.

54. Chicago Surface Lines, *Annual Report*, January 31, 1940, 17.

55. Foster, *From Streetcars to Superhighways*, 116–17.

56. Chicago Surface Lines, *Annual Report*, January 31, 1938, 3.

57. "Plan Spending 172 Million on Transit Lines," *Chicago Daily Tribune*, November 30, 1938, 13.

58. Chicago Surface Lines, *Annual Report*, January 31, 1937, 5.

59. Chicago Surface Lines, *Annual Report*, January 31, 1935, 8–9.

60. Andris Kristopans, "Chicago, Part I," *Motor Coach Age*, January–March 1999, 13.

61. Chicago Surface Lines, *Annual Report*, January 31, 1942, 1–9.

62. Chicago Surface Lines, *Annual Report*, January 31, 1944, 8.

63. Chicago Surface Lines, *Annual Report*, January 31, 1946, 1–7.

Chapter Three

1. James C. O'Connell, *The Hub's Metropolis: Greater Boston's Development from Railroad Suburbs to Smart Growth* (Cambridge, MA: MIT Press, 2013), 73.

2. *Annual Report of the Board of Public Trustees of the Boston Elevated Railway Company*, 1940, 1–11.

3. Boston Population Density per square mile, 1920, Social Explorer, accessed June 30, 2021.

4. "A Comprehensive Development Program for Public Transportation in the Massachusetts Bay Area 1966," MBTA Planning Staff, May 3, 1966, Internet Archive, IV-18.

5. Warner, *Streetcar Suburbs*, 25–28.

6. Warner, 28.

7. Lawrence W. Kennedy, *Planning the City upon a Hill: Boston since 1630* (Amherst: University of Massachusetts Press, 1992), 102.

8. Kennedy, 102.

9. *Annual Report of the Board of Public Trustees of the Boston Elevated Railway Company*, 1933, 9.

10. Metropolitan Transit Authority, *Sixth Annual Report*, 1952, 30. West End becomes Boston Elevated. The first elevated lines opened in 1901 and would reach Forest Hills by 1909 and the Cambridge subway in 1912.

11. John Harriman, "How the MTA Got That Way," *Boston Globe*, November 9, 1948, 1, 20.

12. *Annual Report of the Board of Public Trustees of the Boston Elevated Railway Company*, 1928, 7.

13. *Annual Report of the Board of Public Trustees of the Boston Elevated Railway Company*, 1918, 33.

14. "The Boston Elevated Bill," *Boston Globe*, April 14, 1918, 9.

15. "Ready to Give Hearings, *Boston Globe*, December 16, 1918, 2.

16. See Michael Rawson, *Eden on the Charles: The Making of Boston* (Cambridge, MA: Harvard University Press, 2010).

17. John D. Merrill, "Politics and Politicians," *Boston Globe*, April 7, 1918, 6.

18. "'L' Fare Not Likely Ever to Be More than 10 Cents," *Boston Globe*, August 26, 1919, 9.

19. John D. Merrill, "Politics and Politicians," *Boston Globe*, April 7, 1918, 6.

20. "Protest to Governor on Control of Elevated," *Boston Globe*, August 2, 1918, 9.

21. *MBTA Annual Report*, 1975, 3.

22. *Annual Report of the Board of Public Trustees of the Boston Elevated Railway Company*, 1918, 16.

23. *Annual Report of the Board of Public Trustees of the Boston Elevated Railway Company*, 1940, 16.

24. John Harriman, "Facts of Life about the MTA," *Boston Globe*, July 6, 1953, 6.

25. "Boston Elevated Gains," *Boston Globe*, August 16, 1918, 5.

26. *Annual Report of the Board of Public Trustees of the Boston Elevated Railway Company*, 1928, 5–6.

27. *Annual Report of the Board of Public Trustees of the Boston Elevated Railway Company*, 1928, 5–6.

28. John Harriman, "Facts of Life about the MTA," *Boston Globe*, July 6, 1953, 6.

29. "'L' Fare Not Likely Ever to Be More than 10 Cents," *Boston Globe*, August 26, 1919, 9.

30. "Amounts to Be Paid toward Deficit," *Boston Globe*, August 15, 1919, 4.

31. *Annual Report of the Board of Public Trustees of the Boston Elevated Railway Company*, 1922, 6–7.

32. *Annual Report of the Board of Public Trustees of the Boston Elevated Railway Company*, 1928, 5–6.

33. *Annual Report of the Board of Public Trustees of the Boston Elevated Railway Company*, 1928, 5–6.

34. *Annual Report of the Board of Public Trustees of the Boston Elevated Railway Company*, 1928, 5–6.

35. *Annual Report of the Board of Public Trustees of the Boston Elevated Railway Company*, 1929, 6–7.

36. *Annual Report of the Board of Public Trustees of the Boston Elevated Railway Company*, 1925, 9.

37. *Annual Report of the Board of Public Trustees of the Boston Elevated Railway Company*, 1924, 1.

38. *Annual Report of the Board of Public Trustees of the Boston Elevated Railway Company*, 1932, 9–10.

39. *Annual Report of the Board of Public Trustees of the Boston Elevated Railway Company*, 1920.

40. *Annual Report of the Board of Public Trustees of the Boston Elevated Railway Company*, 1923, 11.

41. *Annual Report of the Board of Public Trustees of the Boston Elevated Railway Company*, 1923, 71.

42. *Annual Report of the Board of Public Trustees of the Boston Elevated Railway Company*, 1924, 1.

43. "Statewide Ballot Question—Statistics by Year: 1919–2018," https://www.sec.state.ma.us/ele/elebalm/balmresults.html#year1919; https://taxfoundation.org/when-did-your-state-adopt-its-gas-tax/.

44. O'Connell, *The Hub's Metropolis*, 101, 95.

45. O'Connell, 101, 103.

46. O'Connell, 89.

47. O'Connell, 79, 84, 85.

48. *Annual Report of the Board of Public Trustees of the Boston Elevated Railway Company*, 1930, 6.

49. *Annual Report of the Board of Public Trustees of the Boston Elevated Railway Company*, 1924, 1.

50. *Annual Report of the Board of Public Trustees of the Boston Elevated Railway Company*, 1933, 9.

51. Metropolitan Transit Authority, *First Annual Report*, 1947, 1–38.

52. *Annual Report of the Board of Public Trustees of the Boston Elevated Railway Company*, 1931, 12–14.

53. *Annual Report of the Board of Public Trustees of the Boston Elevated Railway Company*, 1933, 9.

54. *Annual Report of the Board of Public Trustees of the Boston Elevated Railway Company*, 1933, 9.

55. *Annual Report of the Board of Public Trustees of the Boston Elevated Railway Company*, 1934, 9–10.

56. *Annual Report of the Board of Public Trustees of the Boston Elevated Railway Company*, 1945, 9.

57. *Annual Report of the Board of Public Trustees of the Boston Elevated Railway Company*, 1932, 9–10.

58. *Annual Report of the Board of Public Trustees of the Boston Elevated Railway Company*, 1935, 15.

59. *Annual Report of the Board of Public Trustees of the Boston Elevated Railway Company*, 1939, 15.

60. *Annual Report of the Board of Public Trustees of the Boston Elevated Railway Company*, 1933, 9.

61. *Annual Report of the Board of Public Trustees of the Boston Elevated Railway Company*, 1935, 15.

62. *Annual Report of the Board of Public Trustees of the Boston Elevated Railway Company*, 1936, 17.

63. *Annual Report of the Board of Public Trustees of the Boston Elevated Railway Company*, 1937, 41.
64. *Annual Report of the Board of Public Trustees of the Boston Elevated Railway Company*, 1938, 18.
65. *Annual Report of the Board of Public Trustees of the Boston Elevated Railway Company*, 1942, 6.
66. *Annual Report of the Board of Public Trustees of the Boston Elevated Railway Company*, 1945, 10–15.
67. *Annual Report of the Board of Public Trustees of the Boston Elevated Railway Company*, 1941, 16.
68. *Annual Report of the Board of Public Trustees of the Boston Elevated Railway Company*, 1943, 8.
69. Metropolitan Transit Authority, *First Annual Report*, 1947, 1–38.
70. *Annual Report of the Board of Public Trustees of the Boston Elevated Railway Company*, 1946, 1–19.

Chapter Four

1. Harry Bennett, "Baltimore Transit under NCL," *Motor Coach Age*, November–December 1988, 4.
2. BTC, "Progress in Public Service: Annual Report of the BTC," December 31, 1946, 1.
3. Bennett, "Baltimore Transit under NCL," 4.
4. Fr. Kevin A. Mueller, *The Best Way to Go: The History of the BTC* (Baltimore: Kevin Mueller, 1997), 1–146.
5. J. S. Armstrong, "Modern BTC System Urged," *Baltimore Sun*, March 31, 1946, 17.
6. BTC, "The Rider's Digest of Coordinated Plan for Traffic and Transit Improvement in Baltimore," November 1945, 2.
7. "Coordinate Planning for Traffic and Transit Improvement in Baltimore," 1947, Chief Engineer of Baltimore City, Commission on the City Plan, and City Council, 6, Maryland Room, EPFL.
8. BTC, "The Rider's Digest of Coordinated Plan for Traffic and Transit Improvement in Baltimore," November 1945, 7.
9. BTC, "The Rider's Digest of Coordinated Plan for Traffic and Transit Improvement in Baltimore," November 1945, 2.
10. BTC, "Progress in Public Service: Annual Report of the BTC," December 31, 1946, 1–9.
11. Mueller, *The Best Way to Go*, 1–146.
12. BTC, "Progress in Public Service: Annual Report of the BTC," December 31, 1946, 4.
13. J. S. Armstrong, "Modern BTC System Urged," *Baltimore Sun*, March 31, 1946, 17.
14. BTC, "Modernizing Public Transportation: Annual Report of the Baltimore Transit Company," December 31, 1947, 7.
15. Mueller, *The Best Way to Go*, 1–146.
16. BTC, "Progress in Public Service: Annual Report of the BTC," December 31, 1946, 1–9.

17. Bennett Jr., "Baltimore MTA," 4–21.
18. Mueller, *The Best Way to Go*, 1–146.
19. BTC, "The Rider's Digest of Coordinated Plan for Traffic and Transit Improvement in Baltimore," November 1945, 8–9.
20. BTC, "Progress in Public Service: Annual Report of the BTC," December 31, 1946, 2–3.
21. Mueller, *The Best Way to Go*, 1–146.
22. American Public Transit Association, *Transit Fact Book*, 2006.
23. Report of the Committee on Mass Transportation, Baltimore City Government, December, 1955, Maryland Room, EPFL, 1–94.
24. Report of the Committee on Mass Transportation, Baltimore City Government, December, 1955, Maryland Room, EPFL, 36.
25. Bennett Jr., "Baltimore MTA," 17, 21.
26. Report of the Committee on Mass Transportation, Baltimore City Government, December, 1955, Maryland Room, EPFL, 10.
27. Public Service Commission of Maryland, Case No. 5220, "In the Matter of the Application of the BTC," July 8, 1952, Maryland Room, EPFL, 5–7.
28. Public Service Commission of Maryland, "Preliminary Report: Investigation of the Service and Facilities of the Baltimore Transit Company and the Baltimore Coach Company," January 10, 1953, Maryland Room, EPFL, 19.
29. Mueller, *The Best Way to Go*, 115.
30. Bennett Jr., "Baltimore MTA," 23.
31. "Barnes Is Appointed Transit Director," *Baltimore Sun*, April 6, 1957, 18, 30.
32. Report of the Committee on Mass Transportation, Baltimore City Government, December 1955, Maryland Room, EPFL, 1–94.
33. Dr. Abel Wolman, Statement, GBC, Minutes of Meeting, Mass Transportation Subcommittee, February 2, 1956, University of Baltimore Special Collections Digital Resource (UBSCDR), 2.
34. "Barnes Is Appointed Transit Director," *Baltimore Sun*, April 6, 1957, 18, 30.
35. Bennett Jr., "Baltimore MTA," 4–21.
36. GBC, "Report by Mass Transportation Subcommittee of the GBC on the Wolman Committee Report," March 1956, 3–5. Extensive GBC debate and discussion of the Wolman report and mass transit can be found in the UBSCDR.
37. "Barnes Is Appointed Transit Director," *Baltimore Sun*, April 6, 1957, 18, 30.
38. "Barnes Is Appointed Transit Director," *Baltimore Sun*, April 6, 1957, 18, 30.
39. John Schmidt, "Henry Barnes, He Speeded City Pace," *Baltimore Sun*, January 14, 1962, 42.
40. Barnes cited the exclusive busway plans of Los Angeles as a useful precedent for Baltimore. Henry A. Barnes, Commissioner/Baltimore Department of Transit and Traffic, "Rapid Transit Possibilities for the Baltimore Metropolitan Area," November 1958, UBSCDR, C-6, D-13, D-15, D-17, D-18.
41. John Schmidt, "Henry Barnes, He Speeded City Pace," *Baltimore Sun*, January 14, 1962, 42.
42. BTC, "Improved Transit Service for Baltimore Metropolitan Area," May 1960, Maryland Room, EPFL, 13.
43. BTC, "Improved Transit Service for Baltimore Metropolitan Area," May 1960, Maryland Room, EPFL, 1–38.

44. Henry Barnes to Mayor Thomas D'Alesandro Jr., November 26, 1958, UBSCDR, 1.

45. Report of the Baltimore Metropolitan Area Mass Transit Legislative Commission, 1960, UBSCDR, 6–7.

46. Bennett Jr., "Baltimore MTA," 29.

47. BTC, "Improved Transit Service for Baltimore Metropolitan Area," May 1960, Maryland Room, EPFL, 1–38.

48. Jack O'Donnell to William Boucher, GBC, April 9 1959, UBSCDR.

49. http://www.roadstothefuture.com/main.html.

50. http://www.roadstothefuture.com/main.html.

51. "22-Year Road Plan Backed," *Baltimore Sun*, December 3, 1950.

52. "The JFX Gets the Backing of the Mayor," *Baltimore Sun*, September 26, 1950, 14.

53. "Jones Falls Expressway Plan," *Baltimore Sun*, April 28, 1951, 24.

54. "Mayor against Toll Highway," *Baltimore Sun*, June 21, 1950, 8.

55. http://www.roadstothefuture.com/main.html.

56. "Expressway May Include Fast Busses," *Baltimore Sun*, September 8, 1950, 34.

57. "Mayor to Seek Jones Falls Road Funds," *Baltimore Sun*, September 20, 1959, 32.

58. Russell W. Baker, "All Ten Municipal Bonds," *Baltimore Sun*, May 9, 1951, 10.

59. "Mayor Promises Freeway Survey," *Baltimore Sun*, July 19, 1944, 7, 20. See Caro, *The Power Broker*; Jackson and Balon, *Robert Moses and the Modern City*.

60. "Mr. Moses Reports," *Baltimore Sun*, October 11, 1944, 12.

61. Linda Shopes and Linda Zeidman, eds., *The Baltimore Book: New Views of Local History* (Philadelphia: Temple University Press, 1991), 211.

62. Andrew M. Giguere, "'. . . and Never the Twain Shall Meet': Baltimore's East–West Expressway and the Construction of the 'Highway to Nowhere,'" MA thesis, Ohio University, June 2009, 113.

63. http://www.roadstothefuture.com/main.html.

64. http://www.roadstothefuture.com/Balt_City_Interstates.html; Giguere, "'. . . and Never the Twain Shall Meet': Baltimore's East–West Expressway and the Construction of the 'Highway to Nowhere,'"; and total of cleared houses from Shopes and Zeidman, *The Baltimore Book*, 211.

65. "M-A-D Position Statement," August 2, 1971, UBSCDR.

66. Movement against Destruction, "Mass Transit Committee Report," 1969, UBSCDR, 1.

67. http://www.roadstothefuture.com/Balt_City_Interstates.html; Giguere, "'. . . and Never the Twain Shall Meet': Baltimore's East–West Expressway and the Construction of the 'Highway to Nowhere,'"; and total of cleared houses from Shopes and Zeidman, *The Baltimore Book*, 211.

68. Bennett Jr., "Baltimore MTA," 4–21.

69. Report of the Committee on Mass Transportation, Baltimore City Government, December, 1955, Maryland Room, EPFL, 14.

70. "To Ride or Drive," *Baltimore Sun*, April 24, 1961, 14.

71. Parsons, Brinckerhoff, Quade and Douglas, "Baltimore Area Mass Transportation Plan, Phase II," October 1965, Maryland Room, EPFL.

72. See Edward Orser, *Blockbusting in Baltimore: The Edmondson Village Story* (Lexington: University Press of Kentucky, 1997); Antero Pietila, *Not in My Neighborhood: How Bigotry Shaped a Great American City* (New York: Ivan Dee, 2010).

73. https://www.census.gov/content/dam/Census/library/working-papers/2005/demo/POP-twps0076.pdf.

74. Baltimore City Bus or Streetcar, 1960, Social Explorer, accessed June 26, 2021.

75. Baltimore City Bus or Streetcar, 1960, Social Explorer, accessed June 26, 2021.

76. Baltimore City Bus or Streetcar, 1960, Social Explorer, accessed June 26, 2021.

77. Baltimore Urban Renewal and Housing Agency, "The Residents of Mount Royal-Fremont Urban Renewal Area," 1960, http://archives.ubalt.edu/burha/pdfs/R0019_BURHA_S10_B05_F029.pdf?, 5.

78. http://archives.ubalt.edu/burha/pdfs/R0019_BURHA_S10_B05_F029.pdf?, 59.

79. http://archives.ubalt.edu/burha/pdfs/R0019_BURHA_S10_B05_F029.pdf?, 71.

80. League of Women Voters of Baltimore, "The Crisis in Baltimore . . . Physical Problems," December 10, 1968, UBSCDR, 5. See also Nicholas Dagen Bloom, *Merchant of Illusion* (Columbus: Ohio State University Press, 2005).

81. League of Women Voters of Baltimore, "The Crisis in Baltimore . . . Physical Problems," 5.

82. Shopes and Zeidman, *The Baltimore Book*, 221; Bus or Streetcar, 1970, Social Explorer, accessed June 26, 2021.

83. Baltimore City census tracts 1511 and 1507.1. Bus or Streetcar, 1970, Social Explorer, accessed June 26, 2021. See Andrew Wiese, *African American Suburbanization in the Twentieth Century* (Chicago: University of Chicago Press, 2004).

84. http://archives.ubalt.edu/burha/pdfs/R0019_BURHA_S10_B05_F029.pdf?, 66.

85. Baltimore County Black Population, 1960, Social Explorer, accessed June 26, 2021.

86. League of Women Voters of Baltimore, "The Crisis in Baltimore . . . Physical Problems," 5.

87. Henry A Barnes, Commissioner/Baltimore Department of Transit and Traffic, "Rapid Transit Possibilities for the Baltimore Metropolitan Area," November 1958, UBSCDR, A-1.

88. Baltimore Bus or Streetcar, 1960, Social Explorer, accessed June 29, 2021.

89. BTC, "Improved Transit Service for Baltimore Metropolitan Area," May 1960, Maryland Room, EPFL, 30.

90. "Transit Plan," *Baltimore Sun*, June 7, 1960, 14.

91. BTC, "Improved Transit Service for Baltimore Metropolitan Area," May 1960, Maryland Room, EPFL, 33, 42.

92. D. W. Barrett to Henry A. Barnes, January 9, 1959, UBSCDR, 1–2.

93. See my *Merchant of Illusion* for a more detailed description of Charles Center's development.

94. BTC, "Improved Transit Service for Baltimore Metropolitan Area," May 1960, Maryland Room, EPFL, 19.

95. BTC, "Improved Transit Service for Baltimore Metropolitan Area," May 1960, Maryland Room, EPFL, 19–20.

96. Charles Flowers, "Hearing Set for Countian," *Baltimore Sun*, November 23, 1962, 2.

97. J. L. O'Donnell, "Rapid Transit—a Reality for Baltimore," April 1962, Maryland Room, EPFL, 3–5.

98. "Power to Bar 2 Streetcar Lines Seen," *Baltimore Sun*, April 8, 1962, 46.

99. "In Brief," *Baltimore Sun*, April 8, 1962, 60.

100. "2 Bus Lines to Be Sought," *Baltimore Sun*, April 10, 1962, 14.

101. "The Week in Brief," *Baltimore Sun*, April 22, 1962, 20.

102. Charles Flowers, "3 Million Budget Surplus Is Seen," *Baltimore Sun*, December 4, 1962, 26.

103. "Aid for Transit," *Baltimore Sun*, September 28, 1962, 18.

104. Report of the Metropolitan Transit Authority Maryland, Fiscal Year Ended June 30, 1963, 1–11.

105. Editorial, "Let Us See," *Baltimore Sun*, November 7, 1962, 31.

106. Edgar L. Jones, "What Barnes Did," *Baltimore Sun*, January 6, 1962, 10.

107. "Transit Quandary," *Baltimore Sun*, June 16, 1960, 16.

108. Report of the Metropolitan Transit Authority Maryland, Fiscal Year Ended June 30, 1967, 1–16.

109. Parsons, Brinckerhoff, Quade and Douglas, "Baltimore Area Mass Transportation Plan, Phase II," October 1965, Maryland Room, EPFL, 23.

110. Metropolitan Transit Authority of Maryland, "Baltimore Area Mass Transportation Study: Phase I," prepared by Parsons, Brinckerhoff, Quade and Douglas, 1964, 27.

111. Parsons, Brinckerhoff, Quade and Douglas, "Baltimore Area Mass Transportation Plan, Phase II," October 1965, Maryland Room, EPFL, 23.

112. Metropolitan Transit Authority of Maryland, "Baltimore Area Mass Transportation Study: Phase I" (ii–iii), 28, 30, 35.

113. Harry Bennett Jr., "Baltimore Transit under NCL," *Motor Coach Age*, November–December, 1988, 31.

114. "Public Transit Ownership," *Baltimore Sun*, February 26, 1963, 13.

115. Report of the Metropolitan Transit Authority Maryland, Fiscal Year Ended June 30, 1963, 3.

116. "Grady Sets Transit Bill Talks," *Baltimore Sun*, March 7, 1959, 18.

117. "Baltimore County Group Rejects City Transit Plan," *Baltimore Sun*, March 10, 1959, 15.

118. Report of the Baltimore Metropolitan Area Mass Transit Legislative Commission, 1960, UBSCDR, 1–4.

119. Mayor Harold Grady to Senator Glenn Beall, June 17, 1961, UBSCDR.

120. Statement by W. Arthur Grotz, Chairman, GBC, April 20, 1961, UBSCDR.

121. Andrew Bristow to Herbert Tyler, February 5, 1961, UBSCDR.

122. "Opposing Views," *Baltimore Sun*, April 28, 1960, 18.

123. Draft, House Bill No. 5, dated May 3, 1961, Chapter 670, Article 64B, 2, UBSCDR.

124. Andrew Bristow to Herbert Tyler, February 5, 1961, UBSCDR.

125. Report of the Metropolitan Transit Authority Maryland, Fiscal Year Ended June 30, 1963, 2–3.

126. "Report to the Honorable Theodore R. McKeldin, Mayor of Baltimore, Special Mass Transit Committee of the Committee for Downtown and the Greater Baltimore Committee," February 23, 1967, UBSCDR, 10.

127. *First Annual Report*, 1970, Metropolitan Transit Authority, Baltimore, Maryland Room, EPFL, 1.

128. "The Week in Brief," *Baltimore Sun*, October 26, 1969, 20D.

129. Harry Bennett Jr., "Baltimore Transit under NCL," *Motor Coach Age*, November–December 1988, 4–31.

130. BTC, 1968 Annual Report, University of Baltimore, Landsdale Library, Special Collections Department, 7; GBC Minutes, Mass Transportation Subcommittee, April 15, 1969, UBSCDR, 3.

131. Janelee Keidel, "Bus Service Cuts Okayed," *Baltimore Sun*, April 23, 1969, C28.

132. *First Annual Report*, 1970, Metropolitan Transit Authority, Baltimore, Maryland Room, EPFL, 1. See also GBC Minutes, Mass Transportation Subcommittee, November 7, 1969, UBSCDR, 3.

133. Bennett Jr., "Baltimore MTA," 4–21.

134. Nelson Nygaard Consultants, Baltimore Regional Transit Governance and Funding Study, August 2021, 2-2.

135. *First Annual Report*, 1970, Metropolitan Transit Authority, Baltimore, Maryland Room, EPFL, 1.

136. "Survival Linked to Mass Transit," *Baltimore Sun*, January 8, 1964, 25.

137. "Transit Quandary," *Baltimore Sun*, June 16, 1960, 16.

138. See GBC Minutes, Mass Transportation Subcommittee, November 7, 1969, UBSCDR, 3, and GBC Minutes, Mass Transportation Subcommittee, August 13, 1970, UBSCDR, 4.

139. Report of the Committee on Mass Transportation, Baltimore City Government, December, 1955, Maryland Room, EPFL, 51.

140. Henry A. Barnes, Commissioner/Baltimore Department of Transit and Traffic, "Rapid Transit Possibilities for the Baltimore Metropolitan Area," November 1958, UBSCDR,D-8.

141. "Barnes Still for 'Busway,'" *Baltimore Sun*, March 6, 1959, 8.

142. George Tyson (Transportation Activist), "Making Baltimore's Metro More Effective and Economical," January 1982, Maryland Room, EPFL, 1–31.

143. Report of the Metropolitan Transit Authority Maryland, Fiscal Year Ended June 30, 1967, 1–16.

144. https://www.census.gov/content/dam/Census/library/working-papers/2005/demo/POP-twps0076.pdf.

145. "Report to the Honorable Theodore R. McKeldin, Mayor of Baltimore, Special Mass Transit Committee of the Committee for Downtown and the Greater Baltimore Committee," February 23, 1967, UBSCDR, 11.

146. Parsons, Brinckerhoff, Quade and Douglas, "Baltimore Area Mass Transportation Plan, Phase II," October 1965, Maryland Room, EPFL, v.

147. Parsons, Brinckerhoff, Quade and Douglas, "Baltimore Area Mass Transportation Plan, Phase II," October 1965, Maryland Room, EPFL, v., 117.

148. "Report to the Honorable Theodore R. McKeldin, Mayor of Baltimore, Special Mass Transit Committee of the Committee for Downtown and the Greater Baltimore Committee," February 23, 1967, UBSCDR, 16–17.

149. Report of the Metropolitan Transit Authority Maryland, Fiscal Year Ended June 30, 1966, 1–9.

150. Parsons, Brinckerhoff, Quade and Douglas, "Baltimore Area Mass Transportation Plan, Phase II," October 1965, Maryland Room, EPFL.

151. C. Steele, Executive Director, MTA, Presentation to Metropolitan Area Council, December 31, 1966, Maryland Room, EPFL.

152. "Report to the Honorable Theodore R. McKeldin," 18.

153. "Report to the Honorable Theodore R. McKeldin," 10.

154. Phase 1 Rapid Transit, MTA, ca. 1973, UBSCDR, 2.

155. "Report to the Honorable Theodore R. McKeldin," 20.

156. George S. Smerk, *The Federal Role in Urban Mass Transportation* (Bloomington: Indiana University Press, 1991), 94, 118–20, 219.

157. Baltimore City Department of Planning, T9-2, Transit Planning and Impact Study: Influence Area Analysis, Volume 1, 1970, 20.

158. Baltimore City Department of Planning, T9-2, Transit Planning and Impact Study: Influence Area Analysis, Volume 1, 1970, 9.

159. Report of the Metropolitan Transit Authority Maryland, Fiscal Year Ended June 30, 1967, 7.

160. Tyson, "Making Baltimore's Metro More Effective and Economical," 28–32, 1–31.

161. Frederic B. Hill, "Baltimore Welcomes New Metro as Vital to Continuing Renewal," *Mass Transit*, September 1983, 28–32.

162. Hill, 28–32.

163. Tyson, "Making Baltimore's Metro More Effective and Economical," 11.

164. Hill, "Baltimore Welcomes New Metro as Vital to Continuing Renewal," 28–32.

165. Tyson, "Making Baltimore's Metro More Effective and Economical," 12.

166. Edward Gunts, "The Stations: An Economic Bonanza," *Mass Transit*, September 1983, 36–41.

167. Hill, "Baltimore Welcomes New Metro as Vital to Continuing Renewal," 28–32.

168. Hill, 28–32.

169. Luther Young, "Mapping the Route," *Baltimore Sun*, July 19, 1987, 1H.

170. George Tyson, "Making Baltimore's Metro More Effective and Economical," 14.

171. Hill, "Baltimore Welcomes New Metro as Vital to Continuing Renewal," 28–32.

172. "MDOT MTA Performance Improvement," https://www.mta.maryland.gov/performance-improvement.

173. Ridership in unlinked trips. Eno Center for Transportation, "Transit Reform for Baltimore," November 2020, https://issuu.com/enotrans/docs/transit_reform_for_maryland_-_new_models_for_accou/2?ffEnco, 14–19.

174. See chapters 8 and 9 in Zachary M. Schrag, *The Great Society Subway: A History of the Washington Metro* (Baltimore: Johns Hopkins University Press, 2006).

175. George S. Smerk, *The Federal Role in Urban Mass Transportation* (Bloomington: Indiana University Press, 1991), 226. See also Larry Ford, *Metropolitan San Diego: How Geography and Lifestyle Shape a New Urban Environment* (Philadelphia: University of Pennsylvania Press, 2005).

176. American Public Transportation Association, "2020 Public Transportation Fact Book," https://www.apta.com/wp-content/uploads/APTA-2020-Fact-Book.pdf, 10.

177. Bennett Jr., "Baltimore MTA," 4–21.

178. Colin Campbell, "Light Rail's Promise Remains Unfulfilled," *Baltimore Sun*, April 24, 2017.

179. Luther Young, "Mapping the Route," *Baltimore Sun*, July 19, 1987, 1H.

180. Figures for 2015 from Colin Campbell, "Light Rail's Promise Remains Unful-

filled," *Baltimore Sun*, April 24, 2017; general estimate from more recent figures, 2019, https://www.mta.maryland.gov/performance-improvement.

181. Hill, "Baltimore Welcomes New Metro as Vital to Continuing Renewal," 28–32.

182. Frederic B. Hill, "Riders Swelter," *Baltimore Sun*, July 9, 1982, D1.

183. Editorial, "Worse Bus Service," *Baltimore Sun*, January 23, 1982, 8.

184. Frederic B. Hill, "Bus Woes," *Baltimore Sun*, February 19, 1982, 1.

185. Frederic B. Hill, "Passenger Drop May Raise Fare," *Baltimore Sun*, February 23, 1982, 1.

186. Frederic B. Hill, "MTA Plan Calls for 50 Layoffs," *Baltimore Sun*, May 20, 1982, 1.

187. Hill, "Baltimore Welcomes New Metro as Vital to Continuing Renewal," 28–32.

188. Frederic B. Hill, "MTA Plan Calls for 50 Layoffs," *Baltimore Sun*, May 20, 1982, 1.

189. Editorial, "Raising the Bus Fare," *Baltimore Sun*, September 30, 1986, 18. See also "U.S. Transit Rallies to Take on Reagan Budget Cuts," *Mass Transit*, April 1985, 10–11.

190. Editorial, "Raising the Bus Fare," *Baltimore Sun*, September 30, 1986, 18.

191. Bennett Jr., "Baltimore MTA," 4–21.

192. Luther Young, "Mapping the Route," *Baltimore Sun*, July 19, 1987, 1H.

193. Baltimore Population Density per square mile, 1970, Social Explorer, accessed June 26, 2021; Population Density per square mile, 2019, Social Explorer, accessed June 26, 2021.

194. Jim Titus, "Governor Hogan Thinks . . . ," Greater Washington Blog, February 2, 2015, https://ggwash.org/view/36978/governor-hogan-thinks-only-10-of-marylanders-use-transit-actually-25-or-more-do.

195. "MDOT MTA Performance Improvement," https://www.mta.maryland.gov/performance-improvement; Colin Campbell, "Facing Shortfall," *Baltimore Sun*, July 13, 2020.

196. Ridership in unlinked trips. Eno Center for Transportation, "Transit Reform for Baltimore," November 2020, https://issuu.com/enotrans/docs/transit_reform_for_maryland_-_new_models_for_accou/2?ffEnco, 14–19.

197. https://ggwash.org/view/36978/governor-hogan-thinks-only-10-of-marylanders-use-transit-actually-25-or-more-do.

198. Density of Anne Arundel was 1,396; and Howard County, 1,297. Baltimore County Population Density per square mile, 2019, Social Explorer, accessed June 26, 2021.

Chapter Five

1. ATL stands for Atlanta-Region Transit Link Authority: "The Atlanta-Region Transit Link Authority (ATL) was established by Georgia House Bill (HB) 930 in 2018 as a new regional transit governance agency for the 13-county region of Atlanta." https://atltransit.ga.gov/wp-content/uploads/2019/12/ATL_ARA-Final-11-25-19.pdf, 7.

2. Atlanta Regional Commission, "Transportation Fact Book," December 2014, https://documents.atlantaregional.com/transportation/TFB_2014_v17.pdf, 28–30.

3. Atlanta-Region Transit Link Authority, "2019 Annual Report and Audit,"

December 1, 2019, https://atltransit.ga.gov/wp-content/uploads/2019/12/ATL_ARA-Final-11-25-19.pdf, 15.

4. O. E. Gene Carson, "Atlanta," *Motor Coach Age*, January–March 1997, 3–29.

5. https://atltransit.ga.gov/wp-content/uploads/2019/12/ATL_ARA-Final-11-25-19.pdf, 7.

6. "Municipal Ownership for Atlanta Defeated," *Atlanta Constitution*, July 24, 1919, 1.

7. Carson, "Atlanta," 3–29; "Jitney Buses Are Banned from Operating in Atlanta," *Atlanta Constitution*, February 3, 1925, 1.

8. Ronald Bayor, *Race and the Shaping of Twentieth-Century Atlanta* (Chapel Hill: University of North Carolina Press, 1996).

9. Kevin M. Kruse, *White Flight: Atlanta and the Making of Modern Conservatism*, (Princeton, NJ: Princeton University Press, 2005), 108.

10. Mia Bay, *Traveling Black: A Story of Race and Resistance* (Cambridge, MA: Harvard University Press, 2021), 161.

11. Carson, "Atlanta."

12. Carson, 9.

13. Carson, 17.

14. Georgia Power Company Advertisement, *Atlanta Constitution*, January 5, 1947, 52.

15. Georgia Power Company Advertisement, *Atlanta Constitution*, November 2, 1948, 8.

16. "More Space and Air for Trolleys," *Atlanta Constitution*, September 17, 1948, 1.

17. Carson, "Atlanta," 3–29.

18. Gene Carson, "Atlanta: Part Two," *Motor Coach Age* 49, no. 3 (July–September 1998): 25.

19. "Transit Co. Seeks," *Atlanta Constitution*, June 20, 1952, 1.

20. Wellington Wright, "Georgia Power Transit Systems," *Atlanta Constitution*, February 2, 1947, 4A.

21. "What Are the Facts about Transit Service," *Atlanta Constitution*, June 18, 1952, 8.

22. "How Long Can This Go On?," Georgia Power Company Advertisement, *Atlanta Constitution*, May 7, 1949, 2.

23. Wellington Wright, "Georgia Power May Sell Transit Unit Here," *Atlanta Constitution*, August 6, 1947, 1.

24. "No-Token 10-Ct. Transit Fare," *Atlanta Constitution*, September 23, 1947, 1.

25. Clark Howell Jr., "Transit Volume," *Atlanta Constitution*, August 12, 1949, 14.

26. Paul Jones, "Transit Negotiations," *Atlanta Constitution*, July 31, 1949, 1.

27. "GP to Drop 32 Trolley Runs," *Atlanta Constitution*, June 1, 1949, 21.

28. Carson, "Atlanta: Part Two," 25–45.

29. "A Welcome to Atlanta Riders," *Atlanta Constitution*, June 26, 1950, 6.

30. "No Fare Increase Pledged," *Atlanta Constitution*, June 23, 1950, 20. ATC would also merge with Suburban Coach after a strike on that line in 1951, bringing in sixteen lines, seventy-two buses.

31. Jim Montgomery, "Transit Haul Rises," *Atlanta Constitution*, January 24, 1963, 42.

32. "What Are the Facts about Transit Service," *Atlanta Constitution*, June 18, 1952, 8.

33. M. L. St. John, "Shoppers' Fares Same," *Atlanta Constitution*, June 13, 1953, 1.

34. St. John, "Shoppers' Fares Same," 1.

35. Jackson Dick, "Transit Company Explains," *Atlanta Constitution*, February 23, 1953, 4.

36. Albert Riley, "Transit Troubles," *Atlanta Constitution*, August 3, 1956, 1.

37. Carson, "Atlanta: Part Two," 25–45.

38. "Bob Sommerville," *Atlanta Constitution*, April 2, 1968, 4.

39. Achsah Nesmith, "35-Cent Bus Fare Pressed," *Atlanta Constitution*, July 24, 1969, 1.

40. Carson, "Atlanta: Part Two," 25–45.

41. Carson, 25–45.

42. Kevin M. Kruse, *White Flight: Atlanta and the Making of Modern Conservatism* (Princeton, NJ: Princeton University Press, 2005), 114, 117.

43. "2 Negroes Start Driving Buses Here," *Atlanta Constitution*, June 1, 1961, 1.

44. Carlton Wade Basmajian, *Atlanta Unbound: Enabling Sprawl through Policy and Planning* (Philadelphia: Temple University Press, 2013), 21; Ronald Bayor, *Race and the Shaping of Twentieth-Century Atlanta* (Chapel Hill: University of North Carolina Press, 1996), 85–91.

45. Bayor, *Race and the Shaping of Twentieth-Century Atlanta*, 53–60.

46. Larry Keating, *Atlanta: Race, Class, and Urban Expansion* (Philadelphia: Temple University Press, 2001), 48–49.

47. Carson, "Atlanta: Part Two," 25–45.

48. Rebecca Bellan, "Can Atlanta End Single-Family Zoning?," *City Monitor*, January 15, 2021, https://citymonitor.ai/government/planning-zoning/can-atlanta-end-single-family-zoning.

49. Carlton Wade Basmajian, *Atlanta Unbound: Enabling Sprawl through Policy and Planning* (Philadelphia: Temple University Press, 2013), 23.

50. Bayor, *Race and the Shaping of Twentieth-Century Atlanta*.

51. Advertisement, "How Will the Metropolitan Plan Benefit You," *Atlanta Constitution*, August 12, 1946, 11.

52. Joseph Hurley, "Atlanta's War on Density," *Atlanta Studies*, January 11, 2016, https://doi.org/10.18737/atls20160111   https://www.atlantastudies.org/2016/02/03/atlantas-war-on-density/.

53. "Public Transit Has Major Traffic Role," *Atlanta Constitution*, December 3, 1956, 4.

54. Speech Of Richard H. Rich, Chairman, Metropolitan Atlanta Rotary Club, July 10, 1967, 3. http://allenarchive.iac.gatech.edu/items/show/10009.

55. Carson, "Atlanta: Part Two," 27, 30.

56. Bayor, *Race and the Shaping of Twentieth-Century Atlanta*, 74.

57. Quoted in Lawrence Vale, *Purging the Poorest: Public Housing and the Design Politics of Twice-Cleared Communities* (Chicago: University of Chicago Press, 2013), 40.

58. Bayor, *Race and the Shaping of Twentieth-Century Atlanta*, 84.

59. "Land Use Map of Atlanta," circa 1945, https://album.atlantahistorycenter.com/digital/collection/p17222coll5/id/150.

60. Vale, *Purging the Poorest*, 39.

61. Bayor, *Race and the Shaping of Twentieth-Century Atlanta*, 84.

62. Hurley, "Atlanta's War on Density."

63. Hurley.
64. Bayor, *Race and the Shaping of Twentieth-Century Atlanta*, 69–70.
65. Bayor, 83.
66. Montgomery, "Transit Haul Rises," 42.
67. Carson, "Atlanta: Part Two," 33.
68. Ted Simmons, "Diesel Buses," *Atlanta Constitution*, November 13, 1962, 1.
69. "Coming Sunday," *Atlanta Constitution*, December 11, 1962, 39.
70. "Coming Sunday," *Atlanta Constitution*, December 11, 1962, 39.
71. Simmons, "Diesel Buses," 1.
72. "McWhorter Says Taxes Strangle Transit Systems," *Atlanta Constitution*, October 16, 1957, 5.
73. "Negative Solutions Harmful to Transit," *Atlanta Constitution*, June 8, 1957, 4.
74. "Bus Tax Relief Is Beaten Down," *Atlanta Constitution*, January 30, 1958, 1.
75. Montgomery, "Transit Haul Rises," 42.
76. Alex Coffin, "Bus Fare Increase Asked Here," *Atlanta Constitution*, March 24, 1967, 1.
77. Nesmith, "35-Cent Bus Fare Pressed," 1.
78. Advertisement, "Atlanta Is Going Places, *Atlanta Constitution*, January 18, 1970, 171.
79. Nesmith, "35-Cent Bus Fare Pressed," 1.
80. "City Buses Go 16,000,000 Miles," *Atlanta Constitution*, March 8, 1965, 21.
81. "25-Cent Bus Fare," *Atlanta Constitution*, September 4, 1963, 37.
82. Coffin, "Bus Fare Increase Asked Here," 1.
83. "Atlanta Bus Fares," *Atlanta Constitution*, May 6, 1967, 1.
84. Bob Hurt, "Atlanta Transit Asks Increase," *Atlanta Constitution*, September 17, 1968.
85. Lee Simowitz, "Transit System," *Atlanta Constitution*, July 4, 1969, 1.
86. Nesmith, "35-Cent Bus Fare Pressed," 1.
87. Jack Spalding, "The Next Urban Crisis," *Atlanta Constitution*, December 6, 1970, 18.
88. Tom Linthicum, *Atlanta Constitution*, August 23, 1969, 1.
89. Jack Spalding, "The Next Urban Crisis," *Atlanta Constitution*, December 6, 1970, 18.
90. Nesmith, "35-Cent Bus Fare Pressed," 1.
91. Achsah Nesmith, "New Bus Fares," *Atlanta Constitution*, July 26, 1969, 1.
92. "Bus Drivers Ask Protection," *Atlanta Constitution*, May 29, 1968, 1.
93. "101 Robberies," *Atlanta Constitution*, November 24, 1968, 41.
94. Angelique McMath, "Crowded Buses," *Atlanta Constitution*, October 8, 1968, 4.
95. "Action Lines," *Atlanta Constitution*, June 23, 1970, 1.
96. Larry Keating, *Atlanta: Race, Class, and Urban Expansion* (Philadelphia: Temple University Press, 2001), 113.
97. Basmajian, *Atlanta Unbound*, 25.
98. "MPC Looks toward Improving Truck, Train and Plane Traffic," *Atlanta Constitution*, March 5, 1955, 1.
99. "Traffic Strangling City," *Atlanta Constitution*, October 22, 1959, 11.
100. "This Is the Start of Rapid Transit," *Atlanta Constitution*, August 24, 1961, 4.
101. "President's Message," *Atlanta Constitution*, April 7, 1962, 4.

102. Dick Hebert, "$200 Million Rapid Line Is Outline," *Atlanta Constitution*, August 24, 1961, 1.

103. Parsons, Brinckerhoff, Quade and Douglas, "A Plan and Program of Rapid Transit for the Atlanta Metropolitan Region," December 1962, Prepared for the Metropolitan Atlanta Transit Study Commission, Digital Library of Georgia, 3, 5, 11.

104. Parsons, Brinckerhoff, Quade and Douglas, "A Plan and Program of Rapid Transit for the Atlanta Metropolitan Region," December 1962, Prepared for the Metropolitan Atlanta Transit Study Commission, Digital Library of Georgia, 3, 5, 11.

105. "Hartsfield Asks U.S. Priority," *Atlanta Constitution*, July 21, 1961, 14.

106. Keating, *Atlanta: Race, Class, and Urban Expansion*.

107. "Good to Have a Governor's Help," *Atlanta Constitution*, November 16, 1961, 4.

108. "Had Trouble with Christmas Traffic?," *Atlanta Constitution*, December 27, 1962, 4.

109. "In Battle of Who Run, Vandiver Didn't," *Atlanta Constitution*, November 11, 1964, 4.

110. "State Aid Justified in Rapid Transit," *Atlanta Constitution*, December 13, 1965, 4; Carson, "Atlanta: Part Two," 25–45.

111. Dick Hebert, "Lack of Money Stalls Atlanta's Rapid Transit," *Atlanta Constitution*, September 21, 1965, 30.

112. Carson, "Atlanta: Part Two," 25–45.

113. Duane Riner, "Assembly Panel," *Atlanta Constitution*, September 21, 1967, 16.

114. Carson, "Atlanta: Part Two," 25–45.

115. "Contracts Signed for Transit Study," *Atlanta Constitution*, February 3, 1967, 3.

116. "Transit Should Receive This Additional Relief," *Atlanta Constitution*, February 26, 1958, 4.

117. "Transit Need a Grim Truth," *Atlanta Constitution*, July 28, 1961, 25.

118. Dick Hebert, "Atlanta Transit Maps Rapid Busways," *Atlanta Constitution*, April 19, 1967, 1.

119. Bruce Galpin, Editorial, "Rapid Busways: Chance for Breakthrough," *Atlanta Constitution*, June 29, 1967, 4.

120. Dick Hebert, "Transit Expert," *Atlanta Constitution*, November 16, 1967, 15.

121. Riner, "Assembly Panel," 16.

122. "Semi-Rapid Transit," *Atlanta Constitution*, April 20, 1967, 4.

123. Galpin, Editorial, "Rapid Busways: Chance for Breakthrough," 4.

124. Dick Hebert, "Busways Rejected by Transit Panel," *Atlanta Constitution*, August 2, 1967.

125. Dick Herbert, "Busways' Sommerville," *Atlanta Constitution*, September 22, 1967, 18.

126. "Transit Planners," *Atlanta Constitution*, December 12, 1967, 3.

127. "Transit Squabble Ends," *Atlanta Constitution*, February 1, 1968, 17.

128. Advertisement, *Atlanta Constitution*, October 19, 1971, 12.

129. Keating, *Atlanta: Race, Class, and Urban Expansion*, 123.

130. Speech of Richard H. Rich, Atlanta Rotary Club, July 10, 1967, 4, 7, 8, http://allenarchive.iac.gatech.edu/items/show/10009.

131. Irene Holliman Way, "Creating a City within a City, January 15, 2019, https://www.atlantastudies.org/2019/01/15/creating-a-city-within-a-city-john-portmans-peachtree-center-and-private-urban-renewal-in-atlanta/.

132. Dick Hebert, "Cost of Rapid Transit," *Atlanta Constitution*, July 6, 1967, 1.

133. "People, Not Trains," *Atlanta Constitution*, March 14, 1968, 4.

134. Dick Hebert, "Transit Plans Envision," *Atlanta Constitution*, October 16, 1967, 31.

135. "Extended Rapid Transit," *Atlanta Constitution*, May 15, 1968, 39.

136. Philp Gailey, "Transit Ignores Them, Negroes Say," *Atlanta Constitution*, October 24, 1968, 35.

137. "Opportunity Deferred: Race, Transportation, and the Future of Metropolitan Atlanta," Partnership for Southern Equity, 35, https://psequity.org/wp-content/uploads/2019/10/2017-PSE-Opportunity-Deferred.pdf.

138. Philp Gailey, "Transit Ignores Them, Negroes Say," 35.

139. Gailey, 35.

140. Keating, *Atlanta: Race, Class, and Urban Expansion*.

141. Nat Sheppard, "Vote Rush," *Atlanta Constitution*, December 28, 1970, 8.

142. "Buses, Bennett Urges," *Atlanta Constitution*, August 9, 1969, 8.

143. "Free Fares?," *Atlanta Constitution*, December 28, 1970, 4.

144. Alex Coffin, "Favorable Vote," *Atlanta Constitution*, April 12, 1971, 9.

145. "Transit Queries," *Atlanta Constitution*, April 21, 1971, 6.

146. Jack Spalding, "Public Transportation," *Atlanta Constitution*, May 30, 1971, 26.

147. "On the Move?," *Atlanta Constitution*, March 1, 1971, 4A.

148. "Proposed Transit Net," *Atlanta Constitution*, July 23, 1971, 1; MARTA promises "shorter waits for buses" and longer hours on thirty routes, total of 1,530 route miles up from 1,084. Alex Coffin, "New Bus Routes," *Atlanta Constitution*, July 30, 1971.

149. Alex Coffin, "MARTA Adopts Tax Plan," *Atlanta Constitution*, January 8, 1971, 21.

150. "On the Move?," *Atlanta Constitution*, March 1, 1971, 4A.

151. "Sales Tax," *Atlanta Constitution*, March 5, 1971, 20.

152. Alex Coffin, "MARTA Low Fare Is Pressed," *Atlanta Constitution*, July 29, 1971, 26.

153. Coffin, "New Bus Routes."

154. Coffin, "MARTA Low Fare Is Pressed," 26.

155. Coffin, "New Bus Routes."

156. "Full MARTA Seen by 1980," *Atlanta Constitution*, August 8, 1971, 1.

157. "Transit Plan," *Atlanta Constitution*, October 3, 1971, 16.

158. "City 'Reawakening,'" *Atlanta Constitution*, August 30, 1971, 15-A.

159. Alex Coffin, "Raise Sales or Property Tax," *Atlanta Constitution*, October 6, 1971, 2-A.

160. MARTA Advertisement, *Atlanta Constitution*, October 12, 1971, 18.

161. "Derailed in Outer Counties," *Atlanta Constitution*, November 14, 1971, 2.

162. "Housing Dispersal," *Atlanta Constitution*, October 17, 1971, 79.

163. Alex Coffin, "MARTA Fights," *Atlanta Constitution*, October 26, 1971, 8.

164. "Blacks Claim Credit," *Atlanta Constitution*, November 11, 1971, 13. What architectural historian Matthew Lasner calls an "architecture of enclosure" in Atlanta's suburban apartment communities, reflecting growing racial divisions in the region, may have also contributed to rejection of rapid transit. See Matthew Gordon Lasner, "Segregation by Design: Race, Architecture, and the Enclosure of the Atlanta Apartment," *Journal of Urban History* 46, no. 6 (May 19, 2017): 1222–60.

165. "Maddox Backs Recount," *Atlanta Constitution*, November 14, 1971, 81.

166. "Voters in Fulton," *Atlanta Constitution*, November 10, 1971, 1.

167. "Blacks Claim Credit," *Atlanta Constitution*, November 11, 1971, 13.

168. "Text of Mayor Massell's State of City," *Atlanta Constitution*, January 4, 1972, 7-A.

169. Carson, "Atlanta: Part Two," 25–45.

170. Carson, 25–45.

171. Carson, 25–45.

172. Keating, *Atlanta: Race, Class, and Urban Expansion*.

173. Partnership for Southern Equity, "Opportunity Deferred: Race, Transportation, and the Future of Metropolitan Atlanta," https://psequity.org/wp-content/uploads/2019/10/2017-PSE-Opportunity-Deferred.pdf, 15.

174. William Schmidt, "Racial Roadblock Seen in Atlanta Transit System" *New York Times*, July 22, 1987, Section A, 16.

175. Carson, "Atlanta: Part Two," 25–45.

176. Atlanta Regional Commission, "Regional Transportation Plan," March 2022, https://documents.atlantaregional.com/The-Atlanta-Region-s-Plan/rtp2050/2050-rtp-main-doc.pdf, 12.

177. https://documents.atlantaregional.com/The-Atlanta-Region-s-Plan/rtp2050/2050-rtp-main-doc.pdf, 20.

178. Isadore Barmash, "Rich's Plans to Close Its Main Store," *New York Times*, April 18, 1991, D3.

179. Gene Carson, "Atlanta: Part Two," 25–45.

180. Keating, *Atlanta: Race, Class, and Urban Expansion*, 8.

181. Keating, 8.

182. Hurley, "Atlanta's War on Density."

183. https://www.census.gov/quickfacts/atlantacitygeorgia.

184. Strong, Prosperous, and Resilient Communities Challenge website, https://www.sparcchub.org/communities/atlanta/.

185. https://atltransit.ga.gov/wp-content/uploads/2019/12/ATL_ARA-Final-11-25-19.pdf, 15.

Chapter Six

1. Clayton Kirkpatrick, "How CTA Service Looks to Reporter Who Rode 40 Hours," *Chicago Daily Tribune*, January 20, 1950, 1.

2. Active Transportation Alliance, "2020 Regional Mode Share Report," http://www.activetrans.org/sites/files/2020regionalmodesharereport.pdf.

3. Chicago Surface Lines, *Annual Report*, January 31, 1942, 1–9.

4. Chicago Surface Lines, *Annual Report*, January 31, 1944, 8.

5. Chicago Surface Lines, *Annual Report*, January 31, 1946, 1–7.

6. CTA, "New Horizons for Chicago Metropolitan Area," 1958, 1–32.

7. CTA, "Chicago's Mass Transportation System," February 15, 1957, 4; William Shinnick, "Transit Unity Bill," *Chicago Tribune*, May 28, 1945, 18.

8. "Mayor Daley Remembered," *CTA Quarterly*, 1st Quarter, 1977, NUTL Digital Collections, 23.

9. *Chicago Transit Authority*, February 15, 1957, NUTL Digital Collections, 4.

10. "Alderman Quiz CTA Board on Fares, Service," *Chicago Daily Tribune*, June 17, 1952, 1.

11. Vote included both Chicago residents and those of Elmwood Park. *Chicago Transit Authority*, February 15, 1957, NUTL Digital Collections, 4.

12. Al Chase, "Merged Transit Lines Expected to Help Realty," *Chicago Daily Tribune*, October 5, 1947, SWA.

13. William Shinnick, "Put Chicago 1st in Transit Plan," *Chicago Daily Tribune*, April 2, 1945, 11.

14. Editorial, "This Is What You Will Vote For," *Chicago Daily Tribune*, June 3, 1945, 18.

15. CTA, "New Horizons for Chicago Metropolitan Area," 1958, 10.

16. Chicago Transit Board, *Second Annual Report*, Chicago Transit Board, Fiscal Year Ending December 31, 1946, New York Public Library, 10.

17. "Big Syndicate Quits Transit Issue Bidding," *Chicago Tribune*, July 24, 1947, 33.

18. Paul Hefferan, "Chicago Yardstick for Transit Fares," *Chicago Daily Tribune*, October 16, 1949, F3.

19. CTA, "Chicago's Mass Transportation System," February 15, 1957, 5.

20. "Chicago Acquires Surface, 'El' Lines," *Chicago Daily Tribune*, October 1, 1947, 47.

21. "Riders Assail CTA Fare Hike Plan," *Chicago Daily Tribune*, July 2, 1951, 1.

22. "Heavy Demand Indicated for Transit Bonds," *Chicago Daily Tribune*, July 29, 1947, 24.

23. "City's Traction Lines Merged for New Epoch," *Chicago Daily Tribune*, October 1, 1947, 4.

24. "Syndicate Shuns Big Transit Issue," *New York Times*, July 24, 1947, 31.

25. CTA, "Chicago's Mass Transportation System," February 15, 1957, 4.

26. "Riders Assail CTA Fare Hike Plan," *Chicago Daily Tribune*, July 2, 1951, 1.

27. George Krambles and Arthur Peterson, *CTA at 45* (Chicago: George Krambless Transit Scholarship Fund, 1993), 139.

28. Editorial, "Manhattan Can Do It; So Can Chicago," *Chicago Daily Tribune*, July 1, 1947, 16.

29. Clayton Kirkpatrick, "Buses Superior to Street Cars; This Tells Why," *Chicago Tribune*, November 9, 1947, 1, 6.

30. Thomas Buck, "New Transit Era Credited to Ralph Budd," *Chicago Daily Tribune*, September 22, 1952, 1.

31. Clayton Kirkpatrick, "Passenger Load Main Advantage of Streetcars," *Chicago Tribune*, November 12, 1947, 4.

32. CTA, "Chicago's Mass Transportation System," February 15, 1957, 6, 15.

33. Krambles and Peterson, *CTA at 45*, 6.

34. Krambles and Peterson, 139.

35. Chicago Transit Board, *Second Annual Report*, of Chicago Transit Board, Fiscal Year Ending December 31, 1946, NYPL, 1–12.

36. Chicago Transit Board, *Third Annual Report*, Chicago Transit Authority, For Fiscal Year Ending December 31, 1947, 24.

37. Chicago Transit Board, *Seventh Annual Report*, Chicago Transit Authority, For Fiscal Year Ending December 31, 1951, 1–31. Station closures and estimates of total mileage cut from http://www.chicago-l.org/history/CTA2.html, 13.

38. Chicago Transit Board, *Annual Report*, Chicago Transit Authority, 1956, 1–21.

39. CTA, *Fourth Annual Report*, 1948.

40. "CTA Meeting Today Will Hike Fares to Meet New Pay Scale," *Chicago Daily Tribune*, June 16, 1948, 19.

41. "Profits Rise on Improved Transit Lines," *Chicago Daily Tribune*, January 18, 1948, 28.

42. "Buses on Devon Prove Superior," *Chicago Daily Tribune*, February 9, 1948, 7.

43. "CTA Buys Bus Rival," *Chicago Daily Tribune*, August 21, 1952, 1.

44. Andris Kristopans, "Part Two: Chicago Transit Authority, 1947–1958," *Motor Coach Age*, April–June 2000, 9.

45. Chicago Transit Board, *Seventh Annual Report*, Chicago Transit Authority, For Fiscal Year Ending December 31, 1951, 1–31.

46. Chicago Transit Board, *Tenth Annual Report*, Chicago Transit Authority, 1954, NYPL, 1–36.

47. "Ask 20 Cent Transit Fare," *Chicago Daily Tribune*, July 1, 1951, 1.

48. Andris Kristopans, "Part Two: Chicago Transit Authority, 1947–1958," 3–25.

49. Chicago Transit Board, *Third Annual Report*, Chicago Transit Authority, For Fiscal Year Ending December 31, 1947, 16.

50. "CTA Meeting Today Will Hike Fares to Meet New Pay Scale," *Chicago Tribune*, June 16, 1948, 19.

51. "Losses to Cut CTA Program in '48 $5,000,000," *Chicago Daily Tribune*, March 25, 1948, 22.

52. Chicago Transit Board, *Fifth Annual Report*, Chicago Transit Authority, For Fiscal Year Ending December 31, 1949, 1–26.

53. "Riders Decrease on CTA Lines," *Chicago Daily Tribune*, April 24, 1949, 10.

54. Hefferan, "Chicago Yardstick for Transit Fares," F3.

55. "Assembly Call to Prevent CTA Fare Hike Asked," *Chicago Daily Tribune*, September 27, 1949, 23.

56. "Ask 20 Cent Transit Fare," *Chicago Daily Tribune*, July 1, 1951, 1.

57. "Higher Fares Due Tonight," *Chicago Daily Tribune*, April 21, 1954, 1.

58. Chicago Transit Board, *Eleventh Annual Report of the Chicago Transit Authority*, 1955, 14.

59. "CTA Elevated Workers Ask 15 Cent an Hour Raise," *Chicago Tribune*, April 15, 1950, 3.

60. "17,500 Get 6 Cent CTA Pay Boost Today," *Chicago Daily Tribune*, January 1, 1952, 1.

61. Thomas Buck, "CTA to Give 5.5 Cent Raise to 10,000," *Chicago Daily Tribune*, November 28, 1955, 1.

62. Erik Gellman, "'Carthage Must Be Destroyed': Race, City Politics, and the Campaign to Integrate Chicago Transportation Work, 1929–1943," *Labor: Studies in Working-Class History of the Americas* 2, no. 2 (2005). Brian McCammack, "'My God They Must Have Riots on Those Things All the Time': African American Geographies and Bodies on Northern Urban Public Transportation, 1915–1940," *Journal of Social History* 43, no. 4 (Summer 2010): 978.

63. Chicago Transit Board, *Seventh Annual Report*, Chicago Transit Authority, For Fiscal Year Ending December 31, 1951, 30.

64. "City to Fight Boost to 20c in CTA Fares," *Chicago Daily Tribune*, July 3, 1951, 1.

65. CTA, "New Horizons for Chicago Metropolitan Area," 1958, 7.

66. "Riders Assail CTA Fare Hike Plan," *Chicago Daily Tribune*, July 2, 1951, 1.

67. "Transit Deficits," *Chicago Daily Tribune*, November 16, 1949, 24.
68. Kirkpatrick, "How CTA Service Looks to Reporter Who Rode 40 Hours," 1.
69. "Chicago GOP Leaders Fight CTA Fare Raise," *Chicago Daily Tribune*, July 6, 1951, 1.
70. Thomas Buck, "CTA Assembly Call Refused by Stevenson," *Chicago Daily Tribune*, July 11, 1951, 1.
71. Thomas Buck, "Fares Boosted to 17 Cents on Street Cars," *Chicago Daily Tribune*, July 26, 1951, 1.
72. Robert Howard, *Chicago Daily Tribune*, June 28, 1955, 1.
73. Chicago Transit Board, *Annual Report*, Chicago Transit Authority, 1956, 7.
74. Thomas Buck, "Vote 25 Cent Fare," *Chicago Daily Tribune*, July 3, 1957, 1.
75. Thomas Buck, "25 Cent Fare Cuts Number of CTA Riders," *Chicago Daily Tribune*, July 10, 1957, 1.
76. CTA, "Chicago's Mass Transportation System," February 15, 1957, 4.
77. CTA, "Chicago's Mass Transportation System," February 15, 1957, 1–24.
78. CTA, "Chicago's Mass Transportation System," February 15, 1957, 8.
79. Kristopans, "Part Two: Chicago Transit Authority, 1947–1958," 25.
80. CTA, *New Horizons for Chicago Metropolitan Area*, 1958, 7.
81. Ray Murphy, "Rides the CTA for Two Days and Likes It," *Chicago Daily Tribune*, May 5, 1958, 1.
82. Chicago Transit Board, *Annual Report*, Chicago Transit Authority, 1956, 1–21.
83. Caption, CTA, *Annual Report*, 1967.
84. "Charge Loss in Service as Buses Go In," *Chicago Daily Tribune*, December 7, 1947, 34.
85. Orville Dwyer, "Trolley Riders on Chicago Ave. Shoved Around," *Chicago Daily Tribune*, February 10, 1948, 7.
86. Andris Kristopans, "Part Two: Chicago Transit Authority, 1947–1958," 3–25.
87. Chicago Transit Board, *Annual Report*, Chicago Transit Authority, 1956, 11.
88. "CTA Seeking 15 Million for Subway Links," *Chicago Daily Tribune*, April 18, 1951.
89. CTA, "Chicago's Mass Transportation System," February 15, 1957, NUTL Digital Collections, 12, 16.
90. CTA, "New Horizons for Chicago Metropolitan Area," 1958, 6.
91. *Chicago Area Transportation Study*, Final Report, Volume 2, Data Projections, July 1960, State of Illinois, County of Cook, City of Chicago, 68.
92. Chicago Transit Board, *Annual Report*, Chicago Transit Authority, 1956, 18.
93. Chicago Transit Board, *Annual Report*, Chicago Transit Authority, 1956, 1–21.
94. Chicago Transit Board, *Seventh Annual Report*, Chicago Transit Authority, For Fiscal Year Ending December 31, 1951, 1–31.
95. CTA, "Chicago's Mass Transportation System," February 15, 1957, 11.
96. Chicago Transit Board, *Eleventh Annual Report*, Chicago Transit Authority, 1955, 7.
97. *Chicago Area Transportation Study*, 48–49.
98. Chicago Housing Authority, "Chicago Panorama and Public Housing," 1952, 10.
99. *Chicago Area Transportation Study*, 51.
100. *Chicago Area Transportation Study*, 54.
101. Chicago Transit Board, *Annual Report*, Chicago Transit Authority, 1963, 1–36.

102. Harold M. Mayer, *Chicago: City of Decisions* (Geographic Society of Chicago, Papers on Chicago, No. 1., 1955), 25.

103. Chicago Subway or Elevated, Railroad, Bus and Streetcar 1960, Social Explorer accessed June 29, 2021.

104. Mayer, *Chicago: City of Decisions*, 25–26.

105. *Chicago Area Transportation Study*, 54.

106. Chicago Transit Board, *Annual Report*, Chicago Transit Authority, 1963, 15.

107. CTA, "New Horizons for Chicago Metropolitan Area," 1958, 1–32.

108. "Skokie Swift: The Commuter's Friend," Mass Transportation Demonstration Project, Final Report, CTA, May 1968, NUTL Digital Collections, 4.

109. "Skokie Swift: The Commuter's Friend," 8–9.

110. Chicago Transit Board, *Annual Report*, Chicago Transit Authority, 1963, 15.

111. "Skokie Swift: The Commuter's Friend," 34.

112. Chicago Transit Board, *Annual Report*, Chicago Transit Authority, 1963, 15.

113. Chicago Transit Board, *Annual Report*, Chicago Transit Authority, 1964, 1–26.

114. "Skokie Swift: The Commuter's Friend," 46–48, 53.

115. "Skokie Swift: The Commuter's Friend," 4, 50, 52.

116. *Chicago Area Transportation Study*, 80.

117. *Chicago Area Transportation Study*, 67.

118. "Mayor Daley Remembered," *CTA Quarterly*, 1st Quarter, 1977, NUTL Digital Collections, 23.

119. Caption, CTA, *Annual Report*, 1967.

120. Chicago Transit Board, *Seventh Annual Report*, Chicago Transit Authority, For Fiscal Year Ending December 31, 1951, 1–31.

121. CTA, "New Horizons for Chicago Metropolitan Area," 1958, 6.

122. *Chicago Transit Authority*, February 15, 1957, NUTL Digital Collections, 15.

123. Chicago Transit Board, *Annual Report*, Chicago Transit Authority, 1967, 1–25; cost figures and other details also from George Krambles, CTA, Expressway Rapid Transit, 1971, paper for the National Transportation Engineering Meeting, July 26, 1971, NUTL Digital Collections, 1–12.

124. Chicago Transit Board, *Annual Report*, Chicago Transit Authority, 1969, 4.

125. "Transit Board Approves Changes Affecting 54 CTA Bus Routes," *Transit News*, February 1969, NUTL Digital Collections, 3.

126. Chicago Transit Board, *Annual Report*, Chicago Transit Authority, 1969, 4.

127. Charles Keiser, CTA Operating Manager, "Dan Ryan–Kennedy Impact," Paper for the American Transit Association Meeting, Boston, September 1970, NUTL Digital Collections, 10.

128. Mayer, *Chicago: City of Decisions*, 29, 32. See also Hirsch, *Making the Second Ghetto*, and Bradford Hunt, *Blueprint for Disaster: The Unraveling of Chicago Public Housing* (Chicago: University of Chicago Press, 2009).

129. Mayer, *Chicago: City of Decisions*, 29, 32.

130. Joseph Schweiterman and Dana Caspall, *A History of Zoning in Chicago: The Politics of Place* (Chicago: Lake Claremont Press, 2006), 45–54.

131. Schweiterman and Caspall, 55–66.

132. Schweiterman and Caspall, 55–66.

133. A. K. Sandoval-Straus, *Barrio America: How Latino Immigrants Saved the American City* (New York: Basic, 2019), 27.

134. Kristopans, "Part Two: Chicago Transit Authority, 1947–1958," 3–25.
135. Andris Kristopans, "Part Three: Chicago Transit Authority, 1958–1971," *Motor Coach Age*, April–June 2001, 14.
136. "City Colleges," *CTA Quarterly*, 1st Quarter, 1977, NUTL Digital Collections, 28.
137. Kristopans, "Part Three: Chicago Transit Authority, 1958–1971," 3–19.
138. Chicago Transit Board, *Annual Report*, Chicago Transit Authority, 1962, 7.
139. Chicago Transit Board, *Annual Report*, Chicago Transit Authority, 1962, 28.
140. Chicago Transit Board, *Annual Report*, Chicago Transit Authority, 1964, 6.
141. CTA, "Chicago's Mass Transportation System," February 15, 1957, 15–16.
142. CTA, "Chicago's Mass Transportation System," February 15, 1957, 16.
143. CTA, "New Horizons for Chicago Metropolitan Area," 1958, 9.
144. CTA, "New Horizons for Chicago Metropolitan Area," 1958, 1–32.
145. "CTA Fare Hike Is Opposed by Mayor Daley," *Chicago Daily Tribune*, February 26, 1957, 1.
146. Thomas Buck, "CTA Aid Plan Gets a Mixed Reception," *Chicago Daily Tribune*, March 20, 1957, 1.
147. George Tagge, "Plan Present Gas Tax Use to Help CTA," *Chicago Daily Tribune*, March 28, 1957, 1.
148. Thomas Buck, "Agree on State Aid for CTA," *Chicago Daily Tribune*, March 6, 1957, 1.
149. Thomas Buck, "CTA Subsidy Plan Ok'D," *Chicago Daily Tribune*, March 19, 1957, 1.
150. Buck, "CTA Aid Plan Gets a Mixed Reception," 1.
151. Thomas Buck, "CTA Fare Hike Near as State Subsidy Lags," *Chicago Daily Tribune*, May 3, 1957, 1.
152. Thomas Buck, "Favor Tax Subsidy for CTA," *Chicago Daily Tribune*, April 28, 1961, 1.
153. Thomas Buck, "Four Civic Groups Oppose CTA Subsidy," *Chicago Daily Tribune*, April 29, 1961, 1.
154. Thomas Carvlin, "Gas Tax for CTA Beaten," *Chicago Daily Tribune*, June 23, 1961, 1.
155. Chicago Transit Board, *Annual Report*, Chicago Transit Authority, 1969, 6.
156. Chicago Transit Board, *Annual Report*, Chicago Transit Authority, 1971, 3.
157. Chicago Transit Board, *Annual Report*, Chicago Transit Authority, 1968, 1–12.
158. *CTA Quarterly*, Summer 1975, Vol. 1, No. 3, NUTL Digital Collections, 4, 18.
159. Chicago Transit Board, *Annual Report*, Chicago Transit Authority, 1968, 29.
160. CTA, *Annual Report*, 1973, NYPL, 1.
161. CTA, *Annual Report*, 1973, NYPL, 1.
162. Chicago Transit Board, *Annual Report*, Chicago Transit Authority, 1969, 1.
163. Chicago Transit Board, *Annual Report*, Chicago Transit Authority, 1970, 1–11.
164. Thomas Buck, "CTA Begs for Cash Aid," *Chicago Tribune*, December 15, 1972, 1.
165. CTA, *Annual Report*, 1973, NYPL, 1.
166. Andris Kristopans, "Part Three: Chicago Transit Authority, 1958–1971," 3.
167. CTA, *Annual Report*, 1973, NYPL, 1.
168. CTA, *Annual Report*, 1973, NYPL, 1.

169. Chicago Transit Board, *Annual Report*, Chicago Transit Authority, 1971, 1–29.
170. Chicago Transit Board, *Annual Report*, Chicago Transit Authority, 1971, 1–29.
171. Chicago Transit Board, *Annual Report*, Chicago Transit Authority, 1968, 1–12.
172. CTA, *Annual Report*, 1973, NYPL, 1.
173. "The Lively Loop," *CTA Quarterly*, Spring 1976, NUTL Digital Collections, 12–15.
174. "CTA Is Tops in Sears Tower Survey," *CTA Quarterly*, Spring 1976, Northwestern University Special Collections, Digital Resources, 19.
175. Bounded by North Avenue, Western, Pershing, and the Lake. RTA, Regional Transportation Authority Demographic Atlas, February 1990, NUTL Digital Collections, 3.
176. "Governor Ogilvie Willing to Meet Mayor Daley," *Chicago Tribune*, April 18, 1970, 3.
177. CTA, *Annual Report*, 1973, NYPL, 2.
178. "Transit Mall on State Street," *CTA Quarterly*, 1st Quarter, 1977, NUTL Digital Collections, 22.
179. CTA, *Annual Report*, 1973, NYPL, 5; Andris Kristopans, "Part Four: Chicago Transit Authority, 1972–1982," *Motor Coach Age*, July–September, 2002, 3–13.
180. CTA, "Owl Network Study," February 1980, US DOT Funded Study, 45.
181. Chicago Region Bus or Streetcar; Subway or Elevated; Railroad 1970, Social Explorer, accessed June 29, 2021. Will County was 1.79 percent railroad, 0.33 percent bus or streetcar, and 0.05 percent subway or elevated.
182. David Young, "Chicago: How One City Coped with Transit's Rude Awakening," *Mass Transit*, September 1985, 16.
183. "Walker Set to Back State CTA Subsidy," *Chicago Tribune*, January 30, 1973, 3.
184. https://www.chicago-l.org/history/RTA.html.
185. Young, "Chicago: How One City Coped with Transit's Rude Awakening," 16.
186. David Young, "Without Aid," *Chicago Daily Tribune*, December 19, 1976, 5.
187. John McCarron, "Won't Buy," *Chicago Daily Tribune*, April 17, 1976, 5.
188. Total originating passengers dropped from 523 to 369 million, with the most considerable losses on buses. "1975 Annual Report," *CTA Quarterly*, Spring 1976, NUTL Digital Collections, 28–31.
189. Young, "Chicago: How One City Coped with Transit's Rude Awakening," 16.
190. McCarron, "Won't Buy," 5.
191. "Chicago Goes Regional," https://www.chicago-l.org/history/RTA.html.
192. David Young, "CTA Expects Budget Problems," *Chicago Daily Tribune*, December 16, 1976, 5.
193. Young, 5.
194. Young, "Without Aid," 5.
195. David Young, "See No Fare Increases," *Chicago Daily Tribune*, December 15, 1977, 3.
196. https://www.chicago-l.org/history/RTA.html.
197. Andy Knott, "Why RTA Doesn't Work," *Chicago Daily Tribune*, July 6, 1981, 1.
198. David Young, "RTA Passes," *Chicago Daily Tribune*, July 1, 1977, 1.
199. David Young, "RTA to Seek," *Chicago Daily Tribune*, November 15, 1980, N1.
200. Stanley Ziemba, "RTA Votes," *Chicago Daily Tribune*, December 23, 1980, 1.
201. Stanley Ziemba, "New Transit Fares," *Chicago Daily Tribune*, December 24, 1980, 1.

202. Young, "Chicago: How One City Coped with Transit's Rude Awakening," 16.

203. Gary Washburn, "RTA Enjoying Ridership," *Chicago Daily Tribune*, April 14, 1985, C1.

204. Washburn, C1.

205. Andris Kristopans, "Part Four: Chicago Transit Authority, 1972–1982," 3–13.

206. CTA, "Owl Network Study," February 1980, US DOT Funded Study, iii–vi, 45.

207. Young, "Chicago: How One City Coped with Transit's Rude Awakening," 16; https://rtachicago.org/sites/default/files/documents/businessandfinance/financial reports/RTA-2019-CAFR-Report.pdf.

208. Young, "Chicago: How One City Coped with Transit's Rude Awakening," 16; later fares from https://www.chicago-l.org/history/RTA.html.

209. Washburn, "RTA Enjoying Ridership," C1.

210. Pace Bus System, 1991 Operating and Capital Program, Published 1990, Transportation Library, Northwestern University, 7, 8, 13.

211. Pace Bus System, 1991 Operating and Capital Program, Published 1990, Transportation Library, Northwestern University, 7, 8, 13.

212. Pace 2000 Operating and Capital Program: Proposed October 1999, NUTL Digital Collections, 1–23.

213. RTA, "2019 Subregional Report," https://rtams.org/sites/default/files/digital_documents/2019%20SUB-REGIONAL%20REPORT.pdf.

214. https://rtams.org/sites/default/files/digital_documents/2019%20SUB-REGIONAL%20REPORT.pdf, 34.

215. See, for instance, "Metra Exemplifies Everything That Is Wrong with American Passenger Rail," https://www.youtube.com/watch?v=H2EWqoiLKHU.

216. https://rtams.org/sites/default/files/digital_documents/2019%20SUB-REGIONAL%20REPORT.pdf, 24.

217. CTA, "Moving toward the Future: Mission and Programs," April 1987, NUTL Digital Collections, 1–16.

218. Strategic Planning Department, CTA, "Results of CTA Household Travel Market Survey," Market Opinion Research, August 1989, NUTL Digital Collections, 38.

219. https://www.chicago-l.org/history/RTA.html.

220. Great Cities Institute, "Fact Sheet: Black Population Loss in Chicago," July 2019, https://greatcities.uic.edu/wp-content/uploads/2019/08/Black-Population-Loss-in-Chicago.pdf.

221. https://greatcities.uic.edu/wp-content/uploads/2019/08/Black-Population-Loss-in-Chicago.pdf.

222. CTA, Strategic Planning Department, "Results of CTA Household Travel Market Survey," Market Opinion Research, August 1989, NUTL Digital Collections, 28.

223. Various reports on the CHA's *Plan for Transformation* are here: https://www.thecha.org/about/plans-reports-and-policies.

224. City of Chicago Department of Transportation, *Strategic Plan for Transportation*, June 2021, 6, https://www.chicago.gov/content/dam/city/depts/cdot/CDOT%20Projects/Strategic_Plan/Strategic_Plan_for_Transportation21.pdf.

225. https://greatcities.uic.edu/wp-content/uploads/2019/08/Black-Population-Loss-in-Chicago.pdf.

226. Manny Ramos, "CTA Bus Services Lose Riders in Last Decade," *Chicago Sun Times*, January 4, 2019.

227. https://rtams.org/sites/default/files/digital_documents/2019%20SUB-REGIONAL%20REPORT.pdf, 14–23.

228. CTA, "Annual Ridership Report" 2018, https://www.transitchicago.com/assets/1/6/2018_Annual_Report_-_v3_04.03.2019.pdf.

229. CTA, "Transforming Transit for the 21st Century," 2019, https://www.transitchicago.com/assets/1/6/FY19_Budget_Recommendations_Book.pdf.

230. http://www.activetrans.org/sites/files/2020regionalmodesharereport.pdf.

231. See Lilia Fernandez, *Brown in the Windy City: Mexican and Puerto Ricans in Postwar Chicago* (Chicago: University of Chicago Press, 2012); A. K. Sandoval-Straus, *Barrio America: How Latino Immigrants Saved the American City* (New York: Basic, 2019).

232. Transit Center, "The Chicago Story," https://dashboard.transitcenter.org/story/chicago.

233. https://www.chicagobusiness.com/crains-forum-racial-gaps/latino-chicago-more-suburban-yet-more-segregated; https://latinostudies.nd.edu/assets/95323/original/paral.pdf.

234. Cathy Yang Liu and Gary Painter, "Travel Behavior among Latino Immigrants: The Role of Ethnic Concentration and Ethnic Employment," *Journal of American Planning Association* 32, no. 1 (2012): 62–80. See also Gerardo Francisco Sandoval, "Planning the Barrio: Ethnic Identity and Struggles over Transit-Oriented, Development-Induced Gentrification," *Journal of Planning Education and Research*, 2018, 1–15.

235. http://www.activetrans.org/sites/files/2020regionalmodesharereport.pdf.

236. http://www.activetrans.org/sites/files/2020regionalmodesharereport.pdf.

237. https://rtams.org/sites/default/files/digital_documents/2019%20SUB-REGIONAL%20REPORT.pdf, 14–23.

238. http://www.activetrans.org/sites/files/2020regionalmodesharereport.pdf.

Chapter Seven

1. "Michigan Public Transit Facts Ridership Report, 2019," https://www.michigan.gov/documents/mDDOT/FY_2019_Ridership_Report_692692_7.pdf.

2. See https://dashboard.transitcenter.org/ for recent analysis of equity in transit service.

3. Thomas J. Sugrue, *Origins of the Urban Crisis: Race and Inequality in Postwar Detroit* (Princeton, NJ: Princeton University Press, 1996); Freund, *Colored Property: State Policy and White Racial Politics in Suburban America*; Heather Thompson, *Whose Detroit? Politics, Labor, and Race in a Modern American City* (Ithaca, NY: Cornell University Press University Press, 2001).

4. Foster, *From Streetcar to Superhighways*, 15.

5. See, for instance, Address of Hazen S. Pingree, 1900, "Municipal Ownership of Street Railways and Other Public Utilities," Chicago, January 27, 1900, 16, https://babel.hathitrust.org/cgi/pt?id=mdp.39015071615517&view=1up&seq=1. See also Teaford, *The Unheralded Triumph*; Melvin Holli, *Reform in Detroit and Urban Politics* (New York: Oxford University Press, 1969).

6. "DSR Is Losing Money," *Detroit Free Press*, December 27, 1929, 1.

7. "The Municipal Take-Over of the City Lines," http://www.detroittransithistory.info/TheCityTakeover.html.

8. Jack Schramm, "Detroit's DSR, Part 1," *Motor Coach Age*, January–February 1991, 4–26.

9. "DSR Is Waging an Uphill Battle," *Detroit Free Press*, June 23, 1959, 34.

10. June Manning Thomas, *Redevelopment and Race: Planning a Finer City in Postwar Detroit* (Baltimore: Johns Hopkins University Press, 1996), 14.

11. Schramm, "Detroit's DSR, Part 1," 17.

12. Rapid Transit Commission, "Rapid Transit System for the City of Detroit," August 16, 1926, 17. See also "Voters to Get $187,798,000 Subway Plan," *Detroit Free Press*, August 18, 1926, 1.

13. "Thousands of New Homes Rising in Detroit," *Detroit Free Press*, May 23, 1926, Realty Section, 1.

14. "Suburbs Shy at Subway Tax," *Detroit Free Press*, August 20, 1926, 3.

15. "Grand River Will Get D.S.R. Express Service," *Detroit Free Press*, January 18, 1928, 1.

16. "Let the Voters Decide," *Detroit Free Press*, August 8, 1928, 6.

17. Paid Advertisement, *Detroit Free Press*, March 29, 1929, 9.

18. "Will Draft New Subway Plan," *Detroit Free Press*, April 3, 1929, 1.

19. "Transit Still Biggest Need," *Detroit Free Press*, April 2, 1929, 1.

20. "DSR Express Wins Patrons," *Detroit Free Press*, September 20, 1927, 4; "DSR Adopts 6-Cent Fare for Redford," *Detroit Free Press*, August 31, 1927, 1.

21. Schramm, "Detroit's DSR, Part 1," 4–26.

22. Schramm, 4–26.

23. Rapid Transit Commission, "City of Detroit Vehicular Traffic in 1925," October 8, 1925, https://babel.hathitrust.org/cgi/pt?id=hvd.hndnnl&view=1up&seq=6&skin=2021, 13–14, 24.

24. Rapid Transit Commission, "City of Detroit Vehicular Traffic in 1925," October 8, 1925, https://babel.hathitrust.org/cgi/pt?id=hvd.hndnnl&view=1up&seq=6&skin=2021, 13–14, 24.

25. http://corktownhistory.blogspot.com/2012/11/the-widening-of-michigan-avenue.html.

26. Foster, *From Streetcars to Superhighways*, 116–17.

27. "DSR Is Waging an Uphill Battle," *Detroit Free Press*, June 23, 1959, 34.

28. Jack Schramm, "Detroit's DSR, Part 2," *Motor Coach Age*, March–April, 1992, 4–17.

29. Schramm, 4–17.

30. Manning Thomas, *Redevelopment and Race: Planning a Finer City in Postwar Detroit*, 14.

31. Article quotation from Schramm, "Detroit's DSR, Part 2," 4–17.

32. Manning Thomas, *Redevelopment and Race: Planning a Finer City in Postwar Detroit*, 17, 31.

33. Schramm, "Detroit's DSR, Part 2," 5.

34. Sugrue, *The Origins of the Urban Crisis: Race and Inequality in Postwar Detroit*, 21–22.

35. "In Detroit Field of Building and Real Estate," *Detroit Free Press*, April 3, 1940, 21. See also https://www.canr.msu.edu/news/detroits_land_use_patterns_date_back_to_the_1940s.

36. https://www.census.gov/content/dam/Census/library/working-papers/2005/demo/POP-twps0076.pdf.

37. Manning Thomas, *Redevelopment and Race*, 18.

38. Sarah Forhardt-Lane, "Close Encounters: Interracial Contact and Conflict on Detroit's Public Transit in World War II," *Journal of Transport History* 33, no. 2 (December 2012): 212.

39. Sugrue, *The Origins of the Urban Crisis*, 23.

40. James W. Loewen, *Sundown Towns: A Hidden Dimension of American Racism* (New York: New Press, 2005).

41. Schramm, "Detroit's DSR, Part 2," 4–17.

42. "DSR Picture Is Gloomy," *Detroit Free Press*, April 14, 1946, 16.

43. Schramm, "Detroit's DSR, Part 2," 4–17

44. "Busses on Grand River," *Detroit Free Press*, January 18, 1947, 4.

45. "Busses to Take Over on Grand River 5 May," *Detroit Free Press*, April 15, 1947, 1.

46. "Busses on Grand River," *Detroit Free Press*, January 18, 1947, 4.

47. "Busses to Take Over on Grand River 5 May," *Detroit Free Press*, April 15, 1947, 1.

48. "Night Bus Service," *Detroit Free Press*, January 23, 1947, 11.

49. "Leo Nowicki Named DSR Manager," *Detroit Free Press*, March 31, 1948, 1.

50. Jack E. Schramm, "Detroit's DSR, Part 3," *Motor Coach Age*, May–June, 1993, 4–27.

51. "DSR Routes," *Detroit Free Press*, May 16, 1948, 3.

52. "Figures Cited as Proof DSR Fare Hike Is Needed," *Detroit Free Press*, March 11, 1948, 35.

53. "DSR Hike Blasted by Public," *Detroit Free Press*, February 24, 1948, 1.

54. Editor, *Detroit Free Press*, April 5, 1948, 6.

55. "Mayor and Council Split on Blame," *Detroit Free Press*, March 10, 1948, 5.

56. "Council Attacks DSR Cut," *Detroit Free Press*, October 15, 1948, 3.

57. "Council Attacks DSR Cut," *Detroit Free Press*, October 15, 1948, 3.

58. "Story of DSR: Less for More," *Detroit Free Press*, January 26, 1949, 1.

59. "Cobo Again Turns Down Plea," *Detroit Free Press*, March 21, 1950, 1.

60. "Where Your DSR Dollar Goes," *Detroit Free Press*, April 16, 1950, 27B; Frank Woodford, "The Public Is Tolerant," *Detroit Free Press*, January 19, 1950, 6.

61. "DSR Shows First Profit since '48," *Detroit Free Press*, June 15, 1950, 25.

62. "New Fare Hike Hinted as DSR Losses Soar," *Detroit Free Press*, August 2, 1951, 2.

63. "DSR Picture Is Gloomy," *Detroit Free Press*, April 14, 1946, 16.

64. "DSR to Start Car Conversion," *Detroit Free Press*, March 27, 1947, 13.

65. "As We See It," *Detroit Free Press*, February 24, 1947, 6.

66. "Where Your DSR Dollar Goes," *Detroit Free Press*, April 16, 1950, 27B.

67. "Early Effort to End DSR Crisis Urged," *Detroit Free Press*, December 7, 1951, 14.

68. "DSR Settlement," *Detroit Free Press*, June 20, 1951, 6.

69. "Strike and Aftermath," *Detroit Free Press*, April 30, 1951, 6.

70. Schramm, "Detroit's DSR, Part 3," 4–27.

71. "20 Cent Fare Starts on DSR," *Detroit Free Press*, September 22, 1952, 3.

72. "How about Rapid Transit," *Detroit Free Press*, April 24, 1953, 8; "DSR Earns Biggest Net in History," *Detroit Free Press*, July 25, 1953, 3.
73. "DSR Union Demands," *Detroit Free Press*, July 10, 1954, 6.
74. "DSR's Route to Nowhere," *Detroit Free Press*, June 24, 1959, 6.
75. "Bus or Streetcar for E. Jefferson," *Detroit Free Press*, January 14, 1954, 9.
76. "Jefferson Coaches Win New Backing," *Detroit Free Press*, January 19, 1954, 2.
77. "Hearing Called on Jefferson Bus," *Detroit Free Press*, January 21, 1954, 3.
78. Charles Weber, "East Jefferson Buses Called a Success," *Detroit Free Press*, February 28, 1954, 4.
79. Schramm, "Detroit's DSR, Part 3," 4–27.
80. "Price of Bad Management," *Detroit Free Press*, June 11, 1951, 6.
81. "This Is How DSR General Managers Gets to Work in Morning," *Detroit Free Press*, February 13, 1954, 20.
82. Frank Woodford, "DSR Subsidy," *Detroit Free Press*, October 1, 1951, 6.
83. "If the DSR Pays No Tax," *Detroit Free Press*, November 23, 1957, 6.
84. "DSR Tax Question," *Detroit Free Press*, February 21, 1957, 8.
85. Advertisement, "It's Up to You," *Detroit Free Press*, November 2, 1958, 22.
86. "Fare Hike in Offing for DSR," *Detroit Free Press*, November 30, 1958, 3.
87. "Fare Hike in Offing for DSR," *Detroit Free Press*, November 30, 1958, 3.
88. "DSR Is Waging an Uphill Battle," *Detroit Free Press*, June 23, 1959, 34.
89. "Fare Hike in Offing for DSR," *Detroit Free Press*, November 30, 1958, 3.
90. "DSR Is Waging an Uphill Battle," *Detroit Free Press*, June 23, 1959, 34.
91. "DSR's Route to Nowhere," *Detroit Free Press*, June 24, 1959, 6.
92. "DSR Profit Up Tenfold," *Detroit Free Press*, December 16, 1959, 30.
93. Schramm, "Detroit's DSR, Part 3," 4–27; https://en.wikipedia.org/wiki/Demographic_history_of_Detroit.
94. Charles C. Weber, "Rapid Transit Useless Here," *Detroit Free Press*, April 17, 1961, 21.
95. "A Word in Behalf of Mr. Nowicki," *Detroit Free Press*, December 17, 1961, 5.
96. Detroit Bus or Streetcar, 1960, Social Explorer, accessed June 28, 2021, 23.
97. "Miel Denies Charges," *Detroit Free Press*, June 23, 1963, 3.
98. "Millions Spent—Nothing Built," *Detroit Free Press*, January 14, 1947, 1.
99. "City's Expressways Given Start," *Detroit Free Press*, January 21, 1947.
100. "Jefferson Coaches Win New Backing," *Detroit Free Press*, January 19, 1954, 2.
101. James Ransom, "Additional 3 Million for Streets Is Asked," *Detroit Free Press*, March 12, 1954, 3.
102. "A Word in Behalf of Mr. Nowicki," *Detroit Free Press*, December 17, 1961, 5.
103. "DSR Unions Demand More Parking Space," *Detroit Free Press*, February 3, 1954, 1.
104. Schramm, "Detroit's DSR, Part 3," 18.
105. Frank Beckman, "Detroit of Tomorrow," *Detroit Free Press*, September 8, 1954, 28.
106. "Combine Forces to Push," *Detroit Free Press*, June 26, 1956, 8. See also Roger Biles, "Expressways before the Interstates: The Case of Detroit, 1945–1956," *Journal of Urban History* 40, no. 5 (2014): 843–54.
107. "The Freeway Juggernaut," *Detroit Free Press*, January 5, 1973, 6.
108. Manning Thomas, *Redevelopment and Race*.

109. "Detroit: Ready for Rebuilding," *Journal of Housing*, October 1952, 348.
110. Manning Thomas, *Redevelopment and Race*, 63, 110.
111. "Poletown," *Encyclopedia of Detroit*, https://detroithistorical.org/learn/encyclopedia-of-detroit/poletown.
112. Schramm, "Detroit's DSR, Part 1," 4–26.
113. "Decades Spent on Transit Plans," *Detroit Free Press*, January 16, 1947, 13.
114. "Engineers Blast DSR," *Detroit Free Press*, September 15, 1946, 1.
115. "As We See It—No Rapid Transit," *Detroit Free Press*, March 17, 1947, 4.
116. "Rail System for Parkway Is Rejected," *Detroit Free Press*, March 15, 1947, 9.
117. "Expressway Mall Rebuffed," *Detroit Free Press*, January 23, 1948, 1.
118. "Van Antwerp Plans Study," *Detroit Free Press* December 3, 1947, 21.
119. "DSR Drops Subway Idea into Obscurity," *Detroit Free Press*, December 14, 1947, 9.
120. "Combine Forces to Push," *Detroit Free Press*, June 26, 1956, 8.
121. "Combine Forces to Push," *Detroit Free Press*, June 26, 1956, 8.
122. Jerry Herron, "The Forgetting Machine: Notes toward a History of Detroit," *Places*, January 2012, https://placesjournal.org/article/the-forgetting-machine-notes-toward-a-history-of-detroit/?gclid=Cj0KCQjw9_mDBhCGARIsAN3PaFNxJIaeppvq_KYiF6DjcU_tsT2ePveJaUAobMR6yF8A6t_1MSQD_JsaAi64EALw_wcB&cn-reloaded=1.
123. Manning Thomas, *Redevelopment and Race*, 67.
124. "Those DSR Dreams," *Detroit Free Press*, February 27, 1949, 11.
125. "Freeway Boss Hits 'Impractical' Planners," *Detroit Free Press*, October 23, 1953, 9.
126. Beckman, "Detroit of Tomorrow," 28.
127. Weber, "Rapid Transit Useless Here," 21.
128. Weber, 21.
129. "Dismissed Too Hastily," *Detroit Free Press*, July 18, 1959, 6.
130. https://www.census.gov/content/dam/Census/library/working-papers/2005/demo/POP-twps0076.pdf.
131. https://www.census.gov/content/dam/Census/library/working-papers/2005/demo/POP-twps0076.pdf.
132. Manning Thomas, *Redevelopment and Race*, 84.
133. Detroit Bus or Streetcar, 1960, Social Explorer (based on data collected by the US Census Bureau; data tabulated by DUALabs; accessed June 28, 2021).
134. Manning Thomas, *Redevelopment and Race*, 84. See also the extensive discussion of racial and zoning politics in Detroit in Freund, *Colored Property: State Policy and White Racial Politics in Suburban America*.
135. Manning Thomas, *Redevelopment and Race*, 7.
136. "Passenger Total off 6.8 Million," *Detroit Free Press*, July 7, 1962, 3.
137. George Cantor, "Ex-DSR Riders Rap," *Detroit Free Press*, August 4, 1963, 3A.
138. "Detroit's Long, Rough Transit Ride," *Detroit Free Press*, August 4, 1963, 14.
139. "New DSR Head Proposes Changes," *Detroit Free Press*, September 29, 1963, 3.
140. "Mayor May Ask Voters," *Detroit Free Press*, March 17, 1963, 60.
141. "Free DSR Rides," *Detroit Free Press*, March 18, 1965, 3.
142. Hal Cohen, "$368,000 State Tax Bill," *Detroit Free Press*, January 17, 1964, 14.
143. "Vote on DSR Is Long Overdue," *Detroit Free Press*, August 5, 1964, 6.

144. "Southeastern Michigan Transportation Authority," http://www.detroittransithistory.info/Suburban/SEMTAHistory1.html.
145. "DSR Is Exempt," *Detroit Free Press*, June 9, 1966, 18A.
146. "DSR to Receive $10 million Grant," *Detroit Free Press*, July 9, 1966, 3.
147. "Romney Signs DSR Tax Bill," *Detroit Free Press*, July 5, 1965, 3.
148. "City Asked to Cover DSR Losses," *Detroit Free Press*, August 23, 1969, 3.
149. "City Asked to Cover DSR Losses," *Detroit Free Press*, August 23, 1969, 3.
150. "A Public Interest in Buses," *Detroit Free Press*, October 25, 1969, 8.
151. "Negroes Swell Jobless Ranks," *Detroit Free Press*, September 6, 1967, 8.
152. Michael Maidenberg, "Transportation Is Key to Jobs," *Detroit Free Press*, February 10, 1969, 18.
153. "Transit," *Detroit Free Press*, January 19, 1989, 14.
154. "DSR Hikes Called Tough on Poor," *Detroit Free Press*, October 6, 1970, 36.
155. https://www.census.gov/content/dam/Census/library/working-papers/2005/demo/POP-twps0076.pdf.
156. "Debt-Ridden DSR," *Detroit Free Press*, February 13, 1972, 2.
157. "DSR Raises Fares and Slashes Service," *Detroit Free Press*, August 31, 1972, 4.
158. "How Will Lost DSR Riders Travel?," *Detroit Free Press*, September 4, 1972, 5.
159. "No Buses to Run On Christmas," *Detroit Free Press*, November 28, 1972, 3.
160. "Debt-Ridden DSR," *Detroit Free Press*, February 13, 1972, 2.
161. "The Freeway Juggernaut," *Detroit Free Press*, January 5, 1973, 6.
162. Ridership estimates from Detroit Bus or Streetcar, 1970, Social Explorer (based on data collected by the US Census Bureau; data tabulated by DUALabs.; accessed June 28, 2021).
163. "The Freeway Juggernaut," *Detroit Free Press*, January 5, 1973, 6.
164. "Riders Air Bus Beefs," *Detroit Free Press*, June 19, 1973, 3.
165. William Mitchell, "Ridership Drops as Bus Crime Increases," *Detroit Free Press*, October 1, 1976, 3A.
166. "Transit Plan Recognizes That the Future Is Here," *Detroit Free Press*, April 7, 1962, 4.
167. Kirk Cheyfitz, "Traffic Jams Weaken Auto Autocracy," *Detroit Free Press*, May 12, 1975, 3A.
168. Tim Holland, "Council Refuses Suburban Bus Aid," *Detroit Free Press*, November 15, 1969, 3.
169. "Southeastern Michigan Transportation Authority," http://www.detroittransithistory.info/Suburban/SEMTAHistory1.html.
170. "Trans Authority Gets Ok," *Detroit Free Press*, June 13, 1967, 3.
171. "Rapid Transit in Detroit," *Detroit Free Press*, November 21, 1976, 33.
172. Jim Crutchfield, "Bus Service Is Not Good," *Detroit Free Press*, February 26, 1978, 3A.
173. "Debt-Ridden DSR," *Detroit Free Press*, February 13, 1972, 2.
174. "Purchase of DSR Is Eyed by SEMTA," *Detroit Free Press*, December 17, 1972, 3.
175. Manning Thomas, *Redevelopment and Race*, 7.
176. "How Mayoral Candidates View Major Issues," *Detroit Free Press*, September 9, 1973, 30.
177. "Mayor's Goals," *Detroit Free Press*, November 9, 1977, 1.

178. "Rapid Transit in Detroit," *Detroit Free Press*, November 21, 1976, 33; Ken Fireman, "Transit Merger Is on Hold," *Detroit Free Press*, April 7, 1983, 3A.

179. Kirk Cheyfitz, "SEMTA Unveils First New Buses," *Detroit Free Press*, May 3, 1978, 3A.

180. Bill Laitner, "Commuting," *Detroit Free Press*, October 17, 1983.

181. David Kushma, "SEMTA Manager," *Detroit Free Press*, September 12, 1985, 3.

182. David Kushma, "Give City More Control on Transit," *Detroit Free Press*, April 19, 1985, 3.

183. "Our Bus Systems," *Detroit Free Press*, August 31, 1985, 4A.

184. SMART, "SMART Facts and History," https://www.smartbus.org/About/Our-Organization/SMART-Facts#6615-facts.

185. "Mayor's Goals," *Detroit Free Press*, November 9, 1977, 1.

186. "What the SEMTA Plan Would Mean for Michigan," *Detroit Free Press*, March 29, 1974, 6A.

187. "TALUS Gives Plan to Speed Travel," *Detroit Free Press*, May 14, 1969, 2A.

188. Tim Holland, "Council Refuses Suburban Bus Aid," *Detroit Free Press*, November 15, 1969, 3.

189. William Mitchell, "GM, Ford Back Mass Transit Plan," *Detroit Free Press*, May 25, 1974, 1A.

190. William Mitchell, "U.S. Agency Casts Doubt on Subway," *Detroit Free Press*, September 1, 1975, 3.

191. "Rapid Transit in Detroit," *Detroit Free Press*, November 21, 1976, 33.

192. "It's Time for Action on Rapid Transit Plans," *Detroit Free Press*, September 7, 1976, 8A.

193. William Mitchell, "SEMTA Transit Plan Falls Through," *Detroit Free Press*, September 22, 1977, 1A.

194. "Representative Bonior Favors Buses," *Detroit Free Press*, November 30, 1977, 9D.

195. Ken Fireman, "Macomb County's Isolationists," *Detroit Free Press*, May 16, 1977, 3A.

196. "SEMTA Picks Last Four Plan," *Detroit Free Press*, March 23, 1977, 80.

197. "Transit," *Detroit Free Press*, November 6, 1979, 8A; Bob Campbell, "Future Commuters," *Detroit Free Press*, November 10, 1983, 5A; Rick Ratliff, "SEMTA OKS Transit Plan," *Detroit Free Press*, February 8, 1984, 3A.

198. "People Mover Plan Pushed," *Detroit Free Press*, August 11, 1976, 6C.

199. Kushma, "SEMTA Manager," 3.

200. Ed Bas, "Detroit's People Mover, *Mass Transit*, October 1986, 8–9.

201. "Mover Costs May Derail Transit Aid," *Detroit Free Press*, May 23, 1986, 19.

202. Constance Prater, "Council Cuts Mover Subsidies," *Detroit Free Press*, May 17, 1989, 4.

203. David McHugh, "Rails Move People for Fun," *Detroit Free Press*, July 29, 1988, 3.

204. Cheyfitz, "SEMTA Unveils First New Buses," 3A.

205. Crutchfield, "Bus Service Is Not Good," 3A.

206. "City Buses," *Detroit Free Press*, July 24, 1979, 12A.

207. "600 Pack Hearing," *Detroit Free Press*, July 11, 1979, 3A.

208. Luther Jackson, "Council Switch," *Detroit Free Press*, July 3, 1980, 3A.

209. Laitner, "Commuting."

210. David Kushma, "Young Pins Bad Service on DDOT," *Detroit Free Press*, October 9, 1983, 1.

211. "DDOT Has Fewer Buses, Riders than a Year Ago," *Detroit Free Press*, March 4, 1985, 23.

212. David Kushma, "SEMTA Wants to Cut," *Detroit Free Press*, May 7, 1986, 3A.

213. Bill McGraw, "Ticket to Ride DDOT Bus Guarantees a Long Wait," *Detroit Free Press*, March 4, 1985, 1.

214. McGraw, 1.

215. Dashboard is updated monthly and not archived. https://detroitmi.gov/departments/detroit-department-transportation#DDOT-Performance-Dashboard. https://www.freep.com/story/news/local/michigan/detroit/2021/11/17/ddot-bus-service-changes-2021-ridership-driver-shortage/8643893002/.

216. Steve Neavling, "Two Years In," *Detroit Metro Times*, May 1, 2019, https://www.metrotimes.com/detroit/two-years-in-detroits-qline-falls-far-short-of-expectations/Content?oid=21552552.

Part Four

1. American Transit Association, "Extent of Subsidization of Publicly Owned Transit Systems," February 11, 1959, Massachusetts State Archive (MSA), TC3/382, Box 37, Folder: Associations, 1–2.

Chapter Eight

1. O'Connell, *The Hub's Metropolis*, 184.

2. Kennedy, *Planning the City upon a Hill*, 158.

3. A Comprehensive Development Program for Public Transportation in the Massachusetts Bay Area 1966, MBTA Planning Staff, May 3, 1966, Internet Archive, (III-2).

4. Metropolitan Transit Authority, *Second Annual Report*, 1948, 1–25.

5. "All Five El Trustees Favor Complete Public Ownership," *Boston Globe*, February 19, 1947, 1, 11.

6. Metropolitan Transit Authority, *First Annual Report*, 1947, 77.

7. "The New Approach," *Boston Globe*, August 18, 1952, 10.

8. *MBTA Annual Report*, 1981, 1–368.

9. Metropolitan Transit Authority, *First Annual Report*, 1947, 1–38.

10. Metropolitan Transit Authority, *First Annual Report*, 1947, 1–38.

11. "N.Y. Syndicate Offers to Buy $22,868,000 'El' Bond Issue," *Boston Globe*, August 15, 1947, 8.

12. "Plan to Block Lengthy Parking on Meter Sites," *Boston Globe*, February 6, 1948, 38.

13. Gene R. Casey, "10 Electric-Train Lines Proposed by Board," *Boston Globe*, April 6, 1947, 1, 28.

14. Casey, 1, 28.

15. Metropolitan Transit Authority, *First Annual Report*, 1947, 29, 31.

16. "Plan to Block Lengthy Parking on Meter Sites," *Boston Globe*, February 6, 1948, 13.

17. Metropolitan Transit Authority, *Fifth Annual Report*, 1951, 1–27.

18. Metropolitan Transit Authority, *Sixth Annual Report*, 1952, 30.

19. A. S. Plotkin, "Want to Buy," *Boston Globe*, May 13, 1958, 16.

20. Selected Interview Forms, MTA, March 1962, MSA TC3/382, Box 29, Folder: Schedules and Routes, n.p.; https://www.jphs.org/transportation/streetcars-in-jamaica-plain-a-history.html.

21. John Harriman, "How the MTA Got That Way," *Boston Globe*, November 9, 1948, 1, 20.

22. Metropolitan Transit Authority, *First Annual Report*, 1947, 12.

23. "Alderman Call for Strike," *Boston Globe*, October 23, 1948, 1.

24. "18 More Localities Would Pay One-Eighth," *Boston Globe*, May 21, 1949, 1, 3.

25. Political Advertisement, *Boston Globe*, October 14, 1948, 19.

26. "Governor's Plan for MTA," *Boston Globe*, March 9, 1949, 1, 3.

27. Metropolitan Transit Authority, *Third Annual Report*, 1949, 1–44.

28. Metropolitan Transit Authority, *Third Annual Report*, 1949, 1–44.

29. "Dever Blames MTA Boost Need on Republican Party," *Boston Globe*, August 2, 1949, 3.

30. Metropolitan Transit Authority, *Third Annual Report*, 1949, 1–44.

31. A. S. Plotkin, "Can MTA Hope to Break Even," *Boston Globe*, October 18. 1959, 64.

32. "Summary of the Report by the Mass Transportation Commission to the General Court," February 27, 1961, 1, Massachusetts State Archive, MBTA, TC3/382, Box 6, 14.

33. Statement of MTA Board Trustee, July 29, 1957, TC3/2000, Box 1, MSA, Folder: Advisory Board, Schedule No. 1.

34. Metropolitan Transit Authority, *Fourteenth Annual Report*, 1960, 1–24.

35. "Labor Unions and Public Bodies," *Boston Globe*, August 24, 1960, 26.

36. Metropolitan Transit Authority, *Fourth Annual Report*, 1950, 1–12.

37. Metropolitan Transit Authority, *Eighth Annual Report*, 1954, 1–9.

38. Metropolitan Transit Authority, *Third Annual Report*, 1949, 9.

39. Metropolitan Transit Authority, *Third Annual Report*, 1949, 9.

40. Metropolitan Transit Authority, *Fifth Annual Report*, 1951, 1–27.

41. Metropolitan Transit Authority, *Sixth Annual Report*, 1952, 1–30.

42. Metropolitan Transit Authority, *Eighth Annual Report*, 1954, 4.

43. Metropolitan Transit Authority, *Ninth Annual Report*, 1955, 1–8.

44. "Fare, Please," *Boston Globe*, July 8, 1955, 16.

45. Metropolitan Transit Authority, *Eighth Annual Report*, 1954, 1–9.

46. Metropolitan Transit Authority, *Tenth Annual Report*, 1956, 1–9.

47. Metropolitan Transit Authority, *Eleventh Annual Report*, 1957, 1–8.

48. Plotkin, "Can MTA Hope to Break Even," 64.

49. Metropolitan Transit Authority, *Thirteenth Annual Report*, 1959, 1–27.

50. "McLernon Keeps Ears Open," *Boston Globe*, November 28, 1960, 1, 12.

51. Metropolitan Transit Authority, *Fourteenth Annual Report*, 1960, 1–24.

52. "Summary of the Report by the Mass Transportation Commission to the General Court," February 27, 1961, 1, MSA, MBTA, TC3/382, Box 6, 11.

53. Rosalie Goode to General Manager, November 24, 1961, 1, MSA, TCS/382, Box 29, Folder: Schedules and Routes, 1RR.

54. José Gomez-Ibanez, "Big-City Transit Ridership, Deficits, and Politics," *Journal of the American Planning Association, JAPA* 62, no. 1, (Winter 1996): 30–51.

55. Edward Dana, Article Draft, March 1, 1972, MSA, Box: MBTA Newsletter; Folder: Article, 2–3.

56. O'Connell, *The Hub's Metropolis*, 149.

57. Statement of MTA Board Trustee, July 29, 1957, TC3/2000, Box 1, MSA, Folder: Advisory Board, 4.

58. O'Connell, *The Hub's Metropolis*, 136–37.

59. Boston Region Population Density per square mile, 1970, Social Explorer, accessed June 29, 2021.

60. MTA Advisory Board, Minutes, March 18, 1954, TC3/2000, Box 1, MSA, Folder: Advisory Board, 7.

61. O'Connell, *The Hub's Metropolis*.

62. "Summary of the Report by the Mass Transportation Commission to the General Court," February 27, 1961, 1, MSA, MBTA, Record Identifier: TC3/382, Box 6, 2.

63. Metropolitan Transit Authority, *Eighth Annual Report*, 1954, 5.

64. O'Connell, *The Hub's Metropolis*, 149.

65. Metropolitan Transit Authority, *Ninth Annual Report*, 1955, 1–8.

66. Metropolitan Transit Authority, *Thirteenth Annual Report*, 1959, 1–27.

67. Edward Dana, Article Draft, March 1, 1972, MSA, Box: MBTA Newsletter; Folder: Article, 2–3.

68. MTA Advisory Board, Minutes, March 18, 1954, TC3/2000, Box 1, MSA, Folder: Advisory Board, 7.

69. Plotkin, "Can MTA Hope to Break Even," 64.

70. Metropolitan Transit Authority, *Eleventh Annual Report*, 1957, 8.

71. "Special Study in Depth: The MBTA," Institute for Rapid Transit, Volume 6, No. 2, April 1, 1965, MSA, TC3/382, Box 37, 14.

72. Plotkin, 64.

73. Metropolitan Transit Authority, *Thirteenth Annual Report*, 1959, 1–27.

74. Operating losses of $338,000 and the remainder for interest and amortization. MBTA Public Relations, "Highland Branch," August 26, 1960, MSA, TC3/382, Box 29, Folder: Schedule and Routes, 1–3.

75. Lewis Schneider, "Impact of Rapid Transit Extensions on Suburban Bus Companies," *Traffic Quarterly*, January 1961, 135–52.

76. Editorial, "The Highland Branch Pays Off," *Boston Herald*, August 5, 1960, no page provided in file, MSA.

77. Francis Shepard to Thomas McLernon, December 27, 1960, MSA, TC3/382, Box 29, Folder: Schedule and Routes, 1; Edward McAuliffe to Thomas McLernon, December 9, 1960, MSA, TC3/382, Box 29, Folder: Schedule and Routes, 1.

78. Metropolitan Transit Authority, *Fourteenth Annual Report*, 1960, 15.

79. A. G. Lyons to T. J. McLernon, March 6, 1961, MSA, TC3/382, Box 29, Folder: Schedule and Routes, 1.

80. "The Public Must Be Served," *Boston Globe*, February 26, 1948, 16.

81. "Braintree Also Votes Down Rapid Transit Plan," *Boston Globe*, May 12, 1948, 1.

82. Plotkin, "Can MTA Hope to Break Even," 64.

83. Railroad; Subway or Elevated; Bus or Streetcar, 1960, Social Explorer, accessed June 30, 2021.

84. "Summary of the Report by the Mass Transportation Commission to the General Court," February 27, 1961, 1, Massachusetts State Archive, MBTA, TC3/382, Box 6, Folder: MBTA General Legislation, 1961, 6.

85. Metropolitan Transit Authority, *Sixth Annual Report*, 1952, 1–30.
86. Metropolitan Transit Authority, *Thirteenth Annual Report*, 1959, 1–27.
87. Metropolitan Transit Authority, *Fifteenth Annual Report*, 1961, 6.
88. "The Fare Situation," *Boston Globe*, June 24, 1961, 4.
89. *MBTA Fares: An Analysis of Current Policy and Practice*, Prepared by MBTA Advisory Board, January 1989, 1–25.
90. Gomez-Ibanez, "Big-City Transit Ridership, Deficits, and Politics," 30–51.
91. "The Public Is Sick, Too," *Boston Globe*, February 1, 1961, 38.
92. A. S. Plotkin, "MTA Needs Astute Guidance," *Boston Globe*, October 21, 1959, 10.
93. "Volpe Would Reorganize," *Boston Globe*, January 5, 1961, 19.
94. Robert Hanron, "Green Light for MTA," *Boston Globe*, August 7, 1963, 1, 6.
95. Karen Dacey, *Financing MBTA Operating Costs: Alternatives for the Future*, Prepared by MBTA Advisory Board, January 1989, 1–53.
96. "Inside the Cage," *Boston Globe*, December 6, 1962, 12.
97. "MTA Growing Pains," *Boston Globe*, December 5, 1962, 50.
98. "Special Study in Depth: The MBTA," Institute for Rapid Transit, Volume 6, No. 2, April 1, 1965, MSA, TC3/382, Box 37, Folder: Publications, 3.
99. "The Master Highway Plan for the Boston Metropolitan Area," Charles A. Maguire and Associates, US Public Roads Administration, 1948, https://archive.org/details/masterhighwypla00char, 9.
100. O'Connell, *The Hub's Metropolis*, 184.
101. "Special Study in Depth: The MBTA," Institute for Rapid Transit, Volume 6, No. 2, April 1, 1965, MSA, TC3/382, Box 37, Folder: Publications, 9.
102. Boston Redevelopment Authority, "A Proposal to Develop a Central Area Distribution System," May 1968, MSA, TC3/382, Box 37, Folder: Publications, 9.
103. Kennedy, *Planning the City upon a Hill*, 158. See also Elihu Rubin, *Insuring the City: The Prudential Center and the Postwar Urban Landscape* (New Haven, CT: Yale University Press, 2012).
104. "Special Study in Depth: The MBTA," Institute for Rapid Transit, Volume 6, No. 2, April 1, 1965, MSA, TC3/382, Box 37, Folder: Publications, 4.
105. Metropolitan Transit Authority, *Seventeenth Annual Report*, 1963, 4.
106. See *How States Shaped Postwar America* for an extensive discussion of the relationship between suburban and urban transit in New York.
107. "Making MTA Sense," *Boston Globe*, August 8, 1963, 22.
108. Gomez-Ibanez, "Big-City Transit Ridership, Deficits, and Politics," 30–51.
109. "Making MTA Sense," *Boston Globe*, August 8, 1963, 22.
110. Hanron, "Green Light for MTA," 1, 6.
111. "A Comprehensive Development Program for Public Transportation in the Massachusetts Bay Area," 1–118.
112. Robert Hanron, "Single Transit Authority," *Boston Globe*, December 6, 1963, 1.
113. Robert Hanron, "$200 Million Transit Plan," *Boston Globe*, April 11, 1964, 1, 2.
114. "Newest MTA Plan Eyes Runs to 78 Communities," *Boston Globe*, April 1, 1964, 6.
115. Karen Dacey, *Financing MBTA Operating Costs*, 78.
116. *MBTA Annual Report*, 1981, 1–368.
117. Karen Dacey, *Financing MBTA Operating Costs*, 3.
118. Robert Hanron, "Peabody Unveils Transit Plan," *Boston Globe*, April 17, 1964,

1, 19; "Special Study in Depth: the MBTA," Institute for Rapid Transit, Volume 6, No. 2, April 1, 1965, MSA, TC3/382, Box 37, Folder: Publications, 10.

119. "New Look, Old Habits," *Boston Globe*, August 27, 1965, 12.

120. Department of the State Auditor, "Report on the Examination of the Accounts of the MBTA," MSA, TC/382, Box 6, Folder: MBTA General, State Auditor's Report, 1966–67, 20.

121. "T Subsidy Saves Railroad Service," *Commuter* 3, no. 12 (December 1967): 1, MSA, Box: MBTA Newsletters.

122. *MBTA Annual Report*, 1965, 1–32.

123. John F. Collins to Charles Cabot, January 16, 1967, MSA, Folder: MBTA Advisory Board, TC3 2000, Box 1, 2.

124. See, for instance, Statement of Representative Lincoln Cole, ca. 1968, MSA, Folder: MBTA Advisory Board, TC3 2000, Box 1, 1–3.

125. *MBTA Annual Report*, 1965, 1–32.

126. "A Report by the Board of Trustees of the MBTA to the Advisory Board," January–June, 1965, MSA, TC3 2000, Box 1, Folder: MBTA Advisory Board, 5.

127. *MBTA Annual Report*, 1966, 11.

128. A Comprehensive Development Program for Public Transportation in the Massachusetts Bay Area 1966, MBTA Planning Staff, May 3, 1966, Internet Archive, 1–118.

129. "484,484 HUD Grant," *Commuter* 3, no. 7 (July 1967): 1, MSA, Box: MBTA Newsletters.

130. *MBTA Annual Report*, 1966, 1–32.

131. Metropolitan Transit Authority, *Sixth Annual Report*, 1952, 1–30.

132. A Comprehensive Development Program for Public Transportation in the Massachusetts Bay Area 1966, MBTA Planning Staff, May 3, 1966, Internet Archive, 1–118.

133. A Comprehensive Development Program for Public Transportation in the Massachusetts Bay Area 1966, MBTA Planning Staff, May 3, 1966, Internet Archive, 1–118.

134. "T Express Buses," *Commuter* 4, no. 10 (October 1968): 1, MSA, Box: MBTA Newsletters.

135. See, for instance, General Manager's Activity Reports, May 6–May 12, 1970, MSA, TC3/382, Box 6, Folder: MBTA-General, 1970, n.p.

136. MBTA, "Green Line Car Design Conference," September 14, 1967, MSA, TC3/382, Box 12, Folder Equipment/Cars, 1967–68, 2.

137. Police Progress Report, July 11, 1966, Folder: Complaints, MSA, TC3 382, Box 37, 1–5.

138. MBTA Advisory Board, "Report of the Budget Committee," November 18, 1969, TC3/382, MSA, Box 19, Folder: MBTA Service Costs, 3.

139. *Commuter* 4, no. 6 (July 1968): 1, Box: MBTA Newsletters.

140. "MBTA Looking for Negro Operators," *Boston Globe*, December 8, 1966, 52.

141. Philip Brine to R. F. Walsh, January 19, 1968, MSA, TC3/382, Box 33, Folder: Unions 1968, 1.

142. "T and Roxbury Community," *Commuter* 4, no. 7 (July 1968): 8, MSA, Box: MBTA Newsletter.

143. See, for instance, "Nine Apprentice Machinists," *Commuter* 4, no. 12 (December 1968): 4, MSA, Box: MBTA Newsletters.

144. Robert Hanron, "MBTA Deficit," *Boston Globe*, July 19, 1966, 10.
145. *MBTA Annual Report*, 1969, 9.
146. E. M. Kahoe, Director of Operations, "Minimum Additional Manpower Requirements," June 30, 1969, TC3/382, MSA, Box 19, Folder MBTA Operations' Costs, 1969, 2, 5, 9.
147. MBTA Advisory Board, Minutes of Meeting, November 24, 1969, MSA, Folder: MBTA Operations' Cost, TC3/382, Box 19, 3.
148. *MBTA Fares: An Analysis of Current Policy and Practice*, Prepared by MBTA Advisory Board, January 1989, 1–25.
149. *MBTA Annual Report*, 1971, 1–34.
150. *MBTA Annual Report*, 1972, 1–86.
151. *MBTA Annual Report*, 1971, 1–34.
152. MBTA Advisory Board, "Report of the Budget Committee," November 18, 1969, TC3/382, Box 19, Folder: MBTA Service Costs, 4, 14.
153. MBTA Advisory Board, Minutes of Meeting, November 24, 1969, MSA, Folder: MBTA Operations' Cost, TC3/382, Box 19, 6; also, in same folder, "Mayor Kevin White's Statement to the MBTA Advisory Board," November 24, 1969, 2.
154. MBTA Advisory Board, Minutes of Meeting, November 13, 1970, MSA, Folder: MBTA Advisory Board Budget Information, TC3/382, Box 19, 3.
155. "Statement of Mayor Kevin H. Whites before the Advisory Board," December 22, 1970, MSA, Folder: MBTA Budget Information, TC3/382, Box 20, 1–3.
156. Cambridge Advisory Committee, Memorandum, May 2, 1972, MSA, TC3/382, Box 20, Folder: MBTA Budget Information, 2.
157. Various Operating Tables, etc. in MSA, percentages totaling 100.1 percent reproduced as presented in original document, TC3/382, Folder: Budget Information, Box 20.
158. MBTA Advisory Board, "Report of the Budget Committee," April 19, 1972, Folder: MBTA Budget Information, MSA, TC3/382, Box 20, 1–3.
159. Henry Lodge to Robert Crane, June 1, 1972, MSA, TC3/382, Box 20, Folder: MBTA Budget Information, 1–6.
160. Editorial, "Inviting a Crisis," 1972, Publication Unclear, MSA, TC3/382, Box 20, Folder: MBTA Budget Information.
161. Editorial, "The 'T' Deficit," *Boston Globe*, April 13, 1972, 22.
162. *MBTA Annual Report*, 1973, 5, 10.
163. *MBTA Annual Report*, 1973, 1–52.
164. Francis W. Sargent, "Funding: Transit Goals and Dollar Priorities in Massachusetts," *Mass Transit*, July 1974, 7, 9.
165. *MBTA Annual Report*, 1975, 1–100.
166. Dacey, *Financing MBTA Operating Costs*, 6.
167. *MBTA Annual Report*, 1981, 1–368.
168. *MBTA Fares: An Analysis of Current Policy and Practice*, Prepared by MBTA Advisory Board, January 1989, 1–25.
169. *MBTA Annual Report*, 1982, 1–106.
170. Dacey, *Financing MBTA Operating Costs*, 1–53.
171. *MBTA Annual Report*, 1985, 1–48.
172. *MBTA Fares: An Analysis of Current Policy and Practice*, Prepared by MBTA Advisory Board, January 1989, 10.

173. Analysis with 1970 constant dollars. See Gomez-Ibanez, "Big-City Transit Ridership, Deficits, and Politics," 30–51.

174. State Representative Dave Rogers, "Long History of MBTA Woes," *Wicked local.com*, March 20, 2015, https://www.wickedlocal.com/article/20150320/NEWS/150329162.

175. MBTA, "FY19 Final Itemized Budget," https://cdn.mbta.com/sites/default/files/financials/budgets/fy19-itemized-budget.pdf.

176. O'Connell, *The Hub's Metropolis*, 185.

177. See George Walter Born, "Urban Preservation and Renewal: Designating the Historic Beacon Hill District in 1950s Boston," *Journal of Planning History* 16, no. 4 (2017): 285–304.

178. Kennedy, *Planning the City Upon a Hill*, 187–88.

179. O'Connell, *The Hub's Metropolis*, 138–39.

180. Kennedy, *Planning the City upon a Hill*, 186–87. Transit ridership estimates from Social Explorer, 1960 and 1970 Censuses, accessed June 30, 2021. See also Cohen, *Saving America's Cities: Ed Logue and the Struggle to Renew Urban America in a Suburban Age*, for an extensive description of Logue's work reforming planning in Roxbury and other neighborhoods.

181. Gerald Frug and David Barron, *City Bound: How States Stifle Urban Innovation* (Ithaca, NY: Cornell University Press, 2013), 113.

182. Robert Davidson, "Not Luxury but Utility," *Boston Globe*, December 8, 1963, 6-A.

183. Pamphlet, "The New Orange Line Opening," May 4, 1987, MBTA, 1–12, Internet Archive. See also Crockett, *People before Highways*; Hilary Moss, Yinan Zhang, and Andy Anderson, "Assessing the Impact of the Inner Belt: MIT, Highways, and Housing in Cambridge, Massachusetts," *Journal of Urban History* 40, no. 6 (2014): 1054–78.

184. Pamphlet, "The New Orange Line Opening," May 4, 1987, MBTA, 1–12.

185. Robert Hanron, "MTA Unveiling $330M Expansion," *Boston Globe*, August 14, 1966, 1, 16.

186. *MBTA Annual Report*, 1972, 1–86.

187. Robert Hanron, "MBTA Approves 5-Way Expansion," *Boston Globe*, August 18, 1966, 1, 18.

188. Bresnick Company, "Marketing Services Program," 1967, MSA, TC3/382, Box 37, Folder: Advertising, 6–7.

189. Robert Hanron, "$700 Million Plan," *Boston Globe*, August 21, 1968, 15.

190. *MBTA Annual Report*, 1970, 1–25.

191. *MBTA Annual Report*, 1973, 1–52.

192. *MBTA Annual Report*, 1985, 1–55.

193. O'Connell, *The Hub's Metropolis*, 193.

194. *MBTA Annual Report*, 1983, 1–79.

195. *MBTA Annual Report*, 1985, 1–48.

196. "Boston Trolleys Make a Comeback," *Mass Transit*, June 1974, 34–35.

197. "Boston Trolleys Make a Comeback," *Mass Transit*, June 1974, 34–35.

198. *MBTA Annual Report*, 1985, 1–55.

199. Gomez-Ibanez, "Big-City Transit Ridership, Deficits, and Politics," 30–51.

200. *MBTA Annual Report*, 1971, 1–34.

201. *MBTA Annual Report*, 1982, 20.

202. Red Line *Extension to Alewife: Before/After Study*, December 1987, MBTA Staff, iii–x. Positive coverage of the expansion program can be found in the Burr Carrington, "Boston: Making a Good System Better," *Mass Transit*, September 1985, 12–13.

203. Red Line *Extension to Alewife: Before/After Study*, December 1987, MBTA Staff, iii–x.

204. Selectmen of the Town Milton to Leo Cusick, General Managers, February 5, 1968, MSA, Folder: MBTA Advisory Board, TC3 2000, Box 1, 1–3.

205. *MBTA Annual Report*, 1982, 1–106.

206. Pamphlet, "The New Orange Line Opening," May 4, 1987, MSA, MBTA, 1–12.

207. *MBTA Annual Report*, 1982, 1–106.

208. *MBTA Annual Report*, 1983, 1–79.

209. *MBTA Annual Report*, 1982, 1–106.

210. *MBTA Annual Report*, 1983, 1–79.

211. *MBTA Annual Report*, 1985, 1–55. Total towns from https://mbtaadvisoryboard.org/about-us/. System size description, which can vary slightly depending upon source, from https://www.mbta.com/guides/commuter-rail-guide.

212. Estimate from Lincoln Land Institute, "By the Numbers," January 7, 2021, www.lincolninst.edu/by-the-numbers.

213. https://www.masstransitmag.com/management/news/21252803/ma-175-mbta-communities-will-have-to-start-increasing-multifamily-zoning-this-year.

214. https://blog.mass.gov/transportation/massdot-highway/massdot-mbta-five-year-18-3-billion-capital-investment-plan-approved/.

215. Boston Transportation Department, "Boston Today," March 2017, https://www.boston.gov/sites/default/files/file/document_files/2017/03/go_boston_2030_-_3_boston_today_spreads.pdf.

216. Deloitte, "Deloitte Mobility City Index," https://www2.deloitte.com/content/dam/insights/us/articles/4331_Deloitte-City-Mobility-Index/Boston_GlobalCityMobility_WEB.pdf.

217. Massachusetts Department of Transportation, "Tracker 2019," https://www.mass.gov/doc/2019-annual-performance-report/download#:~:text=Riders%20took%20362%20million%20trips,other%20large%20US%20transit%20agencies, 15–17.

218. https://www.census.gov/quickfacts/chelseacitymassachusetts#qf-headnote-b; https://www.census.gov/quickfacts/fact/table/bostoncitymassachusetts/PST045219#qf-headnote-b.

219. https://publictransitpublicgood.org/wp-content/uploads/2020/12/2020.12.04-job-loss-report-final-REV-SRB.pdf, 4.

Chapter Nine

1. Dick Nolan, "Shed a Tear for Muni," *San Francisco Examiner*, June 30, 1957, 14.

2. Marmion Mills, Consultant, "Report on the Rehabilitation of the San Francisco Municipal Railway from 1947–1951," April 1, 1951.

3. Municipal Railway of San Francisco, *Annual Report*, Fiscal Year 1965–66, Institute of Transportation Studies Library University of California, ITSLUC, 1–46.

4. Marmion Mills, Consultant, "Report on the Rehabilitation of the San Francisco Municipal Railway from 1947–1951," April 1, 1951, 24.

5. A. G. Mott, "Summary of Conclusions and Recommendations Contained in Report Rendered to the Board of Public Boards on the Survey of Municipal Railway of San Francisco," July 1931, ITSLUC, 16.

6. Report of the San Francisco Public Utilities Commission, 1933–34, 209.

7. Report of the San Francisco Public Utilities Commission, 1932–33.

8. Report of the San Francisco Public Utilities Commission, 1933–34, 209.

9. A. G. Mott, "Summary of Conclusions and Recommendations Contained in Report Rendered to the Board of Public Boards on the Survey of Municipal Railway of San Francisco," July 1931, Berkeley Library, 6, 13.

10. "A Wrong Way Out," *San Francisco Examiner*, June 19, 1947, 22.

11. San Francisco Planning Commission, "Centennial Celebration," https://default.sfplanning.org/publications_reports/SF_Planning_Centennial_Brochure.pdf.

12. Indian, Chinese, Japanese, or Other Race, 1930, Social Explorer (based on data from digitally transcribed by Inter-university Consortium for Political and Social Research; edited, verified by Michael Haines; compiled, edited and, verified by Social Explorer; accessed June 30, 2021).

13. Report of the San Francisco Public Utilities Commission, 1933–34, 209–19.

14. Report of the San Francisco Public Utilities Commission, 1933–34, 159.

15. Report of the San Francisco Public Utilities Commission, 1933–34, 209–19.

16. Report of the San Francisco Public Utilities Commission, 1937–38, Internet Archive, 230.

17. John McKane and Anthony Perles, *Inside MUNI: The Properties and Operations of the Municipal Railway of San Francisco* (Glendale, CA: Interurban, 1982).

18. John H. McKane, "San Francisco," *Motor Coach Age*, November 1972, 4–37.

19. Marmion Mills, Consultant, "Report on the Rehabilitation of the San Francisco Municipal Railway from 1947–1951," April 1, 1951.

20. W. Issel, "Land Values, Human Values, and the Preservation of the City's Treasured Appearance: Environmentalism, Politics, and the San Francisco Freeway Revolt," *Pacific Historical Review* 68, no. 4 (1999): 618, 620.

21. Report of the San Francisco Public Utilities Commission, 1947–48.

22. Marmion Mills, Consultant, "Report on the Rehabilitation of the San Francisco Municipal Railway from 1947–1951," April 1, 1951.

23. Report of the San Francisco Public Utilities Commission, 1947–48, 163.

24. Marmion Mills, Consultant, "Report on the Rehabilitation of the San Francisco Municipal Railway from 1947–1951," April 1, 1951.

25. "A Wrong Way Out," *San Francisco Examiner*, June 19, 1947, 22.

26. McKane and Perles, *Inside MUNI*, 128.

27. Report of the San Francisco Public Utilities Commission, 1945–46, 250–60.

28. McKane and Perles, *Inside MUNI*.

29. "Company Seeks Lease of Municipal Railway," *San Francisco Examiner*, June 17, 1947, 5.

30. "Haugh Presses Bid on Transit," *San Francisco Examiner*, August 26, 1947, 3.

31. "Muni Rail Lease Will Hit Taxpayers, City Warned," *San Francisco Examiner*, July 10, 1947, 6.

32. "A Wrong Way Out," *San Francisco Examiner*, June 19, 1947, 22.

33. "Plan to Lease Muni Rejected," *San Francisco Examiner*, September 5, 1947, 14.

34. Dick Nolan, "Muni Lease Deal, "*San Francisco Examiner*, August 2, 1952, 1; Dick Nolan, "Christopher Now Opposed MUNI Lease," *San Francisco Examiner*, August 5, 1952, 1.

35. Report of the San Francisco Public Utilities Commission, 1947–48.

36. McKane and Perles, *Inside MUNI*, 134, 191.

37. Marmion Mills, Consultant, "Report on the Rehabilitation of the San Francisco Municipal Railway from 1947–1951," April 1, 1951, 7.

38. "Plans Started for Use of Sales Tax Revenue," *San Francisco Examiner*, July 15, 1947, 2.

39. "Proposition before Voters," *San Francisco Examiner*, October 21, 1947, 11.

40. "Proposition before Voters," *San Francisco Examiner*, October 21, 1947, 11.

41. Report of the San Francisco Public Utilities Commission, 1947–48, 156.

42. C. D. Miller, "Municipal Railway of San Francisco: Report to Public Utilities Commission," May 17, 1956, Internet Archive. 6.

43. R. W. Jimerson, "Road Budget Proposed," *San Francisco Examiner*, January 22, 1947, 1.

44. Mel Scott, "New City: San Francisco Redeveloped," San Francisco City Planning Commission, 1947, https://archive.org/details/newcitysanfranci1947scot/page/4/mode/2up, 9.

45. Editorial, "Must Muni Railway Pay Its Own Way," *San Francisco Examiner*, November 15, 1949, 22.

46. https://archive.org/details/newcitysanfranci1947scot/page/4/mode/2up.

47. "Old Geary Trolleys Go into Limbo," *San Francisco Examiner*, December 30, 1956, 10.

48. https://default.sfplanning.org/publications_reports/SF_Planning_Centennial_Brochure.pdf.

49. Meredith Oda, *The Gateway to the Pacific: Japanese Americans and the Remaking of San Francisco* (Chicago: University of Chicago Press, 2019), chapter 6, 73–105.

50. Black, 1950, Social Explorer, accessed June 30, 2021.

51. Mel Scott, *New City: San Francisco Redeveloped*, San Francisco Planning Commission, 1947, https://archive.org/details/newcitysanfranci1947scot/page/4/mode/2up, 6.

52. Scott, 3–4, 14.

53. Black, 1950, Social Explorer, accessed June 30, 2021.

54. "The Fillmore," documentary, PBS Thirteen, 2001, https://www.pbs.org/kqed/fillmore/program/index.html; see also Leslie Fulbright, "Sad Chapter in Western Addition History Ending," *SFGATE*, July 21, 2008, https://www.sfgate.com/bayarea/article/Sad-chapter-in-Western-Addition-history-ending-3203302.php.

55. Dick Pearce, "Supervisors Vote Economy Cuts in Cable Car System," *San Francisco Examiner*, January 26, 1954, 1.

56. "Mayor's Suggestions in Traction Problem," *San Francisco Examiner*, January 28, 1947, 2. See D. Scott, "When the Motorman Mayor Met the Cable Car Ladies: Engendering Transit in the City That Knows How," *Journal of Urban History* 40, no. 1 (2014): 65–96.

57. "Are Cable Cars a Luxury?," *San Francisco Examiner*, April 28, 1950, 22.

58. Pearce, "Supervisors Vote Economy Cuts in Cable Car System," 1.

59. "New Bus Plan," *San Francisco Examiner*, March 30, 1948, 8.

60. "Proposed SF Buses," *San Francisco Examiner*, March 31, 1948, 21.

61. Marmion Mills, Consultant, "Report on the Rehabilitation of the San Francisco Municipal Railway from 1947–1951," April 1, 1951.

62. "Subways Planned," *San Francisco Examiner*, February 1, 1949, 1.

63. "New Demands Made for Rise in Muni Fare," *San Francisco Examiner*, May 7, 1948, 1.

64. McKane and Perles, *Inside MUNI*, 1–247.

65. "Better Transportation," *San Francisco Examiner*, December 3, 1952, 28.

66. McKane and Perles, *Inside MUNI*, 1–247.

67. Marmion Mills, Consultant, "Report on the Rehabilitation of the San Francisco Municipal Railway from 1947–1951," April 1, 1951, 11.

68. Marmion Mills, Consultant, "Report on the Rehabilitation of the San Francisco Municipal Railway from 1947–1951," April 1, 1951, 16.

69. Muni Advertisement, *San Francisco Examiner*, March 27, 1951, 12.

70. Marmion Mills, Consultant, "Report on the Rehabilitation of the San Francisco Municipal Railway from 1947–1951," April 1, 1951, 27.

71. Sherman Miller, "Muni Losses Held Stemmed," *San Francisco Examiner*, April 28, 1950, 4.

72. "Muni Expediter Urges More Trolley Coaches," *San Francisco Examiner*, April 1, 1950, 3.

73. McKane, "San Francisco," 4–37.

74. McKane and Perles, *Inside MUNI*, 176.

75. Editorial, "City Could Make It Pay," *San Francisco Examiner*, April 17, 1952, 28.

76. "Lightest Vote in Years," *San Francisco Examiner*, November 4, 1953, 1.

77. Jon Gitlzer, "For Trolley Cars," *San Francisco Examiner*, November 18, 1952, 24.

78. Marmion Mills, Consultant, "Report on the Rehabilitation of the San Francisco Municipal Railway from 1947–1951," April 1, 1951.

79. "Audit Shows Muni Lost," *San Francisco Examiner*, October 27, 1950, 7.

80. McKane and Perles, *Inside MUNI*, 141.

81. Muni Advertisement, *San Francisco Examiner*, June 8, 1950, 14.

82. "Fiscal Plight of Muni Told," *San Francisco Examiner*, March 25, 1955, 11.

83. Municipal Railway of San Francisco, *Annual Report*, Fiscal Year 1963–64, ITSLUC, 61.

84. San Francisco Population per square mile; Bus and Streetcar; Black; White, 1960, Social Explorer (based on data collected by the US Census Bureau; data tabulated by DUALabs; accessed June 26, 2021).

85. C. D. Miller, "Municipal Railway of San Francisco: Report to Public Utilities Commission," May 17, 1956, Internet Archive, 1–130.

86. Municipal Railway of San Francisco, *Annual Report*, Fiscal Year 1959–60, ITSLUC, 1–39.

87. McKane and Perles, *Inside MUNI*, 1–247.

88. C. D. Miller, "Municipal Railway of San Francisco: Report to Public Utilities Commission," May 17, 1956, Internet Archive, 1–130.

89. McKane, "San Francisco," 4–37.

90. Dick Nolan, "Muni Service Cuts," *San Francisco Examiner*, November 15, 1949, 1.

91. Dick Nolan, "Utilities Board Bars Boost," *San Francisco Examiner*, November 17, 1949, 1.

92. C. D. Miller, "Municipal Railway of San Francisco: Report to Public Utilities Commission," May 17, 1956, Internet Archive, 1–130.

93. Dick Nolan, "$6,500,00 Muni Deficit Forecast," *San Francisco Examiner*, January 7, 1958, 1.

94. Nolan, 1.

95. C. D. Miller, "Municipal Railway of San Francisco: Report to Public Utilities Commission," May 17, 1956, Internet Archive, 1–130.

96. "$11,864,400 Bonds Asked," *San Francisco Examiner*, April 14, 1951, 1.

97. McKane and Anthony, *Inside MUNI*, 1–247.

98. C. D. Miller, "Municipal Railway of San Francisco: Report to Public Utilities Commission," May 17, 1956, Internet Archive, 1–130.

99. Nolan, "$6,500,00 Muni Deficit Forecast," 1.

100. Dick Nolan, "Muni Sliding Headlong," *San Francisco Examiner*, November 15, 1953, 21.

101. Nolan, "Shed a Tear for Muni," 14.

102. McKane and Perles, *Inside MUNI*, 1–247.

103. Dick Nolan, "Muni Budget Due Today," *San Francisco Examiner*, January 13, 1949, 1; C. D. Miller, "Municipal Railway of San Francisco: Report to Public Utilities Commission," May 17, 1956, Internet Archive, 1–130.

104. "Manager Surveys 20 Cent Fare Plan," *San Francisco Examiner*, May 24, 1956, 32.

105. "Muni to Add to Tax Rate," *San Francisco Examiner*, October 8, 2020, 18.

106. Municipal Railway of San Francisco, *Annual Report*, Fiscal Year 1959–60, ITSLUC, 13.

107. C. D. Miller, "Municipal Railway of San Francisco: Report to Public Utilities Commission," May 17, 1956, Internet Archive, 1.

108. Dick Nolan, "Officials, Citizens Decry Muni Deficit," *San Francisco Examiner*, January 8, 1958, 7.

109. Nolan, "$6,500,00 Muni Deficit Forecast," 1.

110. Municipal Railway of San Francisco, *Annual Report*, Fiscal Year 1969–70, ITSLUC, 1–46.

111. "San Francisco Metro Area Population, 1950–2022," https://www.macrotrends.net/cities/23130/san-francisco/population.

112. https://default.sfplanning.org/publications_reports/SF_Planning_Centennial_Brochure.pdf.

113. Issel, "Land Values, Human Values, and the Preservation of the City's Treasured Appearance," 611–46.

114. Issel, 611–46.

115. "Against All Odds: San Francisco's Embarcadero Freeway," February 5, 2018, https://americascanceledhighways.com/2018/02/05/against-all-odds-san-franciscos-embarcadero-freeway/.

116. https://default.sfplanning.org/publications_reports/SF_Planning_Centennial_Brochure.pdf.

117. Chester Hartman, *City for Sale: The Transformation of San Francisco* (Berkeley: University of California Press, 2002), 290–324.

118. Editorial, "Muni's Dynamic Role in the City," *San Francisco Examiner*, October 15, 1962, 3C.

119. Hartman, *City for Sale*, 290–324. See also Alison Isenberg, *Designing San Francisco: Art, Land, and Urban Renewal in the City by the Bay* (Princeton, NJ: Princeton University Press, 2017), for debates about skyscrapers.

120. https://default.sfplanning.org/publications_reports/SF_Planning_Centennial_Brochure.pdf. See also Hartman, *City for Sale*, 290–324.

121. Johnson, "Captain Blake versus the Highwaymen," 66.

122. Municipal Railway of San Francisco, *Annual Report*, Fiscal Year 1960–61, ITSLUC, 4.

123. See, for instance, Michal C. Healy and John King, *BART: The Dramatic History of the Bay Area Rapid Transit* (Berkeley, CA: Heyday, 2016).

124. "The Challenge Facing Bart," *San Francisco Examiner*, February 27, 1967, 36.

125. https://www.sfgate.com/bayarea/article/Sad-chapter-in-Western-Addition-history-ending-3203302.php.

126. San Francisco Density per square mile, Public Transportation, Asian and Pacific Islander, 1980, Social Explorer (based on data from US Census Bureau; accessed June 30, 2021).

127. Municipal Railway of San Francisco, *Annual Report*, Fiscal Year 1963–64, ITSLUC, 1.

128. McKane and Perles, *Inside MUNI*, 196.

129. Municipal Railway of San Francisco, *Annual Report*, Fiscal Year 1967–68, ITSLUC, A-J.

130. Municipal Railway of San Francisco, *Annual Report*, Fiscal Year 1963–64, ITSLUC, 1.

131. Municipal Railway of San Francisco, *Annual Report*, Fiscal Year 1964–65, ITSLUC, 1.

132. Editorial, "A Higher Fare for the Muni?," *San Francisco Examiner*, December 19, 1967, 36.

133. "$83 Million in PUC Budget," *San Francisco Examiner*, January 27, 1965, 9.

134. "Shelley Demands His Say on Carfare," *San Francisco Examiner*, January 21, 1966, 10.

135. "Chances Fade for Muni Hike," *San Francisco Examiner*, May 29, 1968, 42.

136. "20 Cent Muni Raise," *San Francisco Examiner*, July 30, 1968, 1.

137. "Action by Board of Supervisors," *San Francisco Examiner*, September 4, 1968, 11.

138. Municipal Railway of San Francisco, *Annual Report*, Fiscal Year 1969–70, ITSLUC, 1–46.

139. Municipal Railway of San Francisco, *Annual Report*, Fiscal Year 1970–71, A-K.

140. Municipal Railway of San Francisco, *Annual Report*, Fiscal Year 1971–72, ITSLUC, 1–37.

141. Municipal Railway of San Francisco, *Annual Report*, Fiscal Year 1971–72, ITSLUC, 1–37.

142. Municipal Railway of San Francisco, *Annual Report*, Fiscal Year 1971–72, ITSLUC, 1–37.

143. Joel Tlumak, "Alioto Asks PUC to Find Muni Funds," *San Francisco Examiner*, March 15, 1972, 1, 8.

144. McKane and Perles, *Inside MUNI*, 203–4.

145. McKane, "San Francisco," 35.

146. McKane and Perles, *Inside Muni*, 1–247.

147. Muni SF Budget, 1974–75, ITSLUC, n.p.

148. In 2017, Governor Brown and state legislators massively expanded state support with passage of SB1; California Transit Association, "Funding," https://caltransit.org/advocacy/key-issues/funding/.

149. "Experts Term Muni Obsolete," *San Francisco Examiner*, November 1, 1966, 26.

150. Municipal Railway of San Francisco, *Annual Report*, Fiscal Year 1966–67, ITSLUC, 1–46.

151. McKane and Perles, *Inside MUNI*, 1–247.

152. Municipal Railway of San Francisco, *Annual Report*, Fiscal Year 1969–70, ITSLUC, 46.

153. McKane and Perles, *Inside MUNI*, 199.

154. Dick Nolan, "Running the Muni," *San Francisco Examiner*, March 5, 1965, 35.

155. McKane and Perles, *Inside MUNI*, 202.

156. McKane and Perles, 168.

157. Advertisement for Bonds, *San Francisco Examiner*, March 26, 1969, 59.

158. Municipal Railway of San Francisco, *Annual Report*, Fiscal Year 1969–70, ITSLUC, 1–46.

159. McKane and Anthony Perles, *Inside MUNI*, 244.

160. McKane and Perles, 244.

161. Joe Fitzgerald Rodriguez, "In 'Shang-Chi,' a Muni Line Made Possible by Chinatown Community Advocacy," KQED, September 3, 2021, https://www.kqed.org/arts/13902470/shang-chi-bus-fight-chase-muni-chinatown-san-francisco.

162. https://default.sfplanning.org/publications_reports/SF_Planning_Centennial_Brochure.pdf.

163. https://default.sfplanning.org/publications_reports/SF_Planning_Centennial_Brochure.pdf.

164. "SFMTA Budget," March 30, 2020, *Mass Transit*, https://www.sfmta.com/sites/default/files/reports-and-documents/2020/06/6-30-20_item_9_fy21_and_fy22_budget.pdf, 16, accessed February 26, 2022.

165. https://www.masstransitmag.com/management/press-release/21131827/san-francisco-municipal-transportation-agency-sfmta-sfmta-budget-revenue-expenditures-and-future-projections.

166. https://www.sfmta.com/projects/central-subway-project.

Conclusion

1. https://transitcenter.org/wp-content/uploads/2020/03/20.03_GND-Transit_use_v4.pdf, 4.

2. See my *How States Shaped Postwar America* for chapter 6 on New York's MTA. See also Michael Manville and Emily Goldman, "Would Congestion Pricing Harm the Poor? Do Free Roads Help the Poor?," *Journal of Planning Education and Research*, 38, no. 3 (2018): 329–44. See also Ezra Klein, "There Has to Be a Better Way to Run the Government," *New York Times*, June 12, 2022.

3. See, for instance, Emily Nonko, "Connecticut Is Considering Statewide Zoning Reform," *Next City*, March 17, 2021, https://nextcity.org/daily/entry/connecticut-is-considering-statewide-zoning-reform-this-map-may-be-why.

4. Michael Manville, "Parking Requirements and Housing Development," *Journal of the American Planning Association* 79, no. 1 (2013): 49–66, DOI: 10.1080/01944363.2013.785346. For a typical planning view of transit oriented development, see Daniel G. Chatman et al., "Does Transit-Oriented Gentrification Increase Driving?," *Journal of Planning Education and Research* 39, no. 4 (2019): 482–95.

5. https://transitcenter.org/wp-content/uploads/2020/03/20.03_GND-Transit_use_v4.pdf, 4.

6. See *Curbing Traffic, the Human Case for Fewer Cars in Our Lives* (Washington, DC: Island Press, 2021).

7. Robert Steuteville, "The Impact of Highway Removal on Cities," April 21, 2020, https://www.cnu.org/publicsquare/2020/04/21/impact-highway-removal-cities; Nadja Popovich, Josh Williams, and Denise Lu, "Can Removing Highways Fix America's Cities," May 27, 2021, *New York Times*, multimedia, https://www.nytimes.com/interactive/2021/05/27/climate/us-cities-highway-removal.html.

8. Adam Millard-Ball, "The Width and Value of Residential Streets," *Journal of the American Planning Association* (2021), DOI: 10.1080/01944363.2021.1903973.

9. Greater Cleveland Regional Transit Authority, "RTA's Healthline—The World-Class Standard for BRT Service," http://www.riderta.com/healthline/about.

10. See Jarret Walker, *Human Transit: How Clearer Thinking about Public Transit Can Enrich Our Communities and Our Lives* (Washington, D.C.: Island Press, 2011).

11. Matt Casale, "Zero Fare Transit Kansas City," May 19, 2020, https://uspirg.org/blogs/blog/usp/zero-fare-transit-kansas-city-case-study-free-public-transportation.

12. Michael Kimmelman, "Los Angeles Has a Housing Crisis: Can Design Help?," *New York Times*, June 22, 2021, C1.

Index

accessory dwelling unit (ADU), 289–90, 292
Alewife (Massachusetts), 229, 243, 252
American Public Transit Association (APTA), 108
Anne Arundel County (Maryland), 98, 105, 111
Arlington (Massachusetts), 229, 252
arterials, 10, 148, 162, 163, 186, 290
Ashburton (Baltimore), 89
Ashmont (Massachusetts), 59, 230, 253
Asian Americans, 256, 261, 268, 271, 279, 286
Atlanta, interwar and postwar transit conditions, 114–46
Atlanta Regional Metropolitan Planning Commission (ARMPC), 131–32, 135, 138
Atlanta Transit Company (Atlanta Transit System, 1955–72), 120, 121–23, 125–30, 133–35, 138–41. *See also* Metropolitan Atlanta Rapid Transit Authority (MARTA)

Baltimore: interwar transit conditions, 25–36; postwar transit, 73–113
Baltimore County (Maryland), 82, 84, 91, 93, 98, 99, 103, 106, 108, 111
Baltimore Transit Company (BTC), 25; interwar operations, 21–37 (*see also* United Railways [Baltimore]); postwar operations, 73–100, 113
Barnes, Henry, 79–82, 86, 91, 92, 94, 95, 97, 98, 102
Bay Area Rapid Transit (BART), 8, 275, 277–78, 284
Berkeley (California), 277, 278
Black (African Americans), 10, 11–16, 18, 23, 70–71, 291; Atlanta, 116–17, 122–27, 131–45; Baltimore, 28–31, 84–91, 104, 106–8, 110, 111; Boston, 52, 63, 249, 256; Chicago, 43–44, 47–48, 162, 169, 170, 172, 185–86; Detroit, 196–97, 203–7, 209–13, 215, 225; San Francisco, 261, 268, 272, 278, 279, 284
Bolton Hill (Baltimore), 28, 104
Boston: interwar conditions, 52–71; postwar conditions, 227–57
Boston Elevated Railway Company (Elevated), 54–63, 228, 230
Boston Redevelopment Authority (BRA), 240, 249
Bouton, E. H., 29, 30
Bronzeville (Chicago), 44, 170
Brookline (Massachusetts), 53, 63, 224, 225, 227, 230, 236, 241
Buchanan v. Warley, 29, 47
Buckhead (Atlanta), 143, 145
Bungalow Belt (Chicago), 43, 44, 47, 163
Burnham, Daniel, 44–45

buses, 11, 14–17, 21, 22, 69, 70, 147, 148, 224, 225, 288, 290, 291; Atlanta, 114, 115, 117, 118, 121–23, 125, 127–45; Baltimore, 31–35, 37, 73–82, 84, 85, 87, 89, 91, 92, 94–106, 109–13; Boston, 59, 60, 66, 228, 230–34, 237, 238, 240, 241, 243–45, 247, 251, 252, 254, 255, 256; Chicago, 43, 44, 46, 48, 50, 51, 150–55, 156, 158–68, 171–74, 176–86, 188; Detroit, 189, 193–203, 205, 207–16, 218–21; San Francisco, 258, 259, 262, 264, 265–75, 277, 278, 281, 283–87. *See also* busways; streetcar substitution (with buses or trolley coaches)

busways, 9, 81, 84, 109–11, 134–36, 139, 140, 160, 177, 290–91

cable cars, 264, 268–70, 272, 280, 287
Callahan, William, 235, 236
Cambridge (Massachusetts), 53, 57, 59, 62, 63, 227, 229, 235, 238, 241, 249–52, 257
Catonsville (Maryland), 31, 91, 93
Charles Center (Baltimore), 92–96, 98, 101, 103–7, 111
Charlestown (Boston), 229, 249
Chicago: interwar conditions, 38–51; postwar conditions, 149–88
Chicago Area Transportation Study, 46, 162, 163, 164
Chicago Motor Club, 153, 174
Chicago Motor Coach (CMC), 46, 155, 158
Chicago Rapid Transit Company (CRT), 41, 49, 150–52
Chicago Real Estate Board, 47, 174
Chicago River, 39, 40
Chicago Surface Lines (CSL), 38–51, 149–52, 158, 160
Chicago Transit Authority (CTA), 49, 50, 91, 229; postwar transit management, 149–88
Chinatown (San Francisco), 261, 280, 286, 287
Citizens for Limited Taxation (Massachusetts), 247

Citizens Planning and Housing Association (Baltimore), 96, 99
Clayton County (Georgia), 124, 133, 139–41, 145
Cobb County (Georgia), 124, 132–34, 143
commuter rail, 2, 8, 9, 31, 38, 44, 47, 48, 105, 108, 149, 154, 163, 164, 166, 174, 176, 178–81, 183, 209, 213, 221, 225, 229, 236, 238, 240–44, 247, 253–54, 291
Congress Street Expressway, 162, 167
Cook County (Illinois), 150, 152, 158, 175
crime (on transit), 14, 108, 130, 142, 174, 213, 244

Dan Ryan Expressway, 162, 163, 167, 168, 171
Dearborn (Michigan), 197, 198, 209
DeKalb County (Georgia), 124, 133, 138–40
Detroit, interwar and postwar conditions, 189–221
Detroit Department of Transportation (DDOT), 189, 215–21
Detroit Street Railway (DSR), 190–215, 220
Dorchester (Boston), 55, 59, 63, 229, 235, 238, 241, 249
Druid Hills (Georgia), 115, 118, 132
DuPage County (Illinois), 48, 178

East Boston, 55, 229, 241, 249
Englewood (Illinois), 170, 185
Evanston (Illinois), 41, 157, 158, 164, 178

fares, 4, 5, 6, 12, 13, 16, 21, 70, 147, 214, 291; Atlanta, 119–21, 128, 129, 130, 138, 139, 140, 141; Baltimore, 27, 32–34, 78, 82, 84, 91, 93, 97, 100, 102, 109–11; Boston, 55, 58, 59, 61, 66, 231, 232–33, 238, 240, 242, 245–48, 256; Chicago, 40, 49, 150–52, 156–58, 161, 165, 175, 179–81, 183, 186, 188; Detroit, 190–94, 197–203, 205, 210, 211–12, 214, 215, 218; San Francisco, 259, 262–64, 271–75, 278, 280–83, 287

Fiscal and Management Control Board (Massachusetts), 248
Ford Motor, 190, 191–92, 194–95, 197, 216
freeway revolt, 10, 86, 104, 239, 267, 275, 287
Fulton County (Georgia), 124, 133, 138–41

Geary Street (California), 259, 267, 268, 276, 287
General Motors (GM), 2, 76, 100, 127, 134, 177, 195, 200, 201, 207, 216, 218, 265, 270, 284
Georgia Power Company (GP), 115, 117–20
Golden Gate Bridge, 263, 267, 276
governors and transit: Jimmy Carter, 139; Paul A. Dever, 231–32; Dwight Green, 150; Endicott Peabody, 241; Hazen S. Pingree, 190–91; Francis Sargent, 247; Ernest Vandiver, 132–33; John A. Volpe, 239
Grand River Avenue (Detroit), 190, 193, 197, 198
Gratiot Avenue (Detroit), 190, 196, 198, 201, 216, 217
Great Depression, 30, 33, 34, 46, 49, 50, 64–66, 117, 193–95, 261–63
Greater Baltimore Committee (GBC), 80–82, 92, 94, 98, 99, 101, 103, 104
Grinnalds, Jefferson C., 28–31
Guilford (Maryland), 29, 30, 87
Gwinnett County (Georgia), 124, 132–34, 139–41, 143

Harvard Square, 55, 252
Hetch Hetchy, 265, 270, 274, 284
highways, 1, 2, 3, 9, 10, 17, 224, 290; Atlanta, 124–26; Baltimore, 82–86; Boston, 233–36, 239, 250–51; Chicago, 161–64, 167; Detroit, 194, 205–6; interwar parkways, 22, 32, 39, 52, 61–62; San Francisco, 258, 263, 267, 275–76
Housing Act of 1949 (United States), 10
Housing Act of 1954 (United States), 10
Howard County (Maryland), 98, 106, 111
Hoyt, Homer, 47, 151

HUD (US Department of Housing and Urban Development), 132, 137

Illinois Institute of Technology, 169, 171
Inner Belt (Massachusetts), 250, 257
interurbans, 9, 21, 38, 48, 164–66, 213, 277

Jefferson Avenue (Detroit), 190, 193, 194, 198, 201
Jim Crow, 12, 13, 23, 31, 43, 70, 116–17, 123, 262
jitney service, 116, 117, 193, 262
Johns Hopkins University, 30, 107
Jones Falls Expressway (JFX), 83–84, 95

King, Martin Luther, Jr., 15, 83, 100, 123, 174

labor costs, 61; Atlanta, 117, 133; Baltimore, 96, 105, 109, 110; Boston, 59, 61, 66, 232, 244, 245, 256; Chicago, 48, 49, 153, 156, 158, 175, 179; Detroit, 195, 199, 200–203, 210, 215; San Francisco, 264, 266, 272, 273–74, 281–83
Lafayette Park (Detroit), 206
Lake Meadows (Chicago), 169
Latinos (Hispanics), 145, 162, 186–87, 256, 279. *See also* Puerto Ricans
light-rail, 11, 108–9, 111, 217, 221, 237–88
Logue, Ed, 240, 249
Loop (Chicago), 38, 41, 44, 45, 49, 149, 151, 154, 165, 176, 178
Los Angeles, 2, 3, 14, 16, 17, 74, 108, 134, 148, 186, 265, 276, 288, 290
Lynn (Massachusetts), 55, 62, 229

Market Street Railway, 259–64, 266, 269
Maryland Area Rail Commuter (MARC), 111
Massachusetts Bay Transportation Authority (MBTA), 8, 54, 227, 228, 230, 238, 239–57, 291. *See also* MBTA rapid transit lines
Mattapan (Massachusetts), 59, 230
mayors and transit: Ivan Allen Jr., 132; Tom Bradley, 16; Jane Byrne, 181;

mayors and transit (*continued*)
Jerome Cavanaugh, 210, 214; George Christopher, 277; Albert E. Cobo, 199, 201, 205; John F. Collins, 240, 245; James J. Couzens, 190; Thomas D'Alesandro Jr., 79, 80, 84; Thomas D'Alesandro III, 101; Richard J. Daley, 150, 167, 178; William B. Hartsfield, 119, 132; Maynard Jackson, 16, 140; Edward Jeffries, 196; Edward Kelly, 50, 150; Roger Lapham, 266; Sam Massell, 138, 139–41; Elmer Robinson, 269, 271, 273; William Donald Schaefer, 108; John F. Shelley, 281; Eugene Van Antwerp, 198, 199, 207; Kevin White, 246; Coleman Young, 215, 217

MBTA rapid transit lines: Blue Line, 229, 241; Green Line, 53, 230, 237, 241, 244, 251, 254; Orange Line, 55, 186, 230, 241, 243, 253, 291; Red Line, 55, 229, 238, 241, 243, 249, 252, 253

MDOT MTA. *See* Metropolitan Transportation Authority (MTA) (Maryland)

Metra (Illinois), 166, 179, 182–83

Metropolitan Atlanta Rapid Transit Authority (MARTA), 13, 114, 125, 130–46. *See also* Atlanta Transit Company (Atlanta Transit System, 1955–72)

Metropolitan Park Commission (MPC) (Massachusetts), 56, 61–62

Metropolitan Transportation Authority (MTA) (Maryland) now MDOT MTA, 79, 80, 95, 97–113

Metropolitan Transportation Authority (MTA) (Massachusetts), 227–41. *See also* Massachusetts Bay Transportation Authority (MBTA)

Middlesex County (Massachusetts), 53, 235

Montgomery (Alabama), 12, 70, 123

Moses, Robert, 85, 167, 235

Mount Royal (Baltimore), 28, 88, 91

MTA (also MBTA) Advisory Board, 238–39, 246–47

Muni, 258–87

Municipal Railway Improvement Corporation (MRIC), 284, 286

National City Lines (NCL), 2, 3, 16, 22, 37, 69, 70, 114, 145, 148, 155, 198, 230; Baltimore, 74, 75, 76, 78, 113; San Francisco, 258, 259, 264, 265, 267, 269, 270, 275

New Haven Railroad, 238, 240, 242

Newton (Massachusetts), 53, 63, 230, 236

New York City, 2, 5–8, 10, 11, 14, 17, 32, 40, 47, 52, 53, 57–59, 63, 66, 76, 85, 86, 99, 133, 136, 153, 157, 166, 193, 208, 209, 213, 223–25, 230, 240, 253, 264, 273, 276, 280, 289

Oakland (California), 224, 258, 259, 264, 265, 275–79

Olympics (Atlanta), 143

one-way streets, 3, 75, 86, 92, 94, 125, 127, 161, 194, 205

Owings Mills (Maryland), 106, 107, 110

owl service, 181, 232

Pace (bus service), 179, 182

Parsons Brinckerhoff: Atlanta, 132, 134; Baltimore, 96–97, 102; Chicago, 45

People Mover (Detroit), 216, 217–18

Perry Homes (Georgia), 123, 137–42

Plan of Chicago, 44–45, 47

President's Conference Committee (PCC) streetcars: Baltimore, 36–37, 76, 77, 93, 94; Boston, 230, 236, 241, 244, 245, 253; Chicago, 50–51, 150, 154, 155; Detroit, 198, 201; San Francisco, 270–72

progressive reform: in Baltimore, 27; in Boston, 56–57; in Chicago, 39, 50

Public Control Act of 1918 (Massachusetts), 56–58

public housing, 70, 88, 123, 124, 127, 140, 162, 169, 178, 185, 196, 207, 210, 224, 249, 279

Public Service Commission (PSC) (Maryland), 27, 33, 76, 78–80, 86, 99, 100

Public Utilities Commission (Illinois), 48
Public Utilities Commission (PUC) (California), 262, 265, 266, 270, 273, 281, 283, 284, 286
Public Works Administration (PWA), 46
Puerto Ricans, 169, 186

Quincy (Massachusetts), 55, 62, 229, 238, 243, 252

rapid transit, 9, 12, 15, 21, 22, 147, 288; Atlanta, 114, 125, 129, 130–43, 291; Baltimore, 28, 32–33, 79, 81, 94, 101–7, 110, 111; Boston, 54–59, 63, 64, 66, 228–30, 231, 233, 236–39, 241, 242–45, 252–54; Chicago, 38, 45–46, 50, 150–51, 153–55, 157, 158, 162–64, 166, 167–71, 173, 174, 176, 177, 185; Detroit, 192–94, 205, 207–9, 213, 215–18, 221; San Francisco, 269, 275, 277, 278, 283
redlining, 14, 22, 44, 47, 71, 87, 127, 261
Regional Transit Authority (RTA), 166, 177, 178–83
Revere (Massachusetts), 53, 62, 229, 236
Richmond District (California), 260, 261, 279, 280, 286
ridership, 1, 5, 6, 7, 11–15, 69, 70, 147, 148, 223–25, 289–92; Atlanta, 115, 117–20, 123–25, 127, 128, 131, 138, 141–44; Baltimore, 32–34, 37, 73, 77–79, 87, 89, 91, 93, 96, 100, 102, 105, 107–13; Boston, 55, 58, 60, 61, 63, 64, 66, 227, 228, 230, 231, 232–34, 236–38, 245, 246, 248, 249, 251–56; Chicago, 38, 41, 44, 48, 49, 51, 149–51, 154, 156, 158, 160, 163–66, 168, 170, 171, 173, 174, 176, 177–79, 181–88; Detroit, 189, 197–99, 203, 206, 209, 210, 212, 213, 214, 219, 220; San Francisco, 258, 259, 261–65, 269, 271–73, 274–76, 279–81, 283, 284
riots, 13, 14, 23, 43, 100, 174, 196, 210, 211, 244
River Rouge, 191, 197
Riverside line (originally Highlands), 237–38, 241

Roland Park (Baltimore), 25, 29, 30, 84, 87
Rouse Company, 106, 107, 251
Route 128 (Massachusetts), 62, 233, 235, 236, 244, 250
Roxbury (Boston), 63, 244, 249, 253, 291

San Francisco: Board of Supervisors, 265, 268, 269, 276, 281; Department of City Planning, 269, 276–77, 286; interwar and postwar transit, 258–87; Municipal Transportation Agency (SFMTA) (*see* Muni); Planning and Housing Association, 263; Real Estate Board, 269, 281
Seattle, 2, 17, 147, 148
segregation, 12, 13; Atlanta, 116, 123, 124, 141; Baltimore, 22, 29, 30, 31, 37, 96; Boston, 59, 63; Chicago, 43, 44, 47; Detroit, 197, 210, 221; San Francisco, 261, 272, 279. *See also* Jim Crow
Shelley v. Kramer, 87
Silver Line (Boston), 253, 290
Skidmore, Owings & Merrill, 167–68, 276
Skokie Swift (Illinois), 164–68, 236
slum clearance, 10, 44, 85, 88, 110, 131, 168–71, 206, 224, 249, 258, 267, 268, 275. *See also* urban renewal
Snell, Bradford, 2–3
Somerville (Massachusetts), 53, 57, 59, 231, 235, 249, 250
Southeastern Michigan Transportation Authority (SEMTA), 213–18
"spatial mismatch hypothesis," 15
state government and transit, 4, 7, 17, 225, 289, 290; California, 283, 287, 289, 290; Georgia, 126, 133, 139; Illinois, 45, 46, 150, 156, 166, 180; Maryland, 27, 31, 100, 108; Massachusetts, 54, 56, 62, 100, 228, 234, 238, 239, 240, 247, 251
"streetcar conspiracy," 2, 3, 5, 6, 8, 9, 12, 60, 74–75, 155
streetcar substitution (with buses or trolley coaches): Atlanta, 117–18,

streetcar substitution (*continued*) 125, 127–28, 130; Baltimore, 34–36, 73–82, 92–95, 97, 113; Boston, 59–60, 66, 230–32, 251–52; Chicago, 50–51, 152–56, 158–61, 176–77, 188; Detroit, 194–202, 207; San Francisco, 258, 263–73, 284–86

subsidies (for transit), 3, 4, 7, 8, 13–17, 21, 22, 50, 147, 148, 223–25, 288, 289, 291; Atlanta, 119, 127, 128, 130, 141; Baltimore, 78, 79, 91, 97, 99, 100–102, 107, 109, 110; Boston, 52–71, 227, 228, 231, 236, 238–43, 245–48, 250–51, 256; Chicago, 51, 157, 162, 163, 171–83, 188; Detroit, 199, 201, 202, 208, 210–12, 214–15, 218; San Francisco, 259, 262, 264, 272–75, 277, 280–87

Suburban Mobility Authority for Regional Transit (SMART), 189, 216

suburbs, 1, 2, 6, 9, 10, 13, 15, 21, 70, 223, 224, 291; Atlanta, 117, 124, 135, 136, 138, 140, 141, 143; Baltimore, 25, 28, 30, 78, 82, 84, 86, 91, 99, 102, 104, 107, 108, 111, 113; Boston, 53, 57, 63, 229, 233, 235–40, 242, 243, 250, 252; Chicago, 41, 47, 48, 50, 151, 152, 154, 157, 158, 162–66, 168, 173, 176–88; Detroit, 192, 195–97, 202, 204, 208–17, 221; San Francisco, 261, 277

subways, 2, 6, 7, 8, 21, 22, 28, 193, 223; Atlanta, 136; Baltimore, 33, 40, 94, 99, 101–4, 107; Boston, 52–55, 57–59, 61, 63–65, 229–34, 236, 237, 241, 251, 252, 255; Chicago, 44–46, 50, 51, 150, 153, 154, 158, 159, 167, 174, 184; Detroit, 192, 193, 195, 198, 208, 216, 217; San Francisco, 265, 269, 271, 277–78, 282, 283, 287

Suffolk County (Massachusetts), 53, 235

Sunbelt, 13, 14, 18, 114, 143, 146

Sunset District (San Francisco), 260, 261, 272, 276, 282

Techwood Homes (Atlanta), 126

Tenement House Act of 1912 (Massachusetts), 62–63

Toronto, 2, 3, 80, 93, 94, 136, 199, 216, 243

Towson (Maryland), 31, 91, 93, 96, 106

transit managers: Sidney Bingham, 269; Edward Dana, 228, 233, 236, 241; Philip Harrington, 50, 55, 153; Jesse L. Haugh, 264–65; Samuel Insull, 40; Marmion D. Mills, 270–71; Fred A. Nolan, 75, 194–95; Leo Nowicki, 197–205; Michael M. O'Shaughnessy, 260; Richard Rich, 125, 131, 135–38; Robert L. Somerville, 121–23, 134–36, 208–9; John Woods, 284; Charles Yerkes, 40

transit-oriented development, 289

transit taxes, 5, 7, 14, 34, 40, 49, 61, 224, 289; Atlanta, 119, 128, 129, 133, 138, 145; Baltimore, 27, 28, 33, 34, 75, 78, 79, 84, 91–92, 95, 97, 99, 100; Boston, 22, 59, 61, 65, 66, 229, 231, 236, 239, 246, 247; Chicago, 40, 41, 49, 151–52, 156, 167, 173, 174, 179, 181; Detroit, 202, 210, 211, 220; San Francisco, 259, 262, 265, 274, 277, 280, 283

trolleybuses (also trackless trolleys or trolley coaches), 8, 17, 21, 147; Atlanta, 117–19, 123, 125, 127–28; Baltimore, 35–36, 73, 76, 82; Boston, 228, 233, 243, 252; Chicago, 153, 155; San Francisco, 258, 264, 266, 270–72, 284, 287

Twin Peaks tunnel, 260, 261, 271

United Railways (Baltimore), 21, 25–37

United Railways (DUR) (Detroit), 190

Urban Mass Transit Administration (UMTA), 105, 108, 286

Urban Mass Transportation Act of 1964 (United States), 7, 211

urban renewal, 17, 44, 53, 70, 88, 224; Atlanta, 115, 125–27; Baltimore, 80, 88, 92, 95, 98, 101, 103; Boston, 53, 227, 248–50, 257; Chicago, 43, 44, 162, 163, 168–71, 186; Detroit, 205–7; San Francisco, 259, 267–68, 275, 278, 283. *See also* slum clearance

US Department of Housing and Urban Development (HUD), 132, 137

US Department of Transportation, 134, 175–76

Wacker, Charles, 45
Warren (Michigan), 209
Washington, DC, 103, 107, 111, 288
Wayne County (Michigan), 205, 211, 216
West End company (Massachusetts), 53–54, 55, 251
Western Addition (San Francisco), 267–68, 271–72, 276, 278–79
Western Transit, 258, 259, 264, 265
white flight, 4, 12, 13, 14
Whitney, Henry, 53–54
Winnetka (Illinois), 48
Wolman, Abel, 79–80, 86, 97

Woodward Avenue (Detroit), 190, 193, 195, 196, 201, 213, 217
Works Progress Administration (WPA), 50, 65

zoning, 3, 9, 10, 12, 16, 17, 22, 70, 224; Atlanta, 115, 116, 124, 126, 133, 140, 145, 146; Baltimore, 28–31, 37, 86–91, 102, 113; Boston, 52, 59, 61–63, 242, 249, 254; Chicago, 38, 46–48, 163–65, 169–70; Detroit, 195–96, 209, 221; San Francisco, 260–61

www.ingramcontent.com/pod-product-compliance
Lightning Source LLC
Chambersburg PA
CBHW071953290426
44109CB00018B/2010